THE CAMBRIDGE COMPANION TO

CLASSICAL ISLAMIC THEOLO

This series of critical reflections on the evolution and major themes of pre-modern Muslim theology begins with the revelation of the Qur'an, and extends to the beginnings of modernity in the eighteenth century. The significance of Islamic theology reflects the immense importance of Islam in the history of monotheism, to which it has brought a unique approach and style, and a range of solutions which are of abiding interest. Devoting especial attention to questions of rationality, scriptural fidelity and the construction of "orthodoxy", this volume introduces key Muslim theories of revelation, creation, ethics, scriptural interpretation, law, mysticism and eschatology. Throughout the treatment is firmly set in the historical, social and political context in which Islam's distinctive understanding of God evolved.

Despite its importance, Islamic theology has been neglected in recent scholarship, and this book provides a unique, scholarly but accessible introduction.

Tim Winter is University Lecturer in Islamic Studies, Faculty of Divinity, University of Cambridge.

CAMBRIDGE COMPANIONS TO RELIGION

A series of companions to major topics and key figures in theology and religious studies. Each volume contains specially commissioned chapters by international scholars which provide an accessible and stimulating introduction to the subject for new readers and non-specialists.

Other titles in the series

THE CAMBRIDGE COMPANION TO CHRISTIAN DOCTRINE
edited by Colin Gunton (1997)
ISBN 0 521 47118 4 hardback ISBN 0 521 47695 x paperback

THE CAMBRIDGE COMPANION TO BIBLICAL INTERPRETATION
edited by John Barton (1998)
ISBN 0 521 48144 9 hardback ISBN 0 521 48593 2 paperback

THE CAMBRIDGE COMPANION TO DIETRICH BONHOEFFER
edited by John de Gruchy (1999)
ISBN 0 521 58258 x hardback ISBN 0 521 58781 6 paperback

THE CAMBRIDGE COMPANION TO LIBERATION THEOLOGY, FIRST EDITION
edited by Christopher Rowland (1999)
ISBN 0 521 46144 8 hardback ISBN 0 521 46707 1 paperback

THE CAMBRIDGE COMPANION TO KARL BARTH
edited by John Webster (2000)
ISBN 0 521 58476 0 hardback ISBN 0 521 58560 0 paperback

THE CAMBRIDGE COMPANION TO CHRISTIAN ETHICS
edited by Robin Gill (2001)
ISBN 0 521 77070 x hardback ISBN 0 521 77918 9 paperback

THE CAMBRIDGE COMPANION TO JESUS
edited by Markus Bockmuehl (2001)
ISBN 0 521 79261 4 hardback ISBN 0 521 79678 4 paperback

THE CAMBRIDGE COMPANION TO FEMINIST THEOLOGY
edited by Susan Frank Parsons (2002)
ISBN 0 521 66327 x hardback ISBN 0 521 66380 6 paperback

THE CAMBRIDGE COMPANION TO MARTIN LUTHER
edited by Donald K. McKim (2003)
ISBN 0 521 81648 3 hardback ISBN 0 521 01673 8 paperback

THE CAMBRIDGE COMPANION TO ST. PAUL
edited by James D. G. Dunn (2003)
ISBN 0 521 78155 8 hardback ISBN 0 521 78694 0 paperback

THE CAMBRIDGE COMPANION TO POSTMODERN THEOLOGY
edited by Kevin J. Vanhoozer (2003)
ISBN 0 521 79062 x hardback ISBN 0 521 79395 5 paperback

THE CAMBRIDGE COMPANION TO JOHN CALVIN
edited by Donald K. McKim (2004)
ISBN 0 521 81647 5 hardback ISBN 0 521 01672 x paperback

Continued at the back of the book

THE CAMBRIDGE COMPANION TO

CLASSICAL ISLAMIC THEOLOGY

Edited by Tim Winter

CAMBRIDGE
UNIVERSITY PRESS

CAMBRIDGE UNIVERSITY PRESS
Cambridge, New York, Melbourne, Madrid, Cape Town, Singapore, São Paulo, Delhi

Cambridge University Press
The Edinburgh Building, Cambridge CB2 8RU, UK

Published in the United States of America by Cambridge University Press, New York

www.cambridge.org
Information on this title: www.cambridge.org/9780521785495

First published 2008

Printed in the United Kingdom at the University Press, Cambridge

A catalogue record for this publication is available from the British Library

Library of Congress Cataloging in Publication Data
The Cambridge companion to classical Islamic theology / edited by Tim Winter.
p. cm. – (Cambridge companions to religion)
Includes bibliographical references and index.
ISBN 978-0-521-78058-2 (hardback : alk. paper) – ISBN 978-0-521-78549-5
(pbk. : alk. paper)
1. Islam–Theology–History. 2. Islam–Doctrines–History. I. Winter, T. J. II. Title:
Classical Islamic theology. III. Series.
BP166.1.C36 2008
297.209–dc22
2008008970

ISBN 978-0-521-78058-2 hardback
ISBN 978-0-521-78549-5 paperback

Contents

Notes on contributors *page ix*

Introduction 1
TIM WINTER

Part I *Historical perspectives*

1 Qur'an and hadith 19
M. A. S. ABDEL HALEEM

2 The early creed 33
KHALID BLANKINSHIP

3 Islamic philosophy (*falsafa*) 55
HOSSEIN ZIAI

4 The developed *kalām* tradition 77
OLIVER LEAMAN (PART I) AND SAJJAD RIZVI (PART II)

5 The social construction of orthodoxy 97
AHMED EL SHAMSY

Part II *Themes*

6 God: essence and attributes 121
NADER EL-BIZRI

7 Creation 141
DAVID B. BURRELL CSC

8 Ethics 161
STEFFEN A. J. STELZER

9 Revelation 180
YAHYA MICHOT

10 The existence of God 197
AYMAN SHIHADEH

11 Worship 218
WILLIAM C. CHITTICK

12 Theological dimensions of Islamic law 237
UMAR F. ABD-ALLAH

13 Theology and Sufism 258
TOBY MAYER

14 Epistemology and divine discourse 288
PAUL-A. HARDY

15 Eschatology 308
MARCIA HERMANSEN

Index 325

Notes on contributors

Umar F. Abd-Allah received his PhD in Arabic and Islamic Studies from the University of Chicago in 1978 with a dissertation on the origins of Islamic law. His principal interests are Islamic intellectual and spiritual history, the history of Islam in the West, and comparative religion. He taught academically in the United States, Canada and Saudi Arabia for more than twenty years before taking up his present post as chairperson and scholar-in-residence of the Nawawi Foundation (Chicago), an educational organisation devoted to exploring Islamic intellectual, spiritual and cultural legacies and making them relevant today. His most recent book, *A Muslim in Victorian America: The Life of Alexander Russell Webb*, appeared in 2006.

M. A. S. Abdel Haleem was educated at al-Azhar, Cairo, and Cambridge Universities, and has taught Arabic at the universities of Cambridge and London since 1966. He is now Professor of Islamic Studies at the School of Oriental and African Studies, University of London. Among his recent publications are *Understanding the Qur'an: Themes and Style* (2001), *English Translations of the Qur'an: The Making of an Image* (2004), and a new translation of *The Qur'an* (2004).

Nader El-Bizri is a Research Associate in Philosophy at The Institute of Ismaili Studies, London, and an Affiliated Lecturer at the Department of History and Philosophy of Science at the University of Cambridge. He is also a Visiting Professor at Lincoln University, and acts as a *Chercheur Associé* at the Centre National de la Recherche Scientifique (CNRS, Paris). He previously taught at the universities of Nottingham and Harvard and the American University of Beirut. In addition, he is an elected member of the Steering Committee of the *Société Internationale d'Histoire des Sciences et des Philosophies Arabes et Islamiques* (CNRS, Paris). His areas of research are Arabic Sciences and Philosophy, Phenomenology, and Architectural Humanities.

Khalid Blankinship obtained his PhD in history in 1988, with a specialisation in Islam, from the University of Washington. Since 1990, he has worked as a professor in the Department of Religion at Temple University in Philadelphia. He has remained active in research and lecturing on religion in general and Islam in particular. His book, *The End of the Jihad State: The Reign of Hisham ibn 'Abd al-Malik and the Collapse of the Umayyads* was published in 1994;

he also translated two of the thirty-eight volumes of *The History of al-Ṭabarī* for the Ṭabarī Translation Project.

David B. Burrell CSC is Theodore M. Hesburgh Professor in Philosophy and Theology at the University of Notre Dame, USA. His publishing career began in 1973 with *Analogy and Philosophical Language*, and led to a series of studies of St Thomas Aquinas. Since 1982 he has worked mainly in comparative issues in philosophical theology in Judaism, Christianity and Islam. His more recent works include *Freedom and Creation in Three Traditions* (1993), and two translations of theological texts by al-Ghazālī.

William C. Chittick is Professor of Religious Studies in the Department of Asian and Asian-American Studies, State University of New York, Stony Brook. He has published twenty-five books and numerous articles on Islamic intellectual history, including *The Sufi Path of Love: The Spiritual Teachings of Rumi* (1983), *The Sufi Path of Knowledge: Ibn al-'Arabî's Metaphysics of Imagination* (1989), and *The Heart of Islamic Philosophy* (2001).

Ahmed El Shamsy is a doctoral candidate in History and Middle Eastern Studies at Harvard University. He received his BA and MSc from the University of London, and has also studied Islamic theology and law in Germany and Egypt. His doctoral research investigates the early social and intellectual history of the Shāfi'ī school of law; in conjunction with this project, he is preparing a critical edition of a ninth-century work by al-Shāfi'ī's successor al-Buwayṭī.

Paul-A. Hardy took his BA/MA from Oxford, and his PhD in Islamic Thought from the University of Chicago. He has lectured at the School of Oriental and African Studies in the University of London and at Hunter College, New York. He is the author of the forthcoming *Avicenna on Self-Knowing*.

Marcia Hermansen is Professor of Islamic Studies and Director of the Islamic World Studies Minor at Loyola University, Chicago. She published *The Conclusive Argument from God: Shāh Walī Allāh of Delhi's* Ḥujjat Allāh al-Bāligha (1996), and is co-editor of the *Encyclopedia of Islam and the Muslim World* (2003).

Oliver Leaman has been Professor of Philosophy at the University of Kentucky, USA, since 2000. Before that he taught in the United Kingdom and Africa. He has written *Islamic Aesthetics: An Introduction* (2004). He edited *The Qur'an: An Encyclopedia*, and the *Biographical Dictionary of Islamic Philosophers*, both published in 2006. He has also written and edited several earlier publications on Islamic philosophy and the philosophy of religion.

Yahya Michot was from 1981 until 1997 Director of the Centre for Arabic Philosophy at the University of Louvain, before taking up his current post as Islamic Centre Lecturer in the Faculty of Theology, University of Oxford. His research interests include the theology of Ibn Taymiyya (d. 1328) and the life and philosophy of Avicenna (d. 1037). Among his recent publications are

Ibn Taymiyya: Un Dieu hésitant? (2004) and *Muslims under Non-Muslim Rule* (2006).

Toby Mayer is currently a Research Associate at the Institute of Ismaili Studies, London, where he works on the esoteric hermeneutics of the Qur'an by figures like Shahrastānī and Āmulī, as well as teaching courses on the Qur'an and Sufism. Until 2003 he held a lectureship at the School of Oriental and African Studies, London, where he taught Islamic philosophy and mysticism. In addition to a number of articles on Islamic philosophy, he is the co-author, with Wilferd Madelung, of *Struggling with the Philosopher: A New Arabic Edition and English Translation of Muḥammad b. 'Abd al-Karīm al-Shahrastānī's* Kitāb al-Muṣāra'a.

Sajjad Rizvi is Senior Lecturer in Islamic Studies at the University of Exeter. He specialises in Islamic intellectual history, in particular the thought of the Safavid period, and is the author of *Mullā Ṣadrā Shīrāzī* (2007) and with Feras Hamza of *Understanding the Word of God* (2008). Current projects include a study of time and creation in Islamic philosophy and Islamic intellectual history in India.

Ayman Shihadeh is Lecturer in Islamic Studies and Arabic at the University of Edinburgh. He specialises mainly in ethical theory in Islam and in the Middle Period of Islamic philosophy and theology, especially twelfth-century interaction between the *kalām* and philosophical traditions, criticism of Avicenna, and the thought of Fakhr al-Dīn al-Rāzī. He is the author of *The Teleological Ethics of Fakhr al-Dīn al-Rāzī* (2006).

Steffen A. J. Stelzer is Professor of Philosophy and Chair of the Department at the American University in Cairo. He obtained his PhD from the Freie Universität Berlin, engaged in research at the École Normale Supérieure in Paris and at Harvard, and has taught at Johns Hopkins University. His areas of specialisation include rationality and revelation, the conditions and constituents of philosophical discourse, concepts of the transmission of knowledge, and comparative analyses of Western philosophical and Islamic models.

Hossein Ziai is Professor of Islamic and Iranian Studies at UCLA. He has published many articles and several books on the Arabic and Persian Illuminationist system of philosophy. He has published several text-editions and translations of Arabic and Persian Illuminationist texts, including Suhrawardī's *Philosophy of Illumination*, Shahrazūrī's *Commentary on the Philosophy of Illumination*, and Ibn Kammūna's *Commentary on Suhrawardī's Intimations*.

Introduction

TIM WINTER

This volume presents a series of critical scholarly reflections on the evolution and major themes of pre-modern Muslim theology. Given Islam's salience in religious history and its role as final religious inheritor of the legacies of monotheism and classical antiquity, such a collection hardly needs justification. The significance of Islamic theology reflects the significance of Islam as a central part of the monotheistic project as a whole, to which it brings a distinctive approach and style, and a range of solutions which are of abiding interest.

Despite this importance it is fair to say that until recently the study of theology was something of a Cinderella subject within Islamic studies, particularly in the Anglo-Saxon world. In part this flowed from the persistence of nineteenth-century assumptions about the marginality of abstract intellectual life in Islam, and about the greater intrinsic interest and originality of Muslim law and mysticism. It was also commonly thought that where formal metaphysics was cultivated in Islamic civilisation, this was done seriously only in the context of Arabic philosophy (*falsafa*), where it was not obstructed by futile scriptural controls, and where it could perform its most significant function, which was believed to be the transmission of Greek thought to Europe.

However, a steady process of scholarly advance over the past two decades, coupled with the publication of critical editions of important early texts, has turned the study of Muslim theology into a dynamic and ever more intriguing discipline. Old assumptions about Muslim theology as either a narrow apologetic exercise or an essentially foreign import into Islam have been successfully challenged. Scholars have moved on from a somewhat mechanical focus on doxography and on tracking the contributions of the Greek tradition, towards the recognition that Islamic metaphysics contain much that is purely indigenous, that is to say, rooted in the language and concerns of the qur'anic revelation.

In decline, likewise, has been the unspoken assumption that what was of value in classical Muslim civilisation was what fed into the story of the West. On that view, the Muslims acted as no more than "go-betweens", a "devious Gulf-stream which brought back to Europe its Greek and Alexandrine heritage".[1] Arabic philosophy after Averroes, and almost the entirety of the formal theology, were thus relegated to the status of an intellectual byway. As we shall see, new research, and a less Eurocentric vision of history and of the remit of scholarship, have done much to challenge this outlook.

CLASSICAL THEOLOGY: A DEFINITION

A word about the title of our collection. The term "classical" is used to cover the era which stretches between the qur'anic revelation and the eighteenth century, with the accent falling on the period between the tenth and thirteenth centuries. For most of this "classical" period the *kalām*, literally "discourse", that is to say, the formal academic discipline which one scholar aptly calls "Islamic doctrinal theology",[2] stood at or very near the apex of the academic curriculum. However, this book does not identify "theology" as coterminous with this *kalām* tradition. Instead, it acknowledges that many issues which most readers will recognise as theological were treated by Muslim civilisation in a wide range of disciplines. As William Chittick defines it in his chapter, theology is "God-talk in all its forms".

The most obvious of these disciplines was Sufism, a category of esoteric and ascetical traditions rather larger than "mysticism" as commonly understood, which frequently addressed issues of creation, ethics, pastoral care, providence, inspiration, miracle and other topics which in medieval Latin cultures would more usually have been dealt with under a theological rubric. Sufism quickly developed to provide a mystical tradition more fully recognised by mainstream thought than was the case with the other monotheisms. It is not entirely clear why this should have been the case, but we may speculate that the process was facilitated by the Qur'an's radical monotheism, which, by resisting any hint of dualism, thoroughly sacralised the world as a matrix of "signs".[3] When integrated into *kalām* through the evolution of doctrines of occasionalism, this resistance in turn gave mainstream theology a natural hospitality to often quite radical mystical concerns.[4]

In this way, and despite their programmatic rationalism, many leading *kalām* thinkers tended to be explicit about their respect for Sufism as a path to knowledge; as David Burrell shows in this volume, Abū Ḥāmid al-Ghazālī (d. 1111) was destined to be the iconic example of this, but his great Ash'arite successor Fakhr al-Dīn al-Rāzī (d. 1210), perhaps Islam's greatest philosophical theologian, also showed increasing respect for Sufi approaches to knowledge in his later works.[5] Recognising that the field now acknowledges the validity and even the centrality of Sufism in constructions of Muslim "orthodoxy", regular references will be made to Sufi discussions, particularly in the chapters on worship and epistemology, and in the long chapter by Toby Mayer which directly addresses *kalām*'s relationship with Sufism, focusing in a particularly helpful way on the Avicennian component of later Sufi thought. Ibn 'Arabī (d. 1240), the Andalusian polymath and esoterist, merits a number of titles, but he is certainly a theologian, despite his regular habit of soaring well beyond the reach of reason. William Chittick, in his chapter, suggests that Ibn 'Arabī may even be viewed as the final summation of Islamic intellectuality. Although Ghazālī, in his *Revival of the Religious Sciences*, had sought to integrate the various exoteric and esoteric disciplines in a way which transcended the boundaries between them, thus claiming a universal coherence for Islamic intellectuality, it was Ibn 'Arabī who brought this ambitious reintegrative initiative to a peak of intricacy, by proposing a detailed mystical theology that seemed to incorporate all the great topics of *kalām*, philosophy, law and Sufism into a vast, brilliant (and hugely controversial) synthesis. It has even been suggested, paraphrasing Whitehead's remark about Plato, that "the history of Islamic thought subsequent to Ibn 'Arabī (at least down to the 18th century and the radically new encounter with the modern West) might largely be construed as a series of endnotes to his works."[6] This view, which is new in the field, is still not universally accepted, and its neglect of later *kalām* makes it an overstatement, but it is noticeably gaining ground.

Paralleling this shift in our understanding of the historical relationship of Sufism to *kalām* has been a maturing grasp of the revealed law of Islam, the *Sharī'a*. The great lawbooks typically included discussions of issues concerning language and human accountability which were purely theological; indeed, the entire remit of Muslim law could be said to be theological, since it takes the function of the law to be the preparation of society and the individual to receive God's grace. A separate chapter, by Umar F. Abd-Allah, engages with this important dimension of Islam's theological history.

There was still another discipline which incorporated theological concerns. This was *falsafa* (Arabic philosophy, from Greek *philosophia*), a tradition substantially borrowed and adapted from late antiquity. Modern scholars take forensic pains to separate *falsafa* from *kalām*, and medieval Muslims usually did the same; yet since its great exponents were Muslims who believed in the Qur'an and the Prophet, it can defensibly be seen as a Muslim theology, as well as an intellectual tradition that constantly informed the *kalām* and, as we are now acknowledging, stood also in its debt.[7]

Altogether it is clear that by limiting themselves to the disciplinary boundaries imposed by medieval Muslims themselves, Western treatments of Islamic theology have often neglected the wealth of properly theological discussions appearing outside the *kalām* in the civilisation's literature. As well as imposing on anglophone readers a division of the sciences which may seem to make little sense in their context, the result has often been a somewhat dry and partial treatment of the great issues of Muslim monotheism, a shortcoming which this volume hopes, in part, to remedy.

THE STATE OF THE FIELD

Drawing together the core topics of Muslim theology from these historically distinct disciplines has brought into sharp relief the very fragmented and sometimes idiosyncratic nature of Western scholarship of Islam, the tradition sometimes known as "Orientalism". Overwhelmingly this discipline has been built up from contributions made by individuals, not by schools. Thinkers and texts are brought to the fore during a scholar's lifetime, and may then quickly sink into undeserved obscurity. Occasionally, cultural prejudices which designate Islam as a "religion of law" with no natural metaphysical concerns have been salient, and on occasion, such presumptions have uneasily recalled anti-Semitic parallels.[8] Yet the huge contributions made by the small number of persistent leaders in this discipline are impossible to ignore: texts have been rescued from obscurity and expertly edited, and important studies have been published on many leading thinkers, particularly al-Ash'arī, al-Māturīdī, al-Ghazālī and Fakhr al-Dīn al-Rāzī, with the pace of publication quickening somewhat in recent years. As this volume demonstrates, many of the younger scholars in the field are Muslims, and the fact that, as in other "Orientalist" disciplines such as qur'anic studies, they have adapted so well to the discipline's paradigms, suggests that older ideas of Western Islamic studies as a monolithic and structurally anti-Islamic project now need to be modified, if not discarded altogether.

Yet the field is visibly deficient. Resources and posts in Muslim theology in Western universities remain woefully inadequate, even when compared to the situation in Chinese and Indic studies, and the appeal of the field to students whose initial interest in Islam, in the imperial and modern periods alike, may have been triggered by contemporary political, social, or legal issues, has been limited. This unfortunate situation has been further exacerbated by the sheer immensity of the literature, most of which remains in manuscript. Attention continues to be focused on the central Islamic lands, and although most accept that the *kalām* curriculum was fairly consistent throughout the "high" institutions of the pre-modern Islamic world,[9] our detailed knowledge of traditional Muslim metaphysics in regions such as South-East Asia must be described as embryonic. As a result, current Western scholarship cannot, with perfect honesty, present anything like a complete synthetic history of Muslim intellectuality, or even a definitive list of the major thinkers. This is particularly true for the later period. Although, thanks to the efforts of Henry Corbin, Hossein Ziai and others, we are aware of the continuing vitality of Islamic philosophy in the later centuries, and indeed, up to the present day, the history of *kalām* after the thirteenth century largely remains *terra incognita*.

CHARACTERISTICS

We need to ask: what is Islamic about Islamic theology? Most evidently, it is Islamic to the extent that it may be traced back in some way to the Prophet Muḥammad and his distinctive vision of the One God. According to his scripture, he was sent "as a mercy to the worlds" (Qur'an 21:107), and one aspect of that mercy, as Muhammad Abdel Haleem suggests in chapter 1, was that he mapped out a religious path of great simplicity. This was to be the simplicity of an Abrahamic and "primordial" monotheism (*milla ibrāhīmiyya ḥanīfiyya*), marked by an iconoclastic rejection of idolatry, a call to repentance, and an unshakeable trust in the justice and mercy of God. Emerging, as Muslims believed, to restore unity and a holy simplicity to a confessional world complicated by Christian disputes over the Trinity and the Incarnation,[10] the qur'anic intervention seemed to its hearers to promise a new age for the human relationship with God, one so straightforward that in the eyes of a small but persistent margin, there would be no need for a "theology" (*kalām*) at all. Voices are therefore raised against the *kalām* enterprise through the Islamic centuries; the angry *Censure of Speculative Theology* by Ibn Qudāma (d. 1223) assumes that scripture alone suffices; al-Harawī (d. 1089) agrees, suggesting that *kalām* is an unreliable substitute for the true gift of mystical illumination. Both men had their passionate supporters.[11]

Monotheism, however, is never as simple as most of its advocates would wish. Its inbuilt paradoxes, which had already exercised and divided Jews and Christians, ensured that most Muslim thinkers came to recognise the need for a formal discipline of argument and proof which could establish the proper sense of a scripture which turned out to be open to many different interpretations. The trigger, in almost every case, was the need to defeat the whims (*ahwā'*) of heretics and innovators. Khalid Blankinship's chapter provides a survey and assessment of the first such debates. God was indeed One, and Muḥammad was His final Prophet: this much was never contested. But were God's names, so abundant in the Qur'an, in existence before the world? If so, was it right to say that they were identical with His essence, or were they in some way distinct? Did the Qur'an pre-date its bearer? Why did God insist on human accountability, when He, as Omnipotent and All-Knowing Creator, is surely not ignorant of what human beings will do? Are good and evil intrinsic, or are they utterly subject to the divine volition? Is faith enough for salvation? In what sense will the Prophet intercede for sinners? What did he envision when he said that God would be seen by the blessed in Paradise?

Many disturbing questions of this kind in turn seemed to be generated by a tension implicit in the Qur'an itself. Some verses spoke of a God who seemed utterly transcendent, so that "nothing is like him" (Qur'an 42:11). Such a deity "is not asked about what he does" (21:23), and appears to expect only the unquestioning submission (*islām*) which seemed implicit in the very name of the new religion. But there were many other passages which implied a God who is indeed, in some sense that urgently needed definition, analogous to ourselves: a God who is ethically coherent, and whose qualities are immanent in his creation, so that "Wheresover you turn, there is God's face" (2:115). This fundamental tension between transcendence and immanence, or, as Muslims put it, between "affirming difference" (*tanzīh*) and "affirming resemblance" (*tashbīh*), became intrinsic to the structuring of knowledge in the new civilisation. As one aspect of this it could be said, at the risk of very crude generalisation, that the Qur'an's theology of transcendence was explored by the *kalām* folk, and its theology of immanence by the Sufis, which is why, perhaps, we should seek for Islam's greatest theologians among those who emphasised the symbiosis of the two disciplines. It may be thus, rather than for any unique originality, that Ghazālī came to be called the "proof of Islam", and Ibn 'Arabī the "greatest shaykh". Their apparent eclecticism was in fact a programmatic attempt to retrieve an original unity, which is why scripture is so central to their respective manifestos.

THE CONSTRUCTION OF ORTHODOXY

If such was the pre-modern culmination of Muslim theology, then its large story, as this volume shows, was that of a white-hot moment of pure revelatory renewal at the hands of a Prophet who, as Hans Küng puts it, was "discontinuity in person",[12] which with remarkable speed systematised itself as a set of contesting but seldom fatally divided schools of law, metaphysics and mysticism, which were then woven together again in the eclectic theologies of Ghazālī and Ibn 'Arabī. For both thinkers, and for the many lesser minds which attempted the same synthetic project, the proof of reintegration was a retrieval of a moral and spiritual understanding of the Law (*fiqh*), and a reinvigoration of the art of qur'anic citation. Ghazālī's *Revival* may, within limits, be read as a qur'anic commentary, and in the case of Ibn 'Arabī, as Mayer attests, his "intensely esoteric hermeneutic of the Qur'an is often strictly in line with the *literal sense of the text*".[13]

The various schools contrived to coexist for centuries, building an intellectual landscape of immense diversity. Ahmed El Shamsy, in his chapter, explains how in the midst of this process of contestation and institution-building an "orthodoxy" came to constitute itself. Lacking sacraments and a true hierarchy, Islam possessed no mechanisms for imposing dogmatic conformity on a society that certainly did not recognise Enlightenment-style "tolerance", but which nonetheless evolved means of allowing and even legitimising profound differences in law, mysticism and doctrine. Hence the four schools of Sunnī jurisprudence came to be seen as equivalently valid, while a less formal attitude presumed the concurrent viability of the major Sufi orders (*ṭuruq*), and of the three great Sunnī theological schools of Ash'arism, Māturīdism and Ḥanbalism. Despite the fury of so much interdenominational polemic, classical Islam knew only two episodes of systematic state-backed inquisition: the Mu'tazilite persecution of their rivals under the Abbasid caliphs between the years 833 and 848, and, in the sixteenth century, the brutal destruction of Iranian Sunnism under the Shī'ī revolutionary regime of the Ṣafavids.[14] Apart from these two experiences, which generated or intensified a bitterness against Mu'tazilism and Shī'ism which lingered for centuries, the central Islamic lands were as religiously diverse as Latin Christendom was religiously homogeneous. Hard-line Mu'tazilism and Shī'ism, which readily invoked the principle of *takfīr* (the anathematisation of fellow Muslims), the move which had characterised the Khārijite revolts of the Umayyad period, were precisely the type of religious extremism (*ghuluww*) which Ash'arite theorists dreaded.[15]

In place of ecclesial authority, medieval Islam came to recognise the infinitely more ponderous and difficult principle of *ijmā'*: the consensus of believers. True belief, it was thought, would always be the belief of the majority (*jumhūr*); sects (*firaq*) were necessarily minorities. The large and detailed heresiographical literature which supplies so much of our information about this history everywhere assumes that God is "with the congregation". His mercy and love for the Muslim community ensure that "it will never agree on an error",[16] and that "the individual who departs from the community departs to Hellfire".[17] Although Sunnī Muslims never agreed on whether the community (*jamā'a*) in question denoted the mass of believers, or only their scholarly representatives, this attitude clearly calmed the psychological fear that heresy might one day prevail. No doubt this supplies one reason why, as van Ess claims, "strictly speaking, Islam had no religious wars like those in Europe",[18] and why Sunnī states seldom ventured to impose doctrines and practices upon the population (*ta'dīb al-'āmma*).[19] Given that the Islamic liturgy does not include the recital of a detailed creed, Muslims of various persuasions could and did attend the same mosque services. Keeping one's own counsel was relatively easy.

Given such opportunities, it is curious that Islamic sectarianism did not develop more exuberantly than in fact it did. It is very difficult to discern, from the pages of the Sunnī heresiographers, the popularity of the early sects. Yet it is clear that the majority of Muslims favoured a simple median interpretation which appeared to be faithful to the plain sense of scripture, but which allowed some room for the formalising of creeds against which error could be defined. Elite Muslims who sought to develop advanced theologies needed to be mindful of the preferences of the believing masses. Perhaps this was seen as fidelity to the Prophet and the original collective spirit of *sancta simplicitas*; perhaps, also, it resulted from the fear that a theology which angered the multitudes might lead to disturbances which could provoke the wrath of a sultan. The Mu'tazilite scholars who successfully persuaded the Abbasid caliph to adopt an elitist and abstract theology which seemed equally far from the scriptures and the comprehension of the masses were obliged to use force to compel conformity, and although most scholars complied, popular incredulity ensured their ultimate downfall.

The power of the masses did much to ensure that mainstream Sunnism developed as a set of median positions. Sayings of the Prophet could be found to support the idea that Islam was a middle way (*wasaṭ*).[20] Perhaps even the "straight path" which Muslims daily prayed to be shown was a middle path, specifically between what were claimed to be the mirrored distortions of historical Judaism and Christianity.[21] So as an awareness grew that there was a tension between the qur'anic verses which saw God as transcendent or immanent, it was thought necessary to chart what Ghazālī called the "just mean in belief" (*al-iqtiṣād fi'l-i'tiqād*), which lay between two forms of *ghuluww*. Theologians who, like the mysterious Jahm ibn Ṣafwān, stripped God of all attributes, transcendentalised Him beyond all possibility of knowledge, while extremist Ḥanbalites who thought that God literally possessed "dimensions", "altitude", a "hand" and a "face", seemed to advocate a finite God, by developing a corporealism which looked like the opposite extreme of the same spectrum.

This was not the only key controversy in which the Sunnī mainstream liked to define itself as a middle position. Addressing the question of the status of sinners, Blankinship's chapter shows how the early community attempted to negotiate a middle path between the Khārijites, who rejected sinners as apostates, and other groups, who held that sin has no effect on an individual's status as a believing Muslim, or that one should simply suspend judgement. Nader El-Bizri, in his chapter on the debate over God's attributes, shows how orthodoxy situated itself between the extremes of either negating the attributes, or concretising them in a way that might compromise the divine unity and transcendence. Similarly, on the free will versus determinism debate, Steffen Stelzer, David Burrell and others show that Muslims tended to favour a median position in the form of the doctrine of Acquisition (*kasb*), and the merits of the *via media* in this context were explicitly extolled by Ghazālī.[22] Overall, it is fair to see the popularity of Ash'arism, Māturīdism and (on a far smaller scale) of moderate Ḥanbalism as the long-term consequence of the community's instinctive dislike of doctrines that seemed to err on the side of excess. It was only in the context of Shī'ism, with its more hierarchical ordering of authority, that the Mu'tazilite doctrines found a permanent place, and even here, as Sajjad Rizvi shows, some of the more austere Mu'tazilite principles were not maintained.

REASON AND REVELATION

Closely linked to this dialectic was the even more taxing balance which high medieval Islam thought it had achieved between "reason" ('*aql*) and revelation (*naql*). Those who stressed the former tended to assume that the Qur'an's arguments for itself proceed on the principle that reason is prior to the authority of revelation; they therefore tended to support a strongly abstract model of God; strict scripturalists, by contrast, often inclined to anthropomorphism. It was generally admitted that metaphysics was primarily the domain of *'aql*, while issues of prophetic authority, and the features of the next world, could be known only through revelation. Marcia Hermansen's chapter on eschatology brings home the strongly scripturalist nature of the arguments here. Such matters were *sam'iyyāt*, doctrines received *ex auditu*, and were acknowledged to be unprovable by reason, although not unreasonable in themselves.

But the *'aql/naql* tension in Islam went far beyond this. To some extent it defined the discipline of *kalām* against the disciplines of law and Sufism, even though, as we have seen, these three were regularly reintegrated and seldom became dangerously divorced. As Ash'arism and Māturīdism evolved, beyond the critical twelfth century they became systematic theologies in the truest sense: in the works of Taftāzānī, Ījī and Jurjānī, scriptural references are common, but the crucial opening treatment of metaphysics (*ilāhiyyāt*) is clearly figured as a reason-based vindication of doctrines which can also be known separately through scripture. The initiative championed by Ghazālī, which sought to show the symbiosis of law, Sufism, scripture and *kalām*, was not incorporated at all into *kalām* in its final stage of development, but flourished, as has been seen, in the tradition of Ibn 'Arabī. *Kalām* remained always a discourse of divine transcendence, of *aporia* and of logic, which vindicated claims made through revelation and mystical insight, but never incorporated them into its epistemology.

The triumph of transcendentalism and of an austere negative theology in *kalām* is striking, and might seem to challenge the claim, made earlier, that doctrines and disciplines tended to emerge as "orthodox" through popular sanction. Certainly it is intriguing that the Ḥanbalī alternative in most places represented no more than a small fringe, just as the Ḥanbalī definition of *Sharī'a* remained the smallest of the rites of law. The iconic hard-line champion of this school, Ibn Taymiyya, whose challenge to Ghazālī's approach is referred to in Paul Hardy's contribution to this volume, is not conspicuous in the catalogues of Islamic manuscript libraries; his current renown is a recent phenomenon.[23] Ibn Taymiyya was, indeed, imprisoned for heresy, a relatively unusual occurrence, and it would be hard to imagine Muslim society, or its rulers or scholars, punishing more philosophical thinkers like Ghazālī, or Rāzī, or Taftāzānī, in the same way. "Hard" Ḥanbalism offered a simple literalism to troubled urban masses, and occasionally won their violent, riotous support, but the consensus of Muslims passed it by.

The community's historic rejection of Mu'tazilism and Ḥanbalism had much to do with distaste at the violence with which those tendencies sought to promote themselves. The demise of Khārijism can probably be attributed to a comparable disenchantment. Very different was the apparent decay of *falsafa*, the Arabic extension of Hellenistic thought, which a much earlier generation of Western commentators, harking back to Ernest Renan if not before, once thought might have been the salvation of an otherwise unreasonable religion. The advocates of *falsafa*'s refined and abstract view of Islam could never have enjoyed much street credibility, and this always told against them. Yet in recent research the important story of the later evolution of this paradigm has emerged as a much more complex process than was once believed.

THE FATE OF *FALSAFA*

As Hossein Ziai demonstrates in his chapter, Abbasid civilisation showed itself willing and able to embark on one of the most ambitious projects of deliberate cultural borrowing known to history. If the Qur'an represents a first moment of Islamic xenophilia, rejecting the indigenous beliefs of the Arabs in favour of the monotheistic worldview and prophetic tales of their neighbours and rivals, then the process whereby Greek texts were translated into Arabic is surely the second. (The third, which is Islam's engagement with modernity, lies outside the scope of this volume.) Oliver Leaman demonstrates that what was at stake in the contest between *kalām*, traditionalism and this imaginative synthesis of Islamic, Neoplatonic and Aristotelian strands was not "reason" against "revelation", but rather the strategy by which these ought to be brought into conversation and synthesis. Even the Ḥanbalites, as he reminds us, could not be said to be "against reason".

Falsafa fascinated many, far beyond the small coteries in which it was formally translated and debated. Yahya Michot has written elsewhere of an "Avicennian pandemic",[24] a rapid spread of Avicenna's system which has no parallel in Islamic intellectual history, apart from the even more sudden diffusion of Ibn 'Arabī's thought which took place in the middle and late thirteenth century. Once believed to have been dealt a mortal blow by Ghazālī, Avicenna's system is now known to have prospered mightily after him.[25] That this should have succeeded is no great surprise; after all, it has been argued that Avicenna had already borrowed from the *kalām* thinkers, for instance in evolving his key essence/existence distinction.[26] If, as one modern historian presents matters, the ancient effort to reconcile Aristotle's various positions was the creation of a "Lesser Symphony", and late antiquity's attempt to reconcile Aristotle with Plato was the "Great Symphony",[27] then it might be said that later *kalām* functioned as a third symphony, whose goal was the completion of the somewhat haphazard attempt by Avicenna to integrate Semitic monotheism into his philosophy.

Even the most superficial perusal of a late *kalām* work will reveal the immense influence which Avicenna exerted on the framing of Muslim orthodoxy. Although the process is still imperfectly mapped, many scholars are accepting a view which presents Avicenna, not Ghazālī, as the watershed between the "ancient" (*mutaqaddimūn*) and "modern" (*muta'akhkhirūn*) theologians, so that "the turn in Sunni *kalām* was therefore Avicennian, not Ghazālian".[28] *Falsafa* as a separate discipline did not die, and, as Ziai shows, it continued to flourish under the name of *ḥikmat* in Iran. Among Sunnīs, Avicenna continued to be taught in tandem with the *kalām* texts which took him, as well as the scriptures, as their point of departure for the study of God, who was now explicitly defined in Avicennian terms as the Necessary Existent. The Ottoman chief judge Molla Kestelli (d. 1495) was proud to have read Avicenna's *Shifā'* seven times,[29] and Avicenna continued to be referred to extensively by some Sunnīs as well as many Shī'īs up to and beyond the dawn of modernity. The field has moved far from older Orientalist images, purveyed notably by Leo Strauss, of a *falsafa* tradition that lived in fear of an orthodox backlash.[30] On the contrary, as we now acknowledge, "there was not a single such philosopher who was ever persecuted, let alone executed, for his *philosophical* views".[31]

The puzzle of the decline of Hellenism in Islam has thus turned out not to be a puzzle at all, for the simple reason that it did not happen. On the contrary, we now know that Hellenism became so dominant in *kalām* that Taftāzānī (d. 1389), author of perhaps the most widely used text of later Muslim theology, wrote that the *kalām* folk had "incorporated most of the physics and metaphysics, and delved deeply into the mathematics, so that but for the *sam'iyyāt*, *kalām* was hardly distinguishable from *falsafa*".[32] The historian Ibn Khaldūn made a very similar observation.[33] In many forms of Sufism, too, we recognise a strong *falsafa* component: there is an Avicennian strand in Ibn 'Arabī, for instance, and Suhrawardī's illuminationist philosophy flourished in Anatolian Sufism, particularly among commentators on Rūmī. Throughout Islamic civilisation the Avicennian insistance on theology as the crown of metaphysics moved Muslim intellectuals towards metaphysical arguments for the existence and nature of God; Ayman Shihadeh, in his chapter, shows the extent to which Avicennism was a major tributary of the later *kalām*, particularly in the key argument from contingency.

Nonetheless, as several authors in this collection demonstrate, *falsafa* as a discipline was progressively overtaken, or perhaps swallowed up, by Sunnī *kalām* at some point after the twelfth century. Perhaps the reason for this was the same factor which had caused the translation movement to wind down two centuries earlier: the ideas had been successfully transmitted. *Falsafa* functioned as an intermediary school, a module provisionally and imperfectly integrated into Muslim culture which allowed Muslim thinkers to entertain Greek ideas and choose those which seemed to them persuasive and true. As a system, however, it did not possess the resources to survive indefinitely. Once Muslims found that their need for a sophisticated philosophical theology was satisfied by the *kalām*, *falsafa* as an independent discipline naturally withered.

This process was no doubt accelerated by the "congregational" principle alluded to above. Although Avicenna and Averroes had both served as religious judges, their systems were hardly calculated to attract the masses. Neither were the complexities of the *kalām* folk, but the latter nonetheless possessed an advantage. *Falsafa* had inherited certain concepts which, reproduced and elaborated by Arabic-speaking philosophers, seemed unacceptable even to eirenically minded Semitic monotheists. The Greek conception of a hierarchy of animate heavens provides one example of an idea of ultimately pagan provenance that was destined to fade away in Islam. Ash'arism and Māturīdism were likewise unhappy with the stark determinism of the Neoplatonists, who had taught that God's actions were the ineluctable consequence of his essence, thus negating both human and divine freedom. With reservations, Ash'arism, and to a lesser degree Māturīdism, accepted a predetermined universe, but this was shaped by God's attribute of power, which for them was separate from his essence.[34] Muslim thought wished to affirm a free and reasonable deity, and this *falsafa* was unable to supply.[35]

A separate category of *falsafa* tenets not only was offensive to Muslim assurances about a morally coherent and autonomous God, but seemed to violate certain fundamental scriptural assurances. As David Burrell notes in his chapter on Muslim doctrines of creation, the qur'anic deity who creates *ex nihilo* was an impossibility for the Greeks, who favoured a model of eternal emanation. Burrell shows how Ghazālī, in his *The Incoherence of the Philosophers*, refutes this belief, together with two others which seemed both un-Qur'anic and metaphysically absurd. Yet the *Incoherence* is not a thoroughgoing manifesto against

Avicennian metaphysics; instead it inveighs against certain ancient Hellenistic principles that seemed to have acquired the status of school doctrines.[36] Ghazālī in fact zealously integrated Greek techniques, the modal logic most notably, into Islamic thought,[37] thus opening the way for the systematic theology of Rāzī, and the thirteenth-century "golden age" of Arabic logic.[38]

The picture that emerges is becoming clearer, and is in fact not terribly surprising. Medieval Muslims treated Greek philosophy rather as modern theologians treat modern secular philosophy. They recoiled at some of its conclusions, and enriched their thought-worlds by constructing imaginative refutations, but they displayed an abiding fascination with its mindset and its methods. While we may, depending on our philosophical preferences, speak of an age of decline, we cannot say that the decline was one of sophistication or of a willingness to use "reason" or "foreign sciences". Muslim orthodoxy did not shed Hellenism, but steadily accumulated it, and continued to extol the core Aristotelian discipline of logic, not only in *kalām*, but in law.[39] The *kalām* had come into being as an apologetic exercise to defeat error, a "therapeutic pragmatism" as Shihadeh puts it,[40] and the absence of major new sectarian movements following its final establishment is presumably a sign that, on its own terms, it did not substantially fall prey to decadence.

Notes

1. Arthur Koestler, *The Sleepwalkers: A History of Man's Changing Vision of the Universe* (London, 1959), p. 105. For the attitude see Dimitri Gutas, "The study of Arabic philosophy in the twentieth century: an essay on the historiography of Arabic philosophy", *British Journal of Middle Eastern Studies* 29 (2002), pp. 10–12.
2. Robert Wisnovsky, *Avicenna's Metaphysics in Context* (London, 2003), p. 301.
3. Louis Massignon, *Essay on the Origins of the Technical Language of Islamic Mysticism*, tr. Benjamin Clark (Notre Dame, 1997), pp. 34–6, 75–6, 94–8.
4. See Michael E. Marmura, "Ghazālī and Ash'arism revisited", *Arabic Sciences and Philosophy* 12 (2002), pp. 91–110. Among other reasons for the acceptability of Sufism one might cite the precedent of the Prophet's own mystical ascension to God (*mi'rāj*).
5. Ayman Shihadeh, "From al-Ghazālī to al-Rāzī: 6th/12th century developments in Muslim philosophical theology", *Arabic Sciences and Philosophy* 15 (2005), pp. 176, 177.
6. James Morris, "Ibn 'Arabī and his interpreters", *Journal of the American Oriental Society* 106 (1986), p. 733.
7. Wisnovsky, *Avicenna's Metaphysics*, pp. 227–44.

8. For the relationship between Christian anti-Semitism and Islamophobia see Achim Rohde, "Der Innere Orient: Orientalismus, Antisemitismus und Geschlecht im Deutschland dem 18. bis 20. Jahrhunderts", *Welt des Islams* 45 (2005), pp. 344–70. Ernest Renan, fountainhead of many Orientalist assumptions about Islamic irrationality, was also given to large theories about the "Semitic mind"; see Charles Chauvin, *Renan* (Paris, 2000), pp. 94–5.
9. Francis Robinson, "Ottomans, Safavids, Mughals: shared knowledge and connective systems", *Journal of Islamic Studies* 8 (1997), pp. 151–84.
10. Cf. Qur'an 19:37; 43:65.
11. Ibn Qudāma al-Maqdisī, *Taḥrīm al-naẓar fī kutub ahl al-kalām*, tr. George Makdisi as *Censure of Speculative Theology* (London, 1962); S. de Laugier de Beaurecueil, *Khwādja 'Abdullāh Anṣārī: mystique Ḥanbalite* (Beirut, 1965), pp. 204–21.
12. Hans Küng, *Christianity and the World Religions* (London, 1984), p. 25.
13. For the centrality of the Qur'an to Ibn 'Arabī, consider C.-A. Gilis, *Le Coran et la fonction d'Hermès* (Paris, 1984). Cf. James Morris: "Nor can one study any work of his for long without developing a transformed awareness of and sensitivity to the words and deeper dimensions of the Qur'an" ("Ibn 'Arabī and his interpreters", p. 551).
14. Jean Calmard, "Les rituals shiites et le pouvoir: l'imposition du shiisme Safavide: eulogies et malédictions canoniques", in Jean Calmard (ed.), *Études Safavides* (Paris and Tehran, 1993), pp. 109–50.
15. For aspects of *takfīr* see Frank Griffel, *Apostasie und Toleranz im Islam: Die Entwicklung zu al-Gazālīs Urteil gegen die Philosophie und die Reaktionen der Philosophen* (Leiden, 2000); for the Mu'tazilite enthusiasm for *takfīr* see pp. 151–64.
16. For the use of this hadith, see the traditional treatment by Mohammed Hashim Kamali, *Principles of Islamic Jurisprudence*, 3rd edn (Cambridge, 2003), pp. 228–63.
17. Hadith in Tirmidhī, Fitan, 7.
18. Josef van Ess, *The Flowering of Muslim Theology* (Cambridge, MA, 2006), p. 43.
19. Van Ess (ibid., p. 142) attributes the *ta'dīb al-'āmma* principle to Iranian, not "indigenous", Islamic sources.
20. Muḥammad al-Sakhāwī, *al-Maqāṣid al-Ḥasana fī bayān kathīrin min al-aḥādīth al-mushtahira 'ala'l-alsina*, ed. M. al-Khusht (Beirut, 1405/1985), p. 332.
21. Abū Ja'far Muḥammad ibn Jarīr al-Ṭabarī, *The Commentary on the Qur'ān*, tr. J. Cooper (Oxford, 1987), pp. 77, 78; and, *Jāmi' al-bayān 'an ta'wīl āyi al-Qur'ān*, ed. M. and A. Shākir (Cairo, 1374 AH), III, p. 142 (to Qur'an 2:143).
22. Marmura, "Ghazālī and Ash'arism revisited", p. 103.
23. Khaled El-Rouayheb, "From Ibn Ḥajar al-Haytamī (d. 1566) to Khayr al-Dīn al-Alūsī (d. 1899): changing conceptions of Ibn Taymiyya amongst Sunnī scholars", in Mohammed S. Ahmed and Yosef Rapoport (eds.), *Ibn Taymiyya and His Times* (Oxford, 2008).

24. Yahya Michot, "La pandémie avicennienne au VIe/XIIe siècle", *Arabica* 40 (1993), pp. 288–344.
25. Dimitri Gutas, "The heritage of Avicenna: the golden age of Arabic philosophy, 1000–*c.* 1350", in Jules Janssens and Daniël De Smet (eds.), *Avicenna and His Heritage* (Leuven, 2002), pp. 81–97.
26. Wisnovsky, *Avicenna's metaphysics*, pp. 16, 145–80. For a challenge to this view see the review by Allan Bäck in *Ars Disputandi*, <www.arsdisputandi.org>, 5 (2005).
27. Wisnovsky, *Avicenna's Metaphysics*, p. 15.
28. Robert Wisnovsky, "One aspect of the Avicennian turn in Sunnī theology", *Arabic Sciences and Philosophy* 14 (2004), p. 65.
29. Mecdī Meḥmed Efendi, *Ḥadā'iq al-Şaqā'iq* (Istanbul, 1269 AH), p. 165. However, after the fifteenth century, references to Ottoman ulema reading independent *falsafa* works are very unusual.
30. Daniel Tanguay, *Leo Strauss: une biographie intellectuelle* (Paris, 2003), pp. 88–9.
31. Gutas, "The heritage of Avicenna", p. 20 (emphasis in original).
32. Sa'd al-Dīn al-Taftāzānī, in Muṣliḥ al-Dīn Muṣṭafā al-Qasṭallānī (Molla Kestelli), *Ḥāshiyat al-Kestellī 'alā Sharḥ al-'aqā'id* (Istanbul, 1326 AH), p. 17.
33. Shihadeh, "From al-Ghazālī to al-Rāzī", p. 175: *falsafa* and *kalām* "came to be as if one and the same discipline".
34. Taneli Kukkonen, "Possible worlds in the *Tahāfut al-Falāsifa*: al-Ghazālī on creation and contingency", *Journal of the History of Philosophy* 38 (2000), p. 484.
35. The idea that *kalām* advocated an arbitrary God whose possible actions are not bound by logic, as in the Ẓāhirite theology of Ibn Ḥazm, is dismissed by Kukkonen, ibid., p. 493, in connection with Ghazālī's thought.
36. Jules Janssens, "Al-Ghazzālī's *Tahāfut*: is it really a rejection of Avicenna's philosophy?", *Journal of Islamic Studies* 12 (2001), pp. 1–17.
37. Michael E. Marmura, "Ghazâlî and Demonstrative Science", *Journal of the History of Philosophy* 3 (1965), pp. 183–204.
38. Tony Street, "Arabic logic", in Dov M. Gabbay and John Woods (eds.), *Handbook of the History of Logic*, 1 (Amsterdam, etc., 2004), p. 527.
39. Khaled El-Rouayheb, "Sunni Muslim scholars on the status of logic, 1500–1800", in *Islamic Law and Society* 11 (2004), pp. 213–32.
40. Shihadeh, "From al-Ghazālī to al-Rāzī", p. 147.

Part I

Historical perspectives

1 Qur'an and hadith

M. A. S. ABDEL HALEEM

THE QUR'AN

The Qur'an is the starting-point of Islamic theology, and indeed of all things Islamic. As technically defined by Islamic theology and law, it is "the corpus of Arabic utterances sent down by God to Muḥammad, conveyed in a way that categorically establishes its authenticity".[1]

For the tradition, this classical definition summarises the basic characteristics of the Qur'an and distinguishes it from anything else the Prophet said. The key phrase is "sent down by God", for God speaks directly in the Qur'an, and Muḥammad is seen as a passive recipient to whom the Book was simply "sent down"; however, it is the last element of the definition which is most significant in considering the historical basis for Islamic beliefs.

According to the Muslim historians, the first revelation consisted of two lines in Arabic: in the year 610, Muḥammad was engaged in a spiritual retreat in a cave outside Mecca when he was approached by an angel who said to him: "Read!" He replied that he could not read, but the angel repeated the command, and received the same response; the third time, the angel recited to him the words: "Read, in the name of your Lord, who created" (96:1–6). This revelatory experience was soon followed by another, when a second short passage was delivered; and between that time and shortly before the Prophet's death at the age of sixty-three years, the entire text of the Muslim scripture gradually appeared. New revelations appeared in order to supply new teaching, commenting on events or answering questions according to circumstance.

That the Qur'an is the Word of God revealed to the Prophet Muḥammad is seen by Muslims to be confirmed by the revelation's language. The first word revealed ("Read!") is an imperative addressed *to* the Prophet, linguistically excluding his authorship of the text. This mode is maintained throughout the Qur'an. The Book speaks to the

Prophet, or talks about him, and nowhere leaves him to speak for himself. The Qur'an describes itself as a scripture which God "sent down" to His prophet, and this expression, "sent down", in its various derivations, is used in the Qur'an well over 200 times. In Arabic this locution conveys immediately, and, implicitly, the principle that the origin of the Book is heavenly, and that Muḥammad is no more than its receptacle. God is the one who speaks in this Book: Muḥammad is addressed as "O Prophet!", "O Messenger!", "Do", "Do not do", "They ask you ... ", "Say!" (this last command appearing more than 300 times). Sometimes the Prophet is reproached (9:43; 80:1–11). His status is unequivocally defined as "messenger" (*rasūl*), and he is often reminded that his duty is simply to communicate (*balāgh*) the message to his community.

A hadith reports that during his first experience of revelation the Prophet was alone in the cave, but subsequent circumstances in which the received episodes of revelation were witnessed by others and recorded. Sometimes these witnesses would report visible, audible and sensory reactions when the Prophet experienced the "state of revelation". His face would "become bright", and he would fall silent and seem to be contemplating distant things; his body would become heavy as though in sleep, a humming sound would be heard around him, and sweat might appear on his brow, even on winter days. This stage would swiftly end, and as it did so he would immediately recite new verses of the scripture. The sources report that this state was not the Prophet's to command: it might descend on him as he was walking, sitting, riding or giving a sermon, and there were occasions when he waited for it anxiously for over a month when he needed an answer to a question he had been asked, or sought an interpretation of some event. The Prophet and his followers understood these signs as experiences accompanying the communication of scriptural verses by Gabriel, the Angel of Revelation; his adversaries explained them as proof that he was "possessed", and in this regard, the Qur'an itself records many claims and attacks made upon it and upon the Prophet in his lifetime.[2]

The evidence suggests that for the Prophet himself, the Qur'an was "sent down" and communicated to him by "the faithful Spirit", Gabriel, and was categorically not his own speech. Stylistically, qur'anic material which the Prophet recited following the states of revelation described above is so evidently different from the Prophet's own sayings as recorded in the hadith, whether uttered incidentally or after long reflection, that the tradition has always ascribed them to two radically different levels of discourse.

For the Qur'an, the Prophet is the passive recipient of a revelation over which he has no control, and which does not allow for dialogue, even between him and the Angel of Revelation. By contrast, a general feature of the hadith is a constant conversation addressed to and reported by named individuals. In hadiths narrating the actions of the Prophet, there is often a description of the setting and the occasion, where the narrator speaks at length, while the Prophet, if he is involved, speaks only a few words, and perhaps not at all.

The Muslim historians report that with each new accumulation in the qur'anic corpus, the Prophet would recite it to those around him, who would memorise it and in turn communicate it to others. Throughout his mission the Prophet repeatedly read the Qur'an to his followers in formal prayer and at other times. An inner circle of his disciples wrote down the verses that he taught them. He himself was assiduous in having the text recorded even in the days of persecution, and he acquired scribes for this purpose (twenty-nine have been counted in the Medina period).

The word 'Qur'ān' itself means "reading", and came to refer to "the text which is read". The Muslim scripture often calls itself *kitāb*, "writing", and this word came to denote the scripture, the "written book". Thus the significance of uttering and writing the revealed scripture was emphasised from the beginning of the new religion, and is locked into the very nouns that designate the qur'anic canon.

Qur'anic revelations are believed to have come to the Prophet piecemeal over a period of twenty-three years. The disparate material is invariably divided into 114 *sūra*s ("sections", conventionally translated in English as "chapters"). A *sūra* may consist of no more than one line, such as *sūra*s 108 and 112; while *sūra* 2, the longest, stretches over dozens of pages. Each *sūra* consists of verses, each known in Arabic as *āya* (a "sign" from God). Some *sūra*s contain Meccan and Medinan *āya*s: the order of material in each *sūra*, according to classical Muslim teaching, having been determined by the Prophet at the command of the Angel of Revelation, who delivered the qur'anic material to him. The hadith record that when each new unit of text was received he would request his disciples to place it in a given chapter, and the result was that material was distributed over the *sūra*s not in chronological order of appearance, but as they were to be read by the Prophet and the believers.[3]

Over the years, in formal liturgical practice and in counselling his followers, the Prophet recited qur'anic material so frequently and at such length that it is reasonable to regard the current sequence of *sūra*s today as faithfully reflecting this original arrangement. By the time of the

Prophet's death in the year 632, the entire scripture had been written down in the form of uncollated sections, but many of his followers, having spent years in his company where the Qur'an was a constant presence, had memorised much or all of the text, and the book was principally experienced as an aural phenomenon.[4] These men and women were members of a cultural world that had a longstanding tradition of committing literature, history and genealogy to memory. Two years after the Prophet's death, the battle of Yamāma against the people of Najd in Central Arabia took place, in which a number of those who knew the text lost their lives, and the sources report that it was feared that parts of the text might be lost. The first caliph, Abū Bakr (632–4), therefore ordered that the Qur'an should be collected in a single written copy, which was then placed in the custody of 'Umar, and, after his death, was left with the Prophet's widow Ḥafṣa. This copy was the basis of the codex issued in several copies by the third caliph, 'Uthmān (644–56), to be distributed to several parts of the Muslim world to ensure that a universal standard text of the scripture would prevail. This has remained the sole canonical text of the Qur'an, recognised by Sunnī and Shī'ī theologians to the present time.[5]

THE HADITH

Although the Qur'an is the unrivalled supreme revelation of Islam, the tradition also recognises a second form of revealed scripture: the hadith (*ḥadīth*). Technically, Muslims came to define the hadith as "the attested reports of the sayings, actions, and tacit approvals and accounts of the Prophet Muḥammad".[6] These present records of the Prophet's statements, as well as statements by his companions relating to him. Collectively the hadith literature provides evidence for the Prophet's way of life (*sunna*), so that the word *sunna* is in the eyes of many synonymous with the word *ḥadīth*.[7] The relationship between the Qur'an and hadith is well defined: the hadith either emphasises what is in the Qur'an (*sunna mu'akkida*), explains the manner in which something should be carried out (*sunna mubayyina*) or introduces teaching based on certain qur'anic verses or principles (*sunna muthbita*). The latter category in particular was to become a prime source of material for the theologians.

The vast corpus of hadith includes reports of the Prophet's childhood and his experiences in Mecca before his prophetic career began; but most hadith refer to the Medina period, when the Prophet had thousands of followers who asked him questions and received instruction from him in all aspects of the new religion.[8] The hadith show the Prophet as a skilled communicator and teacher.[9] In Medina he was with his Companions for nearly all the daylight hours and for much of the evening; his house gave on to the mosque, and some hadith show that even when at home he would sometimes hear heated discussions taking place in the mosque and would come out to resolve the dispute. This constant interaction led to the creation of the immense body of hadith, which he is recorded as urging his followers to pass on to others: "God bless the one who has heard me say something and preserved it [in his memory] so that he can pass it on to others, for many a person carries knowledge to others more knowledgeable than himself."[10]

However, whereas with qur'anic material the sources record that the Prophet was careful to have it written down as well as learnt by heart, this was not the case with the hadith. In fact, there is evidence to suggest that only once the Qur'an was fully recorded did he begin to allow those Companions who could write proficiently to record the hadith in written form.[11] After his death, the caliph 'Umar I (634–44) is said to have debated a scheme to have the hadith collected into a single text; he decided against this, fearing that it might come to rival the Qur'an. The collection of hadith appears not to have received official sanction until the time of the Umayyad caliph 'Umar II (717–19), who seems to have initiated and partly carried out the task of collating the material. But by the beginning of the second Muslim century the writing down of hadith and of other forms of Muslim learning was spreading exponentially. The community came to revere three successive generations who inaugurated and shaped this process. These were the Companions (*ṣaḥāba*) of the Prophet, a category made up of all who saw him or heard him speak (the last is said to have died in the year 110 AH); the Successors (*tābiʿūn*) who received the hadith from the Companions (the last of these, according to some claims, died in 180); and the Successors of the Successors (*atbāʿ al-tābiʿīn*), some of whom allegedly lived until the first quarter of the third century of Islam.

Because of the delay in commencing the authentication process, and because of the sheer size of the hadith material (which was preserved in the form of perhaps a million separate reports), the early Muslim scholars admitted the existence of a large number of forgeries and distortions, many of which echoed early sectarian tensions. In reaction, the growing class of scholars (*'ulamā'*) slowly developed intricate methods for assessing the reliability of individual hadith reports. A tradition of travelling in search of relevant information began, retracing the footsteps of the Companions and others who had migrated to the far corners of the new Islamic world. We are told, for instance, that it took the

Central Asian al-Bukhārī (d. 870) sixteen years of travel and study to assemble his collection.[12]

Bukhārī's criteria for accepting a hadith as sound (*ṣaḥīḥ*) were that it should have reached him from the Prophet on the authority of a well-known Companion, by means of a continuous chain (*isnād*) of narrators who, according to his records, had been accepted unanimously by trustworthy scholars as men and women of integrity, retentive memories and firm faith. If they did not explicitly state that they had received the material from their own teachers, he took care to establish that they had demonstrably met those whom they cited as teachers.

Given the overwhelmingly oral nature of the hadith in the early period, it was only natural that hadith specialists should have begun with the chain of narrators; but their criticism was not limited to this. General principles for the criticism of the transmitted text (*matn*) of the hadiths evolved during the second and third Islamic centuries, and foremost among these principles was the understanding that a hadith should not contradict the Qur'an, or other hadiths which were already and generally accepted as authentic, and that it must not conflict with the absolute consensus of the community (*ijmāʿ qaṭʿī*), or a list of accepted general principles of the religion. For a hadith to be an acceptable source of practice or of doctrine it was thought that it should not contradict the established historical facts known about the time of the Prophet, or report an event that should have been visible to a large number of people yet was not reported by anyone else, or be the result of any demonstrably partisan motivations. Traditional Muslim scholars continue to assert, with some justification, that this insistence on authenticity and exactitude in determining the scriptural canon is unparalleled in other pre-modern cultures. In consequence, a body of accepted hadith was able to form a highly reputable second source of Muslim teaching which, it was thought, should complement and augment the doctrine of the Qur'an itself.

SCRIPTURAL DOGMAS

The most elementary components of Islamic faith might be said to appear in a single qur'anic verse:

> The Messenger believes in what has been sent down to him from his Lord, as do the faithful. They all believe in God, His angels, His scriptures and His messengers: "We make no distinction between any of His messengers." They say: "We hear and obey; grant us Your forgiveness, our Lord. To You we all return." (2:285)

On the basis of this and similar statements, Islamic theology was often broken down into the following five basic components: belief in one God, His messengers, His books, His angels, and the day of judgement.

In traditional Muslim theology, any credal article fundamental enough to distinguish believer from non-believer has to be established by categorical proof-texts which have been rigorously transmitted and which indisputably mean what they are claimed to mean. Accordingly, fundamental matters of creed (*'aqīda*) can only[13] be based on the Qur'an, since it is believed to be categorically authentic in the highest degree, and only on such verses in the Qur'an that are indisputable in meaning (*qaṭ'ī al-dalāla*).[14]

A rather small number of axiomatic beliefs fall into this category. They came to be distinguished from a range of other theological problems, such as whether God can be seen by the human eye, whether His attributes are other than His essence, whether or not a person committing a major sin will be punished everlastingly, whether there will be a *mahdī* who will come at the end of time, whether or not Jesus will return in person, whether or not it is obligatory for God to do what is best for people, whether or not a person creates his own actions voluntarily, and whether or not the sins people commit are willed by God. These issues, which have been disputed by the theologians, are not taken by Ash'arism, the main school of Muslim orthodoxy, to be the most fundamental axioms of the creed, and disbelief in any one of them will not put anyone outside the fold of Islam, since they are not established by absolutely categorical proof-texts in the scriptures.

A salient feature of the qur'anic presentations of doctrines is that they are not treated together and exhaustively in a single *sūra*. Instead, as the medieval exegete al-Rāzī concludes in his account of the "stylistic habits of the Qur'an", they are the armature of other, practical teachings.[15] Thus even in discussions of legal matters, theological statements often come before and afterwards, reminding the reader of God's power and glory, and also of the judgement, both of past nations and at the end of time. It is these scattered declarations, together with the names which God has given Himself in the Qur'an, which form the qur'anic quarry from which Muslim theology is hewn.

The core of Islamic theology is limited to the explanation and defence of the five fundamental beliefs listed above. In the *ṣaḥīḥ* hadith anthologies of Bukhārī and Muslim we find these reiterated; to give but one well-known example, in a hadith related by the second caliph 'Umar, the beliefs given in Qur'an 2:285 are reported in the same order: "When the Prophet was asked: 'Tell me what is faith (*īmān*),' he replied:

'Faith is to believe in God, His angels, His books, His messengers, and the Last Day, and to believe in divine destiny, whether good or bad.' "[16] This hadith merely repeats the information supplied in Qur'an 2:285, adding the belief in destiny established elsewhere in the scripture, as at 57:22–3 and 64:11.

The first belief: monotheism

The Qur'an emerged in contestation with a polytheistic culture, and affirming God's unity (*tawḥīd*) is its most fundamental tenet. A characteristic feature of the Qur'an is that its urging of faith in God is accompanied by an argument, which is a straightforward argument from design.[17] In numerous passages, the Qur'an argues for the existence, unity and grace of God, for example in the many "Signs" verses:

> Another of His signs is the way He created spouses of your own kind for you to find repose with one another – He ordained love and kindness between you. There truly are signs in this for those who reflect. Another of His signs is the creation of the heavens and the earth, the diversity of your languages and colours. There truly are signs in this for those who know. (30:21–2)

the "Who" verses:

> Say [Prophet]: "Who provides for you from the sky and the earth? Who controls hearing and sight? Who brings forth the living from the dead and the dead from the living, and who governs all things?" They are sure to say: "God." Then say: "So why do you not take heed of Him?" (10:31)

and the "It is He" verses:

> It is He who sends down water from the sky. With it We produce the shoots of each plant, then bring greenery from it, and from that We bring out grains, one riding on the other in close-packed rows. From the date-palm come clusters of low-hanging dates, and there are gardens of vines, olives and pomegranates, alike yet different – watch their fruits as they grow and ripen! In all this there are signs for those who would believe. (6:99)

Other inductive arguments:

> If there had been in the heavens or earth any gods but Him, both heavens and earth would be in ruins. (21:23)

> Nor is there any god beside Him – if there were, each god would have taken his creation aside and tried to overcome the others. (23:91)

> Say [Prophet]: "Consider those you pray to other than God: show me which bit of the earth they created or which share of the heavens they own; bring me a previous scripture or some vestige of divine knowledge, if what you say is true. (46:4)

Believing in or calling on any deity other than God is termed *shirk* (partnership), which is the only unforgivable sin (4:116), unless one repents (25:68–70). It is God that should be worshipped: "there is no god but God" (47:19). This mode of expression is the most categorical possible in Arabic grammar. All gods are denied, with the exception of God Himself.

The second belief: in angels

The pagan Arabs of Mecca believed that the angels were the daughters of God; and this met with a qur'anic response.

> One of their fabrications is that they say, "God has begotten" – how they lie! (37:151–2)

The angels exist, and are creatures, not disobeying God's commands (66:6). Some of them convey God's messages to the Prophets (32:51); they encourage and pray for the believers (40:7–9); some record human actions (50:17–18), while others take human souls at death (32:11). Angels praise God (2:30), and carry His throne:

> Those [angels] who carry the Throne and those who surround it celebrate the praise of their Lord and believe in Him. They beg forgiveness for the believers: "Our Lord, You embrace all things in mercy and knowledge, so forgive those who turn to you and follow Your path. Save them from the pains of Hell and admit them, Lord, to the everlasting Garden You have promised to them, and to their righteous forebears, spouses and offspring. You alone are the Almighty, the All-Wise. Protect them from evil deeds: those You protect from evil deeds on that Day will receive Your mercy – that is the supreme triumph." (40:7–9)

The third belief: in scriptures

The Qur'an exhorts its audience to believe in all the scriptures "sent down" by God, and not only in the Qur'an, for the Muslim scripture states that it confirms the scriptures already received by the "People of the Book" (*ahl al-kitāb*):

> Step by step, He has sent the scripture down to you [Muḥammad] with the truth, confirming what went before; He sent down the Torah and the Gospel as a guide for people: He has sent down the distinction [between right and wrong]. (3:3–4)

> We revealed the Torah with guidance and light, and the prophets, who had submitted to God, the rabbis and the scholars all gave judgement by it for the Jews in accordance with that part of the Book of God which they were entrusted to preserve, and to which they were witnesses. (5:44)

> We sent Jesus, son of Mary, in their footsteps, to confirm the Torah that had been sent before him: We gave him the Gospel with guidance, light and confirmation of the Torah already revealed – a guide and lesson for those who take heed of God. So let the followers of the Gospel judge according to what God has sent down. Those who do not judge according to what God has revealed are lawbreakers. (5:46)

The fourth belief: in God's messengers

The recipients of scripture are "messengers" (*rusul*), who are all addressed by God with the words: "This community of yours is one – and I am your Lord: be mindful of Me" (23:52). Those who accept them are asked to profess that they "make no distinction between any of them" (2:284). Over twenty prophets are mentioned in the Qur'an, including Abraham, Moses, Jesus and Muḥammad, and over and over again the text rehearses their stories to emphasise that they brought a shared doctrine, which alone is to be followed.

> We never sent any messenger before you [Muḥammad] without revealing to him: "There is no god but Me, so serve Me". (21:25)

> These were the people God guided, so follow the guidance they received. (6:83)

The qur'anic recitals of the lives of earlier prophets confirm to Muslims that they are adhering to the unalterable message God has made available since the creation of Adam, summed up particularly in the monotheism and self-surrender of Abraham. All the prophets are seen as *muslim*, that is, they are 'submitters' to God, who devote themselves utterly to Him. "Religion in the sight of God is *islām*" (3:19), that is to say, it is devoted submission to Him alone.

The fifth belief: in the day of judgement

The Qur'an frequently evokes the beauty and diversity of the natural world, and belief in a final end gives sense and purpose to the whole creation. But for the judgement, the world would be in vain (23:115–16; 95:7–8), which is why the next life is mentioned in the Qur'an exactly as often as the life of this world. The semantic logic of the qur'anic text makes the domain we presently occupy the "first world" (*al-ūlā*), which exists only with reference to the "other" world which is to come (*al-ākhira*). Almost every page of the scripture presents a direct or implicit reference to the afterlife and the judgement, often in connection with the need to respect a commandment (2:232; 65:2). The Arabs who first heard the revelation found this aspect of its teaching the hardest to accept: "What! When we are dead and turned into dust and bones, shall we be resurrected again? And our fathers and our ancestors too?" (56:47–8).

It is in connection with this Arab inability to imagine a transition from one form of life to another after death that the Qur'an supplies arguments for God's ability to take life from one stage to another, frequently referring to the physical world which the Arabs could not deny.

> People, remember, if you doubt the Resurrection, that We created you from dust, then a drop of fluid, then a clinging form, then a lump of flesh, both shaped and unshaped – We mean to make Our power clear to you. Whatever We choose We cause to remain in the womb for an appointed time, then We bring you forth as babies and then you grow and reach maturity – some die young and some are left to live on to such an age that they forget all they once knew. You can perceive the earth to be barren, yet when We send down water it stirs and swells and yields every kind of joyous growth: this is because God is the Truth; He brings the dead back to life; He has power over everything. (22:5–6; see also 56:57–74)

Insistent arguments for a resurrection are also set out in 36:77–81:

> Can man not see that We created him from a drop of fluid? Yet – lo and behold! – he disputes openly, producing arguments against Us, forgetting his own creation. He says: "Who can give life back to bones after they have decayed?" Say, "He who created them in the

first place will give them life again: He has full knowledge of every act of creation. It is He who produces fire for you out of the green tree: you kindle your fire from it – lo and behold! Is He who created the heavens and earth not able to create the likes of these people? Indeed He is! He is the All-knowing Creator: when He wills something to be, He only says to it, "Be!" – and it is! So glory be to Him whose hand holds control over all things. It is to Him that you will all be brought back.

The hadith material, presumably because it addresses those who already accept the Qur'an's doctrines, does not offer this kind of argumentation, but simply builds on this belief to establish further teachings.

Whoever believes in God and the Last Day, let him speak in goodness, or hold his peace.[18]

Everyone will be resurrected in the state of faith and conduct in which he died.[19]

Finally, the Qur'an and hadith also provide lengthy descriptions of heaven and hell.[20]

In supplying arguments for belief, the Qur'an appears to assume that faith is to be accepted by free and conscientious human agents, since "there is no compulsion in religion" (2:256). The Prophet is addressed as follows:

Had your Lord willed, all the people on earth would have believed. So can you compel people to believe? (10:99)

His task is clearly demarcated:

Say: "Now the Truth has come to you from your Lord: let those who wish to believe in it do so, and let those who wish to reject it do so." (18:29)

SUMMARY

The beliefs commended by the Muslim scriptures appear to share two basic features. They are to be based on revealed texts whose mode of transmission cannot be contested, and they appeal to a thinking, questing humanity. The Qur'an proclaims, but it also offers arguments. It does not merely command faith, but commands the kind of thinking that can lead to the discovery of ultimate truth. When asking its audience to believe, or to adopt a virtue, the Qur'an invariably presents arguments based on premises that it takes to be universally accessible, since it addresses unbelievers as well as those who have accepted it as the word of God. It thus provides an original model for dialectical theology. The hadith, by contrast, are largely addressed to believers, and furnish later generations of theologians with data on which to reflect.

Further reading

Abdel Haleem, M. A. S., *The Qur'an: A New Translation* (Oxford, 2004).
Understanding the Qur'ān: Themes and Style (London, 2001).
Babu Sahib, Moulavi M.H., *The Tenets of Islam: Being a Translation and Extensive Commentary on* Kitab Jawharatu 't-Tawhid *of Imam Burhanu'd-din Ibn Harun al-Laqqani* (Singapore, 2000).
Ibrahim, Ezzedien, and Johnson-Davies, Denys (trans.), *An-Nawawi's Forty Hadith* (Damascus, 1976).
Izutsu, Toshihiko, *God and Man in the Qur'ān: Semantics of the Qur'ānic Weltanschauung* (Tokyo, 1964).
Mahmoud, Abdel-Haleem, *The Creed of Islam* (London, 1978).
Motzki, Harald (ed.), *The Biography of Muḥammad: The Issue of the Sources* (Leiden, 2000).
Rippin, Andrew (ed.), *Approaches to the History of the Interpretation of the Qur'ān* (Oxford, 1988).
Robinson, Neal, *Discovering the Qur'an: A Contemporary Approach to a Veiled Text* (London, 1996).
Robson, James (tr.), *Mishkāt al-maṣābīḥ* (Lahore, 1965).
Siddiqi, A. H. (tr.), *Sahih Muslim* (Lahore, 1973).
Welch, A. T., "Ḳur'ān", *Encyclopedia of Islam*, 2nd edn, VI, pp. 400–29.

Notes

1. Mahmud Shaltūt, *al-Islām 'aqīda wa-sharī'a* (Cairo, 1990), p. 1471; M. S. Lāshīn, *al-La'āli' al-Ḥisān fī 'ulūm al-Qur'ān* (Cairo, 1982), p. 19. To this definition should be added the property of *i'jāz*, inimitability, which makes the text an evidentiary miracle (*mu'jiza*), greater than the Prophet's other miracles of healing the sick, etc.; see Sophia Vasalou, "The miraculous eloquence of the Qur'ān: general trajectories and individual approaches", *Journal of Qur'anic Studies* 4 (2002), pp. 23–53.
2. See for instance 15:6; 21:3–4; 25:4–8.
3. Many have sought to identify a grand thematic or stylistic plan; cf. for instance M. A. Draz, *Introduction to the Qur'an* (London: 2001); Neal Robinson, *Discovering the Qur'an: A Contemporary Approach to a Veiled Text* (London, 1996), pp. 271–83; such attempts remain unproven.
4. Ṣubḥī al-Ṣāliḥ, *Mabāḥith fī 'ulūm al-Qur'ān* (Beirut, 1981), pp. 65–7; William A. Graham, *Beyond the Written Word: Oral Aspects of Scripture in the History of Religion* (Cambridge, 1987), pp. 96–109.

5. Some Shī'ite scholars disputed the canonical text; see Meir M. Bar-Asher, "Shī'ism and the Qur'ān", *Encyclopedia of the Qur'ān*, IV, pp. 593–604. Over the last quarter-century there have been theories contesting the traditional history of the Qur'an, and maintaining that it was canonised at a later date. For a survey and discussion of these views see Angelika Neuwirth, "The Qur'an and history – a disputed relationship", *Journal of Qur'ānic Studies* 5 (2003), pp. 1–18; Harald Motzki, "The collection of the Qur'ān: a reconsideration of Western views in light of recent methodological developments," *Der Islam* (2001), pp. 2–34.
6. Muṣṭafā al-Sibā'ī, *al-Sunna wa-makānatuhā fi'l-tashrī'* (Beirut, 1978), p. 47.
7. Muhammad Zubayr Siddiqi, *Ḥadīth Literature: Its Origin, Development, and Special Features* (Cambridge, 1993), p. 2.
8. Traditional sources suggest that the number of those who saw or heard him exceeded 100,000 by the end of his life; Siddiqi, *Ḥadīth Literature,* p. 15.
9. M. A. S. Abdel Haleem, "The Prophet Muḥammad as a teacher: implications for Hadith literature", *The Islamic Quarterly* 46/2 (2002), pp. 121–37.
10. Tirmidhī, 'Ilm, 7.
11. Siddiqi, *Ḥadīth Literature,* pp. 24–7.
12. Hadith anthologies came to be compiled in a variety of formats, of which the main three are: (1) *Musnad,* where the material is arranged under the names of the Companions who transmitted it. The most famous of these was the *Musnad* of Aḥmad ibn Ḥanbal (d. 855). (2) *Ṣaḥīḥ,* where material is arranged under subject headings. The most influential of these is the *Ṣaḥīḥ* of al-Bukhārī (d. 870). (3) *Sunan,* where the material is arranged under specific legal and doctrinal subject headings. The most reputed of these was the *Sunan* of al-Tirmidhī (d. 892).
13. See the role of the hadith later in this chapter.
14. Shaltūt, 53–65; for the difficulty of declaring someone a non-Muslim see Sherman Jackson, *On the Boundaries of Theological Tolerance in Islam: Abū Ḥāmid al-Ghazālī's* Fayṣal al-Tafriqa (Karachi, 2002).
15. See for instance the opening of his commentary to Qur'an 2:255.
16. Ezzeddin Ibrahim and Denys Johnson-Davies, *An-Nawawi's Forty Hadiths* (Beirut, 1976), p. 30.
17. The scripture's hearers are urged to consider their surroundings and their own selves (e.g. 10:101; 51:21). Scores of rhetorical questions are addressed to disbelievers, such as "Do you not reflect?" "Do you not see?" "Do you not use your reason?" "Do their minds command them to do so?" (52:32).
18. Bukhārī, Riqāq, 23.
19. Bukhārī, Īmān, 70.
20. Soubhi el-Saleh, *La vie future selon le Coran* (Paris, 1971); see also Marcia Hermansen's chapter (15) in the present volume.

2 The early creed

KHALID BLANKINSHIP

BACKGROUND

The intellectual milieu of seventh-century Mecca and Medina into which the Qur'an came was rustic, and bore no resemblance to the environment of the urbanised, far more literate societies of the organised empires of the Romans and Persians to the north. While literacy was nowhere widespread in early medieval times, it seems to have been especially lacking in the Arabian peninsula, where the prevalent Arabic language appears not to have possessed a written literature before the seventh century. On the other hand, the groundwork for Islam had apparently been laid orally, for the Qur'an presupposes a society of a certain sophistication of thought. Part of this sophistication was a familiarity with monotheism (Qur'an 29:61, 63; 31:25; 39:38; 43:9, 87), despite the well-entrenched and confident paganism native to the Arabs. While Arab familiarity with the monotheistic idea is unmistakably the fruit of centuries-old contact with Judaism, Christianity and Zoroastrianism, Arab isolation persisted, and knowledge of the abstract thought of the neighbouring high cultures was limited.

Such a situation of illiteracy and isolation provided the opportunity for the emergence of a new religious movement, precisely because the Arabs were not already committed to one of the existing literate traditions. This opportunity was realised when the Prophet Muḥammad began to proclaim a new message from God, first privately at Mecca, and then publicly in that city, and finally from 622 in Medina. Muḥammad taught that the true religion was that of Abraham, who had been neither Jew nor Christian (3:67), and he proclaimed that the revelation he now bore represented the true, original and unchanging religion established by God for humankind since the beginning of the human story. The older religions of Judaism and Christianity, whose followers were to be styled "People of the Book" (*ahl al-kitāb*), were seen as equally divine in their origin, but corrupted or misinterpreted by their latter-day followers

(2:75, 79; 3:78; 4:46; 5:13, 41), who in any case were now failing adequately to uphold their own teachings. By thus accounting for other faiths, a space was made for an entirely new revelation that would need no further reference to the authority claimed by those religions, their founders and their doctrines, in order to proclaim its message.

As befits a new historical beginning, Muḥammad brought a message of seeming simplicity. He warned the Arabs to renounce their ancestral idolatry, and to turn instead to the worship of the One God. The new revelation was filled with warnings about God's coming judgement on humanity. This would come in the form of a general resurrection of the dead, to be followed immediately by a great day of judgement, at which God would assign all rational beings to either everlasting bliss or torment, on the basis of their actions during their worldly lives. The Qur'an further called on its hearers to repent or face chastisement even in this world, recounting the ways in which God had destroyed several wayward nations of older times who had rejected the messages brought to them by their prophets. Nothing, of course, was original in this overall vision, since ideas of salvation and judgement had long flourished in the Near East, and had been greatly elaborated there by the earlier monotheistic religions.

Although simple on the surface, this qur'anic system of salvation based on divine judgement brought in its inexorable train many complexities that prompted debate and elaboration among later Muslim generations. This process began in the time of the revelation, insofar as many of the divine exhortations it contains reveal a polemical situation of considerable nuance, and periodically respond directly to questions or criticisms. While it is true that the Qur'an, as a text in the genre of Semitic prophecy, does not contain a single sustained argument of the kind familiar in the elite literature of the Greco-Roman world, it nevertheless develops its own themes argumentatively, sometimes at considerable length, to explain its teachings, and to rebut the established anti-monotheistic arguments of its initial target audience. Because the elaborations of the qur'anic vision of salvation stressed different aspects of the message, and reflected different patterns in the reception of the qur'anic text by those who had heard its interpretation from the Prophet, doctrinal stresses became, over time, the nuclei of diverging ideological schools.

In addition to its coherent system of otherworldly salvation, the Qur'an also laid great stress on certain practical prescriptions for life in this world. Originally connected, for the most part, with the events of the Prophet's multidimensional career, the Qur'an's revelations are replete with exhortations to action as well as counsels on human relationships. Some of this advice is couched in the form of exhortations and recommendations, coupled with a general insistence on justice (4:58; 5:8; 6:115, 152; 7:181; 16:76, 90; 42:15; 49:9), which urge the earliest believers to concentrate their minds on the inherent rightness of their actions, rather than on their utility to their tribes, and to insist on such rightness in their rulers, and this is stressed far more than issues of doctrine or ritual. Such a concern ensured that the earliest Muslim schisms emerged over what were in the first instance political matters, and this very early pattern continued profoundly to affect the course of Muslim history and thought. Although the political ructions took on ideological and religious overtones whose later fixity helped to define religious boundaries, it is very doubtful whether such differences can be considered essentially "spiritual", especially in the earliest period, however strongly they may have been felt, since their origins lay in political contestations that had little to do with credal or legal matters.

THE SUCCESSION TO MUḤAMMAD

In this way, there emerged two stresses which led to sectarian and ideological differentiation. First, there were disputes over matters concerning God and the afterlife, and secondly, disputes over the legitimate administration and shaping of the earthly Muslim community (*umma*). The latter preceded the former, but in time the two came to be symbiotically related. Thus the first major rending of the Muslim community arose over the succession to the Prophet at his death in 632. Although Abū Bakr (*c.* 571–634), the father of the Prophet's most influential wife, 'Ā'isha (*c.* 613–78), was able to establish himself as *amīr* (or "commander") with the support or acquiescence of the majority of the community, and thus ensure the continuance of the Muslim polity, his actions were opposed by a minority, including 'Alī (599–661), the husband of Fāṭima (*c.* 604–32), the Prophet's last surviving daughter.

While it appears that these tensions over the succession emerged primarily between dissonant personalities, there were serious political differences at stake as well. The supporters of Abū Bakr included most of the Meccans, and favoured the continued importance of the city's dominant tribe of Quraysh, since it had been the Prophet's tribe, and most of the earliest Muslims had been its members. The party of 'Alī, by contrast, enjoyed the loyalty of many Medinans, and claimed to favour a more inclusive policy in line with the unambiguous universalism of the Qur'an (9:33; 21:107; 34:28; 48:28; 61:9). Though the differences largely lay dormant during the highly successful caliphates of Abū Bakr (r. 632–4) and 'Umar I (r. 634–44), the powers of the ruler, or "the Prophet's successor/deputy" (*khalīfa*), as well as "leader of the believers", grew apace, adding to the tensions, especially as Arab Muslims had no long experience with any central authority. These tensions came to a head as the expansion slowed under the third caliph, 'Uthmān (r. 644–56), leading to his assassination in a revolt which brought 'Alī (656–61) to power.

In fact, the traumatic upheaval of 656 led to the complete breakdown of the system established twenty-four years earlier upon the death of the Prophet, and resulted in a civil war (*fitna*) that lasted the length of 'Alī's reign. The war brought into the open all of the competing groupings, and laid the foundation for many subsequent sectarian alignments. During the war, 'Alī successively confronted, first, Abū Bakr's daughter 'Ā'isha with her relatives Ṭalḥa and al-Zubayr, near Basra (656); second, Mu'āwiya, the governor of Syria, who championed the Umayyad clan within Quraysh (battle of Ṣiffīn, 657); and third, the so-called Khawārij, or "rebels", at Nahrawān in Iraq (658). Those loyal to 'Ā'isha and Mu'āwiya, although representing different nuances of the Qurashī viewpoint, did not co-operate, and may have initially differed on the question of whether 'Uthmān had died as a perpetrator or as a victim of wrongdoing. The parties of 'Alī and the Khawārij both considered the assassination of 'Uthmān to have been just, but 'Alī's willingness to negotiate with Mu'āwiya led the Khārijī purists to rebel against him, on the grounds that there should be no negotiation over what is right.

Such fratricidal events were immensely traumatic for the young community, and many refused to take sides. However, four parties had emerged by the end of 'Alī's reign, driven more by a passionate concern for the qur'anic insistence on justice than by substantial differences over doctrine. Of these parties, it was Mu'āwiya who succeeded in maintaining political control, inaugurating the Umayyad dynasty which endured from 661 until 750; but the other three groups maintained an open or covert existence, and became crucibles within which distinctive doctrinal alignments began to take shape. Thus the mainstream tendency which was to become Sunnism emerged mainly from those loyal to 'Ā'isha, and the Khawārij maintained a powerful presence for several generations, while 'Alī's supporters became known as the *Shī'a*, the "Faction". Within each alignment there was no shortage of internal complexity and shifting allegiances.

Umayyad vigour and acumen permitted the restoration of Muslim political unity, and required control of many of the ideological manifestations associated with the other groups. Under the Umayyads, the caliph acquired the title "God's deputy" (*khalīfat Allāh*), a term probably connected with the one favourable appearance of the term *khalīfa* in the Qur'an, in 38:26: "O David, We have made you a deputy on the earth; therefore judge among the people with truth." Through the use of their claim to a divine stewardship over the earth, as well as ongoing military campaigns to spread their rule, the Umayyads succeeded for a considerable time both in establishing one of the world's great empires, stretching from the Atlantic to the Indus and to the borders of China, and in managing internal opposition to their dynasty. Their political success powerfully strengthened the evident legitimacy of their rule among many Muslims, especially among the Syrian troops who were the mainstay of their dynasty and its chief beneficiaries.

THE KHĀRIJITES

Despite Umayyad success, opposition continued. All three of the groups which had been eclipsed during the First Civil War (656–61) continued to exist and to promote their opposition. All three contended again with the Umayyads during the Second Civil War (680–92), which proved longer and more disastrous than the first. In this period, each of the three oppositions underwent further ideological development. The most confrontational was the radical Khawārij, who initially rejected any compromise with the caliphate, insisting that the sins of the caliphs not only destroyed their legitimacy but imposed a duty of resistance to them upon every individual Muslim. The revulsion felt by the Khārijites against the caliphs was such that they held that the committing of major sins negated faith, and thus placed the sinner outside Islam. Adopting the slogan *Lā ḥukma illā li'Llāh* (judgement is God's alone; cf. Qur'an 6:57; 12:40, 67; 18:26), the Khārijites appeared to vest authority directly in the text of the Qur'an as the primary manifestation of God's will; human political authority was de-emphasised and undermined in consequence.

Nevertheless, any radical Khārijite faction which "came out" to fight the Umayyads would typically elect one of its number as commander, adopting a caliphal title. Those who refused to submit would be considered sinners and apostates, and could legitimately be robbed and killed. Unlike the Shī'a, who insisted that a leader must be a descendant of the Prophet, and the proto-Sunnīs, who required that the caliphs be of Quraysh, the Khārijites elected whomever seemed best for the office, with the condition that his moral character be exemplary. Sometimes this is read as a democratic principle, despite the exercise by the commander of absolute authority on condition that he eschewed major sins. Such groups, however, proved unstable, because of the possibility of undermining or disqualifying a leader by accusing him of sin; and in consequence, the Khārijites were unable to effect any positive political programme. Moreover, their incessant violence against fellow Muslims made them unpopular among the general public, and the government was generally able to marginalise and suppress them.

The Second Civil War also saw the emergence of a more moderate trend among the Khārijites, including groups such as the Ṣufriyya and the Ibāḍiyya, neither of whom required immediate revolution against illicit rulers. The Ibāḍiyya not only preached a patient waiting for the right circumstances, but also declined to regard sinners as apostates, preferring to qualify them as ingrates towards God's blessings (*kuffār bi'l-ni'am*) rather than as polytheists (*mushrikūn*). This offered some scope for peaceful coexistence with other Muslims, and this in turn helped the Ibāḍiyya to maintain an existence as a small but distinctive Muslim sect, which survives to this day in communities in Oman, Libya and Algeria. In time, the Ibāḍīs participated in and influenced the evolution of *kalām* theology, notably through their continuing severe strictures against sin, which helped to maintain the focus of discussion on that issue. The Khārijite focus on sin also implied that human beings were responsible for it (Qur'an 4:79), and this led naturally to a doctrine of free will, which clashed with the more deterministic belief that may have been held by some pre-Islamic Arabs, and by the larger number of early Muslims (4:78). On the issue of free will they thus appear to parallel or to anticipate the position of later alignments such as the Qadarīs and the Mu'tazilites, whom they also resemble in asserting the belief in the created status of the qur'anic text.

THE QADARĪS

It was the tension between free will and determinism that gave rise to the first properly theological dispute in Islam. The pre-Islamic Arabs had tended to believe in a predetermined fate (*dahr*), and hence received the Qur'an in the same spirit. The early caliphs seem also to have upheld this view, particularly Mu'āwiya (661–80), 'Abd al-Malik (685–705), and 'Umar II (717–20), in connection with each of whom epistles or traditions of a deterministic hue have been associated. Usually, modern scholars have seen determinism as a position congenial to the rulers, since it logically appears to diminish concern with the morality of their actions and of one's response to their rule. Determinism also naturally brings to the foreground the principle of the absolute, exalted majesty and power of God.

On the other hand, pietists tended to worry about whether their actions were acceptable to God, and whether they could not do better by increasing their efforts to live in a way pleasing to Him. The origins of such pietism in early Islam are obscure; however, it is quite certain that there were considerable numbers of individuals passionately concerned about their own conduct, and determined to conform their lives to God's will. This tendency is first notably attested at Basra, a city with large concentrations of Khārijites, and of Ibāḍīs in particular. The foundation of this pietistic school in Basra is associated with the name of al-Ḥasan al-Baṣrī (646–728), a non-Arab Muslim (*mawlā*), who was born in Medina but moved to Basra after 663. Al-Ḥasan criticised the Umayyad governors of Iraq, and, despite his opposition to violent rebellion in the Khārijite mode, was forced into hiding between the years 705 and 714. Connected to his political dissent was his rigorist view of sin. With his leading disciple Qatāda ibn Di'āma (d. 735), he denied that a sinner could exculpate himself by claiming that God was the source of all human actions. In an epistle dated to the final years of the seventh century addressed to the caliph 'Abd al-Malik, al-Ḥasan cites numerous qur'anic verses which indicate that humans are responsible for their actions. For him, God creates only good, and evil comes either from humans or from the devil. The human agent chooses freely whether or not to sin, and although God has foreknowledge of that person's choice, it is not a predetermining knowledge.

Shortly after al-Ḥasan's death, a group of Basran Khārijites led by Shabīb al-Najrānī proposed a more thoroughgoing doctrine of free will, in which God neither knows in advance nor decrees human actions. This idea, with its apparent diminution of divine authority over creation, was attacked in an epistle attributed to the caliph 'Umar II. Himself strongly determinist in his convictions, the caliph nonetheless regarded al-Ḥasan's type of moderate Qadarism as acceptable. Qadarī dissent became more active with Ghaylān al-Dimashqī (d. between 731 and 735), a government secretary of Coptic origin, who launched a revolutionary campaign against the Umayyad caliph Hishām (r. 724–43). The movement gained momentum only after Ghaylān's death, and culminated in the coup of Yazīd III against al-Walīd II in 744, which led to a brief implementation of the Qadarī political agenda, including a limited caliphate in which Yazīd agreed to step down if he failed to uphold the programme. This sat well with Qadarī ideas of free will; the caliph was fully responsible for his actions and thus had to remove himself or be removed if he fell into grave sin. However, the political failure of the movement sent Qadarism into a period of eclipse.

The Qadarīs subsequently continued in two forms: a pietistic trend that was eventually re-absorbed by the proto-Sunnī hadith scholars, and a more doctrinally defined alignment that eventually joined Mu'tazilism. The distinction made between the two was marked by the traditionists' subsequent appropriation of al-Ḥasan al-Baṣrī and Qatāda as exemplars of early Muslim piety, and by a condemnation of the hardline Qadarīs who had attempted to revolt against the government: Ma'bad al-Juhanī (d. 699), and Ghaylān.

THE SHĪ'A

The stronghold of ongoing loyalty to the memory of 'Alī was his former capital, the Iraqi city of Kūfa. The Shī'a were convinced that the tragic dissensions among the Muslims following the Prophet's death were the result of a sinful abandonment of the Prophet's own family. All would be well if a divinely chosen, rightly guided imam from the Prophet's house took the reins of power in place of the corrupt and worldly dynasts of the time. In time, this early "philo-'Alism" developed into messianic expectations and an adulation of those who, being descendants of 'Alī, were thought to be the designated leaders of the righteous community.

The catalyst for this process was the traumatic massacre of 'Alī's son al-Ḥusayn (626–80) with his family at Karbalā' in Iraq. Shortly thereafter, a Shī'ite revolt in Kūfa (685–7), led in the name of 'Alī's son Muḥammad ibn al-Ḥanafiyya by al-Mukhtār al-Thaqafī, was already replete with messianic expectations and overtones, which persisted even after its failure. This Shī'ite revolt also saw the emergence of extreme doctrines in some circles, which condemned even the caliphates of Abū Bakr and 'Umar I. Divisions within nascent Shī'ism, and the failure of Mukhtār's revolt, ensured that there were no further Shī'ite rebellions until the Umayyad period had almost drawn to a close, when the revolt of Zayd ibn 'Alī in Kūfa (740) failed as disastrously as had that of al-Ḥusayn sixty years before. Despite its limited geographical spread, and its political failures, the early Shī'a's simple political solution to the problem of Umayyad autocracy gained considerable support, particularly as conditions worsened towards the end of the Umayyad era.

The early Shī'a were heavily subdivided, each group defined by the imam to whom it paid allegiance. These groups differed also in the energy with which they promoted their imam's political leadership, and quiescent groups tended to survive longer. From the point of view of their Sunnī opponents, the most moderate group was the Zaydīs, descended from Zayd ibn 'Alī, who held that an imam could be elected, and that the imamate of an inferior candidate (*mafḍūl*) could be accepted. Such a doctrine readily validated the rule of Abū Bakr and 'Umar I, and thus raised few problems for the rulers and the Sunnī majority. They were opposed by the emerging group of the Imāmīs, also called the Twelvers after the death of their eleventh imam, and the disappearance, or "occultation" (*ghayba*), of their twelfth in 874. A major catalyst in the emergence of Twelver Shī'ite thought was the Kūfan Hishām ibn al-Ḥakam (d. 795 or later). Hishām held that each imam had been designated by his predecessor by a specific appointment (*naṣṣ*). All the imams were infallible, and the imamate was confined to the descendants of 'Alī and Fāṭima. Thus, every elected imam was a usurper, even when "acclaimed" by the troops. Such a hard-line stance necessarily brought the Imāmīs into conflict with the Abbasid state, which had supplanted the Umayyads in the year 750.

Hishām is also thought to have entertained anthropomorphic ideas that Twelvers later discarded, such as the belief that God is contained in a physical body, since only bodies can have existence. He rejected, however, the extreme anthropomorphism which taught that God had a form like a man, which doubtless was too redolent of Christian belief ever to be acceptable among Muslims. Hishām also seems to have been the first to have described the divine attributes as substantives, a theme later taken up in Sunnī discourse. Like proto-Sunnī traditionists, Hishām also favoured predestination over free will, although he also assigned to humans responsibility for their actions. Interestingly, most of these early metaphysical views came to be reversed among the Shī'a, whose continuity was assured more by their definitions of political legitimacy than by an abstract theological programme.

A further important subdivision of Shī'ism after 850 was the Ismā'īlīs, who recognised seven imams culminating in Ismā'īl ibn Ja'far al-Ṣādiq (d. by 765). Once politically inactive, and engaged in esoteric speculations whose history is now obscure, they began an intense and well-organised revolutionary activity around 878, and for much of Islamic history the Ismā'īlīs were the most significant of the many Shī'ite branches. In later times, Abu'l-Ḥasan al-Nasafī and others brought them the Neoplatonist doctrines which have distinguished them since, but which had little or no influence on other Muslims in the early period.

ZUBAYRIDS AND PROTO-SUNNĪS

Just as Umayyad rule had provoked the emergence of Shī'ite and Khārijite movements during the Second Civil War, so it galvanised the party of Qurashīs descended from the followers of Ṭalḥa, Zubayr, and 'Ā'isha, now led by 'Abd Allāh ibn al-Zubayr (624–692). Centred in Mecca, the Zubayrid party failed to offer the ideological force that propelled the Khārijites and the Shī'a, and was readily dealt with by the Umayyad caliphs. Its political significance collapsed, but its erstwhile followers, descended from many of the Companions of the Prophet who had remained in Arabia, and who constituted the largest reservoir of substantial tradition about the earliest period of Islam, appear to have been particularly active in preserving and transmitting information about that period. They were encouraged in this by the growing thirst of many Muslims from the great cities of the Fertile Crescent and beyond for authentic information about earlier times. Muslims from outside Arabia would frequently encounter these traditionists while fulfilling their pilgrimage obligations. The people of Medina, in particular, began to think of themselves as representing the epitome of Muslim authenticity, an oasis of correct memory and practice in a confused and divided world.

Led mostly by descendants of the Companions, some of whom were descended from Abū Bakr and 'Umar I, the Medinans kept alive the memory of those men as exemplary rulers, against the opinions of the Shī'a and others. They also perpetuated a simple and literal-minded understanding of the verses describing God in the Qur'an. Thus, in interpreting Qur'an 20:5: "The All-Compassionate is established (*istawā*) on the throne," Mālik ibn Anas (d. 795), the eventual systematiser of Medinan legal thought, is said to have commented: "This establishment is known; but its mode is unknown; belief in it is a duty; but inquiring about it is a [reproved] innovation."[1] Too much metaphysics, for Mālik, was clearly a bad thing. As is indicated by the many deterministic traditions that came to be circulated, even in the earliest major work of such traditions, the *Muwaṭṭa'* of Mālik, the Medinans also tended to uphold the predestinarian view that was being endorsed by the Umayyad caliphs.

THE MURJI'ITES

Despite its small size and the relative homogeneity of its practices, Medina was host to certain divisive controversies. Again, politics lay at the source of these issues. Which of the protagonists of the First and Second Civil Wars had been right? Had 'Uthmān been a grave sinner, so that he deserved to be overthrown, or even slain; or was he rather an innocent victim, whose killers were the sinners? The Shī'a and the Khawārij were already typically hostile to 'Uthmān, and the Khawārij extended the hostility to 'Alī as well. On the other hand, the Umayyad authorities ordered 'Alī to be ritually cursed on the pulpits throughout the caliphal realms, but justified 'Uthmān.

Many Muslims, however, recoiled in distaste from such polemical and partisan behaviour. Some had objected conscientiously to involving themselves in the First Civil War. This group began to teach that it was best to withhold judgement about the more controversial rulers, especially 'Uthmān and 'Alī. After the Second Civil War, the former Zubayrids gave up their own political claims, and threw in their lot with this anti-polemical movement. They were also joined by al-Ḥasan ibn Muḥammad ibn 'Alī (d. *c.* 718), the son of the discomfited Shī'ite candidate of the Second Civil War, Muḥammad ibn al-Ḥanafiyya, becoming the first to issue a declaration proclaiming "deferment of judgement" (*irjā'*) on 'Uthmān and 'Alī. Adherents of this pietistic solution became known as Murji'a, "Deferrers", a term which is related to a word in Qur'an 9:106. The idea of deferring judgement by leaving it to God seemed particularly to support the defeated political activists in Medina. The Murji'a sought to keep Islam united by avoiding the partisan attacks and the cursing of opponents that had characterised the approach of the Khārijites, the Shī'a, and the Umayyad government. Although, like the Umayyads and the proto-Sunnī traditionists, they remained largely predestinarian, they upheld the principle that the current rulers should recognise the principles of justice, holding only that those of past times could not be judged *in absentia*, and in the absence of certain evidence. Present-day wrongdoers, however, could be condemned, not as unbelievers, but as misguided believers (*mu'minūn ḍullāl*). This was a less harsh judgement than that of the Khārijites, with their near-universal anathemas. On the basis of their understanding that interior faith rather than external actions was the hallmark of a believer, the Murji'ites developed a celebrated line of thinking in which faith and actions were regarded as separate.

The conciliatory principle of Murji'ism made it popular in cities exhausted by sectarian argument. Even in the metropolis of Kūfa, they gained ground at the expense of the Khārijites and Shī'a. Increasing popularity, coupled with their insistence on justice, induced them into greater political activity in opposing the injustices of Umayyad rule, especially with regard to the rights of the non-Arab Muslims (*mawālī*). The Murji'a, holding that the mere confession of belief sufficed for a new Muslim to be acknowledged as a Muslim and indeed as a believer, supported the *mawālī*, even to the point of revolt in the period 728–46, despite the general Murji'ite teaching that a Muslim should not fight another Muslim except in self-defence.

The most radical revolutionary manifestation of the Murji'a in this period is associated with the shadowy figure of Jahm ibn Ṣafwān (d. 746), who was secretary to the rebel al-Ḥārith ibn Surayj (d. 746). Their programme called for a return to the Qur'an and the Sunna, which implied opposition to the worldly Umayyad rulers. Jahm apparently taught that faith is merely an internalised knowledge in the heart, without any outward expression at all, thus reducing the Murji'a's minimal requirements for the outward expression of belief still further. He also affirmed an absolute predestination, together, possibly, with the view that heaven and hell are not eternal, and is said to have held that the Qur'an was created by God, although this seems to anticipate a question that was not discussed until after 800. In fact, Jahm's own teachings are obscure, being mentioned only in much later, hostile sources, and no alleged followers of him are heard of for seventy years after his death. Later, the terms Jahmī and Jahmiyya were used mainly by Ḥanbalites to denounce anyone they accused of Mu'tazilite tendencies; although it is difficult to know if any of the Mu'tazilite positions allegedly anticipated by Jahm, such as the createdness of the Qur'an, were actually held by him; indeed, it is probable that they were not.

On the other hand, the most famous of all scholars associated with the Murji'a, Abū Ḥanīfa (*c.* 699–767), the eponym of the Ḥanafī school of jurisprudence and an important scholar of Kūfa, upheld the pacific doctrine of the mainline Murji'a. Several more of Abū Ḥanīfa's doctrines are laid down very succinctly in an early creed called "al-Fiqh al-Akbar I", which contains ten points that represent perhaps the earliest surviving elaboration of Muslim creed. In this statement, Abū Ḥanīfa opposes the beliefs of the Khārijites, Qadarīs, Shī'ites and Jahmīs. The text also contains an assertion of deferral of judgement with regard to 'Uthmān and 'Alī, an equal regard and respect for all the Companions of the Prophet, a sentence indicating a form of predestinarian belief, and an apparent reference to God being established on His throne in heaven. The document thus shows how close the Murji'a were to later Sunnism. Only an extreme offshoot of the Murji'a, the Karrāmiyya, founded by the Iranian Muḥammad ibn Karrām (*c.* 806–69), continued to hold that God was a body which touches the "throne", although without specific limbs or organs, but this belief was usually condemned by other Muslims.

Later Murji'a went some way in elaborating the earlier doctrines in their debates with the proto-Sunnī traditionists. The original idea of suspending judgement on 'Uthmān and 'Alī disappeared, as both became no less formally justified in the Sunnī community than Abū Bakr and 'Umar I had been. Instead, there came to be a heavy emphasis on faith being separate from works, and an insistence that faith, being an indivisible and uncountable whole, can neither increase nor decrease. Thus, faith (*īmān*) was conceived as perfect, undoubting belief, as portrayed, for example, in Qur'an 49:15. Later Murji'ites somewhat modified this conception in the light of Qur'an 3:173; 8:2; 9:124; 33:22; 48:4; and 74:31, where it is asserted that faith can increase; but the mainstream Murji'a continued to deny that it could decrease.

Most Murji'ite positions were later adopted as part of the mainstream Sunnī synthesis in some form, even though traditionists of the Ḥanbalī type tried to exclude them as heretics, perhaps because of their rationalism in contemplating and considering the problem of divine justice. Although the name "Murji'a" became a pejorative term that no-one cared to apply to himself, later Sunnīs, with the exception of most Ḥanbalites, did not regard the Murji'a as lying beyond the Sunnī pale.

THE LATER MURJI'A

As Muslim acquaintance grew with the urban civilisation of the Near East, with its Hellenistic legacy which had deeply shaped the earlier monotheisms, some Muslims began to develop a high form of religious, doctrinal or theological discourse known as *kalām*. Many of the earliest of these thinkers are broadly characterised as Murji'a, and they emerged from the same general intellectual environment in southern Iraq which had produced Abū Ḥanīfa. Like the Ḥanafīs, they won favour with some of the early Abbasid caliphs and their ministers. Among the earliest and most important of these was Ḍirār ibn 'Amr (*c.* 730–*c.* 800), a Kūfan who migrated to Basra, where he made a considerable contribution to the evolution of a dialectical *kalām* discourse. Ḍirār opposed most of the known trends of his day, and so is hard to classify. Although he was not really a Murji'ite, as he critiqued Murji'ite positions, he was loyal to the memory of both 'Uthmān and 'Alī. A predestinarian opponent of Qadarism, he appears to be the first to have applied the doctrine of the qur'anic verb *kasaba* (Qur'an 2:286), meaning "to acquire", to human actions, as a means of resolving the antinomy between determinism and free will. Thus, like his contemporary, the Shī'ī Hishām ibn al-Ḥakam, he held that God creates all human actions, but human beings "acquire" them, together with a sufficient degree of responsibility for them. A human's ability to perform an action exists only because God wills it at the moment the act is performed. Beyond this, Ḍirār also held that immaterial "accidents" (*a'rāḍ*) could not exist from moment to moment, but rather had to be recreated by God in each moment, a decision which He was free to revoke at any time. This was the origin of the famous theory which came to qualify Sunnī theology, that time consists of a series of individual, indivisible points, and thus is not a continuum.

Ḍirār also adopted the idea that between the two categories of believer and unbeliever there is a third possibility, "a state between the two states" (*manzila bayn al-manzilatayn*), which is the place of the believer who is an unrepentant mortal sinner. In his view, such a person is beneath believing status, because of his sins and failure to repent. Partly paralleling Khārijite strictures against mortal sinners, Ḍirār taught that such would be eternally in hell, a view that Sunnism was to reject. Furthermore, Ḍirār rejected the belief in an intermediary punishment of sinners in the grave before resurrection, and did not accept that the believers would apprehend or "see" God on the day of judgement in a literal way, but only through a sixth sense. Regarding God's attributes, Ḍirār taught that these were only to be understood negatively, that is, as denying their opposites. This approach, taken in opposition to a literalist understanding of the sacred texts, considerably deflated the importance of the attributes.

Differing from Ḍirār was Bishr al-Marīsī (*c.* 760–833), a Murji'ite and hence a predestinarian in creed and of Ḥanafī tendency in law. An advisor to the Abbasid caliph al-Ma'mūn (r. 813–33), Bishr may have played a major role in inducing that ruler to accept the doctrine that the Qur'an had been created. Other teachings of Bishr resembled those of Ḍirār, such as his denial of the "torment of the tomb", a pre-resurrection punishment for sinners. However, he anticipated later Sunnī systematisation by also denying, against Ḍirār and the Khārijites, that major sinners among the Muslims would be eternally in hell, basing his view on Qur'an 99:7. He also held that faith consisted only of belief plus its verbal expression, and not other works; thus, bowing to the sun or to an idol could be only an indication of unbelief, and not unbelief itself, since that had to be expressed verbally. He also recognised only four essential attributes of God: will, knowledge, power, and creativity, and considered all other attributes to be figurative. This contribution anticipated the later discussion over the essential versus the active attributes of God.

The most prominent student of Bishr was al-Ḥusayn al-Najjār (d. *c.* 833–6), who was in most respects more influenced by Ḍirār, particularly on the subject of determinism, which he elaborated more fully than Ḍirār had done. Al-Najjār tended to see God's power as His overriding attribute, just as later Sunnīs would do. He specified that the human being's power to act only arose simultaneously with the act itself and did not endure but had to be granted again by God at the time of a second action. This fitted with Ḍirār's atomistic view of time and also anticipated later Sunnī orthodoxy. Al-Najjār's view of faith grew perhaps out of the Ḥanafī one, in that he taught that faith is only in belief and profession, and thus cannot decrease except through a complete denial, although it can increase. But he appended to his definition of it some qualities which are also "acts of obedience" (*ṭā'āt*), which seems to come closer to the later Sunnī majority, which included acts in the definition of faith. Al-Najjār also upheld Ḍirār's idea of a negative understanding of the divine attributes, but stated that humans seeing God on judgement day would be doing so with the eye which God would imbue with the power of knowing, which seems to be a concession to the Sunnī traditionists. Contrary to the Mu'tazila, al-Najjār maintained that God could bestow on human beings unmerited blessing or grace (*luṭf*). He also denied the "torment of the tomb", like his two predecessors, and followed Bishr in stating that neither believers nor unbelievers would suffer in hell forever. Thus in many but not all ways, he anticipated the eventual Sunnī–Ash'arī discourse against the Mu'tazila.

MU'TAZILISM

Mu'tazilism, as already noted, was in significant ways a continuation of Qadarism, the upholding of a doctrine of free will. But it went far beyond the simple free-will ideas of the early Qadariyya, to become the first fully elaborated, quasi-rationalistic defence of the faith.

The Basran Wāṣil ibn 'Aṭā' (d. 748), an associate of al-Ḥasan al-Baṣrī, is traditionally considered the originator of Mu'tazilism, along with 'Amr ibn 'Ubayd (699–761). Slightly later, another Basran, who moved to Baghdad, Abu'l-Hudhayl al-'Allāf (*c.* 753–841), more thoroughly developed the main early doctrines. Abu'l-Hudhayl was probably the originator of the "Five Principles" (*al-uṣūl al-khamsa*) of Mu'tazilism: (1) God's unity and uniqueness (*tawḥīd*); (2) His justice (*'adl*); (3) the eternity of Paradise for the righteous and hell for sinners (*al-wa'd wa'l-wa'īd*, literally "the promise and the threat"), (4) the intermediate state of the Muslim sinner, between belief and unbelief; and (5) the command to enjoin goodness and to forbid iniquity (*al-amr bi'l-ma'rūf wa'l-nahy 'an al-munkar*). In general, it is the first two of these principles which define the Mu'tazilite position, which is why the Mu'tazilites called themselves the "People of [God's] Unity and Justice" (*ahl al-tawḥīd wa'l–'adl*).

For the Mu'tazila, God was unique (Qur'an 42:11), and nothing should be permitted to compromise this uniqueness and unity. Thus they disdained the grossly anthropomorphic explanations that were favoured by some traditionists and early Shī'a, which they saw as insults to God's transcendence. They taught that God was indivisible into parts (Qur'an 114:1–4), and that He could not even have an indivisible body, because such corporeality would also compromise his transcendent totality. Thus the Mu'tazila asserted that any anthropomorphic descriptions of God in the Qur'an must be explained as purely metaphorical or allegorical. To support this concept, a theory of language was elaborated, whereby utterances were divided into literal (*ḥaqīqī*) and figurative (*majāzī*), using Qur'an 3:7 for textual evidence.

Furthermore, the numerous adjectives and verbs by which God and His actions are qualified in the Qur'an do not point to the separate existence of the things described, any more than verses invoking God's hands (Qur'an 5:64, etc.) mean that God possesses actual hands. Such descriptions can be no more than symbols of his action. This interpretation was easy enough on those points where God was clearly acting to produce something else, as in his roles as creator and provider. But it was less obvious on the issue of those characteristics essential to his own being that produced no necessary outside effects, such as knowing and living. Abu'l-Hudhayl at first insisted that each of these internal attributes (*ṣifāt dhātiyya*) acted through an entity that was identical with God Himself. That is, God knows through a knowledge that is identical with Him. Such a locution in effect disposed of these attributes. Later Mu'tazilism dropped this claim, holding that God knows through Himself. The Mu'tazilite view was denounced by the Sunnī traditionists as a "denial" (*ta'ṭīl*) of God's attributes, which many of them thought placed the Mu'tazila beyond the pale of Islam. The Sunnīs held rather that the internal attributes were coeternal with God. Perhaps in concession to Sunnī criticisms, the later Mu'tazilite, Abū Hāshim al-Jubbā'ī (d. 933) opined that the attributes represented "states" (*aḥwāl*) that had a real existence and served as the basis for the adjectives describing God. However, this concession did not win the assent even of all the Mu'tazila, and was insufficient to encourage the Sunnī traditionists to end their anathematisation of the Mu'tazilite school.

One of the internal attributes of God that the Mu'tazila debated with the Sunnīs was that of God's speech, as evidenced by the existence of the Qur'an. The Mu'tazila famously insisted that the Qur'an was created by God, while the Sunnīs held it to be uncreated. The Mu'tazilites supported their claim with the rational supposition that God's Book was subordinate to God and not coeternal with Him, while their Sunnī adversaries adduced a range of hadith in response, to the effect that there could never have been a time when God did not speak and "know" the Qur'an, so that it had existence before creation. After the Abbasid caliph al-Ma'mūn adopted Mu'tazilism as state doctrine in 827, the religion's scholars were required to conform to it, particularly on this issue. An inquisition (*miḥna*) was instituted to enforce this in 833, the year of his death, and Aḥmad ibn Ḥanbal (780–855), the leading Sunnī traditionist, was arrested. After al-Ma'mūn's death, the new caliph, al-Mu'taṣim, attempted to force Ibn Ḥanbal to acknowledge the createdness of the Qur'an, and unsuccessfully resorted to torture in an attempt to make him submit. Although Mu'tazilism remained the state doctrine until 851, the effort to impose it on the scholars proved counterproductive, and led to a hardening of the emerging Sunnī resistance to Mu'tazilism as a principle. Whatever the original theological merits of either position on the qur'anic text, they were soon submerged when each side became embroiled in a partisan struggle with strongly political implications.

Although not so salient in the official ideological struggle, the Mu'tazilī doctrine of God's justice was perhaps even more central to the overall system, because of its practical implications. The Mu'tazila stated that God, having declared Himself to be just (Qur'an 6:115; 16:90; 21:47; 57:25), was constrained to follow His own declaration. Therefore, being good, He could will and do only that which is good, a view already embraced by deterministic Murji'a. As developed by Abu'l-Hudhayl, the idea of God's justice led, however, to a rather mechanistic view of how that justice operated. That is, instead of God having the power to consider each case and to be merciful to whomever He would, He was constrained always to judge exactly according to the just deserts of each soul at the judgement, so that there would be no escape for the impenitent sinner. Verses stating that God pardons whom He will and punishes whom He will (2:284) mean only that He will pardon those deserving pardon, in other words, the repentant, and will punish those who deserve punishment. The doctrine of the Prophet's intercession (*shafā'a*) for sinners, set forth in many hadith, could have no place in this system. While such a vision could have terrifyingly serious implications in one's daily life, as one would want always to avoid having sins unrepented and unatoned for, it also presented God as a kind of cosmic justice machine, rather than a free and conscious being. In other words, Mu'tazilism tended to lean towards portraying God as a dharmic force, rather than as the personal deity most Muslims conceived Him to be.

However, in reducing God to a mechanistic justice device, the Mu'tazila also resoundingly affirmed human free will. However human beings might act, their fate in eternity lies entirely in their own hands, and their acts are their own creations. God only creates in humans the power or ability to act, not the acts themselves. The Mu'tazilites demonstrated this theory by an atomic theory of time which may originate ultimately in Greek philosophy. Thus, God's empowerment precedes the acts rather than operating concurrently with them. Being thus empowered to act, humans do so at a later moment of their own volition. Furthermore, according to a doctrine first stated by Bishr ibn al-Mu'tamir (d. between 825 and 840), secondary consequences arise from one's own actions, and one is responsible for these consequences too, as suggested by Qur'an 16:25. The Mu'tazila also held that potentially deterministic verses suggesting that God guides whom He will to the right or the wrong are to be explained as actions God takes after the human concerned has already acted. Thus, they are more like rewards and punishments. God's grace, in this view, consists in His blessings, including His revelations, which may help to guide people if they choose to heed them. A related idea is that such guidance is available to all in equal measure, so that each soul will have an equal chance to achieve Paradise and will have only itself to blame for failing to heed the signs.

Also bound up with the idea of free will and human responsibility was the Mu'tazilite adoption of the "intermediate degree" doctrine. Wāṣil ibn 'Aṭā' and early proto-Sunnīs are said to have described this as "deviant" (*fāsiq*), but the later Mu'tazila followed Ḍirār in calling it "a state between the two states". Sunnī traditionist critics also contended with the Mu'tazila over this issue, insisting that the unrepentant mortal sinner was a believer, while the Khārijites considered such a person to be an apostate. The Mu'tazilite polemic on this point eventually led some Sunnīs to state that the mortal sinner is not a believer while he is committing the act, but afterwards returns to believing status. Thus did inter-group polemic trigger fine adjustments to the creeds of all the contending parties.

Underlying many of their characteristic doctrines was the Mu'tazilite introduction of a rational element into their religious discourse. While the early Mu'tazilīs cannot be shown to have drawn substantially on Greek learning, and may have taken their logic, terminology and style of argument from evolving Iraqi systematisations of Arabic grammar and law, the mature Muʿtazilite school armed itself with the Hellenistic methodology which became increasingly popular as Abbasid rule progressed. Thus, while most of them were not themselves philosophers, or interested in philosophy as such, the Muʿtazila benefited from the study of logic and physics, and speculated about perception and language, as well as philosophical problematics such as the composition of bodies from atoms, substance versus accident, and the nature of the will. However, those inclined to philosophy itself, such as the earliest major Muslim philosopher, al-Kindī (d. 866), and the philosophically inclined theologian al-Naẓẓām, upheld many of the key principles of Muʿtazilism.

The later Muʿtazila such as Abū ʿAlī al-Jubbāʾī (d. 915) tempered the mechanistic understanding of God's justice by adding that God could grant unmerited grace (*tafaḍḍul*) to whomever He might. Other Sunnī concerns were also incorporated into some Muʿtazilite systems, making their God more personal, and although the school declined after the ending of the Abbasid inquisition, it eventually found new followers in both Twelver and Zaydī Shīʿism, which frequently adopted it as their doctrine in place of their own earlier theological views. The only major Shīʿite group which did not substantially engage with Muʿtazilism was the Ismāʿīlīs, increasingly drawn to Neoplatonist formulations.

SUNNĪ TRADITIONIST TRIUMPH AND ASHʿARITE SYNTHESIS

While Abū Ḥanīfa, Mālik, al-Shāfiʿī (767–820) and others elaborated schemes of legal thought that favoured the revealed sources of the Qurʾan and the Sunna but employed reason in varying degrees (the school of Abū Ḥanīfa being at the forefront in this regard), Aḥmad ibn Ḥanbal was regarded as the champion of a traditionism that sought to minimise the use of reason and to seek religious unity by applying literalist explanations. In his confrontation with Muʿtazilism, however, Ibn Ḥanbal had been obliged to take a clear stand on all the issues at stake, and hence was publicly associated with a kind of Sunnī traditionist creed. In general, his teaching simply opposed Muʿtazilism on most points. First came the issue of the Qurʾan, for which Ibn Ḥanbal had been imprisoned. He insisted that not only was the Qurʾan uncreated and therefore coeternal with God, but that its oral recitation was likewise uncreated. However, even some traditionists, such as al-Bukhārī (810–70), who assembled the most authoritative of all hadith collections, found this excessive.

Generally the Ḥanbalites promoted anthropomorphic ideas about God. Their conflict with the Mu'tazila made them ever more insistent on this stance, which was elaborated in large quantities of traditions which they circulated. For example, the traditionist Abu'l-Shaykh al-Iṣbahānī (887–979) compiled a large collection of anthropomorphic hadith which he entitled *The Book of Majesty* (*Kitāb al-'Aẓama*). Against the Mu'tazila, such traditions had the advantage of fitting better with the popular conception of deity held by the masses: that of an immediately available personal God, enthroned above the heavens. These anthropomorphisms also included graphic pictures of resurrection, judgement, heaven and hell which extend considerably beyond the qur'anic picture. In fact, the Qur'an is notably lacking in anthropomorphisms, despite the bare mention of a few suggestive themes, such as God's "throne", or His "hands", which are never graphically pictured or described in the Qur'an in the way they appear in the Bible.[2] Not even the Ḥanbalites circulated hadiths as unambiguously anthropomorphic and picturesque as can be found in certain Biblical passages.

The Sunnī traditionists also objected to the Mu'tazilite concept of human free will, which seemed to compromise God's majesty, power and sovereign freedom. The mechanistic image of a deity constrained by His own laws and incapable of true mercy because of the demand for the absolute mathematical requital of deeds appalled them likewise. For the traditionists, God had ultimate power to will every event and act, in effect overriding His other attributes, such as His justice, which the Mu'tazila said must constrain the divine agency.

Ibn Ḥanbal had himself condemned the use of *kalām* methods in defence of the faith, but this prohibition proved impossible to uphold, and later Ḥanbalīs could be intensely concerned to define the details of Muslim belief dialectically. Thus, while Ibn Ḥanbal condemned the pietistic ascetic and proto-Sufi, al-Ḥārith al-Muḥāsibī (*c.* 781–857), for engaging in *kalām* discourses in defence of the faith, he was not able to find other points of dispute to hold against al-Muḥāsibī. While Muḥāsibī's contribution to *kalām* discourse may have been considerable, his contemporary Ibn Kullāb (d. after 854) evidently formulated the Sunnī doctrine of the divine attributes, holding that, contrary to the teaching of the Mu'tazila, they have real existence. He also distinguished the essential from the active attributes, the former being of more importance as coeternal with God, and defined as "neither God, nor other than God".

The decisive *kalām* formulation of Sunnī belief was made by Abu'l-Ḥasan al-Ash'arī (874–936). Beginning his career as a moderate

Mu'tazilite and a student of Abū 'Alī al-Jubbā'ī, al-Ash'arī seems to have undergone a spiritual transformation about 913, and outwardly became a Ḥanbalite, although he is also claimed by the Shāfi'īs. Al-Jubbā'ī himself had already moved away from some Mu'tazilite positions, as in his doctrine of unmerited grace, and al-Ash'arī's conversion can be seen as a culmination of a longstanding trend. Al-Ash'arī now propounded Ḥanbalī doctrines, but defended them with the highly developed Mu'tazilite methods of argumentation. Thus he affirmed that God was all-powerful, that His eternal, essential qualities were coeternal with Him, and were neither God Himself nor other than Him, that all descriptions of God in the Qur'an and hadith were actual but were to be understood "without specifying how" (*bi-lā kayf*), that is, "amodally," that the images of resurrection, heaven and hell are factual, that the gravely sinning believer remains a believer but may be punished for a limited period in hellfire, that the believers will gain actual sight of their Lord in Paradise, albeit amodally, that the Qur'an is uncreated, that God is the creator of all human acts, making them actual by creating in humans the ability to perform each act at the time of the act, and that faith consists of both belief and acts, increasing and decreasing according to the righteousness of the latter. Ash'arī's system became the basis of belief among the Mālikīs and Shāfi'īs among the Sunnīs, although the Ḥanbalīs continued ostensibly to reject the methodology of rational argument, even though they often indulged in it, rather claiming to rely entirely on the plain sense of scripture as they understood it.

Most Ḥanafīs, on the other hand, reached an accepted summation of their beliefs in the doctrines of Abū Manṣūr al-Māturīdī (d. 944), whose teachings flourished especially in Turkestan and the Muslim East. While close to Ash'arī on many points, Māturīdī continued to maintain more rationalising views on many others. Thus in many cases he allowed that anthropomorphic descriptions in the Qur'an had to be taken literally but amodally, while elsewhere he admitted allegorising strategies not countenanced by Ḥanbalites or Ash'arites. He considered both the essential and the active attributes of God to subsist with God eternally, whereas the Ash'arīs permitted only the former. He accepted that the believers would see God, but not by eyesight. The Qur'an was uncreated, but not the sound of its recitation. Thus the voice of God heard by Moses in Qur'an 4:164 was created speech. Most importantly, Māturīdī continued to affirm that human works, although decreed by God, were ultimately attributable to their human authors. Human ability to act both precedes the act and is simultaneous with it.

Thus, by the mid-tenth century, the Muslim world had begun to settle on several defining and immensely enduring doctrinal alignments that have not been substantially altered since: the Ash'arī, Māturīdī and Ḥanbalī Sunnīs, two varieties of Mu'tazilism among the Twelver and the Zaydī Shī'a, the Neoplatonism of many Ismā'īlī Shī'a, and the Ibāḍī doctrines among the residual Khārijites. All other early formulations in that period of intense competition and energy eventually passed into extinction, although, as in the case of the Murji'a, they made substantial contributions to the schools that were able to survive.

Further reading

Encyclopedia of Islam, 2nd edn, 12 vols. (Leiden, 1986–2004), articles "Abu'l-Hudhayl al–'Allāf"; "Aḥmad b. Ḥanbal"; "al-Ash'arī, Abu'l-Ḥasan"; "Bishr b. Ghiyāth al-Marīsī"; "Bishr b. al-Mu'tamir"; "Djahm b. Ṣafwān"; "*Djahmiyya*"; "Ghaylān b. Muslim"; "al-Ḥasan al-Baṣrī"; "Hishām b. al-Ḥakam"; "*Ikhtiyār*"; "*Istiṭā'a*"; "Ḳadariyya"; "Karrāmiyya"; "*Kasb*"; "al-Māturīdī "; "Murdji'a"; "Mu'tazila"; "al-Nadjdjār"; "Shī'a".

Cook, Michael, *Early Muslim Dogma* (Cambridge, 1981).

Ess, Josef van, 'Das Kitāb al-irǧā' des Ḥasan b. Muḥammad b. al-Ḥanafiyya', *Arabica* 21 (1974), pp. 20–5.

Theologie und Gesellschaft im 2. und 3. Jahrhundert Hidschra: eine Geschichte des religiösen Denkens im frühen Islam, 6 vols. (Berlin, 1991–5).

Frank, Richard M., "Remarks on the early development of the *kalām*", *Atti del terzio congresso di studi arabi e islamici* (Naples, 1967), pp. 315–29.

"The science of *kalām*", *Arabic Sciences and Philosophy* 2 (1992), pp. 7–37.

Gimaret, Daniel, *Dieu à l'image de l'homme: les anthropomorphismes de la sunna et leur interpretation par les théologiens* (Paris, 1997).

La doctrine d'al-Ash'ari (Paris, 1990).

Mourad, Suleiman Ali, *Early Islam between Myth and History: al-Ḥasan al-Baṣrī (d. 110 H / 728 CE) and the Formation of His Legacy in Classical Islamic Scholarship* (Leiden and Boston, 2006).

Nagel, Tilman, *The History of Islamic Theology: From Muḥammad to the Present* (Princeton, 2000).

Watt, W. Montgomery, *The Formative Period of Islamic Thought* (Edinburgh, 1973).

Notes

1. 'Uthmān ibn Sa'īd al-Dārimī, *al-Radd 'ala'l-Jahmiyya*, ed. Badr al-Badr (Kuwait, 1405/1985), p. 56, para. 104 and fn. 58.
2. Ezek. 1:4–28; 8:1–4; 10:1–22; Dan. 7:9–14; Rev. 1:12–16; 4:2–11; 19:1–8; 20:11–15.

3 Islamic philosophy (*falsafa*)

HOSSEIN ZIAI

GENERATIVE INFLUENCES: AN OVERVIEW

The initial conditions leading to the formation of the discipline and study of philosophy in Islam were complex, but in general it can be said that this philosophical tradition was almost entirely based on Arabic translations of Greek texts. What is commonly designated as "Islamic philosophy" is marked by wide-ranging textual traditions in the genesis and development of a predominantly syncretic yet systematic philosophy in Islamic civilisation from Andalusia to India from the ninth century to the present. The majority of its texts are in Arabic, but a large number came to be written in Persian, a process which accelerated after the twelfth century.

Islamic philosophy grew out of the desire by learned members of the community to uphold the authority of Islamic revelation against arguments increasingly posed by members of the many divergent peoples who were living in lands united by the conquests of the seventh and eighth centuries. After the establishment of the Abbasid caliphate in Baghdad (750), subjects of various faiths contributed to an atmosphere of relatively free debate concerning the main constructs of religion, such as God, creation, causality, free will and divine authority. Increasingly, Muslims were forced to uphold the universalist ideology of Islam from a rational perspective and within civil institutions. Thus, although the majority of the practitioners of philosophy in the Islamic world were Muslims of differing cultural, social and linguistic backgrounds, their ranks also included many notable members of other religions.

The formative period of philosophy in the Islamic world was shaped by problems posed by the *kalām* scholars. Two groups of theologians whose rationalist position was sometimes called the "Primacy of Reason" (*aṣālat al-ʿaql*), and who had the most lasting effect on the origination of philosophical trends, were first the Muʿtazila, and later the

Ismā'īlīs. However, Islamic philosophy taken as a whole cannot be defined by Islam as a religion, nor did it ever become the "handmaiden of theology". Certain later trends did confine philosophical investigation within structures guided by the theologians, but a genuinely philosophical tradition distinct from theology continued, although in the later centuries this was cultivated by fewer and fewer scholastic figures, whose main investigations lay in the religious sphere and who were known to the community as ulema.[1]

After the thirteenth and fourteenth centuries philosophy as a distinct discipline died out almost entirely in Sunnī Islam outside Iranian centres of learning, such as Shīrāz, Iṣfahān, Tabrīz, Marāgha, and Zanjān, where it was kept alive in scholastic centres, despite being marginal to mainstream scholastic activity. While Muslim thinkers were very careful to distinguish theology from philosophy, and some addressed this point in their writings,[2] the most enduring sets of problems that formed the core of philosophical activity were all defined by early theological debates. These were first posed by the Mu'tazila, then studied and re-examined by perhaps the most philosophically inclined religious thinkers in early Islam, the Ismā'īlīs,[3] and later emphatically debated by the Ash'arite theologians, whose methods in the early period to some extent restricted philosophy. These problems included (1) creation, (2) atomism and the nature of reality, (3) causality, (4) anthropomorphism, (5) God's attributes, (6) God's knowledge, (7) free will and predestination, and (8) issues of immortality, resurrection, and reward and punishment. Questions of methodology were also posed: for example, the applicability of analogy to doctrine and the necessity of defining a technical vocabulary capable of expressing abstract concepts beyond the semantics of ordinary speech.

In addition to these fundamentally significant problems in the determination of normative Muslim behaviour and the limits of human thinking and action, the theological outlook as a whole determined once and for all the two main types of authority in Islamic intellectual history: the transmitted (*naqlī*), and the rational (*'aqlī*). The tension between these two types of authority has played a significant role in the unfolding Muslim attitudes within political and ethical as well as more abstract domains to the present. Later philosophers addressed this issue, but adherents of the supremacy of transmitted authority finally prevailed, albeit in the context of the large-scale integration of *falsafa* issues within later *kalām*. This framework, as broadly described here, forever marked philosophical investigation in the religion.

TERMINOLOGY

The term *falsafa* is an Arabised form of the Greek *philosōphia*. The Arabic *ḥikma* may also be used more or less synonymously with the same term, although more often the intended meaning is closer to the word "wisdom". Used in numerous Arabic and Persian texts, *falsafa* indicates an inclusive rational process aimed at knowing the nature of things and expressing the result in a systematic way. The term *ḥikma*, by contrast, is used in several ways, some of them not related to the science, or the art, of systematic philosophy. Some historians have used words such as "theosophy" to translate the term *ḥikma* as a means of explaining the presumed esoteric and mystical dimensions of Islamic philosophy, but such usage is not justified in the actual Arabic and Persian texts. Based on the Greek term, an agent noun *faylasūf* was coined, which means "philosopher". In relation to the Arabic term *ḥikma*, the adjectival form *ḥakīm* may be used in the same sense as *faylasūf*, but it is mainly employed to denote a special, often religious quality associated with the practitioner/follower of *falsafa* or *ḥikma*.

Throughout history Islamic philosophers sought to construct holistic philosophical systems, and some made special efforts to harmonise philosophical principles with religion. Following Avicenna (Abū 'Alī ibn Sīnā, 980–1037), the story of Islamic philosophy can best be understood as the quest to refine and construct holistic philosophical systems that have also served to uphold the deduced validity of revealed truths.

EARLY TRANSLATIONS AND STATE PATRONAGE

From as early as the late decades of the seventh and early decades of the eighth century evidence exists that Arabic translations were being made from the Syriac and perhaps also from the Greek. No sources are known from earlier periods, however, and our knowledge of the earliest translations is limited to later accounts. One superb source, cited in every study of the intellectual history of Islam, is a work known as the *Fihrist*, a Persian term meaning "list" or "outline". This work was compiled in the tenth century by the famous Baghdad book-dealer Ibn al-Nadīm (d. 995).[4] It notes the first instance in which a member of the Arab ruling elite, Khālid ibn Yazīd (d. 704), commissioned the translation of medical, astrological and alchemical treatises, allegedly from the Greek.[5] The text further reveals that under the patronage of the Umayyad caliph Marwān (683–85) the earliest translations of medical compendia from the Syriac were produced.[6] The most significant personality in this earliest period of translations into Arabic was 'Abdullāh ibn al-Muqaffa' (d. 757). His translations from Sanskrit, best exemplified by the *Kalīla wa Dimna* of Bidpai, and from Pahlavi, best exemplified by a version of *Khudāy Nāmeh*, indicate an early intellectual curiosity about the cultural heritage of non-Muslim nations.

The caliphs became increasingly interested in commissioning translations of works of all kinds from various disciplines into Arabic, the newly declared language of state. This interest intensified during the reign of al-Manṣūr (754–75), when the first Arabic translations of philosophical texts appear. Ibn al-Muqaffa', or his son Muḥammad, translated a good number of Aristotle's texts, including the *Categories* and the *Posterior Analytics*, as well as one of the philosophical tradition's most widely read works, the *Isagōgē* of Porphyry. After the reign of al-Manṣūr, attention paid to the scientific and medical heritage of all nations took on a new dimension.

Beginning with the reign of the caliph Hārūn al-Rashīd and reaching an apogee under his son, the caliph al-Ma'mūn (r. 813–833), translations and the study of non-Muslim intellectuality became institutionalised. Several factors contributed to this period's spirit of discovery and genuine regard for scholarship beyond the limits imposed by most juridical interpretations of Islam.

The triumph of the Abbasids over the Umayyads was in no small measure due to the Persian armies led by Abū Muslim of Khurāsān. The Persians subsequently played a very significant role in early Abbasid rule, and when the new capital of Baghdad was built, many learned Persian families involved themselves in all types of state institutions. In the domain of science, the famous Nawbakhtī family, many of whom were physicians at the still functioning medical complex and university of Jundī Shāpūr, built by the Sasanian emperor Anūshiravān, served the period's medical needs. This scientific centre had furnished a refuge for many Greek philosophers who had fled the theological tyranny of Justinian, and when Baghdad was built, a degree of scholarship and the study of the sciences and philosophy was still alive there. Learned members of this centre joined the retinue of the Abbasid caliphs, and some served important functions at court. One example was Faḍl al-Nawbakhtī, a celebrated Persian astronomer, who was assigned to the court of al-Manṣūr; others are supplied by the Bokhtishū' family of scholars and medical doctors, such as Georgius ibn Jibrā'īl, head of the medical school, and his pupil 'Īsā ibn Shahlāthā, who were among the eminent physicians who found employment at the Abbasid court. In addition, the Barmecide family of Persian Buddhists, who had converted to Islam, assumed leadership roles in Baghdad.

The atmosphere at court, certainly during Ma'mūn's period, was that of an active interest in and overt support and patronage for the scientific, medical and various other accomplishments of other nations and cultures, as well as of individuals. The caliphate as a state did not attempt to label as "heretic" those of its subjects who were active in philosophical and scientific endeavours.

This early period represents the Islamic state's height of self-confidence, in which ideas and traditions of all kinds were permitted to be debated in forums often presided over by the caliph himself. During this time, religious and juridical scholarship was also gaining in definition, and gradually the four schools of Islamic law were developed. The idea of a single, Islamic, all-inclusive legal system symbolised by these schools had not yet taken hold, and every aspect of the principles and practices of statecraft, including the foundations of belief itself, were subject to debate and intensive examination.

The reasons for the birth of Islamic philosophy in such an environment are clear. By sanctioning and even promoting a culture of debate, the state encouraged the expression of a wide range of beliefs, arguments and doctrines originating in different religious and scientific views. To maintain its authority, the Islamic state increasingly found it necessary to defend its position against well-argued but diverse challenges on a range of theological topics. Very soon, therefore, the need emerged for a much more powerful tool than *qiyās*, or analogy, which the Muslim scholars had employed successfully up to that time in the science of hadith and in the codification of Islamic law.

THE RISE OF THE ACADEMY

Ma'mūn's state-sponsored translation movement was centred in a new Academy of Philosophy, the "House of Wisdom", in Baghdad. Ma'mūn appointed the well-respected court physician of Hārūn al-Rashīd, Yūḥannā ibn Māsawayh, as the Academy's first head.[7] Skilled translators under the direction of Yūḥannā himself were actively engaged in translating texts from the Syriac and subsequently from the Greek in the identified philosophical tradition. The most important translator of this period was Ḥunayn ibn Isḥāq (809–73). His Arabic versions of the Greek philosophical tradition, executed in a highly refined, scholarly manner, contributed immensely to the rise of philosophy in Islamic lands.[8]

In addition to Ma'mūn, other members of the Arab tribal aristocracy, such as the Banū Mūsā family, also patronised translators and scholars from a range of ethnic and religious backgrounds. The participation of learned scholars and members of religions other than Islam in the state-endowed centres and in scholarly activity in general had a very positive effect on the rise of *falsafa*, and prominent Jewish and Christian philosophers are counted among those responsible for contributing to its refinement in Islamic history.

Baghdad exercised power over vast regions from the Indus valley to North Africa, and an Islamic universal worldview was sought to uphold the legitimate authority of the caliphate as world power. Umayyad factions which had questioned the caliphate's authority of universal rule from different points of view, including the doctrinal, persisted, and in some cases became more refined. This led to the definition of a set of critical political issues, which were later addressed by theologians such as al-Bāqillānī and 'Abd al-Qāhir al-Baghdādī. In addition to doctrinal issues a set of political-philosophical questions concerning rule and legitimacy, justice, knowledge, the role of leadership in the city, law and the position of lawgiver was stated within an Islamic framework. These questions were later examined systematically by Islam's greatest political philosopher, al-Fārābī, whose Platonist-inspired principles of politics became the standard for all later Islamic political theories.

This Greek heritage became the most sought-after tool in the construction of a rational base for the revealed teachings of a defined Islamic theology, thus serving to defend it.[9] As an example, the religious doctrine of creation and the position of a willing and knowing creator possessing choice came to be discussed in terms of Aristotelian notions of causality and of the position of the cause of causes. The creator's "attributes" (*ṣifāt*), and one in particular, that of the qur'anic "All-Knowing" (*'alīm*), were discussed in terms of Aristotelian principles of intellectual knowledge as interpreted by the later Peripatetic commentators of the school of Alexandria.

Dependence on Greek philosophy had a two-sided impact. The Greek philosophical methods, principles and techniques were hailed for their power, demonstrating solutions to problems of immense value to the Muslim community. At the same time they caused a reaction from the traditionalist segments of society along with literalist religious scholars, particularly the Ḥanbalites. This polarity has forever defined the position of philosophy in Islam.

THE IDEA OF VALIDITY

The formative period was distinguished by the role played by Abū Yūsuf ibn Isḥāq al-Kindī (d. *c.* 866), sometimes referred to as the "philosopher of the Arabs", whose works introduced the idea of the validity of philosophical investigation *per se*, independently of formal *kalām* affiliation. This notion of the validity of philosophy as an independent discipline has been fundamental to its development in Islamic history.

Of lasting significance to the position of philosophy is Kindī's principal view, which upholds the validity of revealed truth and at the same time holds that the demonstrative method, known by the term *burhān* (Arabic for *Posterior Analytics*, the title of Aristotle's most important book on logical method), is equally capable of recovering the highest form of knowledge. Kindī did not, however, attempt a systematic "harmonisation" of revealed truth with philosophy (one of Islamic philosophy's primary goals, also known as the "rational proof of prophecy"). His main contribution was to identify Greek texts and refine their Arabic translations (some of which he had commissioned). These texts include extensive paraphrases of pre-Socratic authors, Plato's *Laws*, *Timæus* and *Republic*, plus paraphrases of the *Phaedo* and other Platonic texts; almost the entire Aristotelian corpus minus the *Politics*; and selected Neoplatonic texts, some incorrectly identified (e.g., parts of Plotinus' *Enneads* IV–VI, thought to be "Aristotle's Theology"); as well as works by Porphyry, notably the *Isagōgē*, and by Proclus, together with many other texts and fragments of the Greek philosophical heritage, including some elements of Stoic logic and physics associated with the late antique schools of Alexandria and Athens. In addition, Aristotelian commentaries, including those of Alexander of Aphrodisias along with their Neoplatonist interpretations, were identified and translated.[10]

The basic character of this period's philosophical method is shown in Kindī's own syncretic approach to the presentation and discussion of philosophical problems. The first attempt to construct a metaphysical system is seen in Kindī's best-known text, *On First Philosophy*, in which he defines a framework based on Neoplatonist theories of emanation and the concept of the One, plus the basic Aristotelian principles of being and modality as well as the metaphysics of causality and of intellectual knowledge. The latter are given an Arabic version that partially incorporates the Aristotelian and Platonic theories of the soul and the Platonic dialectical method. Kindī argued for creation *ex nihilo*, based on the Platonic emanation of intellect, soul and matter from the One, but not as any natural causation in which the First Being is created simply by God's eternal will.[11] On one of Islamic philosophy's other lasting problems, namely the nature of resurrection, he affirmed the immortality of the individual soul and claimed this to be the rational explanation for resurrection.

Kindī's work thus represents the first serious philosophical discussion of a set of problems formulated by the earlier Mu'tazilite theologians and marks the true genesis of philosophy in the Islamic world. In addition to his attention to cosmological problems surrounding creation *ex nihilo*, Kindī also addressed epistemological problems that relate to revelation, prophecy and human knowledge.[12] His philosophical analysis and the construction of arguments in Arabic, in which he introduces for the first time a well-defined technical language, set the scene and contributed to the acceptance of *falsafa* as an independent, *bona fide* science. His arguments plus their corollaries (such as the identification of the God of revelation with the One of Greek cosmological systems on the one hand and with the First Cause of Aristotelian metaphysics on the other), the crucial distinction between divine knowledge and human knowledge, and other analyses, were later rejected, redefined or refined, but his writings, especially in the theoretical domain, describe the basic frame of reference for Islamic philosophy.[13]

THE CREATIVE PERIOD: LATE NINTH TO EARLY TWELFTH CENTURY

The first theological movement in Islam, best exemplified by the work of the Mu'tazila as noted earlier, ushered into the Islamic intellectual domain a strong rationalist tendency. The dominant view of this movement was heralded as the "Primacy of Reason". The rationalist direction was partially curtailed, however, by a second theological principle, known as "Primacy of Revelation" (*aṣālat al-waḥy*). This position was publicly proclaimed by Abu'l-Ḥasan al-Ash'arī (912), the movement's exemplum figure. Political trends and populist movements, directed by the increasingly influential Ash'arite theologians, reined in what they saw as the excesses of rationalism, and Ḥanbalite anti-rationalist zeal as well as theological decrees aimed against the Greek and "pagan" sciences presented a powerful challenge to the *falsafa* movement.

The creative genius of the two exemplar philosophers of this period, Fārābī and Avicenna, met this challenge by their holistic and systematic philosophical constructions aimed, among other things, at harmonising reason with revelation. Their work also manifested innovations and refinements in philosophical technique and analysis, and thus permanently defined major trends in Islamic philosophy. Three general areas of inquiry together indicate the apogee of Islamic philosophy's creativity during this period: (1) logic and philosophy of language; (2) political philosophy, including questions of prophecy and conjunction with the Active Intellect; and (3) holistic systems and the study of being.

A PHILOSOPHY OF LANGUAGE

Abū Naṣr al-Fārābī (875–950) (Abunaser, or Alfarabius in medieval Latin texts), often esteemed as the "Second Teacher", is one of the most original thinkers in Islamic philosophy. His commentaries on the Aristotelian logical texts of the *Organon* were pivotal in the process of refining Arabic logical terminology and formal techniques.[14] For example, he elaborated and refined the rules of inference with clearer identifications of valid moods. One of his major theoretical works, *The Book of Letters* (*Kitāb al-Ḥurūf*), represents the first attempt to study language in relation to logic in a clear and systematic way.[15] Together with his other independent technical work, *Utterances Employed in Logic*, Fārābī defined a new style and structure for the study of logic in which he introduced linguistic transformations in ascertaining the meaning of philosophical terms. These texts represent perhaps the first technical examination of how many ways a thing can be said. They include a critique of predication, an examination of truth-value and meaning, and an analysis and refinement of many other formal logical arguments and problems.

POLITICAL PHILOSOPHY

Fārābī was the first thinker to define the classical political philosophy of Plato's *Republic*, harmonised with Aristotelian epistemological, ontological and cosmological principles within the broader frame of Islamic religion. While political philosophy in the structure presented in Fārābī's independent studies does not continue after him, his study of the typology of political regimes, the concept of law and the role of the lawmaker, and the identification of an ideal form of Islamic government, called the "Virtuous City", has indirectly but permanently marked the fundamental ideas of political philosophy in Islam.

For example, Fārābī's entirely new types of works on political philosophy, such as the *Attainment of Happiness* and the *Political Regime*, include a novel approach to technical discussions of prophecy and creation, the role of the lawgiver and divine law in the city.[16] For the first time, political thought is presented in a framework defined by the metaphysics of the one and the many, integrated with Aristotelian theories of intellectual knowledge. Here the domains of practical philosophy are redefined in a metaphysical system designated and named the "science of politics". These are put forth as a means for the attainment of happiness and identify the institution of just rule. In fact the entire range of political views concerning the role of the human being in the "city", of the enlightenment of the citizen through knowledge and justice, and of human salvation in resurrection, is stipulated as the end of the process and practice of philosophy.

Fārābī's most technical work in political philosophy explores the foundations of the ideal city and relates the study of being and of cosmology to politics by constructing interconnected realms of the soul, the city and the cosmos. These highly refined texts impacted a limited audience, and influenced the Latin tradition more than they did the Islamic. Islamic political philosophy was defined almost entirely by Fārābī's most popular work, *The Ideas of the Inhabitants of the Virtuous City,*[17] a text that employs a less technical language and so was more accessible to a wider intellectual audience. As an expression, the "Virtuous City" is invoked continuously to indicate the ideal Islamic state. This text had an essential impact in the spread of political doctrines of just rule by allowing philosophical discourse about the Islamic revelation, prophecy and law, and of the beliefs and actions of the Muslim community as a whole within a rational system.

In *The Virtuous City* Fārābī describes prophecy as a type of knowledge based on Aristotelian theories of intellectual knowledge and later formulations by the Peripatetic commentators of the Active Intellect. These theories make it possible for the human being, not restricted by God's will and the action of God's choice, to obtain unrestricted, "prophetic" knowledge. Here Fārābī, in a novel philosophical way that is unique in the Islamic intellectual tradition, integrates Plato's ideas of the ideals of the Republic and the rank of the philosopher-king/philosopher-ruler with Aristotelian metaphysics and epistemological theories. Fārābī argues that anyone who is devoted to philosophical inquiry and undergoes a rigorous intellectual training can experience conjunction with the Active Intellect. Anyone who achieves this – which, as an epistemological principle, acts as a "giver of forms" or "giver of science" (the *dator formarum* and *dator scientias* of the Latin texts) – will come to know all the intelligibles and will gain perfect knowledge. This bestows the authority to rule the ideal city.

This epistemological theory forms the core of Fārābī's political thought and is later taken up by Avicenna, who refines and reformulates the structure of union with the Active Intellect into a unified theory of prophecy. Avicenna's work in this regard is incorporated in his discussions of psychology and epistemology and is regarded as one of the most significant components of Islamic philosophy as a whole. Avicenna's doctrine of prophecy serves the later definition of seventeenth-century Shī'ite political doctrine. In all subsequent refinements of intellectual Shī'ism, the "Virtuous City" concept describes legitimate, divinely inspired, just rule by the philosopher-ruler, now called the "jurist-guardian".[18]

HOLISTIC SYSTEMS

Islamic Peripatetic philosophy is defined by the highly creative work of Avicenna. Avicenna's corpus sets him apart from all his predecessors because it represents the first complete system within which every aspect of philosophical inquiry from logic to metaphysics is well defined, systematically argued and properly situated within the structure of existing philosophical systems.

The holistic system is best exemplified in his work known as the *Healing* (*al-Shifā'*), in which the entire range of philosophical subjects is reconstructed in Avicenna's own style, rather than as a non-argumentative commentary on the texts of Greek masters. In this system, political theory is incorporated within metaphysics, and prophecy is described in terms of a generalised theory of intellectual knowledge. This generalised theory is also capable of defining mystical knowledge.

The other most significant features of Avicenna's system are a number of innovative analyses of being, modality and the determinants of being. These include the distinction between essence and existence and the ontological distinction between contingent and necessary being, which leads to the logical construction of the "Necessary Being", all described by Avicenna for the first time in history.[19] This ontological construct serves to harmonise philosophy with religious ideas, especially since the Islamic intellectual tradition accepts the identification of the Necessary Being with God, who is responsible for a necessary and eternal creation, beginning with the intellects, souls and the heavenly spheres.

Avicenna's novel and famous thought-experiment known as the "Flying Man Argument" served to define the idea of primary self-consciousness as an act of self-identification. Avicenna was the first thinker to state that an individual suspended with no spatial or temporal referents will necessarily affirm his or her own being. This served as the model for the later Illuminationist views of identity relations in being and knowing as foundations of knowledge.[20] Many problems related to religious notions such as prophecy and immortality are also analysed in Avicenna's system and provided a basis for later thinkers to make philosophy more easily integrated into religion. His theories of prophetic knowledge, for example, are based on the notion of "holy intellect", and he is the first philosopher to express the idea that through exegesis of qur'anic teachings, the validity of demonstrated, rational truth may be further proved.[21] Avicenna's students, notably Bahmanyār, continued his systematic philosophical work, which served to solidify the definition of Islamic Peripatetic philosophy and contributed to its acceptance as the first clear "school" of *falsafa* in Islam.

REACTION AND RECONSTRUCTION: TWELFTH TO SEVENTEENTH CENTURIES

The twelfth century was marked by a myriad political and intellectual currents. The caliphate grew weaker, regional dynasties seized the chance to assert their independence, and the caliphs increasingly proclaimed *kalām* theological positions as the official doctrine of state. Many jurists followed, and at times initiated, trends that considered the Greek sciences and especially the Greek-inspired philosophical worldview to be heretical. However, the pursuit of the sciences and of philosophy, including medicine, that once thrived exclusively under the patronage of the caliphs and other Arab overlords, continued to be supported by a range of princes, rulers and kings in centres in Iran, Central Asia, Anatolia and elsewhere.

Three types of reaction to philosophy were initiated by three figures whose work has forever defined normative Islam and emerged as predominant doctrinal processes that gained strength with every passing century in the religious, juridical and legalist domains. These trends are briefly indicated here in relation to the principal views of a proponent of each one: (1) Abu'l-Ḥasan al-Ash'arī, (2) Abū Ḥāmid al-Ghazālī and (3) Ibn Taymiyya.

THE REFORMIST REACTION

Abu'l-Ḥasan al-Ash'arī represents a theological trend that sought to reform the dominant rationalist Mu'tazilite thinking of the time and secure a more qur'anically faithful style of monotheism. Ash'arī, whose work *The Treatise* (*al-Risāla*) is still studied in Sunnī institutions, was sceptical about any systematic recourse to Greek thinking to explain Islamic revelation and to prove the validity of its tenets. The Ash'arite tradition succeeded in diminishing the study of philosophy as an independent discipline, and to this day traditional theological learning in Islam often rejects not only *falsafa* but also the thoroughgoing rationalist doctrine espoused by the Mu'tazila, even though Ash'arism did come to incorporate major areas of Greek logic, and much of the metaphysical terminology and categories.

THE REVIVALIST REACTION

The second trend was initiated by the creative Abū Ḥāmid al-Ghazālī (d. 1111), an influential scholar who was born in Ṭūs in the heart of the Iranian sphere of intellectual life. He was employed by the state, and was encouraged to define a concordist Islamic theology that would define a legitimate place for Sufism, tradition and rationality, to provide a stable and inclusive official creed for the Sunnī rulers. His theological work, *The Revival of Religious Sciences* (*Iḥyā' 'Ulūm al-Dīn*), achieved this; it is still actively studied and serves as a lively source for interpretation and opinion in mainstream Sunnī Islam.

Ghazālī's philosophical work has had an impact in defining, one way or another, the direction of all subsequent philosophical composition in Islam. This work may be divided into two main types, both of them demonstrating an extremely sophisticated analysis of philosophical problems, whether aimed at the refutation of *falsafa* doctrine or at teaching an "accepted" type of philosophy. The first type is his famous anti-*falsafa* polemic, *The Incoherence of the Philosophers* (*Tahāfut al-falāsifa*), in which Avicennan propositions and problems are identified and expressed in a refined philosophical language, and then shown to be self-contradictory.[22] Among these problems three stand out, which have subsequently inspired philosophers to present analyses of them in ways deemed harmonious with religion: creation and eternity, God's knowledge of particulars, and the immortality of the human soul and resurrection. In each case Ghazālī seeks to demonstrate that the philosophers' position of (1) eternity over creation, (2) God's knowledge as limited to universals and (3) the rejection of an individuated immortality of the soul and bodily resurrection are both rationally untenable and tantamount to infidelity (*kufr*).

Ghazālī's second type of work consists of independent texts on philosophy in which the approach is not polemical, but seeks to analyse and explain philosophical arguments. These include his *Aims of the Philosophers* (*Maqāṣid al-falāsifa*) and *The Straight Method* (*al-Qisṭās al-Mustaqīm*). Thus Ghazālī's work actually ensured in more ways than one the continuity of philosophy in Islam, perhaps even providing it with a new impetus and energy. In practice, this second aspect of Ghazālī's work defined a "textbook" genre of *falsafa*, accepted and studied in scholastic traditions, albeit not in all Islamic centres. The usual Ottoman approach to *falsafa*, for instance, took Ghazālī's position to be definitive. The best example is the textbook by Athīr al-Dīn al-Abharī, called *Guide to Philosophy* (*Hidāyat al-ḥikma*), which has been widely studied together with numerous commentaries, glosses and superglosses. Many scholastic centres used these texts as part of an accepted syllabus on philosophy.

Another outcome of Ghazālī's critical analysis was that many thinkers responded by seeking to remove the inconsistencies in the Peripatetic philosophical corpus that Ghazālī had demonstrated, and in so doing made significant contributions to the refinement of *falsafa* and thus to its creative existence. For example, Shihāb al-Dīn Suhrawardī (d. 1191), the innovative Persian founder of the new system called the "Philosophy of Illumination" (*Ḥikmat al-ishrāq*), was able to "solve" many logical gaps and metaphysical and epistemological inconsistencies and so help to remove doubts as to *falsafa*'s legitimacy.[23]

The great Andalusian philosopher Averroes (Ibn Rushd) (d. 1198) wrote one of *falsafa*'s most creative works as a direct response to Ghazālī's polemics, *The Incoherence of the Incoherence* (*Tahāfut al-tahāfut*), a text that also wielded influence in Latin translation. This, together with the Latin translations of his commentaries on many of Aristotle's texts, and on Plato's *Republic*, contributed significantly to the development of Latin philosophy.[24] In his Aristotelian commentaries Averroes aimed to cleanse the Islamic philosophical corpus of Neoplatonist, emanationist views, to separate pure philosophy from the more explicitly theological arguments of Fārābī and Avicenna, and hence to construct a "pure" Aristotelian philosophical system.

Later philosophers were also inspired to meet the challenges of Ghazālī's texts and constructed elaborate arguments to prove the validity of accepted philosophical positions. For example, in the seventeenth century, Mīr Dāmād's highly refined theory of "Temporal Generation" (*ḥudūth dahrī*) once and for all harmonised the idea of creation with the philosophers' views on eternity and becoming. And in the nineteenth century Hādī Sabzevārī's construct, called "Formal Body" (*badan mithlī*), helped to demonstrate that the philosophers do believe in a kind of bodily resurrection, which caused an even greater degree of acceptance of philosophy by the powerful Shī'ite ulema. In short, the continuation of the study of a religiously accepted Islamic philosophy to this day, albeit in a limited way and confined mostly to Shī'ite scholastic centres, has been both directly and indirectly shaped by Ghazālī's work.

THE FUNDAMENTALIST REACTION

Although Ḥanbalism faded before the appeal of Ash'arism, it retained its appeal in certain Syrian circles. Its most distinguished interpreter, Ibn Taymiyya (d. 1326), was a staunchly anti-*falsafa* jurist and ideologue of scriptural literalism. Ibn Taymiyya produced a harsh attack on philosophy, entitled *al-Radd 'alā al-manṭiqiyyīn* (*Refutation of the Rational Philosophers*), which exercised some influence in the complex and divided world of Ḥanbalī literalism.[25] From the eighteenth century, such movements, including the Wahhābī and the Salafī, have shared this dogmatic ideology and actively preach on the need to rid Islam of all forms of innovations deemed to be un-Islamic, including any recourse to reason (*'aql*). Naturally, such militantly fundamentalist views, while generally opposed by mainstream ulema, have served to curtail the study of philosophy in any of its forms.

RECONSTRUCTION, CONTINUITY AND "ILLUMINATION"

Philosophy continued in Andalusia, where the texts of Averroes were instrumental in its development. Other types of philosophical writing emerged in Andalusian centres such as Cordoba and Seville in the twelfth century. The dominance of legal strictures, among other reasons, ensured that the production of philosophical writing by Ibn Bājja (d. 1138) and Ibn Ṭufayl (d. 1185) took the form of individual works rather than a trend or school.

Ibn Bājja's writings were an interpretation of Fārābī's political philosophy. Ibn Bājja reaffirms the supreme virtues of the perfect, ideal city, but does not think that it will ever be realised. He argues that darkness prevails in all actual cities, whose inhabitants live in the cave (after Plato), perceiving only the "shadows" and not the "good". He does not accept Fārābī's view of a leadership role for the philosopher in the city but argues instead that the philosopher's activity is limited to the solitary pursuit of theoretical knowledge. His teaching accepts Avicenna's notion of experiential knowledge, explained as "enlightenment", through conjunction with the Active Intellect (e.g. Avicenna's *Directives and Remarks*, IX, X), but this "prophetic" knowledge serves only the individual philosopher rather than a political system, or a state.

Ibn Ṭufayl continued Ibn Bājja's political interpretations. He was more inclined towards Avicenna's philosophical allegories and composed a philosophical story of a solitary man who is suckled by a deer on an isolated island, reared in the wild, and finally acquires complete theoretical knowledge based on his own self-abilities in unaided reason. This enlightenment, however, does not affect society; he fails on his mission to bring wisdom to the inhabitants of an adjacent island, and is forced to return to his solitary life.

In the East, philosophy mainly continued through Suhrawardī's Illuminationist philosophical system. The Philosophy of Illumination is a holistic, constructed system that aims to refine the period's Peripatetic philosophy, which was known mainly through Avicenna. Illuminationism is critical. Had it not been for Suhrawardī's definition and construction of the Philosophy of Illumination, the creative endeavour of philosophy as a distinctive branch of knowledge might have died out altogether in Islam.

For the most part, Aristotle's authority was unquestioned among devotees of *falsafa*, and Avicenna's work was considered the perfect and consistent Arabic and Persian expression of his system. Suhrawardī was among the very first philosophers, as opposed to theologians, to raise well-reasoned objections to Aristotle. His aim – to refine philosophical arguments by rethinking the set of questions that constitute holistic systems – generated novel analyses covering the principles of knowledge, ways of examining being, and new cosmological constructs.

The most important and clearly stipulated aim of the philosophy of Illumination is the construction of a holistic system to define a new method of science, named the "Science of Lights" (*'ilm al-anwār*), a refinement of Aristotelian method that is capable of describing an inclusive range of phenomena in which Peripatetic theory is thought to have failed. Suhrawardī's novel ideas were expressed in four major texts that together constituted the new system. The first of these texts was *The Intimations* (*al-Talwīḥāt*); the second, its addendum, was entitled *The Apposites* (*al-Muqāwamāt*). The latter was composed with a standard Peripatetic structure and language with the aim of presenting a working synopsis of Avicenna's philosophical system, to bring out the elements in which the Illuminationist position differs from that of the Peripatetic, and also to introduce arguments to prove the former. The third text, the *Paths and Havens* (*al-Mashāri‘ wa'l-Muṭāraḥāt*), is the longest of Suhrawardī's compositions. Here he presents detailed arguments concerning Illuminationist principles in every domain of philosophical inquiry set against those of the Peripatetics, mainly the strictly Avicennan.

The fourth text of the corpus is the text eponymous with the system itself, *The Philosophy of Illumination* (*Ḥikmat al-ishrāq*); this is the best known of all of Suhrawardī's works. The book is the final expression and systematic construction of the new analysis. Its structure differs from the standard, three-part logic, physics and metaphysics found in Peripatetic texts and employs a constructed, symbolic metalanguage, called the "Language of Illumination" (*lisān al-ishrāq*). All things pertaining to the domains of knowing, being and cosmology are depicted as lights in which distinction is determined by equivocation; that is, in terms of degrees of intensity of luminosity. The One origin of the system is the most luminous, hence most self-conscious light, named the Light of Lights, and all other entities are propagated from it in accordance with the increasing sequence 2^n, where n is the rank of the propagated light starting with the First Light; and together they form the continuum, the luminous whole of reality.

The Illuminationist ontological position, called "primacy of quiddity", was a matter of considerable controversy. Those who believed in the primacy of being, or existence (*wujūd*), considered essence (*māhiyya*) to be a derived, mental concept (*amr i‘tibārī*, a term of secondary intention); while those who believed in the primacy of quiddity considered existence to be a derived, mental concept. The Illuminationist position was this: should existence be real outside the mind (*mutaḥaqqaq fī khārij al-dhihn*), then the real must consist of two things: the principle of the reality of existence, *and* the being of existence, which requires a referent outside the mind (*miṣdāq fī khārij al-dhihn*). Moreover, its referent outside the mind must also consist of two things, which are subdivided, and so on, *ad infinitum*. This is clearly absurd. Therefore existence must be considered an abstract, derived, mental concept.

Mongol rule over eastern Islam witnessed the emergence of noted thinkers who, starting in the thirteenth century, wrote commentaries on Suhrawardī's texts and also composed independent works, some distinctly inspired by the Illuminationist system. Among the Ottomans, too, Illuminationism continued to be cultivated, as exampled in the figure of Ismāʿīl Ankarawī (d. 1631), whose commentaries on Suhrawardī perpetuated this important branch of the *falsafa* tradition in Ottoman lands.[26] In this respect an Illuminationist-inspired analytical trend can be seen to have helped to rescue genuine philosophy from being assimilated entirely into either dogmatic theology or mysticism. In part, the origins of Illuminationist philosophy may be viewed as attempts to respond to anti-*falsafa* polemics. The daring Illuminationist philosophical position, however, insisted that Peripatetic philosophy itself needed to be reconstructed in order to remove a set of presumed logical gaps and to provide epistemological and other theories better able to explain being, knowing and cosmology.

THE METAPHYSICAL SCHOOL OF IṢFAHĀN

During the late sixteenth century in Iṣfahān, the beginnings of a remarkable, widespread and prolific philosophical activity are in evidence. Safavid rulers initiated a new era in Iranian intellectual life by their lavish endowment of many new centres of scholarship, as in the previous century when the mother of the ruling Timurid Shah, Shāhrokh, had been the prime mover in large endowments given to scholarship and the founding of religious colleges (*madrasas*). One of the major results of this enhanced level of intellectual life in Iran has been described as a period of "revival" in the history of post-Avicennan philosophy. Philosophy in this period took the form of the widespread study and teaching of philosophical subjects, in a way quite distinct from the earlier limited engagement of a few thinkers. Also, many of the *falsafa* works produced in this period are superior to the scholastic textbooks that were generated in Iran from the thirteenth to the late sixteenth century. As intense as the period was, however, it did not last long, and by the late seventeenth century the creative side of the activity gave way to a scholastic trend that continued the philosophical endeavour through the composition of commentaries, glosses and superglosses.

The impact of the School of Iṣfahān is evident in many intellectual domains in Iran up to the present, most of all in the acceptance and incorporation of a reformulated Islamic philosophy into higher level syllabuses of Shīʿite *madrasas* (studied by a few pre-eminent religious scholars *after* completing the study of formal theology and law). Twelver Shīʿism, as we know it today, is the result of work done by sixteenth- and seventeenth-century scholars, most of whom were trained in the "intellectual sciences" (*al-ʿulūm al-ʿaqliyya*) and in juridical domains called "transmitted sciences" (*al-'ulūm al-naqliyya*). Philosophy in this period was believed to be a comprehensive and scientific (*'ilmī*, which also means "philosophical" in the classical sense) system, and intellectual Shī'ism drew from it considerably in many ways that were not confined to jurisprudence and theology, thus distinguishing it from Sunnī Islam.

The manifest results of the philosophical activity and creation of the rationalist principles of Shī'ite theology were based on multiple sources. In the domain of political thought, Shī'ite scholars equipped with the method of demonstration defined a place for Fārābī's concept of learned reformers of law and elaborated on it by formulating the role of a supreme source of authority, whose authority was established by unified epistemological theories. The view of knowledge employed here combined the Peripatetic with the Illuminationist, and the legalist tradition that drew on revealed authority was also incorporated into the system. The widespread scholarly work of this period gave rise to the recovery and study of the entire range of Islamic philosophy's texts and also led to the definition of the third synthesis and restructuring of a holistic system. This was a major achievement in the development of philosophy in Islam, as it was finally proven to be "harmonious" with revelation and therefore accepted by more and more Shī'ite clergy. The seventeenth-century philosophical texts, mostly composed in the Safavid capital of Iṣfahān, continued the examination of the earlier trends but also included the elaboration and refinement of a number of added problems, often in line with the period's characteristic preoccupation with uniform theories and holistic systems.

Mīr Dāmād (d. 1630) and his acclaimed pupil Mullā Ṣadrā (1571–1640) were the two most creative philosophers of this period and together defined the School of Iṣfahān's analytic summit. Other members of this school included Mīr Fendereskī (d. 1640) and Shaykh Bahā'ī (d. 1621), who excelled in scientific and mathematical discoveries. The main outcome of this period was the construction of a system called "Metaphysical Philosophy", which is also part of the name given to Mullā Ṣadrā's best-known text, *The Four Journeys* (*al-Asfār al-Arba'a*).[27] This system is structurally distinct from both the Peripatetic and the Illuminationist systems. It commences with the study of being and places a special emphasis on metaphysics. The structure of Peripatetic texts, where the study of logic forms the first of the three sciences is changed, and a considerably shortened logic is studied as part of independent textbooks with an emphasis on formal techniques.

Further reading

Adamson, Peter, and Taylor, Richard C. (eds.), *The Cambridge Companion to Arabic Philosophy* (Cambridge, 2005).

Daiber, Hans, *Bibliography of Islamic Philosophy*, 2 vols. (Leiden, 1999).

Fakhry, Majid, *A History of Islamic Philosophy*, 2nd edn (New York, 1983).

Gutas, Dimitri, *Avicenna and the Aristotelian Tradition* (Leiden, 1988).

Greek Thought, Arabic Culture: The Graeco-Arabic Translation Movement in Baghdad and Early Abbasid Society (2nd–4th/8th–10th centuries) (London, 1998).

"The study of Arabic philosophy in the twentieth century: an essay on the historiography of Arabic philosophy", *British Journal of Middle Eastern Studies* 29 (2002), pp. 5–25.

Nasr, Seyyed Hossein, and Leaman, Oliver (eds.), *History of Islamic Philosophy*, 2 vols. (London, 1996).

Sharif, M. M., *A History of Muslim Philosophy*, 2 vols. (Wiesbaden, 1963–6).

Wisnovsky, Robert, *Avicenna's Metaphysics in Context* (London, 2003).

Notes

1. For a discussion of theology in relation to and its impact on philosophy see Majid Fakhry, *Philosophy, Dogma, and the Impact of Greek Thought in Islam* (Aldershot, 1994).
2. An important discussion of the relationship between *falsafa* and *kalām* was presented by Averroes (Ibn Rushd), who believed that philosophical investigation should be kept distinct from theological premises. See Averroes, *Decisive Treatise and Epistle Dedicatory*, tr. Charles E. Butterworth (Provo, UT, 2001).
3. For a comprehensive study of the Ismā'īlī doctrines including their philosophical and theological views see Farhad Daftary, *The Ismā'īlīs: Their History and Doctrines* (London, 1990). See also S. M. Stern, *Studies in Early Ismā'īlism* (Jerusalem, 1983).
4. Muḥammad ibn al Nadīm, *al-Fihrist* (Cairo, n.d.).
5. Ibid., p. 511; also Majid Fakhry, *A History of Islamic Philosophy*, 2nd edn (New York, 1983), p. 5.
6. Fakhry, *History*, pp. 5–12.
7. The official institution of Bayt al-Ḥikma was directed by Māsawiyah, had a "keeper" named Yaḥyā ibn al-Biṭrīq, and was protected and supported by Ma'mūn, whose love of "ancient wisdom" led him to send officials to Constantinople and other regions in Byzantium to seek out and purchase books of the ancient sages and scholars. These were then brought to the Academy and translated into Arabic. See Fakhry, *History of Islamic Philosophy*, pp. 12ff.
8. For a comprehensive presentation of translations from Greek sources to Arabic see Franz Rosenthal, *The Classical Heritage in Islam*, tr. Emile Marmorstein and Jenny Marmorstein (London, 1975).
9. Fakhry, *Philosophy, Dogma*.

10. The Aristotelian and other philosophical texts translated are discussed in F. E. Peters, *Aristotle and the Arabs: The Aristotelian Tradition in Islam* (New York, 1968).
11. See al-Kindī, *On First Philosophy*, tr. Alfred L. Ivry (Albany, NY, 1974). An excellent account of the crucial set of philosophical questions concerning Kindī and the Mu'tazila is given by P. Adamson, "Al-Kindī and the Mu'tazila: divine attributes, creation, and freedom", *Arabic Sciences and Philosophy* 13 (2003), pp. 45–77.
12. For a discussion of creation and other problems significant in the development of early Islamic philosophy see Herbert Davidson, *Proofs for Eternity, Creation, and the Existence of God in Medieval Islamic and Jewish Philosophy* (Oxford, 1987).
13. For a general discussion of Kindī's works and philosophical method see George N. Atiyeh, *Al-Kindī: The Philosopher of the Arabs* (Rawalpindi, 1966).
14. See Shukri Abed, *Aristotelian Logic and the Arabic Language in Alfarabi* (Albany, NY, 1991).
15. This is one of medieval philosophy's most creative texts. It has not been translated, nor has it as yet been the subject of an analytical study in Western scholarship. The Arabic text represents the apogee of refined technical language; and Fārābī's penetrating analysis of being, and of the theoretical foundations of state and religion, set the standard for philosophical expression in Islam. See al-Fārābī, *Kitāb al-Ḥurūf*, ed. Muhsin Mahdi (Beirut, 1970).
16. Richard Walzer, *Alfarabi on the Perfect State* (Oxford, 1985), and Muhsin Mahdi, *Alfarabi's Philosophy of Plato and Aristotle*, revised edn (Ithaca, 2002).
17. Richard Walzer, *On the Perfect State*, revised edn (Chicago, 1998).
18. See Hossein Ziai, "Knowledge and authority in Shī'ī philosophy", in Lynda Clarke (ed.), *Shiite Heritage: Essays in Classical and Modern Traditions* (Binghamton, NY, 2002), pp. 359–73.
19. See for example Fazlur Rahman, "Essence and Existence in Avicenna", in *Mediaeval and Renaissance Studies* 4 (1958), pp. 1–6, continued in "Essence and Existence, I: Ibn Sīnā: the myth and the reality", in *Hamdard Islamicus* 4/1 (1981), pp. 3–14. See also Michael E. Marmura, "Avicenna's proof from contingency for God's existence in the *Metaphysics* of the *Shifā*", *Medieval Studies* 42 (1980), pp. 337–52.
20. Avicenna's views of a primary and intuitive act of self-identification impact the Illuminationists' famous unified theory of knowledge by presence, and anticipate the Cartesian *cogito*. See Thérèse-Anne Druart, "The soul and the body problem: Avicenna and Descartes", in Thérèse-Anne Druart (ed.), *Arabic Philosophy and the West: Continuity and Interaction* (Washington, DC, 1988), pp. 27–49.
21. See Fazlur Rahman, *Prophecy in Islam* (London, 1958).
22. Ghazālī's text is available in a bilingual edition: *The Incoherence of the Philosophers*, tr. Michael E. Marmura, 2nd edn (Provo, UT, 2000). His polemical theological views concerning how philosophy should be positioned and studied are discussed by Michael E. Marmura in

"Ghazālī and Ash'arism Revisited", *Arabic Sciences and Philosophy* 12 (2002), pp. 91–110. Ghazālī's doctrinal positions on creation and related problems argued against Avicenna are discussed by Richard M. Frank, *Creation and the Cosmic System: Al-Ghazālī and Avicenna* (Heidelberg, 1992).

23. For a general account of the new Illuminationist system see Hossein Ziai, *Knowledge and Illumination: A Study of Suhrawardī's Ḥikmat al-Ishrāq* (Atlanta, 1990).
24. The Arabic text of Averroes' *Tahāfut al-tahāfut* has been translated by Simon Van Den Bergh, *The Incoherence of the Incoherence* (London, 1969).
25. Ibn Taymiyya attacks the philosophers by paraphrasing their arguments, taken from a host of sources, which he then presents as his own, claiming that they are indications of the heretical positions held by philosophers. His work is a prime example of sophistry, distorting the philosophers' views to serve his own anti-rationalist ideology. See Wael B. Hallaq (tr.), *Ibn Taymiyya against the Greek Logicians* (Oxford, 1993).
26. Bilal Kuşpinar, *Isma'il Ankaravi on the Illuminative Philosophy: His Izahu'l-Hikem: Edition and Analysis in Comparison with Dawwani's* Shawakil al-Hur, *together with the Translation of Suhrawardi's* Hayakil al-Nur (Kuala Lumpur, 1996).
27. There are no comprehensive, analytical studies of this work, and to date only the older philosophical study by Fazlur Rahman captures Ṣadrā's stipulated and textually valid philosophical aim. See Fazlur Rahman, *The Philosophy of Mullā Ṣadrā* (Albany, 1975).

4 The developed *kalām* tradition

OLIVER LEAMAN (PART I) AND
SAJJAD RIZVI (PART II)

PART I: SUNNISM

A few initial points need to be made about the nature of Islamic theology in its later stages before a discussion of some of its main themes and thinkers can be attempted. First, there often exists no clear distinction between Islamic theology, in the sense of *kalām*, and the other Islamic and not so Islamic sciences, such as grammar, jurisprudence (*fiqh*), philosophy (*falsafa/ḥikma*), Sufism, and the even more specific activities of learning how to operate with the Traditions of the Prophet, and how to assess and rank the chains of narrators which differentiate their levels of reliability. Islamic theologians did not usually strictly separate what they did from all these other activities, and so it is not easy to provide a neat account of precisely what is "theological" and what is not.[1]

The first four centuries of Islamic theology had been a time of vibrant creativity. The whole structure of the subject was being created, with its novel vocabulary and its distinctive hermeneutic techniques, but by the time of Ghazālī the basic paradigms were already well established, and *kalām* was rivalling or outstripping *falsafa* in intellectual eminence. It is often said that the assault of Ghazālī on philosophy destroyed the latter in the Islamic world until (and perhaps even in) modern times, and that he replaced philosophy with theology and Sufism.[2] This is not true; for one thing *falsafa* as a discipline did not die; it continued to flourish in the Persian world and to some extent among the Ottomans, and it was only in the Arabic-speaking regions of Islam that it sank into a marked decline, until reviving in the nineteenth century as part of the *Nahḍa* or Arabic-Islamic "renaissance". However *falsafa*'s key concerns and methods lived on, and flourished, within developed *kalām*.

THE IMPACT OF AL-GHAZĀLĪ

Ghazālī (d. 1111) certainly did attack what he saw as the leading theses of *mashshā'ī* or Peripatetic philosophy, as represented by

Avicenna, and in his attack he asserted what I shall argue is a defining characteristic of *kalām*, namely, its reliance on rational argument of what might be regarded as a dialectical type. According to Ghazālī some of the theses of *falsafa* are merely *bid'a* or heretical innovation, but there are three graver positions which they uphold which actually constitute *kufr* or unbelief. These are the denial of God's knowledge of particulars, the claim that the world is uncreated, and the insistence that a physical afterlife is impossible. What is most interesting about Ghazālī's approach is that he does not argue that because certain conclusions are beyond the pale from the point of view of Islam it follows that they are not to be believed, drawing a line under the matter. He argues, quite brilliantly, that on the criteria which the philosophers themselves adduce, these conclusions do not follow from their premises and so may safely be denied. In fact, so ready is Ghazālī to put his toes in the water of philosophy that some of the most distinguished scholars of his thought have considered him to be a *faylasūf*, rather than the chief nemesis of *falsafa* in the lands of Islam.[3] (Interestingly, this was a view shared by Christian Europe, so impressed was it by the fairness with which he described the theses of Avicenna in his *Maqāṣid al-falāsifa*, later to be translated as the *Intentiones Philosophorum*.)

What was the impact of Ghazālī's critique of *falsafa*? His arguments were subsequently attacked by Averroes,[4] but Ghazālī's view largely prevailed in the Islamic world, at least within its Arabic segment, in suggesting that *falsafa* as a total system had really nothing to offer in the understanding of religion or religious texts, and so was best abandoned. These strictures do not apply at all to much of the metaphysics, or to what he did not see as an inseparable part of *falsafa*, namely logic (*manṭiq*), which he argued forms a vital part of theology and can even be derived from Islamic texts itself. His arguments for the importance of logic, derived in part from the methods of his teacher al-Juwaynī (d. 1085), known as the Imam of the Two Sanctuaries (*Imām al-Ḥaramayn*), proved persuasive in an intellectual context that had already internalised logic in the area of jurisprudence. This deep internalisation of logic, the core rationalist technique, within the fundamental disciplines of the religion, ensured that later *kalām* texts were well equipped to present a systematic theology which progressed on strictly ratiocinative lines to prove the truths of religion, as well as deploying reason to interpret the content of revealed doctrine. It is true that some Ḥanbalite thinkers came to attack logic also, arguing that it was so infected by metaphysics that it cannot furnish a neutral tool of analysis but instead serves to smuggle improper ideas into the discussion of a religion which has been definitively expounded in scripture.[5] For the great majority, however, logic continued to enjoy a high level of respect among the exponents of *kalām*, albeit often under disparate labels. On balance, this outcome is hardly surprising, since the whole *modus operandi* of theology was to establish conclusions about Islam through some form of argument, and to defeat the advocates of error using universally accessible techniques.

It is difficult to know precisely how to assess Ghazālī's arguments, since he seems to be operating on two levels at once. In the first instance, he needs to disprove the arguments of his opponents using their own techniques, an ambitious strategy which denies the opponent the refuge of disagreeing with the methodology employed. Yet he then wants to argue that the conclusions of Avicennan *falsafa* are not only improperly derived, but also constitute unbelief or at the very least *bid'a*. So even if these conclusions followed logically from their premises, there must be something wrong, since it could hardly be the case that one could validly derive propositions which contradict the clear meaning of God's speech. The philosophers, then, had not only to argue that their conclusions were logically valid, but also that they did not contradict Islam. They were also obliged to defend the view that ratiocination is a perfectly acceptable method for Muslims to use.

It has often been stated in the literature that those critical of reason are "anti-rationalist" and "traditionalist", but this is not necessarily the case. If the results of deductive reason go against what we know through some other method, then one might well wonder how far deductive reason is useful. After all, we do not come to know most of the important features of our lives through the use of reasoning at all; they are more intimate and closer to us than that. It would, for example, be difficult for someone to persuade me under normal circumstances that my name was not Oliver Leaman, however good at reasoning she was, nor that I was not working right now on a desk in Lexington, Kentucky. Everything around me suggests that I am Oliver Leaman and that I am typing this in Lexington, and I do not find this out through reasoning. (Wittgenstein's *On Certainty* is full of examples like this.[6]) So if reasoning suggested I was wrong I might well come to suspect reasoning as a useful route to the truth in such cases, and this would not be "anti-rationalist" or "traditionalist" in any meaningful sense.

THE RESPONSE OF THE PHILOSOPHERS

The philosophers tended to argue that where there was an apparent conflict between Islam and *falsafa* this conflict was only apparent, and that a correct understanding of philosophy would resolve the tension. It is the theologians, in particular those labelled by Averroes the people of *kalām* (for him definitely a derogatory term), who unnecessarily complicate the matter by their analyses of particular theological doctrines. It is the philosophers who should be left to sort out these doctrines, since only the philosophers have the ability and the training to resolve them once and for all in a demonstrative fashion. The theologians with their dialectical (*jadalī*) methodology are unable to resolve issues comprehensively, and leave an abundance of loose ends. This not only results in a lack of closure, but also threatens to provoke doubts in the mind of the hearer about the truth of Islam itself, since questions which cannot be settled appear to have been raised. One might think Averroes was trying to evade the issue by making this point, but he does point to a characteristic feature of *kalām*, the fact that it tends to be directed against some other position, and so is dialectical in form. The trouble with such arguments is that they are only as strong as their premises, and since these may be vulnerable, theological arguments are not always impressive in their analytical depth.[7]

It is important to bear in mind that many of the arguments which appear to be theological in Islamic culture operate at a number of levels (no doubt this is true of theology in general). The debate between Ghazālī and Averroes on, say, the nature of prophecy (*nubuwwa*) is not just philosophical and theological, but also legal and political. According to Ghazālī, God chooses who will prophesy, and He provides that person with the information he requires in order to set out on his task. According to Averroes and most of the *falāsifa*, the prophet is the sort of person who through self-perfection is fit to receive prophecy, and so receives it automatically, in the same way that I will receive a cold if I am in a fit state to catch one and the appropriate germs are in my vicinity. Prophecy is always available to those who are capable of reaching out to it intellectually. Ghazālī insists that this is far from the Islamic view, since it implies that God has no choice of prophetic recipients, and this conflicts with the way in which the scriptural texts describe the process. But then, as Averroes suggests, perhaps these texts need to be interpreted in different ways for different audiences. Those who are able to understand the real basis of prophecy will not object if the community at large is given an account of the process which it can understand and which has within it the important features of what is true, but which otherwise they would not comprehend.

THEOLOGY AND "RATIONALITY"

What was the Arabic for "theology"? The obvious answer is *kalām*, or speech, which represents well the scope of early theology, which was to confront the arguments of non-Muslims in the vastly expanding Islamic empire, and to deal with the early polemics between the Ash'arites, the Mu'tazilites and the Qadarites over the nature of the basic concepts of Islam itself. This was taken in two directions, the first allowing the use of reason, as in the case of the followers of Shāfi'ī and Abū Ḥanīfa, and the second based on a literal reading of hadith, as with the supporters of Ibn Ḥanbal. It is worth pointing out that both approaches were rational, in that they both relied on the rational resolution of theoretical issues, but they applied reason to different sets of issues. For the Ḥanbalīs it is primarily to be applied to the issue of hadith verification and the precise relationship between the Traditions as bequeathed by the Prophet, his Companions and their Successors.

In Western accounts these two groups of thinkers are sometimes called Rationalists and Traditionalists (terms commended by Abrahamov and Makdisi, among others), but these labels are not always helpful. It is not that some scholars known as Traditionalists favoured irrationality, or that "Rationalists" did not use the hadith; it was more a matter of emphasis than a difference in kind. The way in which these two approaches developed came to be subsumed under *uṣūl al-dīn*, the "roots of religion", which until the eleventh century tended to be rather thin philosophically but placed the emphasis on understanding the structure of religion and how its different areas of discourse were related.

As theology evolved, the early years of *kalām* came to be seen as a very free period of thought indeed, as evidenced by the popular slogan *man ṭalaba al-dīn bi'l kalām tazandaqa* (whoever seeks religion through *kalām* becomes a heretic). What this referred to was not the whole project of theology itself as represented by *uṣūl al-dīn*, but the investigation of basic features of the nature of God which some early Muslim thinkers engaged in, something which later generations often felt to be presuming too much about the accessibility of the divine nature. Despite the increasing incorporation of *falsafa* topics and methods into later *kalām*, the institutionalisation of forms of Ash'arism and even more "traditionalist" approaches such as that of Ibn Ḥanbal has led some recent commentators on Islamic theology like Muhammad Iqbal to contrast the relative freedom of discussion of the early years with a *kalām* equivalent of the "closure of the door of *ijtihād*", or interpretation, a move which allegedly ended juridical innovation approximately a thousand years ago.[8]

THE ROLE OF IBN TAYMIYYA

In particular, there emerged a few late medieval thinkers like the Syrian Ḥanbalite Taqī al-Dīn Ibn Taymiyya (d. 1328) whose campaign to critique theology was more radical than that found in earlier generations.[9] He criticised the very basis of *kalām* by attacking the notion of definition, that is, specifying a clear and distinct meaning for abstract concepts; and without the possibility of definition there is no possibility of theological discussion, since one is then without the basic materials for such an activity. Ibn Taymiyya directly attacked the Aristotelian notion of definition (*ḥadd*) for assuming that there is a basic distinction between essential and accidental properties which a thing has. That is, there are properties everything has which are incidental to its being the sort of thing it is, to be contrasted with properties which are definitive of its being that kind of thing. In order to understand what a thing is we have to be able to distinguish between its essential and merely accidental qualities. According to the philosophers and theologians who used this notion of definition, what it does is to provide us with information about the nature of concepts, not about whether those concepts actually exist. For us to discover whether the latter is the case we need to examine the world and see whether those concepts are actually instantiated. These defining general ideas or universals are taken to have a type of being which is entirely independent of their actual existence in the world of generation and corruption. We can use concepts even if there are no instances of them in our world, and even fictitious concepts have essential and accidental features. In addition to this, Ibn Taymiyya also criticised the notion of syllogism, the basis of reasoning in *falsafa* and also in *kalām*, which, he thought, even were it to be combined with an acceptable notion of definition, would not be capable of working its way to irrefutable conclusions.

Perhaps, though, it would be better to concentrate not on the critique of definition, but rather on the theory of universals which Ibn Taymiyya sees as part and parcel of that critique.[10] He is a firm nominalist, and argues that universals should be analysed entirely in terms of the individuals which constitute them. We can construct universals, but we should always be aware that they are merely a shorthand for grouping together particulars, and possess no independent existence of their own. The trouble with the *kalām* folk, Peripatetics, mystics and the *ishrāqīs* is that they all use universal notions as though these represent something which really exists. We should be aware, he tells us, of the role of God in creating the particulars out of which the universals are abstracted, and not go on to make the next mistake of assuming that the universals have independent existence and in fact influence or restrict the activity of God.

The notion of definition underpins what looks like the independent existence of the essences; but it might be argued that there is no problem in being a nominalist and combining this with the Aristotelian notion of a universal. There is nothing wrong with generalising over individuals and constructing as a result a universal concept, which then represents the common features which all the particulars possess. Of course, for a nominalist like Ibn Taymiyya the problem would ensue that one could never be sure that one had really acquired an accurate view of what the particulars had in common, so that any such construction of universals would need to be provisional. This is the problem with the notion of the definition, in that we would never know whether we were correct in distinguishing between its essential and its accidental properties, since our experience will hardly be a useful guide to this distinction. Experience would give us evidence of the existence of objects, but what features they must possess and which they could do without, and still be the same sort of object, is not information provided by experience. Knowledge should be identified with our experience and its basis in divine grace. Ibn Taymiyya uses this theory to develop an account of how one must trust certain kinds of authority on the meaning of the Qur'an by going straight to the interpretive tradition itself, as opposed to reason (*'aql*). All that can be acquired through reason is confusion and contradiction. It is revelation which provides a secure source of information and instruction, and any attempt to replace or supplement revelation by having recourse to logic is to be avoided. The idea that revelation could be supplemented is unacceptable to him, and he was just as hostile to the forms of Sufism which he saw as transgressing the bounds of what can be said and known about the nature of reality, and our place in it, as he was of logic, philosophy and theology of the more ambitious variety.

ISLAMIC THEOLOGY AS A SYSTEM

It is important to see how the ontology of those critical of much Islamic philosophy, mysticism and even logic fits in with this critique. Since the argument is that the world is at root atomistic, and so is kept together in its present fairly stable form only by the constant intervention of the Deity, the reification of concepts is even more inaccurate than treating the material world as though it were independently subsistent and real. The developing line of broadly Ash'arite thinkers defended this view of the world as constituted of atoms and accidents, and so entirely dependent on God's grace for its continuing existence. Ghazālī turned these various aspects of the defence of Ash'arism as theology into something of a system, one which was to survive for a long time in the various schools of theology in the Islamic world, and indeed continues to have resonance today.

Most commentators on Islamic theology offer a fairly neat idea of how it developed. First there existed a variety of views, with Mu'tazilism becoming politically dominant, emphasising the significance of reason in discussing religious issues. Then Ash'arī (d. 936) established a critique of Mu'tazilism, not just of its doctrines but also of the implications of those doctrines for the relative significance of reason and tradition (*'aql* and *naql*, a familiar binary addressed in the theology texts and discussions), and for a period Ash'arism predominated. This in turn was criticised for being too liberal by a small revival of Ḥanbalī fortunes, in particular through the work of the Ẓāhirite literalist Ibn Ḥazm of Córdoba (d. 1064)[11] and Ibn Taymiyya, both of whom criticised the ability of intellectual argument to resolve deep-seated difficulties in understanding the Qur'an. They rejected the methods of *falsafa* and Ash'arite theology and advocated in their place a reliance on the ancestors, the *salaf*, who understood the language of the Qur'an and the practices of the Prophet in ways which we do well to emulate, and who were not troubled by the sorts of issues raised by later sects.

Although in recent times this approach has become important politically due to its acceptance in simplified form by the Wahhābīs, who in 1924 achieved control over the holy sites in Arabia (the present-day Saudi Arabia), Ibn Taymiyya was always a marginal figure, and the Ash'arite school proved far more acceptable to the ulema, quickly developing into a complex system at the hands of thinkers such as Abū Bakr al-Bāqillānī (d. 1013), whose *Prolegomena* (*Kitāb al-Tamhīd*) systematically laid out the basic principles of Ash'arism, a process further refined by 'Abd al-Qāhir al-Baghdādī (d. 1037) and probably reaching its completion as an original form of thought in the *Guidance* (*Kitāb al-Irshād*) of al-Juwaynī, to be vigorously defended by al-Shahrastānī (d. 1153), Fakhr al-Dīn al-Rāzī (d. 1209), Najm al-Dīn al-Nasafī (d. 1142) and 'Aḍud al-Dīn al-Ījī (d. 1355). Al-Ghazālī is perhaps too original a thinker to be subsumed completely beneath an Ash'arite or Māturīdite rubric, but he did a great deal to suggest that it might be possible to integrate *kalām* with other approaches to the question of how to be a Muslim, such as Sufism. This project for a spiritual reanimation of *kalām* had ramifications for later Sufi metaphysics, but was not much taken up within the schoolbooks of Ash'arism itself.

THE LATE PERIOD

Later Ash'arism was dominated by creeds and their commentaries. The Ash'arī thinker al-Taftāzānī (d. 1389 or 1390) is particularly worth mentioning for his commentary on Nasafī's famous *'Aqīda* or creed, a broadly Māturīdī work. Al-Ījī's work *The Stations* (*al-Mawāqif*) was the subject of many commentaries, of which perhaps the most widely used was the Ash'arite commentary by al-Sharīf al-Jurjānī (d. 1413), which made extensive use of *falsafa*. Like many other works of the late period, Jurjānī's text is marked by the systematic and detailed use of logic, drawing in particular on a logic manual which was to become standard in the *madrasa* curriculum, *al-Risāla al-Shamsiyya* by Najm al-Dīn al-Kātibī (d. 1276).[12] The late thirteenth-century Ash'arī theologian, al-Ījī's teacher 'Abdallāh al-Bayḍāwī, wrote a handbook entitled *Rising Lights* (*Ṭawāli' al-anwār*), which again attracted several commentaries. Abū 'Alī al-Sanūsī (d. 1490) and Ibrāhīm al-Laqānī (d. 1641) also authored influential creeds. Such creeds and their commentaries, studied intensively in the *madrasa*s until the present day and the subject of innumerable supercommentaries, established a tradition of the production of creeds which laid out the basic principles of Islam in a way which reflects earlier polemics, particularly against Mu'tazilism, and which provided the commentator and the teacher with the opportunity to display Sunnism as the final resolution of the divisions which rent the early community.

The development of broadly Ash'arite theories still continues today, something which commentators sometimes see as a victory for an anti-rationalism which has retarded Islam's development. This, however, is an entirely misleading view. For one thing, even the critics of *kalām* defended their arguments rationally. Even today those who advocate a return to the *salaf*, to the ancestors, argue for this. They argue against alternative views, and defend their approach to the understanding of the Qur'an, in such a way as to make it difficult straightforwardly to identify one side of the debate as "rationalist" and the other as "traditionalist" or "fundamentalist". It might even be argued that it is those who are not normally seen as rationalists who are in fact the most concerned with reason, since they are prepared to be critical of reason and argue (but note the term here, argue) that we should acknowledge its severe limitations. So the "traditionalists" are able to view the use of reason critically, unlike their "rationalist" opponents, something which might be considered an even more rational strategy than that of their adversaries, who evince an uncritical enthusiasm for rationality itself.

A good example of this ability to couple a scepticism about the range of reason metaphysically with its acceptability in other areas of intellectual inquiry can be found in the work of the Ash'arī thinker Ibn Khaldūn (d. 1406). Ibn Khaldūn is best known as a highly innovative social historian and philosopher of history, but he also served as a distinguished judge, and in that capacity wrote extensively on theology. He was critical of the unbridled use of reason, and offered perfectly rational arguments for his critique. Logical techniques, he tells us, are important if we are to secure clarity on the nature of any subject of discussion, but it does not follow that we must have confidence in the capacity of reason to unveil to us the ultimate truths which are accessible to us only through religion. Often called an anti-rationalist position, this view is in fact something quite different. It is a rational position based on concerns about the range of reason when this is used by itself to come to conclusions. To argue that there are limits to reason is not to attack reason but is rather to suggest that it be employed in tandem with something else, perhaps religious knowledge, and most importantly that it be employed critically.

THE MURJI'Ī CONTROVERSY REVISITED: MĀTURĪDISM

To give another example of how misleading the nomenclature often used in theology can be, let us examine briefly the controversy over *irjā'* or "postponement".[13] As Khalid Blankinship has outlined in chapter 2 of the present volume, a central controversy in early Islam had evolved over the nature of belief (*īmān*): was it primarily a matter of belief and acts, or of beliefs alone? Could one be a sinner and yet at the same time remain a sincere Muslim? An important school which was initiated by Abū Ḥanīfa (d. 767) and provided with a solid intellectual foundation by Abū Manṣūr al-Māturīdī (d. 944) argued that even the worst sinner cannot be treated as an unbeliever, and that the decision as to whether he is really a believer should be left to God (compare Qur'an 9:106). Ḥanafī jurists, basing themselves largely on Māturīdī's work, argued that *īmān* does not genuinely increase or decrease, unlike *taqwā* or piety, which does fluctuate. The Ash'arites took the opposite view on *īmān*, arguing also that we are strictly limited in what we can work out by ourselves using reason alone. For the Māturīdīs, by contrast, even without religious instruction or revelation we can know that some things are just wrong. This has interesting implications for the fate of those who do not receive the message of Islam and then die. The Māturīdīs argued that how one ought to live is broadly so obvious that those who do not live appropriately will be sent to hell, despite their lack of access to revelation. The Ash'arites would assign them elsewhere, perhaps to a kind of limbo, since they cannot be blamed for their actions.[14] The Māturīdī strategy was strongly opposed by the Ḥanbalites, who cited hadith statements against the Murji'ī hesitancy to define belief. In particular, the Qur'anic idea that "judgement is God's alone" (6:57; 12:40, 67) does rather suggest that scripture monopolises the answer to all such controversies. Whatever the purport of the scriptures, however, it is worth pointing to a feature of the Murji'a which is interesting. At the end of most accounts of *īmān* which are sympathetic to the Murji'ī perspective comes a political chapter, and this tends to argue for a quietist approach to an evil ruler. The Ḥanbalite position is more revolutionary, often arguing that the believer does not owe allegiance to a sinful ruler if the latter can be classified as *kāfir* (unbeliever); on the contrary, the Muslim may well have a duty of disobedience. It is perhaps not surprising that the Ḥanafī, and so largely Murji'ī, climate of the Ottoman Empire was much better able to incorporate diversity within its borders than other Muslim regimes which emphasised the significance of the ruler being a particular kind of believer. A regime is likely to tolerate more diversity if it leaves the decision as to precisely who is a believer and who is not to the Almighty, refusing to claim the ability to decide on such issues on the basis of the actions of the agent himself. Only God can look into the heart of the individual, and even the Almighty will wait until his death before deciding the issue. How much more incumbent it is on us, the Murji'ites and their successors would say, to postpone the decision also. Yet many Ḥanbalī rigorists, harking back to the Khārijites, had good arguments for deducing character from actions; and we are helped by scripture in making our judgement on that character rational and just. If the only thing of importance is the intention of the agent, then it would not matter, they argue, whether Muslims who pray are actually praying in the right direction or whether they are praying behind a just imam. One could abandon all ritual and good works if the only thing of significance was intention (as some ridiculed the Māturīdī doctrine, it would not matter if one bowed down in front of a shoe, provided that one had the right intention!); and there are many sayings of the Prophet and his Companions which emphasise the importance of correct action in any definition of being a Muslim. What needs to be noted about this fascinating debate is that it is far from obvious which protagonist is the more "rational" and which the more "traditional". Both positions take themselves to be both reasonable and grounded in revelation.

The *īmān* controversy shows how Māturīdism may broadly be considered a natural derivation from the Murji'ī position. Māturīdī had provided a secure intellectual basis for the Ḥanafī school of jurisprudence, which made much space for reason and individual judgement.[15] He played an active role in the theological controversies of his time, and in particular argued with the Mu'tazilites who were then well ensconced in Basra. However, while he often agreed with Ash'arī, he was by no means a slavish follower, and sought to establish something of a middle ground between the Mu'tazila and the Ash'arites. This middle ground turned out to be the source of fertile conceptual work for many of the next centuries of Islamic theology, and it is worth looking at the structure of Māturīdism to understand how it was able to establish such a presence in the intellectual world of the time, and indeed ever since.

The principles of evolved Māturīdite theology are quite simple. First, knowledge can be acquired by using our senses, accepting reports and, most importantly, through the use of reason. This is why the Qur'an itself places such reliance on reason, and constantly calls on its hearers and readers to think rationally about what is set before them. Reason alone is not enough, though, since it needs to be combined with revelation, and this leads to a very productive form of *tafsīr* or exegesis (Māturīdī himself wrote a pioneering work of theological commentary on the Qur'an). Where a passage in the Qur'an is clear, it must be accepted as it stands. Where it seems to run foul of another clear verse, something has to be done: at least one of the verses needs to be reinterpreted. This may mean that we are constrained to admit that we do not fully understand it, but it could also be that there exists an interpretation that would reconcile the two verses, even if this is not the most obvious one. As in the case of the Mu'tazilites, a good deal of reliance is placed on reason, but unlike them this is not allowed complete sway over the process of interpretation. Reason and revelation working in tandem resolve theological difficulties, and it is important to get the balance right between the two.

What is the problem with clinging only to literal and clear meanings? This is very much the demand of those of Ibn Taymiyya's persuasion who see the Book as perfectly easy to understand and in no need of the importation of any specific rational methods of interpretation. But the Māturīdīs point out that reason is something that God has given us, since it is conformable to his nature; and he expects us to use it. Some of the anthropomorphic passages in the Book cannot be taken literally unless we think that God has a body, and this cannot be what we are supposed to believe. So exegesis has to be used to make sense of such passages, unless we will merely say that they have to be taken *bi-lā kayfa*, without knowing how they are to be taken, which does not advance us at all, although sometimes this is something that just has to be accepted. This traditionalist response to difficult passages is, in Māturīdī eyes, just as generally unsatisfactory as the Mu'tazilite principle that ascribing names to God as though this were to describe Him is to damage the idea of the unity of the divine. Where they both go wrong, the Māturīdīs argue, is in not providing an appropriate balance between reason and revelation. Those theologians who want to emphasise the significance of tradition tend to downgrade reason because they suggest that only revelation can help us to know how we should act and what we can know. After all, if reason were sufficient to acquire such information, we would hardly need revelation to guide us through life. However, the idea that reason alone might provide the knowledge we require is vacuous, since we live in a divinely created world and require information about and from our creator in order to make sense of it. We can certainly use reason in that enterprise – God did after all create us with it for a purpose – yet by itself it is insufficient to provide a route through life. Like the Murji'īs, the Māturīdīs think that *īmān* does not increase or decrease, does not depend on action and can survive sin. It is worth pointing out how this strategy, which suggests a clear division between faith and works, provides an effective arena for further debate, since on this rather relaxed criterion for membership of the religious community a good deal of backsliding can be tolerated.

This is the Māturīdī strategy that helped the doctrine to become so dominant in the Sunnī world. It is a strategy of balance and practicality. Although the Māturīdīs are undoubtedly closer to the Ash'arites than to the Mu'tazilites, they differentiate themselves from the extremes of both sides, seeing in their doctrine a faithful but rational response to the Qur'an's description of the desirability of being in the middle (2:143). Māturīdism came to dominate Turkey, and through the Ottoman Empire much of the Islamic world.

STRATEGIES OF REVIVAL

There is a well-known hadith in which the Prophet predicts that during each century God will send someone to the community of Islam in order to revive its religion.[16] "Reviving" religion involves, first, showing its capacity to achieve something which alternative systems cannot, namely, to provide spiritual guidance to the community. There is also the need to demonstrate that the arguments of those hostile to religion fail to persuade. Finally, it is important that the reviver can express himself in a way which resonates with the *umma* (community) as a whole, and not only with a part of it. It is a characteristic of many such revivers that they take seriously a system of thought which is apparently opposed to Islam, and do not dismiss it merely as unbelief or blasphemy.

The epitome of this style is Ghazālī's *Revival of the Sciences of Religion* (*Iḥyā' 'ulūm al-dīn*), an extraordinary work consisting of four parts, each of which comprises ten books. In this encyclopaedic text he deals with every conceivable aspect of Islamic belief and practice. This has been the model for many other works with the same synthetic and totalising purpose, none of which, however, is said to have surpassed it. His work as a whole does not amount to a rejection of the "modernity" of his day, since he showed how aspects of *falsafa* such as Aristotelian logic and ethics might be profitably employed in theology, and argued that the *falāsifa* themselves err in their use of the philosophical principles to which they are committed. As such, they could not help to revive a moribund Muslim world. But neither could the *'ulamā'*, many of whom were trapped in formalistic, polemical exercises, both legal and theological. The solution was to be sought in a moral and spiritual rebirth.

There can be little doubt that the dominance of Ash'arism and Māturīdīsm led to a certain amount of repetition in theology, and to a formalism of the kind that Ghazālī deplored. For one thing, the popular form of literary expression was often the *ḥāshiya*, a kind of supercommentary, which was often itself the subject of further glosses. Often these hermeneutic accretions were lively and innovative; frequently, however, they were not. This stylistic feature was also present in the Shī'ite theological world, where commentary and supercommentary prevailed and defined the curriculum in those colleges and schools that developed a form of theology that fitted in with the Shī'ite view of God and the world.

PART II: LATER SHĪ'Ī THEOLOGY

The development of theology among the Shī'a was a function of the historical and intellectual encounter with Mu'tazilite rational (and philosophical) theology, and later with the *falsafa* traditions. The key feature of early theology had been the defining feature of Shīʿism itself: the imamate, particularly discussions of its necessity and the identification of the holders of legitimate divinely ordained authority (*walāya*).

Two (complementary and often mutually nourishing) strands of theological reasoning were inherited from the formative period: the first was a focus on narratives from the Shīʿite Imams on the nature of theology and in particular on the nature of the Imamate, covering issues such as infallibility, the miraculous knowledge of the Imams, their designation and succession both political and spiritual to the Prophet and their relationship to the scripture; the second tendency was born out of inter-sectarian disputations and revolved around rational defences of the logical necessity of the imamate, the nature of human value, ability (*istiṭāʿa*) and responsibility for actions and the afterlife, the nature of God and the possibility of His changing His mind (*al-badāʾ*). The earliest theologians were companions of the Imams who engaged in debates (mainly in the Islamic heartlands of Iraq) on these issues using a variety of traditional and rational modes: Muʾmin al-Ṭāq, Hishām ibn al-Ḥakam (d. 796), and Muḥammad ibn Abī ʿUmayr and Yūnus ibn ʿAbd al-Raḥmān in the generation after.[17] Their presence in polemics began to shape not only Twelver theology but also the identity of the community with respect to the majority and to rival Shīʿite groups such as the Zaydīs and the Ismāʿīlīs. The Zaydīs rejected the principle of the infallibility of the Imam and argued that any descendant of the Prophet with the requisite knowledge and piety could claim the imamate and ought to establish it by force. (An imam who did not wield political power was not an Imam.) The Zaydīs proceeded to establish states in northern Iran and Yemen from the ninth century. The Ismāʿīlīs understood the Imam to be primarily a spiritual leader and shared many of the theological positions of the Twelvers. Although they did in fact establish a Shīʿī Fāṭimid state in North Africa from 909 and thus were not devoid of political ambitions, the failure of that state in the twelfth century and their internal divisions led to a fragmentation of the Ismāʿīlī imamate.[18] The key feature of Twelver doctrine in the intra-Shīʿī polemic was the belief in the occultation of the twelfth Imam after 874 and his messianic function as a redeemer of the Last Days, expounded in traditionalist fashion by al-Shaykh al-Ṣadūq (d. 991) in his *Completion of the Faith* (*Kamāl al-Dīn*) and revised in a more rational manner by al-Shaykh al-Ṭūsī (d. 1067) in his work on the Occultation (*al-Ghayba*).[19]

Traditionalism and rationalism were not absolute opposing values that expressed, as some have argued, the difference between the parochial tradition of Qum and the rational cosmopolitanism of Baghdad.[20]

Both agreed on the twin exceptionalist pillars of Twelver doctrine: the imamate and divine justice (*'adl*). The codification of the Twelver tradition of narrations within the Four Books was concurrent with the development of theology; in fact, the latter two of these hadith compilations were formed by a significant Twelver Mu'tazilite, al-Shaykh al-Ṭūsī (d. 1067). But it was the adoption of Mu'tazilism, the school *par excellence* of divine justice, that signalled the true development of Twelver theology. Although the Twelver encounter with the Mu'tazila had begun with the courtly family of scholars, the Banū Nawbakht in the tenth century and the theologian Ibn Qiba al-Rāzī, who had been Mu'tazilite before he became Twelver, it was the pivotal role of al-Shaykh al-Mufīd (d. 1022) that reconciled Twelver theology with this school.[21] Al-Mufīd had studied with Abu'l-Jaysh al-Muẓaffar al-Balkhī (d. 977), a student of Abū Sahl al-Nawbakhtī (d. 923) and of Abu'l-Qāsim al-Ka'bī (d. 931), the leader of the Baghdad Mu'tazila. The teaching of this school is evident in al-Mufīd's works such as *First Discourses* (*Awā'il al-maqālāt*). The traditionalists had acquired a reputation for believing in determinism, literalism and anthropomorphism: al-Mufīd's *Correction of the Treatise on Beliefs* (*Taṣḥīḥ al-i'tiqādāt*) of his teacher al-Ṣadūq is a significant attempt to distance Twelver theology from such forms of irrationalism. Al-Mufīd trained a number of students who perpetuated the Mu'tazilite tendency, such as al-Sharīf al-Murtaḍā (d. 1044), al-Shaykh al-Ṭūsī (d. 1067) and al-Karājakī (d. 1057). Al-Murtaḍā's own taste was for the Bahshamiyya (Basran Mu'tazilite) school of his other teacher, 'Abd al-Jabbār (d. 1025).

The adoption of Mu'tazilite ideas was never wholesale or uncritical. Particular Shī'ite doctrines such as the imamate remained distinctive; different also were teachings relating to prophecy such as miracles and intercession, and wider aspects of eschatology touching on the status of sinners, intercession and the afterlife. Al-Mufīd felt strongly about the role of reason in theology but did not allow for the supremacy of unaided reason as a source for discovering truth. He defended the role of the intercession of the Prophet and the Imams as a means for sinners to escape hellfire, in opposition to the Mu'tazilite teaching of the unconditional punishment of the unrepentant sinner. He promoted some distinctively Twelver doctrines rejected by the Mu'tazila such as *raj'a*, the return to life of the pious at the time of the messianic appearance of the twelfth Imam, and *badā'*, the possibility of God abrogating human history in response to human free will, a doctrine that he explained as a form of "textual abrogation" that was similar to the Mu'tazilite notion that God changes human life-spans in accordance with their actions.

Among the Zaydīs, the adoption of Muʻtazilite teachings seems to have begun rather earlier. It is questionable whether the early Zaydī Imam al-Qāsim ibn Ibrāhīm (d. 860) was a Muʻtazilite, but he was open to rationalising theology.[22] His successors aligned themselves closely to the Muʻtazila: al-Ḥasan ibn Zayd (d. 884), the founder of the Zaydī state in northern Iran was associated with the Basran Muʻtazila, and Yaḥyā ibn al-Ḥusayn (d. 911), the founder of the state in Yemen, was influenced by the Muʻtazila of Baghdad. Later, the Zaydī Mānkdīm Shishdev (d. 1034) wrote a famous paraphrase of ʻAbd al-Jabbār's exposition of the five central theological principles of the Muʻtazila. Ibn al-Murtaḍā (d. 1437), a Zaydī imam in the Yemen, wrote extensive Muʻtazilite theological treatises.

Among the Ismāʻīlīs, theology took a Neoplatonic philosophical turn from the tenth century onwards.[23] God was placed outside the cosmos as the One beyond being, and the Imam became the teacher and god revealed to humanity. Ismāʻīlī theology also proposed an esoteric hermeneutics in which the spiritual significance of doctrine, ritual and event as defined by the imam began to take precedence over the exoteric meaning. This became more acute after the Ismāʻīlīs went into schism in 1094 over the succession: the major group were the Nizārīs, located mainly in Iran, who proclaimed the 'Resurrection' in 1164, meaning that ultimate truth had been revealed and the law was abrogated, as believers now lived in a kingdom of heaven presided over by the Imam.[24]

Later on, from the twelfth century, the Muʻtazilite teachings of Abu'l-Ḥusayn al-Baṣrī (d. 1044), himself a dissident student of ʻAbd al-Jabbār, became more significant among the Twelvers, partly because of his openness to philosophy, and theologians such as Sadīd al-Dīn al-Ḥimmasī al-Rāzī (d. after 1204), Naṣīr al-Dīn al-Ṭūsī (d. 1274), Maytham al-Baḥrānī (d. 1300), Ibn al-Muṭahhar al-Ḥillī (d. 1325) and later al-Miqdād al-Suyūrī (d. 1423) were at the forefront of his school.[25] This trend ushered in a sophisticated philosophical theology in which the metaphysics of God as a Necessary Existent who produces a contingent world was incorporated into a theology of divine nature and human agency. In particular, al-Ṭūsī's short *Epitome of Doctrine* (*Tajrīd al-iʻtiqād*) had an enormous impact, and Twelver and other scholars, including Sunnīs, wrote commentaries upon it up to the modern period. Al-Ḥillī's commentary on this text was influential, as was his short "creed", *The Eleventh Chapter* (*al-Bāb al-ḥādī ʻashar*). This creed is divided into the five standard divisions of Twelver theological texts: divine unity and attributes, divine justice, prophecy, the imamate and the afterlife. The central relationship between the concepts of the imamate and divine justice is expressed in terms of the dynamic of the Mu'tazilite concept of *luṭf* or facilitating grace. Divine justice demands that humans can be held responsible for, and requited for, only actions that they could be expected to perform. This expectation results from their ability to discern good from evil through their rational faculty and through the guidance bestowed upon them by God through his sending of prophets and imams. Reason and guidance are thus facilitating graces that determine the realisation of human doctrine and agency and the afterlife.

Although Ṭūsī's school was dominant, there were rivals. A group of scholars in al-Ḥilla associated with the al-'Awdī family were hostile to philosophy, although they accepted the Basran turn in theology.[26] Other thinkers, such as 'Abd al-Razzāq Kāshānī (d. 1336) and Sayyid Ḥaydar Āmulī (d. after 1385), sought to reconcile Twelver theology with the Sufi metaphysics of monorealism espoused by Ibn 'Arabī.[27] Later, a further synthesis between Sufi metaphysics, theology and philosophy was initiated by Ibn Abī Jumhūr al-Aḥsā'ī (d. 1501).[28] Finally, traditionalism did not die out but re-emerged with the Akhbāriyya movement in the seventeenth century and its rejection of rational theology and philosophy and other "alien" forms of learning in favour of a pristine adherence to the narrations of the imams.[29]

Further reading

Sunnism

Abrahamov, Binyamin *Islamic Theology: Traditionalism and Rationalism* (Edinburgh, 1998).

al-Bayḍāwī, *'Abd Allāh, Ṭawāli' al-anwār min maṭāli' al-anẓār*, tr. Edwin E. Calverley and James W. Pollock, as *Nature, Man and God in Medieval Islam: Abd Allah Baydawi's Text* Tawali al-Anwar min Matali' al-Anzar, along with Mahmud Isfahani's commentary *Matali' al-Anzar Sharh Tawali' al-Anwar* (Brill, 2002).

Cerić, Mustafa, *Roots of Synthetic Theology in Islam: A Study of the Theology of Abū Manṣūr al-Māturīdī* (Kuala Lumpur, 1995).

Dabashi, Hamid, *Authority in Islam* (London, 1989).

Frank, Richard M., *Creation and the Cosmic System: Ghazālī and Avicenna* (Heidelberg, 1992).

al-Ghazālī and the Ash'arite School (Durham, NC, 1994).

al-Ghazālī, Muḥammad, *Tahāfut al-falāsifa*, ed. and tr. Michael E. Marmura (Provo, UT, 1997).

Leaman, Oliver, *Averroes and His Philosophy* (London, 1997).

A Brief Introduction to Islamic Philosophy (Oxford, 1999).

Madelung, Wilferd, *Religious Schools and Sects in Medieval Islam* (London, 1985).

Makdisi, George, *Ibn ʿAqīl: Religion and Culture in Classical Islam* (Edinburgh, 1997).
Nagel, Tilman, *History of Islamic Theology from Muhammad to the Present* (Princeton, 2000).
Ormsby, Eric, *Theodicy in Islamic Thought* (Princeton, 1984).
al-Shahrastānī, Muḥammad, *The Summa Philosophiae of al-Shahrastānī, Kitāb nihāyat al-iqdām fi ʿilm al-kalām*, tr. Alfred Guillaume (London, 1930–4).
Watt, W. Montgomery *Islamic Creeds: A Selection* (Edinburgh, 1994).
Wolfson, H., *The Philosophy of the Kalām* (Cambridge, MA, 1976).

Shīʿism

Antes, Peter, *Zur Theologie der Schīʿa: eine Untersuchung des Ǧāmiʿ al-asrār wa-manbaʿ al-anwār von Sayyid Ḥaidar Āmulī* (Freiburg, 1971).
Daftary, Farhad, *The Ismāʿīlīs* (Cambridge, 1990).
Jafri, Husain M., *The Origins and Early Development of Shīʿa Islam* (London, 1979).
McDermott, Martin, *The Theology of al-Shaikh al-Mufid* (Beirut, 1978).

Notes

1. See on this the various entries on theology in Oliver Leaman (ed.), *The Qur'ān: An Encyclopedia* (London, 2006). For information about the major theologians Oliver Leaman (ed.), *Bibliographical Dictionary of Islamic Philosophy* (London, 2006) may be consulted.
2. Massimo Campanini, "Al-Ghazzālī", in Seyyed Hossein Nasr and Oliver Leaman (eds.), *History of Islamic Philosophy* (London: 1996), pp. 258–74.
3. Richard M. Frank, *Al-Ghazālī and the Ashʿarite School* (Durham, NC, 1994).
4. Especially in his *Tahāfut al-tahāfut*, discussed in detail in Oliver Leaman, *Introduction to Classical Islamic Philosophy* (Cambridge, 2002).
5. Oliver Leaman, "Islamic philosophy and the attack on logic", *Topoi* 19 (2000), pp. 17–24.
6. Ludwig Wittgenstein, *On Certainty*, tr. G. Anscombe and G. Wright (New York, 1969).
7. A point made forcefully by Averroes in his short essay designed to put theology decisively in its place, the *Faṣl al-maqāl*, in G. Hourani (tr.), *Averroes on the Harmony of Religion and Philosophy* (London, 1976).
8. Muhammad Iqbal, *The Reconstruction of Religious Thought in Islam* (Lahore, 1930).
9. James Pavlin, "Sunnī *kalām* and theological controversies", in Nasr and Leaman, *History*, 1, pp. 105–18.
10. On the significance of Islamic texts on definition see Kik: Kennedy-Day, *Books of Definition: The Limits of Words* (London, 2003).
11. Roger Arnaldez, *Grammaire et théologie chez Ibn Hazm de Cordoue: essai sur la structure et les conditions de la pensée musulmane* (Paris, 1956).

12. Tony Street, "Logic", in Peter Adamson and Richard C. Taylor (eds.), *The Cambridge Companion to Arabic Philosophy* (Cambridge, 2005), pp. 247–65.
13. I owe much of my interest in the Murji'a to conversations with Ibrahim Hakki Inal, to whom I am grateful.
14. Tim Winter, "The Last Trump Card: Islam and the Supersession of Other Faiths", *Studies in Interreligious Dialogue* 9 (1999), pp. 147–50.
15. See in particular his *Kitāb al-Tawḥīd* (Book of Unity), ed. Bekir Topaloğlu and Muhammad Aruçi (Ankara, 2003).
16. Abū Dāūd, Malāḥim, 1; al-Ḥākim, *al-Mustadrak 'alā al-Ṣaḥīḥayn* (Hyderabad, 1334–42 AH), IV, p. 522.
17. Josef van Ess, *Theologie und Gesellschaft im 2. und 3. Jahrhundert Hidschra: eine Geschichte des religiösen Denkens im frühen Islam* (Berlin, 1991), I, pp. 278–316, 336–92; Wilferd Madelung, 'Imamism and Mu'tazilite theology', in *Le Shī'isme imamite*, ed. T. Fahd (Paris, 1979), pp. 13–29.
18. Farhad Daftary, *The Ismā'īlīs* (Cambridge, 1990).
19. See Abdulaziz Sachedina, *Islamic Messianism: The Idea of the Mahdi in Twelver Shi'ism* (Albany, 1981).
20. On Qum versus Baghdad, see Andrew J. Newman, *The Formative Period of Twelver Shī'ism: Ḥadīth as Discourse between Qum and Baghdad* (London, 2000).
21. On al-Mufīd, see Martin McDermott, *The Theology of al-Shaikh al-Mufid* (Beirut, 1978); Sayyid Waheed Akhtar, *Early Ṣhī'ite Imāmiyyah Thinkers* (New Delhi, 1988); Tamima Bayhom-Daon, *Shaykh Mufīd* (Oxford, 2005).
22. The best introduction to him and to Zaydī theology remains Wilferd Madelung, *Der Imam al-Qāsim ibn Ibrāhīm und die Glaubenslehre der Zaiditen* (Berlin, 1965).
23. Paul Walker, *Early Philosophical Shiism* (Cambridge, 1994).
24. Christian Jambet, *La grande résurrection d'Alamut* (Paris, 1990).
25. Sabine Schmidtke, *The Theology of al-'Allāma al-Ḥillī* (Berlin, 1991).
26. Sabine Schmidtke, "Introduction" to *Khulāṣat al-naẓar*, eds. Sabine Schmidtke and Hasan Anṣārī (Tehran, 2006), pp. xiii–xiv.
27. Peter Antes, *Zur Theologie der Schī'a: eine Untersuchung des Ǧāmi' al-asrār wa-manba' al-anwār von Sayyid Ḥaidar Āmulī* (Freiburg, 1971).
28. Sabine Schmidtke, *Theologie, Philosophie und Mystik im zwölferschiitischen Islam des 9./15. Jahrhunderts: Die Gedankenwelt des Ibn Abī Ǧumhūr al-Aḥsā'ī* (Leiden, 2000).
29. Devin Stewart, 'The genesis of the Akhbārī revival', in Michel Mazzaoui (ed.), *Safavid Iran and Her Neighbors* (Salt Lake City, 2003), pp. 169–94.

5 The social construction of orthodoxy

AHMED EL SHAMSY

Orthodoxy as a social phenomenon is not a "thing" but rather a process. For theological doctrines to become established as orthodox, they must find a place in the constantly changing net of social relations and institutions that constitute society. This is a two-way process: ideas can reconfigure these relations and institutions, but the social context also actively receives ideas and promotes, channels and/or suppresses them. Thus the history of orthodoxy cannot be simply a history of ideas, but a history of how, in particular situations, claims to truth came to be enshrined in social practices, such as rituals, and in institutions, such as the "community of scholars".

This chapter seeks to provide an overview of the social and institutional environment in which discourses of orthodoxy in Islamic theology were formed, propagated and resisted between the ninth and nineteenth centuries CE. In each of the disciplines which touched upon the realm of theology, scholars (*'ulamā'*) were socialised into a specific culture of learning, with established modes of inquiry and standards of authenticity. Within these parameters, they developed and defended notions of orthodoxy and sought to marginalise those they defined as heretics, sometimes by drawing on executive power or the muscle of the mob. The government, in turn, employed its coercive potential to influence the definition of theological orthodoxy in order to defuse perceived threats to social order, often by means of its executive prerogatives (especially the appointment of judges and other authorities), and occasionally through the outright persecution of those whose unorthodoxy was deemed too dangerous. Finally, ordinary believers were not passive recipients of ideals of orthodoxy proffered by scholars and rulers: they were actively engaged in evaluating, propagating and forging beliefs and rituals that contributed substantially to the construction of orthodoxy in any given time or place.

THE TRANSMISSION OF KNOWLEDGE

From the emergence in the eighth century of the traditional "Islamic sciences", which include grammar (*naḥw*), exegesis (*tafsīr*), dialectic theology (*kalām*), study of hadith, and jurisprudence (*fiqh*), the establishment and maintenance of a connection to the event of revelation became the central preoccupation of those who dedicated themselves to learning. If revelation represented a special infusion of knowledge into the world, this knowledge had to form the basis of human scholarly endeavours, and therefore had to be transmitted accurately from generation to generation.

The fundamental method of transmission at the heart of the emerging Islamic disciplines was the face-to-face encounter of teacher and student. Students took private lessons with their teachers or – more frequently – participated in their mentors' teaching circles, in which the master would deliver a lecture, seated, to a cluster of students, the most advanced of whom sat closest to him. Lectures were typically, though not always, based on a text or texts, which the teacher read out in sections, explaining and commenting on each segment. Students took notes, or had notes taken for them by professional scribes. Depending on the nature of the subject and the disposition of the teacher, students could participate by asking questions, voicing their disagreements and engaging the teacher in debate. At the conclusion of each class, students would revisit their notes, ideally committing them to memory, and discuss their contents with fellow students. Many of the classical works of Islamic scholarship that can still be accessed today originate in such lecture notes.

The medieval Islamic world was a manuscript culture: the texts studied had to be copied by hand, often by the students themselves. Given the many pitfalls inherent in copying a handwritten text, a variety of techniques aimed at minimising and detecting mistakes in manuscripts was developed in order to safeguard the integrity of the transmitted text. This was particularly important for the two sacred texts, the Qur'an and the hadith. The content of the former was preserved both orally and in written form in countless identical copies, and it was thus considered secure. Individual prophetic traditions, on the other hand, numbered in the hundreds of thousands, and were in most cases known by only a few people. Their accurate transmission was thus a matter of paramount importance. It was, accordingly, the traditionists (*muḥaddithūn*) who devised a protocol for the authoritative transmission of texts from teacher to student that rested on the direct aural link between transmitters.

There were two ways in which an individual could claim truly to know a text. Either he had heard the text read aloud by its author or by someone who had received it through authoritative transmission (a process known as *samāʿ*), or he had himself read the copied text aloud to such a person, who could correct any mistakes (a method termed *qirāʾa*). At the end of a manuscript produced by the student through one of these forms of transmission, a certificate was added. This specified whether the text was the product of *samāʿ* or *qirāʾa* and gave the names of the teacher and the student as well as the date of completion. Through such a certificate, the student was incorporated into a chain of transmission (*isnād*) that linked the student to the original author of the text, thus preserving an authoritative connection to the past. This was a crucial feature in the self-understanding of medieval Muslim scholars, who proudly proclaimed that the maintenance of chains of transmission was a unique characteristic of the Muslim community. At the same time, these certificates functioned as important tokens of authority and permission for the student to transmit the work further. When the newly appointed chief judge of Egypt, Muḥammad al-ʿAbādānī, began to offer lessons in hadith in 891, local experts noticed that he was teaching from books that he had simply bought but never studied with a teacher who was part of an *isnād*. As a result, the Egyptian scholarly community branded al-ʿAbādānī an imposter and boycotted his lessons.

Transmission via *samāʿ* and *qirāʾa* remained the primary mechanism for ensuring the authenticity of seminal or sacred texts well into the Mamlūk period (1250–1517). However, for the bulk of scholarship these methods soon gave way to a more thoroughly literate modus of textual transmission. Already in the beginning of the ninth century, the famous jurist al-Shāfiʿī granted an *ijāza* – a general permission to teach one of his books – to a particularly gifted scholar even though the latter had never studied the work in question with him. In subsequent centuries, the practice of granting such permissions became widespread. A student could receive an *ijāza* in a number of ways. Often, it was granted once a teacher was familiar enough with a student to have sufficient confidence in the latter's general academic potential. However, it was also not uncommon for teachers to award *ijāza*s in response to well-phrased letters of request, or to bestow *ijāza*s on the children of friends, colleagues and notables, even if the "student" was still an infant or indeed unborn.

Western scholarship has generally interpreted the spread and seemingly unconstrained use of the *ijāza* as a sign of the degeneration and growing decadence of Islamic scholarship from the tenth or eleventh century onwards.[1] However, while there is no doubt that the significance of the *ijāza* as a genuine indicator of competence declined, this does not necessarily imply a corruption of the culture of scholarship itself. First, with the explosive growth of the Islamic sciences, both the number and the length of the available works increased to the point where it was no longer possible for an individual scholar to study all the works he desired to master by reading them aloud to a teacher or having them read to him. Second, as the disciplines matured and grew more sophisticated, they acquired common terminologies and accepted paradigms. A student could familiarise himself with the technical vocabulary particular to his subject by studying a short basic text (*matn*) with a teacher, and then go on to read more extensive works on his own. The decline of *samā'* and *qirā'a* in the Islamic sciences may thus be an indication not of decadence but of the development of a more mature, literate, scholarly culture.

A side-effect of the emergence of the *ijāza* system was the decline – though not disappearance – of an important educational institution of the first centuries of Islamic scholarship, the "journey in search of knowledge" (*al-riḥla fī ṭalab al-'ilm*, or simply *riḥla*). This practice had developed among traditionists who, having gathered the prophetic traditions circulating in their own locales, set out to collect and bring back the traditions of the other major centres of learning. The *riḥla* was more than a business trip; it often had a penitential aspect. Thus, Abū Ḥātim al-Rāzī, who lived in the ninth century, chose to undertake his four *riḥla*s entirely on foot, travelling from his native Rayy near present-day Tehran westwards as far as Egypt. With the growing acceptance of the practice of granting by correspondence the licence to transmit works (known as *ijāzat al-riwāya*), the motivation for undertaking a *riḥla* diminished. In addition, by the end of the ninth century most of the localised prophetic traditions had been collected, evaluated and disseminated. In its heyday, however, the *riḥla* played an important role in the creation of a cosmopolitan class of traditionists who were united by a common ethos that embodied shared notions of theology, law and ethics.

Another institution that contributed to the training of young scholars was the apprentice-like relation of *ṣuḥba* ("companionship") into which a student who sought to learn a particular subject in depth entered with a senior scholar. In such a relationship, the apprentice (*ṣāḥib* or *ghulām*) was socialised into the culture and proper etiquette of the field by his mentor, whose role was not limited to the academic guidance of his pupil. In the classical Islamic sciences, knowledge was not defined simply as the possession of an ability to process information, but rather rested on a holistic model of personal transformation that was to accompany and give meaning to the acquisition of information. Medieval theoretical manuals of education thus stress that the teacher needs to serve as a role model and a guide for the student's personal growth. On a more mundane level, scholars used their apprentices as teaching assistants who handled the supervision of ordinary students, explained to them the master's lectures, and were available to answer questions. Apprentices also typically took on the role of personal servants to the master. Famous examples of this relationship in the ninth century are the jurist al-Shāfiʿī and his close student al-Rabīʿ (who was instrumental in spreading al-Shāfiʿī's teachings after the latter's death), and the prominent Muʿtazilite theologian al-Naẓẓām and al-Jāḥiẓ, the apprentice who was to become one of the most influential figures of classical Arabic *belles-lettres*.

PLACES OF LEARNING

In the pre-Ottoman Islamic world, scholarship was not rooted in any single specific venue. Nevertheless, the mosque has always been, and remains to this day, an important place of teaching. In the first Islamic cities, particularly the garrison towns built by the early Arab-Muslim conquerors in the seventh century, the mosque represented the public space *par excellence*. It was in the mosque that scholars sat between the five daily prayers, lecturing to their students as well as to interested passers-by. In the early centuries of Islam (and in some locations to the present day) each city had a single central mosque where the communal Friday prayer was held, which was at least in theory attended by every free and healthy resident Muslim man. These central mosques were places infused with the authority of the government. Only the representative of the government, or someone appointed by it, could give the Friday sermon, and the mentioning of the caliph or sultan in the sermon was one of the most important insignia of government authority and legitimacy. Such mosques were the preferred venues for teaching, as they permitted teachers to attract the attention of ordinary worshippers. There are countless anecdotes of distinguished scholars who had been drawn into their fields by passing a mosque teaching-circle by chance and pausing to listen in.

The importance of the congregational mosque as a teaching venue declined in the following centuries. The growing population of Baghdad and other urban centres simply could no longer fit into a single building, so the various urban quarters began to acquire their own Friday mosques. As a result, the unified public space represented by the single Friday mosque was fragmented. In eleventh-century Baghdad, the mutually hostile Shīʿite and Ḥanbalite quarters each had their own mosques, with their restricted "public" spaces that excluded the other. Such particularist venues allowed minorities, including the various Shīʿite groups, to develop their own legal and theological doctrines.

The privacy of the home was no less important as an environment of learning and scholarship. Intensive and advanced instruction was often carried out in the homes of scholars or wealthy patrons, as were formal scholarly debates. The seclusion of the home offered a sheltered space for the airing of controversial arguments beyond the reach of governmental interference: the state had limited ability and, in cases of non-political "heresy", little incentive to police and enforce orthodoxy in the private realm. The home also typically represented the first or even the only place of education for children, with family members serving as the first teachers. The acquisition of certain basic facts was considered a religious obligation for every Muslim, whether male or female. At the minimum, children were taught the basic tenets of belief and the correct performance of duties such as purification, prayer, almsgiving and fasting, but beyond this the content of study was not determined.

For girls, the home was particularly important as a place of learning. Given that the process of transmitting knowledge was based on an intimate relationship between student and teacher, the socially prescribed distance between the sexes severely curtailed women's opportunities to become apprentices to famous scholars. In effect, such apprenticeships were possible only in the rare instances when the senior scholar was female or the student's close relative. This is not to deny that women attended the public lectures of jurists, traditionists, theologians, Sufis and other scholars. However, women were rarely among the closest or most advanced students of the teacher. In general, although there are countless examples of highly educated women in the medieval Islamic world, they are conspicuously absent in the production of scholarly literature and do not feature in the top echelons of any field of study.

The only real exception to this trend is represented by the study of prophetic traditions. Most notably in the Mamlūk period, women played a significant role in this field and it is not uncommon to find in the biographies of the top male scholars of the time that a quarter or even a third of their teachers in hadith were women.[2] A good example of a female traditionist is Umm Hāniʾ Maryam al-Hūrīnīya (1376–1454), an extraordinary woman whose education had been supported from childhood by her grandfather, an influential judge. She was well travelled (she performed the pilgrimage to Mecca from Egypt thirteen times), wealthy, and one of the most important transmitters of hadith of her time. Her many students, both male and female, show deep reverence when mentioning her name in their writings, praising her learning and piety. Nevertheless, she seems never to have authored a book herself, and her training in other fields appears to have been basic. The only formal training beyond traditions that she is known to have received consisted of the study of a short and basic text on Shāfiʿī jurisprudence. This suggests that while she was a learned individual and a much-loved teacher, as a woman she lacked proper socialisation and entrance into the predominantly male scholarly discourse. This discourse was multidisciplinary and expressed itself most significantly in the publishing of literary works that either advanced the field or served as textbooks that synthesised earlier scholarship.

Between the public mosque and the private home, the tenth and eleventh centuries saw the appearance of semi-public venues for scholarship. The economic basis of these institutions was formed by pious foundations (*awqāf*, sing. *waqf*) established by private individuals who set aside a source of revenue, such as a market, a mill or a parcel of agricultural land, and dedicated the funds to the establishment and upkeep of a recognised pious cause, such as the support of religious learning.[3] The founding deed drawn up by the benefactor specified the nature of the activities that would be supported by the foundation. We know that at least by the tenth century, *awqāf* provided wages for teachers and financial aid for students, and from the eleventh century onwards they enabled the emergence of specific institutions of learning, most prominently the *madrasa* and the Sufi lodge (*zāwiya*, *tekke*, *khānqāh*, *ribāṭ*).[4]

A typical *madrasa* came to consist of a common prayer area similar to that of a mosque, with dedicated classrooms in which teaching took place, and lodgings for teachers and students, all within a single building or complex. Some *madrasa*s were built adjacent to the shrines of famous scholars, such as those of the Shīʿite imam al-Riḍā in Mashhad and of al-Shāfiʿī in Cairo. The richest *madrasa*s, often founded by sultans and other prominent figures, incorporated charitable institutions such as hospitals and soup kitchens that catered for the general public. Sufi lodges became especially widespread with the emergence of organised Sufi orders in the twelfth and thirteenth centuries. They were usually headed by a master who instructed a group of devoted students in the theory and practice of the "path to God". There were also regular occasions on which the public was able to participate in the ceremonies by listening to spiritual poetry, celebrating the birthday of the Prophet or a saintly individual, or simply by enjoying the blessed presence of the master. Certain particularly influential orders even counted sultans among their members. In addition, Sufi lodges functioned as places where unmarried or widowed women found shelter, where the wealthy distributed food in times of famine, and where people sought refuge from the law or from persecution.

Even within these new institutions, however, education, learning and research remained fundamentally informal in nature up to the Ottoman period. Institutions of learning never developed a corporate character: students did not graduate with "degrees" from particular *madrasa*s, but rather received a number of certificates and teaching licences from individual, named teachers. *Madrasa*s and Sufi lodges functioned as meeting-points for scholars and students and were a source of income for both, but they never monopolised higher education. Their contingent nature is evident in the format of the pre-modern version of the academic *curriculum vitae,* namely the relevant entry in a biographical dictionary. In such entries, we learn the names of the scholar's teachers, and the titles of the books taught; but whether this instruction took place in a mosque, a private home or a *madrasa* does not seem to have been thought relevant and is rarely mentioned. While institutions such as *madrasa*s contributed to the professionalisation of the scholarly community by providing funding that liberated scholars from the need to practise other occupations, they did not initially change the personal nature of Islamic education.

A significant shift in the nature of the *madrasa* took place with the maturation of the imperial Ottoman educational system. Sultan Meḥmed II (d. 1481) established a hierarchy of *madrasa*s within the empire and outlined a fixed career path that permitted students and teachers to move gradually up the ladder according to merit and/or personal connections: the higher the position of the *madrasa* in the hierarchy, the higher the wages paid to its teaching staff. The *madrasa* hierarchy corresponded to a hierarchy in the judicial system, determining the level of position within the judiciary to which a *madrasa* teacher could transfer. The curriculum, hitherto determined by the interests and expertise of individual students and teachers, was standardised, with digests written by fourteenth- and fifteenth-century authors such as al-Ījī, al-Taftazānī, and al-Sharīf al-Jurjānī underpinning the theological syllabus. The driver of this unprecedented formalisation was the Ottoman Empire's continuous need for uniformly trained and loyal administrators for its immensely complex and highly centralised bureaucracy. However, although the formal training of the *'ulamā'* was oriented towards a likely career as civil servants, a minority of scholars and students continued to follow the traditional paradigm based on the personal teacher–student bond.

THE *'ULAMĀ'* AND DISCOURSES OF ORTHODOXY

Within the informal and decentralised institutional framework of the pre-Ottoman period, several divergent discourses of theological orthodoxy could emerge and flourish, both competing and overlapping with one another. Two of these, the discourses of the traditionists (*muḥaddithūn*) and the dialectic theologians (*mutakallimūn*), stood at the heart of the debate that eventually yielded an extent of common ground between Sunnī theologians of all persuasions. This shared understanding formed the theological core of what is commonly termed the "Sunnī consensus".

The discipline of the traditionists rested on a shared methodology, an accepted body of material, and a minimum set of doctrines that together rendered the discourse remarkably stable and cohesive. Extensively travelled and cosmopolitan, the traditionists formed a transnational network of like-minded scholars whose focus was on gathering and then ascertaining the authenticity and accuracy of reported prophetic traditions. The emerging corpus of agreed-upon hadith and the conclusions drawn from these regarding correct belief and action formed the theological core of the traditionists' discourse. This core was articulated in the form of succinct credos (*'aqā'id*, sing. *'aqīda*), which were designed for easy memorisation by students and served as important pedagogical tools. The universally accepted methodology that was developed for the evaluation of prophetic traditions and their transmitters (*'ilm al-rijāl*, literally "the science of men"), and its application to a finite body of material, provided a centripetal force that ensured the cohesion and integrity of the discipline.

The discourse of the early dialectic theologians, and particularly those who adhered to Mu'tazilism, was in many ways diametrically opposed to that of the traditionists. The theologians focused not on a substantive set of materials but rather on a formal methodology of reasoning and debate. As a consequence, a student of *kalām* who attached himself to a teacher could not simply adopt and internalise authoritative statements regarding belief from his teacher in the way that students of traditions, who would memorise their teachers' credos, could. Instead, the aspiring theologian would be introduced to and trained in the theoretical paradigm developed by his master and the rational arguments that underpinned that paradigm. If he was intellectually capable, he could disagree with his master and eventually develop his own theory.

This rationalist methodology was appealing to scholars in other fields, such as grammar and law, who incorporated elements of the approach and techniques of the *mutakallimūn* into their works. However, within *kalām* it created a centrifugal effect, which led to the emergence of countless schools and sub-groups of theologians. In contrast to the established schools of legal thought, the early theological schools did not possess an ethos of mutual toleration comparable to the jurists' principle that the considered judgement of a competent scholar was always valid,[5] nor could they call upon a shared corpus of material like the traditionists. The uncompromising rationalist stance of the theologians further augmented the divisiveness of their approach. The assumption that the acquisition of rational proof for the existence of God and the truthfulness of the Prophet were prerequisites of genuine adherence to the Qur'an led many early *mutakallimūn* to dismiss any faith not thus grounded as deficient, if not invalid. The resulting sectarianism and intellectual radicalism among dialectical theologians, exemplified by the three members of the prominent Mu'tazilite family of al-Jubbā'ī, who denounced one another as heretics, gradually alienated them from scholars of other backgrounds. The legal scholar al-Shāfi'ī advised his student al-Muzanī to engage in jurisprudence and to avoid theology on the grounds that if he, al-Shāfi'ī, were to give the wrong answer to his student's question, he would rather be told "You are wrong!" than "You have uttered disbelief!"[6]

The stark distinction between the approaches of the traditionists and the *kalām* folk disappeared with the emergence of the Ash'arī and Māturīdī schools of theology in the tenth century and the acceptance of these two schools into the mainstream scholarly community. An important reason for the success of this integration was the deliberate inclusiveness of Ash'arī and Māturīdī theologians, who explicitly disavowed the denunciation of fellow Muslims. A particularly clear statement of this policy can be seen in the book *The Decisive Criterion for Distinguishing Belief from Unbelief* (*Fayṣal al-tafriqa bayna al-islām wa'l-zandaqa*) of al-Ghazālī: the author declares not only Muslims but also most non-Muslims to be assured of eventual salvation.[7] Although the Ash'arīs and Māturīdīs continued to maintain that rational investigation was necessary for complete belief, they adopted the traditionist practice of authoring and teaching basic credos for memorisation. They argued that such texts served to implant the correct tenets of belief in the mind of the believer who would come to understand them more fully through reason at later stages in his intellectual development.

By the end of the tenth century, the broad outlines of the developed Sunnī orthodoxy had taken shape. This orthodoxy was structured around several established schools of law, which defined right action, and the three main "schools" of theology (Ash'arīs, Māturīdīs and traditionists) that defined right belief. Over the next few centuries, the *'ulamā'* worked out a system of mutual tolerance that was based on universal agreement regarding the sacred sources, a pragmatic acceptance of and respect for differences of opinion, and an ideal of intellectual humility that was expressed by al-Ghazālī as follows:

> I advise you, my brother, to have a good opinion of all people, especially the scholars. And it is part of having a good opinion of someone to look for the most positive possible interpretation of his words, and if you cannot find [one], then blame your own inability to find it [rather than him].[8]

The scholarly culture of Twelver Shī'ites developed roughly a century later. The primary reason for this lay in the role played by the infallible Imams as supreme guides for the community until 940: in the presence of a living, unerring religious authority, the cultivation of religious scholarship was not perceived as a pressing need. Only after the withdrawal into occultation of the twelfth and final Imam and the consequent disappearance of the Shī'ī community's focal point did Twelver scholars set out to formulate the basis and content of Shī'ī orthodoxy. The development of Twelver scholarship was facilitated by a unique source of funding: the *khums*, a fifth of all profits from trade, agriculture and crafts, which lay Twelvers had traditionally given to the Imam and which in the Imam's absence was argued to be due to his representatives, the *'ulamā'*. By deriving their primary means of support directly from the population, Twelver scholars were able to retain a higher degree of independence than their Sunnī colleagues, who were often dependent on *waqf* funding, direct patronage or appointments in the state-controlled judicial system.

Like early Sunnism, which was characterised by a tension between the discourses of the traditionists and the theologians, Shī'ism was also divided between two conflicting understandings of the nature of religious knowledge. The Akhbārīs held that the basis of religious life – the traditions of the Prophet and the twelve Imams – could be accessed and grasped directly by ordinary believers, rendering the development of a specialised and authoritative scholarly class obsolete. Uṣūlīs, on the other hand, viewed theology and law as highly complicated disciplines requiring the rational investigation and evaluation of sources. Such erudition, they believed, could be reached only by a minority, leaving the general populace with no option but to follow the lead of the scholars who held a monopoly over religious authority in the absence of the Imam. Although both streams of thought coexisted in Twelver Shīʿism from early on, the great Twelver scholars in Baghdad under the Buyids, such as Abū Jaʿfar al-Ṭūsī, and later key scholars who originated from the Jabal ʿĀmil area in Lebanon, were all Uṣūlīs. Although Akhbārism experienced a renaissance in the Twelver heartlands of Iran and southern Iraq in the seventeenth and eighteenth centuries, its brief dominance ended with the reassertion and establishment of Uṣūlī doctrine by a number of prominent scholars in the late eighteenth century, leading to the virtual extinction of Akhbārism. The Uṣūlī model, based on a rigidly hierarchical scholarly class headed by the "Object of Emulation" (*marjiʿ al-taqlīd*), forms the core of Twelver religious orthodoxy to the present day.[9]

The question that I will now turn to is how the orthodox positions were enforced by the community of scholars, both Sunnī and Shīʿī. The primary mechanism of enforcement available to scholars was exclusion. On the simplest level, basic human courtesies were denied to those who were deemed to have moved outside the boundaries of orthodoxy: smiling at them, initiating the Islamic greeting and participating in their funerary prayers. Going a step further, scholars sought to dissuade the public from accepting certain heretics as qualified to lead communal prayers (a qualification possessed in principle by every Muslim). According to the twelfth-century Sunnī scholar Ibn Qudāma, this prohibition applied to those heretics who practised and professed their beliefs openly. The most severe measure of exclusion available to scholars within the purely academic realm was exclusion from the community of *ʿulamāʾ* itself. The traditionist method of categorising hadith by assessing the reliability of the individual transmitters featured in the chains of transmission provided a mechanism for this, as those whose views were considered too unconventional were discredited as transmitters. Similarly, given that the majority of Muslims considered the consensus of the community to have binding force, the views of heterodox individuals could be excluded from the consensus, meaning that their objections to the prevailing position could be ignored and the consensus declared valid. In addition, unorthodox scholars could be posthumously returned to the fold through the attribution of a deathbed recantation. Thus, for example, the great eleventh- and twelfth-century theologians al-Juwaynī and Fakhr al-Dīn al-Rāzī were alleged to have repented of their engagement in dialectic theology and to have affirmed the non-speculative approach of the traditionists. Conversely, later Shāfiʻī scholars such as Ibn ʻAsākir attempted to explain away the critical stance taken by al-Shāfiʻī and many of his successors towards *kalām*. These examples demonstrate that the struggle for the definition of orthodoxy was not only a struggle that took place in each moment, but also involved a re-evaluation and sometimes a rewriting of the past.

In order to carry out more drastic forms of exclusion, the *ʻulamāʼ* required the support of the government. This was a delicate arena: early on, Muslim scholars had already developed a disdain for the corrupting effect of worldly power, and the emerging scholarly ethos prescribed the maintenance of a circumspect distance from government, the source of this corruption. The reluctance to accept prestigious state-appointed judgeships became a frequent theme in the biographies of pious scholars, and suspicion of the government and of its motives usually prevented scholars from appealing to the authorities to punish or persecute heretics. Nevertheless, scholars did occasionally join forces to demand that a particularly threatening figure be chastised; this was the case, for example, in 922, with the execution of the famous Sufi al-Ḥallāj. Those scholars who did serve as judges also held considerable power to enforce orthodoxy. They had the authority to appoint court witnesses, a status that was considered an emblem of moral and religious uprightness, and whose denial consequently implied a loss of social standing. Most dramatically, if the judge determined someone to have crossed the ultimate line from heresy to all-out disbelief, he could demand a recantation or sentence the offender to death.

In addition to judgeships, the informal role of advisor to powerful government officials could provide individual scholars with significant powers of enforcement. An extreme example of such a scholar is Ibn al-Jawzī, who lived in twelfth-century Baghdad and enjoyed the patronage of some of the most influential figures of his time, including the caliph al-Mustaḍīʼ and two viziers. Ibn al-Jawzī was a gifted speaker whose core teachings consisted of a strict version of Ḥanbalism, a traditionist school that had not yet reached a *modus vivendi* with Ashʻarism or Māturīdism. He first laid out his ideas in talks that he gave at the homes of his patrons, then he lectured in the caliphal palace mosque, in *madrasa*s, and finally in public places in the presence of the caliph. Through this gradual movement from the private to the public sphere,

Ibn al-Jawzī's teachings reached an ever wider audience, and the caliph eventually granted him legal powers to pursue heretics. Initially, Ibn al-Jawzī's campaign was directed against Shīʿīs, but soon also non-Ḥanbalite Sunnī scholars began to feel marginalised. Eventually the persecution touched also the Ḥanbalī community, when heretical philosophical works were discovered in a *madrasa* led by a prominent Ḥanbalī scholar: the latter was relieved of his directorship and the *madrasa* was turned over to the direct control of Ibn al-Jawzī. However, while Ibn al-Jawzī's career is not unique, his inquisitorial powers represent an exception that was enabled not by the strength and dominance of the views he represented, but by the force of his personal charisma.

THEOLOGY IN SOCIETY

There are few direct sources which shed light on the reception of theology by ordinary believers in the pre-modern period. Most of what can be discovered on this subject must be gleaned from the writings of scholars; these, however, had little interest in popular religion and generally mention the beliefs of the common people only in the context of bemoaning ignorance and superstition among the masses. Consequently, not much is known about how ordinary Muslims received, understood and contributed to theological orthodoxy, and this section is thus inevitably little more than a sketch.

What we do know is that the discourse of the hadith folk enjoyed immense legitimacy and popularity among ordinary people from its very beginning. The traditionists were perceived as safeguards of the information through which the model embodied by the life of the Prophet (*sunna*) could be accessed. Recitations of prophetic traditions, covering a wide variety of subjects including theological issues, were often attended by thousands if not tens of thousands of listeners. In contrast, the public generally shunned the debates of the early *mutakallimūn*. The latter's elitist discourse and their acerbic public exchanges which easily turned to polemics and sophistry alienated ordinary believers, who, it seems, often considered such bold speculation regarding the nature of God to border on the impious and thus viewed the theories of the theologians with suspicion.[10]

With the gradual development of the Sunnī consensus, the public confrontations of the *kalām* experts died down, and basic Ashʿarī and Māturīdī doctrines were eventually absorbed into the evolving Sunnism of the ordinary Muslims. There was, however, a period of transition as the scholars negotiated the contours of a common ground, and the differing doctrinal orientations of social groupings such as neighbourhoods could turn into civic conflict. In a number of instances, the power of communal religious identity was harnessed by members of the *'ulamā'* to draw support from the masses for their campaigns against perceived heresy or immorality in society. An illustration is provided by the events following the arrival of Abū Naṣr al-Qushayrī, an avid Ash'arite, in Baghdad in 1067. Qushayrī used his public lectures to extol Ash'arite teachings and to castigate the dominant Ḥanbalī theology, which was highly critical of Ash'arism, as anthropomorphic. In response, a large number of residents from the Ḥanbalite quarters of Baghdad – a significant force in Baghdādī politics – took to the streets under the leadership of the Ḥanbalī scholar al-Sharīf Abū Ja'far. They were met by a mob of adherents of the Shāfi'ī school of law, who had come to the defence of their fellow Shāfi'ī Qushayrī. In the ensuing street battle, several people were killed, and order was restored only through the intervention of vizier Niẓām al-Mulk, who briefly imprisoned Abū Ja'far and persuaded Qushayrī to return to his native Nīshāpūr. Such clashes between rival schools were also not uncommon in other urban centres. There is a heated but as yet inconclusive debate among historians regarding whether these sprang primarily from the public's will to defend its notion of orthodoxy, or whether religious claims were in fact deployed to mask social and ethnic divisions that were the true root causes of these conflicts.[11]

Outside the sphere of scholarly discourse, lay Muslims developed their own religious practices and convictions, giving rise to localised forms of popular religion that at times were at odds with the sober orthodoxies of the *'ulamā'*. A prominent example is the longstanding Cairene tradition of visiting the graves of saintly individuals buried in al-Qarāfa, the "City of the Dead", located next to the old city. Such visits were fuelled by the belief that the *baraka*, special grace bestowed by God on certain individuals during their lifetimes, lingered at the sites of their interment. Prayers performed at these sites (for example for recovery from an illness or for success in conceiving a child) were thus believed to be particularly potent. Over time, grave visits developed into an established form of pilgrimage, with prescribed rituals to be performed at set days of the week.

The majority of the *'ulamā'* reacted to the popularity of grave visitation by seeking to impose "orthodox" limits on the rituals through their sermons and through the composition of written manuals for grave visits. A vocal minority of scholars insisted that the visitation of graves was a reprehensible religious innovation and should be shunned altogether. However, the fact that grave visits had become such an integral part of popular religion and were based on such entrenched beliefs meant that the practice continues to the present day.[12]

Ordinary believers also played a role in the social definition of the boundaries of orthodoxy through their perception and treatment of marginal elements of society, such as certain controversial Sufi groups who were frequently viewed with suspicion or even condemned by the *'ulamā'* and, in some cases, also by other Sufis. Being oriented towards the goal of direct experience of the divine, Sufism could allow for a high degree of subjectivity and idiosyncrasy in the definition of individual "orthodoxy". Overcome by his experience, the Sufi could even utter apparent blasphemies in his inability to express his experience in ordinary language. By and large, Islamic societies acknowledged the validity of these experiences and expanded the realm of the socially acceptable to accommodate such anomalies. This created an inclusive social space in which even the marginalised and the antisocial were tolerated in an act of suspended judgment. Even if the behaviour of people such as the Qalandars, wandering dervishes with hedonistic tendencies, appeared scandalous, they were usually given the benefit of the doubt.[13]

THE GOVERNMENT AND ORTHODOXY

The scholarly discourses generated the content of theological orthodoxy: only the *'ulamā'* were recognised as possessing the competence to make authoritative statements about matters of religion. Attempts by rulers to overrule the consensus of the majority of scholars and to impose a minority theological position by force – such as Ma'mūn's infamous Inquisition (*miḥna*) – were generally unsuccessful when confronted by determined opposition from the scholarly establishment. However, executive power played a crucial role in promoting and enforcing favoured theological ideas, and in suppressing rival doctrines.

A crucial vehicle for this influence was the government's right to appoint judges and other public officials who could wield considerable power. Beyond the basic requirement that appointees be recognised scholars and meet the minimum qualifications for office, rulers could select officials based on their school and doctrinal affiliations, and personal beliefs and characteristics, as well as social connections. For instance, the ninth-century governor of Egypt, Aḥmad ibn Ṭūlūn, chose to appoint a Shāfi'ī scholar – a representative of a minority school – as the first teacher in the central mosque of his newly built capital city, even granting him the unprecedented support of an annual stipend.

As the Shāfiʿīs were linked neither with the central Abbasid government nor with the indigenous Egyptian aristocracy, this appointment served to bolster Ibn Ṭūlūn's drive for greater independence from the Abbasid empire.

Similar considerations applied in the appointment of teachers for *madrasas* that were sponsored by state officials in a nominally private capacity. The eleventh-century Abbasid vizier Niẓām al-Mulk founded the prestigious network of Niẓāmiyya *madrasas* at a time when Ashʿarite theology was struggling to establish itself. In a successful effort to support the spread of Ashʿarism, he staffed the new institutions only with scholars who were favourably inclined towards its doctrines. In general, any *waqf* benefactor was entitled to select the personnel for the new institution. Thus, the setting up of *awqāf* for the purpose of founding and financing *madrasas* and, to a lesser extent, Sufi lodges permitted government officials to exercise significant but indirect influence on the composition and fortunes of the scholarly class.

Going beyond the fulfilment of individual judiciary and teaching appointments, the Ottoman government exerted an unprecedented degree of control over the scholarly establishment via the creation of the centralised *madrasa* network described earlier and via the position of the *şeyhülislam* (from the Arabic *shaykh al-islām*). The *şeyhülislam* was the highest religious authority in the empire; he was appointed by the government and his edicts were backed up by state power. Like the government-controlled *madrasa* system, this post was an Ottoman invention. The *şeyhülislam* was a *muftī*, that is, he could respond authoritatively to legal questions, whether asked by the ordinary man or woman on the street or by the sultan, by issuing a *fatwā*, a legal opinion. These questions were collected from around the empire, rephrased, and brought to the *şeyhülislam* by an army of assistants, who also collated his replies for later reference. What in the early centuries of Islam had been an informal phenomenon, consisting simply of a questioner submitting a legal dilemma to someone whom he considered knowledgeable, had under the influence of the centralising Ottoman state become a formal state institution.

On occasion, the state employed violence in the enforcement of acceptable limits on heterodoxy. The state held the sole authority to carry out executions of heretics, though the sentence itself had to be handed down by a qualified judge. The ruler could ban the public airing of certain ideas, and – through the government-appointed judiciary – persecute those who violated the ban. A dramatic illustration of such state action is the Abbasids' ninth-century *miḥna*, which sought to impose by force the minority theological doctrine of the createdness of the Qur'an throughout the judicial system. In Egypt, for example, the Abbasid-appointed chief judge of Egypt banned scholars of the Mālikī and Shāfi'ī schools who refused to endorse the doctrine from teaching in the central mosque. The judge had the text of the doctrine inscribed over the entrance of the mosque and sentenced those who dared show their disagreement to public whipping and humiliation.

The *miḥna* eventually foundered due to sustained resistance by the majority of the *'ulamā'*. However, the much more radical project of the sixteenth-century ruler of the Safavid empire, Shāh Ismā'īl, to force the overwhelmingly Sunnī population of Iran to embrace Shī'ism was successful. This was in part due to the determination and military strength of Shāh Ismā'īl, who imported a contingent of prominent Twelver scholars from Lebanon, equipped his army with firearms, and declared adherence to Sunnism within his realm a capital offence. A second crucial factor in this momentous development lay in the lack of effective opposition from the Sunnī *'ulamā'*, whose numbers and vigour had not recovered from the severe social dislocation and depopulation that followed the Mongol invasion of the region in the thirteenth century.

The motive for the state's intervention in the arena of theological scholarship was often the need to defuse perceived political threats. This need was underpinned by the frequent intertwining of state legitimacy with religious authority: the state bolstered its domestic sovereignty by portraying itself as the guardian of orthodoxy. As a result, political opposition to the ruling regime easily acquired an air of heresy. Unsurprisingly, therefore, political rebellions often appeared in alliance with heterodox movements. An example is the revolt led by the tribal chief Muḥammad ibn Sa'ūd and the religious scholar Muḥammad ibn 'Abd al-Wahhāb against the Ottomans in the Arabian region of Najd in the eighteenth century. Ibn 'Abd al-Wahhāb contested the status of the Ottomans as defenders of Sunnī Islam, claiming that the Ottomans' principle of religious tolerance had allowed heresy to flourish in the empire. This theological challenge was harnessed by Ibn Sa'ūd to legitimise his plans of territorial expansion, and it infused his fighters with the iconoclastic zeal that led to the wholesale destruction of Sufi shrines, the bloody sacking of the Shī'ite town of Karbalā' in 1801, and the occupation of Mecca from 1803 to 1812.[14] The Ottomans succeeded in countering the politico-religious threat posed by Ibn Sa'ūd and Ibn 'Abd al-Wahhāb's movement. Only after the demise of the Ottoman Empire in the aftermath of the First World War could Ibn Sa'ūd's descendants, still armed with Wahhābī ideology, make a successful bid for power on the peninsula, leading to the eventual establishment of modern Saudi Arabia.

OVERALL TRENDS

I have argued above that the social construction of theological orthodoxy took place at the intersection of three primary societal arenas, comprising the scholars, the ordinary believers and the government. To conclude, I will briefly summarise some broad historical trends that can be observed in these arenas during the millennium between the ninth and the nineteenth centuries.

The history of the *'ulamā'* is marked by the progressive professionalisation of scholarly activity: while early scholars enjoyed no formal distinction and made their living through trade or industry, most later scholars were career academics who dedicated their time to research, teaching and writing and vied for lucrative positions at well-endowed *madrasa*s. This development permitted the increased sophistication and explosive growth of the Islamic sciences and their literatures, but it also left the scholarly class dependent on society's capacity to produce a sufficient surplus to support its scholars. The consequent vulnerability of scholarship was demonstrated by the decline in scholarly activity and output that accompanied the economic crises experienced by Muslim countries in the seventeenth and eighteenth centuries.

The nature of the *umma*, the community of believers, underwent constant change due to successive waves of conversion to Islam. In the year 700, most ordinary Muslims were Arabs with strong tribal identities and a shared language and culture, living as tiny, close-knit minorities among non-Muslims. Two centuries later, the majority of Muslims were non-Arabs, representing a variety of cultural and religious backgrounds and thus bringing to the community a range of different preconceptions regarding God and the nature of religion. The geographical spread and cultural diversification of Islam supported the proliferation of localised forms of popular religion, even as the unification of the Islamic realm enabled the diffusion of official orthodoxy to all corners of the Muslim world.

Finally, the role played by the state in the construction of orthodoxy depended on the nature and strength of the government. From 750 until roughly 950 the early Abbasids ruled over an empire that was in medieval terms both powerful and highly centralised. The middle period between 950 and 1450, on the other hand, was characterised by small, often ephemeral states or statelets, frequently ruled by foreigners with slave backgrounds. Consequently, while an Abbasid caliph such as Ma'mūn could hope to refashion the definition of orthodoxy by fiat, the later rulers could realistically cherish no such ambitions. The latter were constrained by an acute need to gain and maintain legitimacy in the eyes of the population and thus were compelled to present themselves as guardians of the theological status quo, leaving the definition of orthodoxy in the hands of the *'ulamā'*. Following the appearance in the fifteenth century of the mighty gunpowder empires ruled by firmly established ruling dynasties, executive power began to gain the upper hand in relation to the scholars. The dynasties claimed the role of defenders of Islam and thus succeeded in intertwining religious orthodoxy with their own legitimacy. With the coming of the modern era and the rise of nationalism as the primary legitimising discourse of the nation-state, the question of religious orthodoxy was eventually pushed out of the centre of the political arena.

Further reading

Berkey, Jonathan Porter, *The Transmission of Knowledge in Medieval Cairo: A Social History of Islamic Education* (Princeton, 1992).

Chamberlain, Michael, *Knowledge and Social Practice in Medieval Damascus, 1190–1350* (Cambridge and New York, 1994).

Ess, Josef van, *The Flowering of Muslim Theology*, tr. Jane Marie Todd (Cambridge, MA, 2006).

Theologie und Gesellschaft im 2. und 3. Jahrhundert Hidschra: eine Geschichte des religiösen Denkens im frühen Islam, 6 vols. (Berlin and New York, 1991–5).

Güzel, Hasan Celal, Cem, Oğuz C., and Karatay, Osman, (eds), *The Turks*, 6 vols. (Ankara, 2002).

Lapidus, Ira M., *Muslim Cities in the Later Middle Ages* (Cambridge and New York, 1984).

Makdisi, George, *Ibn Aqîl et la resurgence de l'Islam traditionaliste au xie siècle* (Damascus, 1963).

The Rise of Colleges: Institutions of Learning in Islam and the West (Edinburgh, 1981).

Mottahedeh, Roy P., *The Mantle of the Prophet: Religion and Politics in Iran* (New York, 1985).

Nagel, Tilman, *Die Festung des Glaubens: Triumph und Scheitern des islamischen Rationalismus im 11. Jahrhundert* (Munich, 1988).

Repp, Richard C., *The Müfti of Istanbul: A Study in the Development of the Ottoman Learned Hierarchy* (London and Atlantic Highlands, NJ, 1986).

Shoshan, Boaz, *Popular Culture in Medieval Cairo* (New York, 1993).

Taylor, Christopher Schurman, *In the Vicinity of the Righteous: Ziyāra and the Veneration of Muslim Saints in Late Medieval Egypt* (Boston, 1999).

al-Zarnūjī, Burhān al-Dīn, *Instruction of the Student: The Method of Learning*, tr. G. E. von Grunebaum and Theodora M. Abel, 2nd revised edn (Chicago, 2001).

Notes

I would like to thank Dr Aron Zysow for his helpful comments on a draft of this chapter.

1. See, for example, Ignaz Goldziher, *Muslim Studies*, ed. S. M. Stern, tr. C. R. Barber and S. M. Stern (London, 1967–71).
2. Omaima Abu Bakr, "Teaching the Words of the Prophet: Women Instructors of the Hadith (Fourteenth and Fifteenth Centuries)," *Hawwa* 1/3 (2003), pp. 306–28.
3. There were also state-funded institutions, such as the Ismāʿīlī Dār al-Ḥikma in eleventh-century Cairo.
4. For an explanation of the differences between these terms, see Leonor E. Fernandes, *The Evolution of a Sufi Institution in Mamluk Egypt: The Khanqah* (Berlin, 1988), ch. 3.
5. *Kullu mujtahid muṣīb*; see Josef van Ess, *The Flowering of Muslim Theology*, tr. Jane Marie Todd (Cambridge, MA, 2006), p. 20.
6. Shams al-Dīn al-Dhahabī, *Siyar aʿlām al-nubalā'*, ed. Shuʿayb al-Arnā'ūṭ and Muḥammad al-ʿArqasūsī (Beirut, 1413/1992), x, p. 28.
7. Sherman A. Jackson, *On the Boundaries of Theological Tolerance in Islam: Abū Ḥāmid al-Ghazālī's Fayṣal al-Tafriqa bayna al-Islām wa'l-zandaqa* (Karachi, 2002).
8. Abū Ḥāmid al-Ghazālī, *Ḥaqīqat al-qawlayn* (MS, Princeton University, Yahuda 4358, fols. 3b–4a).
9. Roy P. Mottahedeh, *The Mantle of the Prophet: Religion and Politics in Iran* (New York, 1985).
10. Van Ess, *Theologie und Gesellschaft*, iv.
11. See, for example, Richard W. Bulliet, *The Patricians of Nishapur: A Study in Medieval Islamic Social History* (Cambridge, MA, 1972); and Ira M. Lapidus, *Muslim Cities in the Later Middle Ages* (Cambridge and New York, 1984).
12. Christopher Schurman Taylor, *In the Vicinity of the Righteous: Ziyāra and the Veneration of Muslim Saints in Late Medieval Egypt* (Boston, 1999).
13. Ahmet T. Karamustafa, *God's Unruly Friends: Dervish Groups in the Islamic Later Middle Period, 1200–1550* (Salt Lake City, 1994).
14. See, for example, Esther Peskes, *Muḥammad b. ʿAbdalwahhāb (1703–92) im Widerstreit: Untersuchungen zur Rekonstruktion der Frühgeschichte der Wahhābīya* (Beirut, 1993).

Part II

Themes

6 God: essence and attributes

NADER EL-BIZRI

GENERAL BACKGROUND

The question of God's essence (*dhāt*) and attributes (*ṣifāt*) confronted Muslim scholars with perplexing paradoxes touching on the divine unity (*tawḥīd*) and transcendence (*tanzīh*).

Since the earliest decades of Islamic speculation, in the seventh and eighth centuries, the question of God's essence and attributes constituted one of the axial themes of the scriptural exegesis and hermeneutics that influenced the unfolding of Islamic thought. This was most manifestly the case with the sharp disputes that arose between Muʿtazilism and Ḥanbalism, which later led to the emergence of Ashʿarī *kalām* and its subsequent debates with the Peripatetic philosophers, paradigmatically culminating in Ghazālī's critique of Avicenna.

The essence–attributes question reflected the variant dimensions of scriptural interpretation and its grounding theories of meaning. According to heresiographic accounts, it was the distinction claimed between the exoteric, apparent (*ẓāhir*) meaning of scripture, and its esoteric, hidden (*bāṭin*) sense which generated extremist doctrinal positions, most emblematically the anthropomorphists (*mushabbiha*) and corporealists (*mujassima*) at one extreme, ranged against various esotericists (*bāṭiniyya*) on the other.

From an abstractive philosophical standpoint, the question of God's essence and attributes points to the dialectical concepts of unity/multiplicity, identity/difference, or sameness/otherness that had constituted universal categories of analysis in the intellectual history of a variety of doctrines from the time of the ancient Greeks, and which continued in the work of modern thinkers of the calibre of Hegel, Heidegger and Levinas. An adaptive appropriation of these notions served the purposes of monotheistic speculation about God's essence and attributes, a process that most radically manifested itself in the intricate Muslim theological disputes over the nature of revelation as manifested by and in the Qur'an.

THE MU'TAZILITES AND THE DISPUTES OVER THE QUR'AN

In addressing the question of divine essence and attributes, the Mu'tazilites typically stressed the equivalence between *ṣifa* (attribute), *waṣf* (description) and *ism* (name). Based on this principle of sameness, the Mu'tazilites held that if we converse about divine attributes we ultimately describe divinity. The Ḥanbalites, and most Ash'arites, opposed this claim by drawing a thoughtful distinction between *ṣifa* and *waṣf*, positing the former as being "what is intrinsically in something", while taking the latter to denote "what is given as a descriptive report (*khabar*) about something".[1] However, any account of the attributes has to pass by a hermeneutic or exegetical position with regard to scripture.

Given that the Qur'an (as God's Word) mentions the divine attributes in conjunction with His "most beautiful names" (*asmā' Allāh al-ḥusnā*), one could easily assert that this entails an affirmation of the ontological reality of these attributes. However, this will require a particular method of reading the Qur'an that affirms the attributes without undermining transcendence and unity, or implying anthropomorphism. Inevitably, one wonders how successfully anthropomorphism can be avoided when accounting for verses like "your Lord's Face ever remains" (55:27), or "I created with My own hands" (38:75). In addition, it is hardly evident how the multiplicity which is implied by any affirmation of the attributes might be reconciled with the idea of God's absolute unity.

From a religious perspective, the Qur'an sets canonical measures for the human condition, while being the locus of textual hermeneutics. Hence, faith is grounded by textuality along with its determining semantics and semiotics. Yet the Qur'an, as God's Word, is manifested in a "language" that is grasped religiously as being unlike any human idiom. As a divine "language", revelation is not part of the created world of composite substances or contingent beings that are subject to generation and corruption. Any account of the question of God's essence and attributes thus requires some uneasy meditations on the reality of divine speech (*kalām*). Centrally, the essence–attributes question calls for thinking about the nature of the Qur'an as God's Word. Historically, this tension soon broke surface in the radical disputes that occurred between the Mu'tazilites and the early Sunnī theologians.

To defend the divine transcendence and unity against misreading the divine attributes in anthropomorphic terms or unguardedly hinting at multiplicity, the Mu'tazilites concluded that the Qur'an had been created (*makhlūq*). The argument may be reconstructed as follows: if the Qur'an is God's speech, then it is either coeternal with God, and thus uncreated, or it is not coeternal with God. To maintain pure monotheism one must concede that it is created. On this inference, if the Qur'an is coeternal with God, then in order to eschew plurality in the divine oneness, one has to say that the scripture, as God's speech, is one with God. To avoid affirming contraries (unity and multiplicity), a Mu'tazilite would assert that it is not coeternal with God and must therefore be created. This argument is seconded by qur'anic proof-texts that point to the descent of revelation in the Arabic tongue that is constrained by place and time, as to its accessibility to finite human apprehension.

This reasoning, however, is problematic, since it begs a further question: if the Qur'an is created, does this then entail that it is no longer God's Word? The Sunnīs radically opposed this controversial thesis. Yet if they refuted it on the basis of arguing that the Qur'an was not created, would this not entail that the Qur'an is coeternal with God? And, hence, would it not compromise the all-important principles of unity and transcendence?

The Mu'tazilite thesis regarding the creation of the Qur'an appears as ill founded on the same grounds that it presupposes, namely, the radical observance of God's transcendence. By stressing transcendence, the belief in the scripture's created status implies that the divine attributes are not real, but are rather revealed in a worldly language for the convenience of human comprehension. The reality of divinity seems to be determinable by the judgements of human reason, which see fit to reject multiplicity even to the point of refuting the attributes and affirming that God's Word was created. The Mu'tazilites censored, through rational directives, the classes of meaningful propositions that could be uttered about the divine. However, by believing that "human reason" sufficiently measures what is applicable to God, transcendence became paradoxically delimited by a negation of the attributes. Furthermore, the unfolding of this rationalist impetus resulted in picturing the Qur'an as a creature.

In an archetypal Mu'tazilite move, Wāṣil ibn 'Aṭā' (d. 748) is believed to have rejected the affirmation of the attributes of knowledge (*'ilm*), power (*qudra*), will (*irāda*), and life (*ḥayāt*), in order to negate a "plurality of eternals". Some later Mu'tazilites restricted the totality of the attributes to knowledge and power, while others reduced them to unity. According to the sources, Abu'l-Hudhayl al-'Allāf considered the attributes and the essence to be identical, al-Naẓẓām denied that God has power over evil, Mu'ammar refuted will and knowledge in order to free God's essence from multiplicity, while al-Jubbā'ī and Abū Hāshim asserted that God possesses a knowledge that is identical with His essence and not subsisting beside it. In principle, the Mu'tazila believed that God's *'ilm* (omniscience), *ḥayāt* (life), *qudra* (power), *irāda* (will), *baṣar* (sight), *sam'* (hearing), and *kalām* (speech), are all reducible to the *dhāt* (essence). To account for these attributes they stated that God is *'ālim bi-'ilm huwa huwa* (knowing by a knowledge that is Him), *qādir bi-qudra hiya huwa* (powerful by a power that is Him), *ḥayy bi-ḥayāt hiya huwa* (living by a life that is Him) and so on.

One of the major difficulties that confronted Mu'tazilism was manifested in the denial of the personal, intimate and uncanny "relation" of the worshipper with God, as what grounds the realities of religious experience. By reducing the attributes to the essence, the Mu'tazila seemed to deny worshippers the object of their praise, exaltation and piety. On their view, God is no longer truly seen as the Beneficent, Ever-Merciful Almighty, to whom believers turn in their supplications and invocations in seeking mercy and salvation. Unlike the traditionalists, the Mu'tazilites might even have subverted the obligatory nature of prayer by indirectly emptying it of its content. By replacing the personal character of the Exalted One with a neuter qualification, their opinions became unintentionally closer to the outlook of the pagan Greeks than to the fundamental perspective of monotheism. One wonders how some qur'anic verses would be meaningfully interpretable if God's attributes and names were reducible to His essence. How would a believer heed, with intimacy, fear and hope, verses like: "He is the Beneficent (*al-barr*), the Ever-Merciful (*al-raḥmān*)" (52:28), "God warns you against His Chastisement" (3:28), "All praise belongs to God" (17:111), "Ask forgiveness of God, surely God is Most Forgiving" (4:106)?

THE ḤANBALITE POSITION

The Ḥanbalites believed that God's revelation is there to be recited, and that no interpretations will exhaust its sense. The ontological status of the attributes will remain concealed, and the most that one can affirm about them is their existence, on the grounds that they are mentioned in the Qur'an. Nonetheless, in the eyes of many this does not entail that believers must not exercise a pious effort to comprehend their meaning. It is in this sense that Ash'arites progressed further than Ḥanbalites in terms of establishing the affirmation of the attributes on theological grounds. Their typical line of interpretation avoided placing believers in a constraining position which stripped them of any say regarding matters of their faith; particularly with respect to their religious experience and its implicitly presupposed conceptions of divinity. The divine attributes are thus not submissively affirmed on the basis of mere imitation (*taqlīd*) or dogma. While conceding that human understanding is restricted whenever it attempts to elucidate the essence–attributes question, they held that this need not entirely disrupt rational inquiry. Consequently, *kalām* speculative theology was positively endorsed by Ash'arī on the basis that human reason exists to be celebrated despite its "limited" nature.

Prior to the concretisation of the Ash'arite school the Ḥanbalites opposed speculation in religious matters. However, with Ash'arism, theological inquiries were encouraged, although there was no presupposition that they necessarily yielded definite clues about the nature of the divine essence or readily facilitated the acquisition of real knowledge about God. Yet the Ḥanbalite line continued to maintain that any such moves would be mere linguistic, grammatical or conceptual verbiage, which might well lead to repugnant errors in matters of faith. The truth of the divine essence is veiled, and the principle of transcendence is not to be compromised by speculation. Even if attributes are disclosed in a language accessible to humans, their meaning is not exhaustible by reasoned explications. Given that the divine names and attributes are revealed through God's words in the Qur'an, it becomes religiously obligatory to affirm their reality with conviction and sincerity in belief.

Returning to the polemics posited by the Mu'tazilite thesis concerning the creation of the Qur'an, God's words are pictured as being expressions of a sensory language ("We made it an Arabic Qur'an", 43:3), which is heard, seen and recited, and, despite its superlative subtleties, can be rationally assessed from the standpoint of human linguistics, grammar and logic. In this sense, whatever is mentioned about the divine attributes, or names, forms part of a spatial-temporal idiomatic structure whose intricate significance may potentially be brought to light by human understanding. According to this doctrine, the attributes and names are reducible to the essence, which remains veiled in its transcendence, even though what can be uttered about divinity is ultimately apportioned by human reason.

By asserting that "whatever is *sensory* is created", Ash'arism occupied an approximately median theological ground between Ḥanbalism and Mu'tazilism. Consequently, what is recited, heard, read and copied of God's words is created without this entailing that the Qur'an is itself a "creature". It may thus be said that the sensible pronunciation (*lafẓiyya*) in the recitation (*qirā'a*) of the divine words is created, while divine speech, as what is recited (*maqrū'*), is uncreated. God's attributes can thus be affirmed without being reducible to the essence or being separate from it, and unity is not undermined by the "semblance" of multiplicity. One notices here a clear departure from the Mu'tazilite refutation of the reality of the attributes coupled with a simultaneous avoidance of the pitfalls of anthropomorphism. It is nonetheless still the case that in general the Ash'arites adhered in broad terms to the Ḥanbalite credo, while being moderately open to the use of reasoned discussion in its defence. For the strict Ḥanbalite fringe, however, God's words are brought forth by way of "letting them be without how"; namely, without speculating about what they mean whenever confusion or dissent might arise from speculation. One has to submit to the words in faith even where no sufficient explanation is available. Hence, the controversies of *kalām* may well run the risk of bordering on heretical innovation (*bid'a*). Ḥanbalites typically affirm that the Qur'an is not created, and caution that anyone who holds that the scripture or its utterance (*lafẓ*) is created will be an infidel (*kāfir*).[2] For instance, Ibn Ḥanbal held that one could not think that there would be someone other than God who would say to Moses, "I am your Lord."[3] This is the case given that the Ḥanbalites hold that God speaks with an uncreated voice (*ṣawt*) or letter (*ḥarf*).[4] In this regard, they reject the Ash'arite claim that the qur'anic *lafẓiyya* (enunciation) is created. Although Ḥanbalites emphasise the literal and apparent (*ẓāhir*) meanings of the Qur'an, they also stress that one must ground them by exegesis (*tafsīr*) based on the canonical tradition of the Prophet and his Companions.[5]

According to the Ḥanbalite scholar Ibn Badrān, a modest form of ratiocination in "representation", called *tamthīl*, may be used, under restricted circumstances, in rejecting the arguments of the dialecticians (*ahl al-jadal*). However, he adds that those curious about the nature of the divine attributes should reverently recognise that such matters are necessarily veiled from the workings of reason. In addition, no questions like "why?" (*limā*?) or "how?" (*kayf*?) may apply in this context. When asked about divine speech, one should reply that God spoke to Moses in a way that befits His divine essence; hence, one must restrict one's answer to this: "And to Moses God spoke directly" (4:164). God's speech, what He uttered, what is written in the "Preserved Tablet" (*al-lawḥ al-maḥfūẓ*), what is manifest in the earthly codices of the Qur'an (*al-maṣāḥif*) and is recited by humans, all point to non-creation. Ibn Badrān adds that "whosoever believes that any of these aforementioned matters are created, should be charged with infidelity, and whoever does not declare that person infidel, shall himself or herself be an infidel".[6] In the same thrust of strictures, it is also mentioned that Ibn Ḥanbal was once asked: "What ought we do with the one who [even] holds that the enunciation (*lafẓiyya*) of the Qur'an is created?" He replied: "You are not to pray behind him, nor to sit next to him, nor talk to him or salute him."[7]

In another Sunnī traditionalist context, the Māturīdī school associated with the legacy of Abū Ḥanīfa permitted a greater use of speculation; although the Māturīdīs continued to uphold the belief that God is known "without qualification" (*bi-lā kayf*).[8] Māturīdīs also objected to the Mu'tazilite claim that "God is everywhere", by saying that this formulation, which is not mentioned in the Qur'an, undermines the divine exaltedness, given that God is "on the Throne" (*al-'arsh*) and does not commingle with worldly profanities.[9] The remark is also seconded by later more philosophically oriented Ash'arites of the calibre of al-Āmidī, al-Ījī and al-Sharīf al-Jurjānī, who argued that God does not join worldly beings nor is He infused in the universe. Māturīdī also asserts that the divine attributes are "neither Him nor other than Him" (*lā huwa wa-lā ghayruh*), adding that God is pre-eternally qualified by all His attributes (*mawṣūf bi-jamī' ṣifātih fi'l-azal*).[10] It is impossible for the attributes not to be coeternal with God, for that would entail deficiency. However, the coeternal status of attributes does not imply that they are the same as the essence. As Abū al-Muntahā al-Maghnisāwī put it, the attributes are not the same as the essence nor are they other than it. He furthermore cautions that "we should not inquire about such matters".[11] Moreover, when considering the attributes any talk about "howness" is to be avoided, since speculations in this regard may result in repugnant innovations. All the divine names are equal in greatness without distinction in rank, since they are attributable to God in His words, while being neither Him nor anything other than Him.[12] This is also confirmed in the Ḥanbalite position, which according to Ibn Baṭṭa is best defined by attributing to God what He attributed to Himself in the Qur'an, and following what the Prophet attributed to Him in the hadith, without asking *limā* (why?) or *kayf* (how?). One thus ought to submit to God's *qudra* (power) by way of having simple faith in what is absent and unseen (*al-ghayb*):[13] "sights cannot attain Him; He can attain sights" (Qur'an 6:103). The Ḥanbalite tradition ultimately affirms a belief in all that is mentioned in the Qur'an, be it in its definite (*muḥkam*) senses or its equivocal ambiguities (*mutashābih*),[14] while fundamentally consigning (*tafwīḍ*) the "meaning and howness" of the attributes to God alone.

THE ASH'ARITE POSITION

Unlike the Ḥanbalite view, the distinctive position of al-Ash'arī is best expressed by way of his support of *kalām* methods in elucidating the essence–attributes question. After all, he disapproved of unreflective deference to doctrinal dogmas by way of mimetic assent (*taqlīd*), given his firm belief that Muslims have the duty to reason about what it means to know God, since knowing God amounts to knowing the truth (*al-ḥaqq*).[15]

In response to the Mu'tazilite reductive overemphasis on transcendence, Ash'arī argued that God's words about God, as manifested in the Qur'an, set up the directives by virtue of which reasoned judgements about the essence–attributes question are to be measured. The affirmation of God's attributes should be coupled with the negation of implied anthropomorphic determinations. Analogy is problematic when it hints at any form of similitude between God and anything in His world of creation. Authentically to believe that "nothing is like Him" (42:11) obligates a refutation of *tashbīh* and *tamthīl*. If the attributes are examined through a radically literal reading, heretical innovation may ensue, as exemplified in the unsustainable doctrines of anthropomorphists (*mushabbiha*) and corporealists (*mujassima*). Yet some attributes retain the semblance of carrying anthropomorphic meanings when judged from the standpoint of generic resemblances.

Ash'arism established a refined nuance between attributes of action (*ṣifāt al-fi'l*), which come to be when God intends something and acts, and those of essence (*ṣifāt al-dhāt* or *ṣifāt al-nafs*). The contraries of the attributes of action are permissibly attributable to God. For instance, it is admissible to state that God is *forgiving* of repentant believers (as a reward; *thawāb*), while also affirming that He may be *unforgiving* of unrepentant transgressors who break the covenant of God after its binding (as retribution; *'iqāb*). Forgiveness is thus an attribute of action that admits negation without its resulting contrary being unattributable to God. As for attributes of essence, their contraries are repugnant: the negation of *omniscience* entails *ignorance*, while the denial of *power* results in *weakness*. Hence the attributes of action are "negational" (*salbiyya*), while the attributes of essence are classed as "existential" (*wujūdiyya*). In this regard, it was commonly held that the *ṣifāt al-dhāt* consisted of the following seven attributes: *'ilm* (omniscience), *ḥayāt* (life), *qudra* (power), *irāda* (will), *baṣar* (sight), *sam'* (hearing), and *kalām* (speech). An internal controversy emerged over "willing", some holding that it is unlike the other essential attributes, given that it hints at action or intention rather than being everlasting and unchanging (*thābita*).

Strict literal exegesis (*tafsīr*), or excessive hermeneutics (*ta'wīl*), may result in groundless extremisms. In emphasising the literal exoteric meaning (*ẓāhir*), the exegete might present anthropomorphist accounts that compromise transcendence (*tanzīh*), while the stress on the esoteric hidden sense (*bāṭin*) might lead the hermeneutic interpreter to accord with the outlooks of the various *bāṭiniyya* sects. Moderation in scriptural readings is to be situated between two extremist poles in interpretation that might lead to heresies, in the form either of a literal anthropomorphism or of the overcoming of its entailments through an excessive allegorical overemphasis on transcendence. This semantic tension characterises the reception of revealed texts and their multilayered readings.

Faced with the difficulty of interpreting expressions like "God's hand" ("I created with My own hands" [38:75]) or "God's face" ("your Lord's Face ever remains" [55:27]), Ash'arī does not question the realities to which they point, since these are qur'anic statements. However, he again seeks a middle path, refusing to affirm that the referents of God's "hand" or "face" are either corporeal members or mere metaphors. Again he is guarding against excess in literal exegesis, while being suspicious of allegorical hermeneutics. Despite this desire for a median position, however, he proclaims that any departure from literal readings must be based on valid reasons. When any form of resemblance, similitude or analogy between God and anything in the world of His creation is refuted, this applies to linguistic, ontological and logical reflections on the essence–attributes question. There is an unbridgeable existential-essential gap between creator and created. To hint that God resembles worldly beings is absurd. A semblance of linguistic affinity in reference to attributes does not affirm a similitude in signification. As Ash'arī holds, "God is not in His creatures nor are His creatures in Him." In his *Letter to the Frontiersmen* (*Risāla ilā ahl al-thaghr*), he refutes any mode of equivalence between the divine essence and the divine attributes.[16] Yet while the attributes are not reducible to the essence, they are not accidents that are other than it. This ontological *difference* is not simply a mode of *separation* in being. In elaborating his thesis, Ash'arī considered with care and thoughtfulness the conditions by virtue of which inferences may be drawn with respect to what is absent and transcendent, on the basis of what is phenomenally experienced; following in this the classical method known as "*al-istidlāl 'alā al-ghā'ib bi'l-shāhid*".

In his *Exposition of the Fundamentals of Faith* (*al-Ibāna ʿan uṣūl al-diyāna*), Ash'arī's views seem to come nearer to the apologetics of the Ḥanbalites. Here he affirms that God does indeed possess a face, eyes and hands. He adds that the divine words are not created and that God will be seen in the afterlife. This latter proposition, derived from a number of hadith, continued to exercise scholars perplexed by the paradoxical nature of this visualising experience. After all, if physical bodies are the only visible entities in the phenomenal universe, what sort of "vision" (*ru'ya*) is implied in affirming that God will be seen in the afterlife? And if this "visual" experience is not sensory, and hence does not accord with the science of optics (*ʿilm al-manāẓir*), what might its nature be? In response, Ash'arī's affirmation of visibility in the hereafter is coupled with the assertion that its "nature" remains inexplicable and beyond human grasp.

In contrast with the text-based position that Ash'arī advocates in his *Exposition*, the arguments of his *Concise Remarks* (*Kitāb al-Lumaʿ*) proceed by way of rational evidences (*adilla ʿaqliyya*) and systemic *kalām* speculations. Moreover, in refuting *tashbīh* (anthropomorphism) and *tajsīm* (corporealism) he offers statements such as "The face is an attribute that God ascribed to Himself and only God knows its significance."[17] The Arabic utterance *wajh* ("face"), may thus be posited as an allegory that does not undermine *tanzīh*. In this specific case, hermeneutics must be exercised to shield the principle of transcendence. In the *Remarks* Ash'arī asserts that God is unlike anything else and that it is irreverent to imply any analogy, resemblance or similitude in connection with His exaltedness.[18] He also argues that corporeity (*jismiyya*) entails composition (*tarkīb*) and multiplicity (*kathra*), which contradict the principles of simplicity and unity, and this rational argument is strengthened by the traditionalist point that since God has not referred to Himself as being a "body" (*jism*), we ought not to ascribe any name to Him that He has not applied to Himself, nor should we utter propositions in this regard that are not conformable to the Muslim consensus.[19] Ash'arī thus affirms God's attributes, while rejecting the attribution to Him of qualities associable with created beings.[20] Moreover, all attributes are coeternal with the essence without being marked by otherness (*ghayriyya*) or privation (*ʿadam*).[21]

Furthermore, Ash'arī asserts in his *Remarks* that "God's speech is uncreated and is coeternal with His essence." However, as noted earlier, he posits a controversial problem regarding the actual enunciation (*lafẓiyya*) of the divine words. He consequently differentiates the createdness of utterances (*ḥudūth al-alfāẓ*) from the beginninglessness of their meanings (*qidam al-ma'ānī*). God's speech is inherent in Him, and in itself it is neither a sensory sound (*ṣawt*) nor a graphical trace that is manifested in the form of a letter (*ḥarf*). Being of the order of human doings, sounds and letters are created expressive traces of the uncreated divine word.

Ash'arī proposes a further argument. Reflecting on the qur'anic verse 16:40, "For to anything which We have willed, We but say "Be!", and it is", it might be said, based on the generative command "Be!" (*kun!*), that if the Qur'an were created, then it was commanded to come into being by the saying "Be!" This would imply that God's words are themselves generated by His word "Be!" and that redundantly, the command "Be!" itself is generated by another command "Be!", *ad infinitum*. Yet would this not imply that we are faced with a purposeless infinite regress, which is inapplicable in reference to divinity? Therefore, God's words must be coeternal with Him, and He is the exalted eternal speaker who possesses the creative command.

FALSAFA VIEWS ON THE ESSENCE–ATTRIBUTE PROBLEM

Reflections on the essence–attribute question were not restricted to *kalām* deliberations but were also systemically debated by the exponents of *falsafa*. For instance, Avicenna addressed this question in terms of an ontological analysis of the modalities of being; namely impossibility, contingency and necessity. Avicenna argues that the impossible being is that which cannot exist, while the contingent in itself (*mumkin bi-dhātihi*) has the potentiality to be or not to be without entailing a contradiction. When actualised, the contingent becomes a "necessary existent due to what is other than itself" (*wājib al-wujūd bi-ghayrihi*). Thus, contingency-in-itself is potential *beingness* that could eventually be actualised by an external cause other than itself. The metaphysical structures of necessity and contingency are different. Necessary being due to itself (*wājib al-wujūd bi-dhātihi*) is true in itself, while contingent being is "false in itself" and "true due to something other than itself". The necessary is the source of its own being without borrowed existence. It is what always exists.[22] The Necessary exists "due-to-Its-Self", and has no quiddity/essence (*māhiyya*) other than existence (*wujūd*). Furthermore, It is "One" (*wāḥid aḥad*),[23] since there cannot be more than one "Necessary-Existent-due-to-Itself" without differentia (sing. *faṣl*) to distinguish them from one another. Yet to require differentia entails that they exist "due-to-themselves" as well as "due to what is other than themselves"; and this is contradictory. However, if no differentia distinguish them from each other, then there is no sense in which these "Existents" are not one and the same. Avicenna adds that the "Necessary-Existent-due-to-Itself" has no genus (*jins*), or definition (*ḥadd*), or a counterpart (*nidd*), or an opposite (*ḍidd*), and is detached (*barī'*) from matter (*mādda*), quality (*kayf*), quantity (*kam*), place (*ayn*), situation (*waḍʿ*) and time (*waqt*).[24]

Avicenna's "Necessary-Existent-due-to-Itself" differs from the Ultimate Being of monotheistic orthodoxy, in the sense that it is ontologically derived from a "naturalised knowledge of God". Accordingly, the concept of the world is essentially contained in the Avicennan notion of divinity, and it is not "logically" plausible that God exists and that the world does not exist. The very being of the "Necessary Existent" implies by necessity the existence of an emanated world. Moreover, salvation is not dependent on grace but is rather dependent on the subject as agent, and any communication with the ontological modality of "Necessary Being" represents a philosophical mistake of category. However, although Avicenna's metaphysics is not representative of a *kalām* ontotheology, his thought is not isolated from the religious context in which it was historically situated. An affirmation of the divine attributes preserves the personal Exalted One of the monotheistic faith, as the Absolute, All-Mighty, All-Wise, who creates by will, without how or why. Hence Avicenna's "Necessary-Existent-due-to-Itself" may still be pointing to "God", even though this does not readily transform his metaphysics into a convincing exegesis of Revelation. However, like that of the Muʿtazila before him, Avicenna's ontology undermines the personal character of God, as well as compromising the positive determinations of fear, hope and expectation which experientially characterise the manner by which the sense of divinity announces itself within the lives of believers.

Countering this turn in philosophical thinking, one of the major developments in the history of classical thought in Islam is exemplified by Ghazālī's critique of the philosophers in general and Avicenna in particular. In his *The Incoherence of the Philosophers* Ghazālī holds that the philosophers agree on the impossibility of affirming knowledge, power, and will for the First Principle, though the divine names, which are given in revelation, are to be used "verbally" while being reduced "referentially" to one divine essence (*dhāt wāḥida*). He then adds that the philosophers believe that a substantive affirmation of the attributes leads to a multiplicity that undermines divine unity.[25] Ghazālī objects by saying that they have opposed all the Muslims in this, with the exception of the Muʿtazila.

To show their "incoherence", Ghazālī summarises their arguments as follows. If an attribute and that to which it is attributed are not the same, then each one will dispense with the other, or each one will need the other for it to be, or one will dispense with the other while the other will be in need of the former. In the first of these cases, both will be necessary existents due to themselves, and this is implausible. In the case where each one of them needs the other, then neither is a "Necessary-Existent-due-to-Itself", and this is impossible in the case of the divine. However, if one has no need of the other, but is needed by it, then one of them acts as the cause of the other. So in this case, if what is ascribed with an attribute is in need of it, the one in need is characterised by a lack, and this does not apply to the divine.[26] Ghazālī's reply to these speculations is that the essence of the Necessary Existent is eternal without agents, and so are His attributes.[27] He also objects to the *falāsifa*'s claim that the affirmation of the attributes entails that the First Principle cannot be absolutely self-sufficient, given that since the First does not need anything other than Himself, therefore He would not need the attributes. Ghazālī thinks that these philosophical sophistications are part of a mere "rhetorical preaching that is extremely feeble". After all, he asserts that "the attributes of perfection are not separate from the essence of the Perfect, so as to say that He is in need of another". Like Ash'arī, he holds that the attributes are not reduced to the essence itself while being coeternal with it without cause. When the philosophers affirm that God is a knower, they face the problem of admitting that there is something superadded to the essence, namely knowledge.

Most adherents of *falsafa* hold that God knows only Himself. However, Avicenna argues that God knows Himself as well as knowing everything else in a universal manner, given that the knowledge of particulars implies change in the divine essence. In response, Ghazālī asks whether God's knowledge of Himself is identical with His knowledge of all genera and species. If the philosophers reply that His knowledge of Himself is indeed identical with His knowledge of everything else, then their position is untenable. If they say that they are not identical, then multiplicity is implied. Neither reply convinces. Furthermore, it cannot be the case that God would know only Himself given the scriptural affirmation that "not even the weight of an atom in the heavens or the earth escapes His knowledge" (10:61). Unlike other philosophers, Avicenna is "ashamed" of asserting that God knows only Himself and does not know anything else, given that this implies deficiency. Therefore, in avoiding assertions that might imply change or multiplicity in the essence, he reaches the conclusion that God knows everything other than Himself in a universal way.[28]

Nevertheless, according to Ghazālī, Avicenna's views result in a contradiction. This is the case given that, according to the philosophers and the Mu'tazila, the affirmation that God possesses the attribute of knowledge implies multiplicity. And, following in Mu'tazilite footsteps, the philosophers exaggerated their strict avoidance of plurality to the point of claiming that "if the First were to have a quiddity characterized by existence this would constitute multiplicity". This position is based on the widespread Avicennan view that the "Necessary Existent" is without quiddity (that its essence is none other than its existence). Attributes need a subject to which they are attributed, which is called *al-mawṣūf*. To say that the essence of the First Principle is His intellect, knowledge, power or will is to say that these attributes are self-subsisting. However, it is impossible that the attributes are self-sustaining because they would then be multiple necessary existents, and as Avicenna has shown, this is not possible. Consequently, attributes subsist in the divine essence; and as Ghazālī asserted, the First Principle cannot be denied His attributes, quiddity or reality.[29]

Ghazālī's critique of Avicenna's metaphysics resulted in a dialectical integration of selected *falsafa* notions within the *kalām* tradition. For instance, the celebrated author of the *Book of Religions and Sects* (*Kitāb al-milal wa'l-niḥal*),[30] Muḥammad al-Shahrastānī (d. 1153), was one of the enigmatic theologians who incorporated elements of *falsafa* in his deliberations in *kalām*. Some believe that he was an Ash'arite theologian, given that he was an eminent scholar at the Niẓāmiyya School in Baghdad, while others claim that he practised *taqiyya* (religious dissimulation), and that there are signs of Ismā'īlī influences in his writings, particularly in his *Struggling with the Philosopher* (*Kitāb al-muṣāra'a*).[31] In this text of theosophy, Shahrastānī critically interrogated Avicenna's metaphysical conception of *wājib al-wujūd* (Necessary Being), on the grounds that it entailed a compromising of the observance of absolute divine transcendence (*tanzīh*). Shahrastānī affirmed the reality of the divine attributes without directly applying them to the divine essence, which he believed was absolutely unknowable and indefinable. He also advocated a philosophical conception of a gradation in creation (*khalq*), and argued that the divine Command (*amr*), Words (*kalimāt*) and Letters (*ḥurūf*) are eternal and pre-existent.[32] He also held that the divine Names bear manifestations (*maẓāhir*) in terms of what he referred to as *al-kalimāt al-qawliyya* (verbal allocutions), corresponding with revelation, and *al-kalimāt al-fi'liyya* (active allocutions), which translate into corporeal individuals (*ashkhāṣ*) in the persons of prophets, imams and spiritual guides. He moreover argued that the enunciation of the divine word (*lafẓ al-kalima*) is created, while its inherent meaning or intention (*al-ma'nā al-nafsī*) is eternal.[33] In delimiting the furthest possibilities of theology, and in pointing towards the boundaries of philosophical deliberation, he attempted to effect an equipoise between *'aql* (intellect) and *sam'* (audition of the recitation of the revealed word), whereby, when rational explications reach an end, an attentive *listening* to the recitation of revelation ought to be exercised.[34]

The historical integration of philosophy into theological reflections on the essence–attribute problem found its most pronounced systemic expressions in the legacy of Fakhr al-Dīn al-Rāzī (d. 1209), who, like his predecessor Ghazālī, was an adherent of Shāfi'ī jurisprudence and an exponent of Ash'arī theology. Unlike some early conventional exponents of *kalām*, Rāzī did not reject Greek philosophy, and, as he indicated in his *Oriental Investigations* (*al-Mabāḥith al-Mashriqiyya*), he delved deep into the writings of the ancient philosophers, affirming their true propositions and rejecting the ones that were false.[35] Following Ghazālī's legitimisation of the use of logic, and the acceptance of most of the premises of natural philosophy *qua* natural sciences (*al-'ulūm al-ṭabī'iyya*), Rāzī was an outstanding dialectical *mutakallim* who established his Sunnī theological investigations on philosophical foundations, combining rational proofs (sing. *dalīl 'aqlī*) with scriptural evidences (sing. *dalīl naqlī*). He refuted the anthropomorphism of the Karrāmiyya and the Ḥanbalīs. He doubted the hermeneutic intricacies of the Ismā'īlīs. His engagement with metaphysics was primarily articulated in his critical commentary (*sharḥ*) on Avicenna's *Book of Remarks and Admonitions* (*Kitāb al-Ishārāt wa'l-tanbīhāt*).[36] He also developed his own philosophical notions in his influential theological text *Harvest of the Thought of the Ancients and Moderns* (*Muḥaṣṣal afkār al-mutaqaddimīn wa'l-muta'akhkhirīn*).[37] In addressing the essence–attribute question, Rāzī criticises Avicenna's claim that God knows only universals and not particulars. He thus postulates that knowledge involves a relation *qua* connection (*ta'alluq* rather than *iḍāfa*) between the knower and the known, and that this state of affairs entails that a change in what is known would result in an alteration of the relation *qua* connection that binds it with the knower, rather than producing a transformation in the knower as such.

The examination of the essence–attribute question continued to preoccupy philosophically oriented theologians like the Ash'arite *mutakallim* Sayf al-Dīn al-Āmidī (d. 1233), the author of *Novel Thoughts on the Fundamentals of Religion* (*Abkār al-afkār fī uṣūl al-dīn*),[38] a text that impacted upon the intellectual development of another Ash'arite thinker, 'Abd al-Raḥmān al-Ījī (d. 1355). For instance, Ījī's *Stations in the Science of Theology* (*Kitāb al-Mawāqif fī 'ilm al-kalām*), which constituted a *Summa Theologiae* of its era, and was principally based on Rāzī's *Harvest* and Āmidī's *Novel Thoughts*, continued to be used until modern times as a textbook of theology at al-Azhar University in Cairo. Furthermore, al-Sayyid al-Sharīf 'Alī ibn Muḥammad al-Jurjānī (d. 1413) wrote an influential commentary (*sharḥ*) on Ījī's *Stations*, while reinforcing his own theology with *falsafa*. Al-Jurjānī was also a challenger of the theological authority of al-Taftazānī (d. 1390), a student of Ījī who combined Māturīdism and Ash'arism in developing the anti-Mu'tazilite arguments of the Sunnī tradition in *kalām*, particularly in the course of his commentaries on the legacy of Najm al-Din al-Nasafī (d. 1142).[39] Taftazānī argued that the divine words were uncreated, and that they resided in the divine essence, even though they are written in the volumes, preserved in the hearts, heard by the ears and recited by the tongues. The Qur'an as God's speech is also uncreated (*ghayr makhlūq*), while its enunciation (*lafẓiyya*) is not eternal. He moreover affirmed that divine speech is not of the genus of letters and sounds, and is rather one of *eight* divine attributes (*ṣifāt*) from all eternity besides omniscience (*'ilm*), power (*qudra*), life (*ḥayāt*), hearing (*sam'*), sight (*baṣar*), will (*irāda*) and creation (*khalq*: differing in this from the customary *kalām* theses by adding *khalq* to the other seven attributes).[40]

HERMENEUTICS AND GOD'S ESSENCE AND ATTRIBUTES

God's words find expression in language by virtue of which they are communicatively preserved in the supplements of writing and recitation: "*Read!* In the Name of thy Lord" (96:1). However, the divine words, which are expressed phonetically and graphically, are not necessarily appropriated by the anthropocentric nature of language, nor are they readily measurable by its grammatical-logical criteria. Religiously, the divine words are not semantically exhausted; their meaning remains open to indeterminate interpretations, without being reduced to a univocal sense, either in literal readings, or in the esoteric folds of allegory or metaphor. The revealed word finds its trace in a language that acts as a supplemental image to what is eternal. By their concealed character, and their withdrawal from anthropocentric appropriation, the divine words reveal language as being what is not at our disposal, or of our mere authorship. The Prophet was called upon in revelation to read and to deliver the message, to rise and warn: "Nor does he speak of his own desire" (53:3). The divine Word exposes the insufficiency of anthropocentric measures, and this reveals the Book as being unlike any text. In this sense, no principle of analogy between human language and divine "Language" is readily conceivable. As with the attributes, no human similitude is to be implied, given that analogy is stamped herein by anthropocentricity. Based on this, the revealed scripture cannot be coherently interpreted in the sheltering of its integral "sacredness" by simply using the methods of human textuality. God's words are religiously approached by way of acceptance (*qubūl*) "without why or how", while being recited and memorised. Nevertheless, any reading is already interpretive, and is determined by projective conceptual foresights or intellective prejudices, which frame doctrinal disputations. This calls for the strictness and restraint that are manifested in the adherence to the literal sense of scripture. This is especially the case when no reasons arise to hold that this sense is not adequate; and yet these reasons are often central. One salient instance where a literal sense may mislead is where it implies that the divine qualities are anthropomorphic. Accepting the literal meaning may express a declared conviction associated with the testimonial attestation to the truth of revelation. Yet such a religious mood and attitude need not force a disclosure of the literal meaning in anthropocentric terms. God's words, in their literality, are not simply posited as utterances of human idioms. Their literal sense must be received with thoughtfulness, by recognising with integrity the fragility of our readings, since "none knows its interpretation save God" (3:7). Regarding allegorical interpretations, these have generally proceeded from the hypothesis that literal meanings are misleadingly anthropocentric. Yet from a philosophical standpoint, language itself is mysteriously neither of our own mere human doing, nor simply subordinate to our skill. Furthermore, caution and sound judgement must be exercised in any attempt at resolving the ambiguous verses of the Qur'an (*al-mutashābihāt*) because of the need to avoid dissension (*fitna*).

Although the question concerning God's essence and attributes has primarily remained a classical *madrasa* problem that has been peripheral to modern reformist deliberations, it nevertheless confronts us with exacting metaphysical riddles. Attempts to advance a definite thesis in this regard are likely to be part of a call for a conversion to one doctrine or another. The atmosphere is one of ideological indoctrination preoccupied with historicity rather than a commitment to the uncanny realities of this question. This should, as a minimum, be replaced with a restraint in taking conclusive positions, and by resisting intellective haste, given that the doctrinal unfolding of this question did not always maintain, with purity, the indeterminacy, indecision, openness and submission that befit a genuine experience of the holy.

Further reading

Allard, Michel, *Le problème des attributs divins dans la doctrine d'al-Ash'arī et de ses premiers grands disciples* (Beirut, 1965).
Avicenna, *Metaphysica of Avicenna*, tr. Parviz Morewedge (New York, 1973).
al-Bukhārī, *Kitāb al-jāmi' al-ṣaḥīḥ*, partial tr. by Muhammad Asad as *The Early Years of Islam* (Gibraltar, 1981).
Ess, Josef Van, *Die Erkenntnislehre des 'Adudaddīn al-Īcī* (Wiesbaden, 1966).
The Flowering of Muslim Theology (Cambridge MA: 2006).
al-Ghazālī, Abū Ḥāmid, *The Incoherence of the Philosophers*, tr. Michael E. Marmura (Provo, UT, 1997).
Gimaret, Daniel, *La doctrine d'al-Ash'arī* (Paris, 1990).
Graham, William A., "Qur'an as Spoken Word", in Richard C. Martin (ed.), *Approaches to Islam in Religious Studies* (Tucson, 1985).
Laoust, Henri, *Le précis de droit d'Ibn Qudāma* (Damascus, 1950).
La profession de foi d'Ibn Baṭṭa (Damascus, 1958).
Wisnovsky, Robert, "One aspect of the Avicennian turn in Sunnī theology", *Arabic Sciences and Philosophy* 14 (2004), pp. 65–100.

Notes

1. Daniel Gimaret, *La doctrine d'al-Ash'arī* (Paris: 1990), pp. 240–1.
2. Ibn Abī Ya'lā ibn al-Farrā', *Ṭabaqāt al-Ḥanābila* (Damascus, 1350/1931), pp. 12, 24, 41, 62–3, 78–82, 101–2, 115, 125, 204, 217, 238, 240, 247, 276.
3. Ibid., p. 311.
4. Ibid., pp. 134–5.
5. Ibid., p. 325.
6. Ibn Badrān al-Dimashqī, *al-Madkhal ilā madhhab al-imām Aḥmad Ibn Ḥanbal* (Cairo, 1919), pp. 7–10, 12–14.
7. Isḥāq ibn Ibrāhīm al-Nīsābūrī, *Masā'il al-imām Aḥmad ibn Ḥanbal*, ed. Zuhayr al-Shāwīsh (Beirut, 1979), p. 60. The strictures of traditionalists with respect to the practice of *ijtihād* and *ta'wīl* also found radical expressions in the legacy of Muwaffaq al-Din Ibn Qudāma (d. 1223) in his *Taḥrīm al-naẓar fī kutub ahl al-kalām* (*The Censure of Speculative Theology*), ed. and tr. George Makdisi (London, 1962).
8. Abū Manṣūr al-Māturīdī, *Sharḥ al-fiqh al-akbar* (Hyderabad, 1948), p. 6.

9. Māturīdī, *Sharḥ*, p. 15; Abū al-Ḥasan al-Ash'arī, *Kitāb al-ibāna 'an uṣūl al-diyāna* (Hyderabad, 1948), p. 38.
10. Māturīdī, *Sharḥ*, pp. 18–19.
11. Maghnisāwī, as noted in ibid., p. 36.
12. Ibid., pp. 41, 57, 69.
13. Laoust, Henri, *La profession de foi d'Ibn Baṭṭa* (Damascus: 1958), pp. 57–8, 87.
14. "We believe in it; all is from our Lord" (3:7).
15. Gimaret, *Doctrine d'al-Ash'arī*, pp. 211–12.
16. Michel Allard, *Le problème des attributs divins dans la doctrine d'al-Ash'arī* (Beirut, 1965), p. 199.
17. al-Ash'arī, *Kitāb al-luma'*, ed. Ḥammūda Ghurāba (Cairo, 1955), p. 9.
18. Ibid., p. 20.
19. Ibid., p. 24.
20. Ibid., pp. 24–6.
21. Ibid., pp. 28–31.
22. Ibn Sīnā, *Kitāb al-shifā': Metaphysics*, II, ed. G. C. Anawati, Ibrahim Madkour and Sa'id Zayed (Cairo, 1975), p. 36.
23. Ibn Sīnā, *Metaphysica of Avicenna*, tr. Parviz Morewedge (New York, 1973), p. 43.
24. Ibn Sīnā, *Kitāb al-Hidāya*, ed. Muḥammad 'Abduh (Cairo, 1874), pp. 262–3; Sālim Mashrān, *al-Jānib al-ilāhī 'inda Ibn Sīnā* (Damascus, 1992), p. 99; Ibn Sīnā, *Shifā'*, p. 354.
25. Abū Ḥāmid al-Ghazālī, *The Incoherence of the Philosophers*, tr. Michael E. Marmura (Provo, UT, 1997), p. 97.
26. Ibid., pp. 98, 109.
27. Ibid., pp. 99–100.
28. Ibid., pp. 101–4.
29. Ibid., pp. 105–10.
30. Muḥammad ibn 'Abd al-Karīm al-Shahrastānī, *Kitāb al-milal wa'l-niḥal* (*Livre des religions et des sectes*), tr. Daniel Gimaret and Guy Monnot, 2 vols. (Paris, 1986–93).
31. al-Shahrastānī, *Kitāb al-muṣāra'a* (*Struggling with the Philosopher: A Refutation of Avicenna's Metaphysics)*, ed. and tr. Wilferd Madelung and Toby Mayer (London, 2001).
32. al-Shahrastānī, *Nihāyat al-iqdām fī 'ilm al-kalām: The Summa Philosophiae of Shahrastani*, ed. with partial tr. Alfred Guillaume (Oxford, 1934), p. 316.
33. Ibid., p. 320.
34. Guy Monnot, "Shahrastānī", *Encyclopedia of Islam*, 2nd edn, 12 vols. (Leiden, 1986–2004), IX, pp. 214–16.
35. Fakhr al-Dīn al-Rāzī, *al-Mabāḥith al-mashriqiyya* (Hyderabad, 1924), I, p. 4.
36. For instance, Rāzī attempted to refute the philosophical Neoplatonist emanation principle that from Unity only unity issues forth (*ex uno non fit nisi unum*).

37. Fakhr al-Dīn al-Rāzī, *Muḥaṣṣal afkār al-mutaqaddimīn wa'l-muta'akhkhirīn min al-'ulamā' wa'l-ḥukamā' wa'l-mutakallimīn* (Cairo, 1323/1905).
38. Sayf al-Dīn al-Āmidī, *Abkār al-afkār fī uṣūl al-dīn*, ed. Aḥmad Muḥammad al-Mahdī (Cairo, 2004).
39. Sa'd al-Dīn al-Taftazānī, *Sharḥ al-'aqā'id al-Nasafiyya* (*A Commentary on the Creed of Islam*), ed. and tr. Earl Edgar Elder (New York, 1950).
40. Taftazānī, *Sharḥ*, p. 78ff.

7 Creation

DAVID B. BURRELL CSC

"Originator (*Badī'*) of the heavens and earth. When He decrees a thing, He says only 'Be!' And it is."

(Qur'an 2:117)[1]

There are eight names for God, among the canonical ninety-nine, which direct our attention to Allah as the source of all that is: *al-Badī'* (Absolute Cause), *al-Bāri'* (Producer), *al-Khāliq* (Creator), *al-Mubdi'* (Beginner), *al-Muqtadir* (All-Determiner), *al-Muṣawwir* (Fashioner), *al-Qādir* (All-Powerful) and *al-Qahhār* (Dominator), each with various connotations of creating.[2] Nothing seems simpler than identifying the one God as creator of all that is; indeed, that has ever been the preferred route for calling attention to the fact of divinity, as in the so-called "proofs" that there is a God. And understandably, since the standing link between such a One and everything else is its origin in that One, so that originary fact connects the revelations proper to each Abrahamic faith tradition with everything we encounter: "the heavens and the earth", as well as the human speculation which attends everything that surrounds us, and especially ourselves as the portion of creation impelled to that speculation. Moreover, when one is urged by those revelations to make the fantastic attestation of a single creator of all, what results is an ontological divide between the one creator and everything else. For if the God of Abraham can be defined, as Thomas Aquinas does at the outset of his *Summa Theologiae*, as "the beginning and end of all things, and especially of rational creatures", that lapidary formula has but one clear implication: God is not one of those things, and this affirmation sums up Islamic *tawḥīd*.[3] For confessing divine unity (*tawḥīd*) entails removing all so-called "gods" from the world; indeed, replacing them all with One whose originating relation to the universe will never cease to occupy thinkers in each of these traditions, as an enduring testimony to the utter uniqueness of the attestation "There is no God but God", its novelty and its intractability in human discourse. Yet as congruent as this affirmation may be to human reason, by contrast to a mythological proliferation of gods, it will also prove to be its stumbling-block, and so testify that its corollary, creation, must properly be rooted in revelation.

This proposed account of various Muslim understandings of creation will corroborate that intractability, as diverse schools of thought stumble in their attempts to articulate the unique relation introduced by the simple assertion, "God says 'Be!' and it is." The conceptual conundra follow from the ontological divide which the "fact" of creation introduces: if God is not one of the things which God creates, what sort of a thing is God? No *sort* of thing, of course, so the initial task will be properly to distinguish this one God from all else. Yet doing that will involve adapting categories from human speculation to this unprecedented task, for the very drive to unity which human reason displays has not proved able, of itself, to attain the celebrated "distinction" which *tawḥīd* and its corollary, creation, demand.[4] Yet unsurprisingly, that same distinction will turn out to defy proper conceptualisation, as the various attempts to adapt the categories of human speculation will testify, so there will be no one Muslim account of creation. And the burden of this chapter will be to show that there can be no fully adequate account, so the plurality of accounts is less a sign of the inadequacy of Muslim thinkers to their task than it is of their fidelity to the founding revelation of their tradition: to *tawḥīd* and its corollary, creation. For irony reigns here: any pretension to have articulated the founding relation adequately will have reduced that relation to one comprehensible to us, and so undermine and nullify the distinction expressed by *tawḥīd*, the heart of this tradition. The stumbling-block which *tawḥīd* becomes as one tries to render it conceptually may be identified by its sharp edges: everything which is not God comes forth from God yet cannot exist without God, so how are they distinct when they cannot be separated? If God is eternal and everything else temporal, how does the act of creating bridge that chasm? If God alone properly exists, and everything else exists by an existence derived from divine existence, how *real* are the things we know? And the clincher: if God makes everything else to be, including human actions, how can our actions be properly our own? That is, how can we be responsible for what God makes to be? How can God's actions, in other words, be imputed to us? And if they cannot, to what end is the Qur'an a warning and a guide? This last conundrum proved to be the crux because it directly affects human lives, and also seems to prove that any metaphysical account which tries to be faithful to the original revelation will end up undermining the point of that very revelation. So unless that sharp edge is negotiated, there could be no room for Islamic theology, properly speaking, but only for the preachers' insistence on the bare assertions of revelation in the face of an uncomprehending philosophical ethos. That is the formula for what we have come to call "fundamentalism", of course; yet while one can identify the tendency in Islam, we shall see that it represents a marginal cul-de-sac in the rich territory of Muslim reflection on the intractable legacy of *tawḥīd* and creation. What Islam has missed is a single towering figure among the plurality of intellectual traditions (or "schools"), and that may well be accounted for by the vast difference between ways of organising and supporting scholarship in the Jewish, Christian and Muslim worlds. Yet as we negotiate our way from one school to another, the capacity given us to read between them may help us find a rich fertility in that absence.

The question elicited by the straightforward insistence that "God says 'Be!' and it is" will require, of course, all the philosophical sophistication one can muster, yet Islamic thought can too readily divide into *kalām* ("theology") and *falsafa* ("philosophy"). Two notable exceptions to this apparent polarisation in the Sunnī world were Ghazālī and Fakhr al-Dīn al-Rāzī, whose familiarity with the thought of Islamic "philosophers" is evident. Yet the clear division between *kalām* and *falsafa* may also be one of those illusions created by handy teaching devices, as we look far back across cultural divides. Just as masters of the arts faculties and of theological faculties in medieval Paris can be distinguished by their different preoccupations, so can these two groups of Islamic thinkers (or for that matter those who self-identify as "philosophers" or "religious thinkers" today), yet their intellectual cultures were bound to intersect. This chapter, then, will proceed by identifying those issues which tended to preoccupy a specific group, as those preoccupations came to direct their respective treatments of creation, and so add yet another dimension to the intellectual tracery emanating from that lapidary qur'anic pronouncement: "God said 'Be!' and it is." A roughly chronological treatment is inevitable, given that earlier thinkers often prepared the ground for later reflection, yet the shadow of Hegel can all too easily obscure real differences in favour of an ineluctable "development". So our treatment will consciously proceed both diachronically and synchronically, calling attention to the points where concerns intersect, and where recognisable tendencies display complementary aspects of the relation between a creator God and creation itself. Here Ian Netton's formulation of "the Qur'ānic Creator Paradigm", as he puts it, can usefully guide our inquiry by forming the undeniable setting for further conceptual quandaries. It "embraces a God who (1) creates *ex nihilo*; (2) acts definitively in historical time; (3) guides His people in such time; and (4) can in some way be known indirectly by His creation".[5] It should be clear how many philosophical conundra lurk in each of these assertions. What is it to create? How does an eternal God act in time? How can divine guidance be carried out and received? What are the ways in which created things can entice a created intellect to some knowledge of their divine source? As we canvas the usual groupings of Islamic thinkers reflecting on such matters – *kalām*, *falsafa* and *ishrāq* – we shall not lose sight of the fact that those whom history has put in one camp or another were all concerned to parse the four compass points of the paradigm.

SCHOOLS OF *KALĀM*

Early Islamic reflection on these matters (broadly identified with the Mu'tazilites) emanated from Basra. Mu'tazilism in this period was not demonstrably the result of Hellenic influence, and was probably an indigenous Islamic development connected with local grammatical and linguistic speculation. These Mu'tazilites starkly contrasted the creator God with everything else, including the Qur'an itself. Since the being of the One has neither beginning nor end, existence belongs to God essentially.[6] But how is that existence bestowed on things which come into existence and depart from it? Put even more finely: how can the existence of things we encounter be traced to its source in the one creator? These early thinkers were reluctant to adopt a view of substance which would have been consonant with Aristotelian thought, whereby things enjoy a consistency (by virtue of the formal cause inherent in them) and an internal dynamic (by virtue of their inherent final cause), perhaps fearing for the resultant consistency of a cosmos which failed to display its provenance from a unitary source. So they identified substance with primitive atoms, notwithstanding Aristotle's trenchant critique of indivisible physical particles as oxymoronic. Rather in the spirit of Leucippus, they saw what Aristotle took to be paradigmatically substances, large-scale living things capable of generating their kind, to be configurations of primitive "substances", called "atoms", to underscore their primitive metaphysical status. What the creator created, then, would be the atoms, while the configurations indicate the various ways in which that creation is conserved in being. So the actual configuration of the manifold possibilities of atomic arrangement best displays the agency proper to the creator, which must be immediate and so cannot be identified with the causal chains which operate in the created universe.

For they understood "cause" in the Greek manner, as a virtual synonym with "reason" and "condition", thus implying a systemic treatment. But the one creator cannot be part of the cosmic system, so (in Richard Frank's words) "the programmed sequence of sufficient causes and fulfilled conditions represented in the causation of the *'illa* and *asbāb* does not offer an adequate model for an explanation of the grounding of the possible that exists, i.e., does not give an adequate account of ... its original possibility and the ground of its actuality in being".[7] Creation must be *sui generis* since the creator is. They were to find an analogue of God's activity in creating, however, in the free actions of human beings, whom the Qur'an demanded to be the true initiators of their actions, for otherwise they could not rightly be held accountable for them. This analogy quickly became an identification, equating authentic agency with creating, an identification which was to help bring about the demise of this school. The contrast of agency with causality would become even more significant, however, in contrasting the later *kalām* thinkers (Ghazālī and Rāzī) with philosophical accounts of origination.

Identifying acting with creating gave the Mu'tazilites a way of keeping the divine agent from being ensnared in evil, as well as of justifying the rewards and punishments promised in the Qur'an to creatures who perpetrate good or evil acts. The key belief here is that God must be able to be justified in whatever God does, and so can in no way be associated with evil, nor can divine justice be arbitrary. It is the presence of this conceptual framework bridging the divide between Creator and creature which a trained Mu'tazilite, al-Ash'arī, will question as he proceeds to found the successor school which bears his name. Two signal implications of the school of his formation can be identified, which also explain why Ash'arism quickly became identified with the consensus position in Sunnī Islam. The first was the stark insistence on the fact that everything which is not God must be created, including the Qur'an itself. Apparently a simple corollary to the *shahāda*'s witnessing that there can be no God but God, this uncompromising teaching unfortunately left Islam with a mute divinity, so it seemed far preferable to grasp the nettle and affirm God's Word to be coeternal with God. In the political climate of Baghdad, blood was initially spilt over this view, but it held firm. The identification of acting with creating, however, instigated an unending debate, which has not yet been decisively settled. For if any authentic action, be it of creator or of creature, must be tantamount to an unconditioned origination, or creation, then the actions of creatures must be attributed to them alone, unduly restricting the sovereignty of the creator of all by removing all deliberate human actions from His purview. Such a restriction hardly befits the qur'anic divinity and directly contradicts the qur'anic creator paradigm. Some other way, therefore, must be found to conciliate divine sovereignty with human responsibility, and much of the ingenuity of the Ash'arite school will be absorbed in this endeavour. The more significant shift by Ash'arī which became imbedded in Sunnī orthodoxy, however, is that which denies an overarching conceptual scheme for creator and creature. As Daniel Gimaret puts it, nothing can be obligatory for God, for there is no one above Him to whom He is accountable.[8] So the recompense accorded to the faithful is always pure favour, on God's part; moreover, should God be obliged to reward us in a patterned way, we would have no obligation to be grateful to Him.[9] One might ask, of course, whether God does not owe whatever God does to God's own self (cf. Qur'an 6:12), but it seems that the Ash'arites were reluctant to pursue questions which led into the very constitution of divinity. What resulted seemed to be a creator for whom will predominated over wisdom, however; something which later *kalām* theologians like Ghazālī and Rāzī would work to correct. The scheme which the Ash'arites proposed to conciliate divine sovereignty over all things with human responsibility, so that actions created by God could nonetheless be imputed to human agents, turned on a novel adaptation of the qur'anic expression *kasb*, and its cognate form *iktisāb*. Its lexical meaning is "acquisition", so that one may say that human beings *acquire* the actions which God creates. (Richard Frank, however, has proposed a more functional translation, "performance", according to which human beings perform the actions which God creates.[10])

One might regard this ploy as a way of properly parsing created action, without questioning the Mu'tazilite identification of acting with creating. Any created action takes place by a power created in the human person who actually performs the act, since the causality of the created agent is not sufficient to determine the entire reality of the act, notably, its very existence. So given the identification of acting with creating, it must be said that God alone is the agent (*fā'il*), determining through a created power (*qudra*) the individual existence of each act in all its particulars. Yet "the act is created as belonging to another, not by God as His own act", so one may also say that "the act is the act of the ... subject in which it is realised as an act".[11] There is, of course, an unavoidable ambiguity in the use of "act" here, as this school struggles to articulate a notion of created agency, which Frank suggests might be disambiguated by rendering the human role as the performance of an action created by God. As should be evident, this ploy is also designed to meet the Mu'tazilite concern to remove all trace of the perpetration of evil from the creator of all: the action created by God cannot, however, be predicated of God (by saying that God did it), but must be imputed to the one performing it. What sounds like double-talk can be explained as an attempt to formulate the relation between creating agent and created agent, using the crude instrument of a created power to perform this act (*qudra*). A comprehensive study of the work of the Egyptian reformer Muḥammad 'Abduh (1849–1905) and his disciple, Rashīd Riḍā (1865–1935), in their modernist qur'anic commentary *The Beacon* (*al-Manār*) (itself intended as a continuing elaboration of the Sunnī position on these matters), pinpoints the key issue as the relation between created and uncreated agents: "By their acquisition [*kasb*], human beings are indeed autonomous agents, yet hardly independent; they are only agents because God wills it and creates them as free agents." Riḍā underscores the non-concurrence of these two concepts: creation and the created free act.[12] So a coherent presentation of the intent of the Ash'arite analysis will require a semantics able to account for the inherently analogous sense of "act", "action", and "acting". Yet such a presentation might also applaud one implication of that analysis for ethics: actions as properly described are what they are, and so retain (as the actions they are) their orientation towards or away from the properly human good. In this sense the actions we perform can indeed be said to be "created by God" in the sense that we are unable to change them into something else by evasive descriptions which seek to accommodate our wishes at the moment of performing them. Indeed, one might well discern these ethical echoes in the overtly theological overtones of continuing Islamic discussions of human life and action.

Another strain of *kalām* reasoning can be identified as Māturīdism, being traceable to Abū Manṣūr al-Māturīdī's *Book of Affirming God's Oneness* (*Kitāb al-Tawḥīd*).[13] Originating in the region of Samarkand, this school was continued by others, and offered itself as the doctrine of Abū Ḥanīfa, thus imbibing the spirit of one of the four schools of Muslim law. In essence, this school tended to reaffirm the twin assertions that "human beings are truly the agents of their actions, while these actions are at the same time created by God".[14] Their insistence that the divine act of *takwīn*, or bringing into existence, is eternal, and so to be distinguished from existing things, became a point of controversy with Ash'arism, as did their understandable avoidance of the ambiguous language of *kasb*/*iktisāb* to account for free created actions of human beings. Yet for our purposes they cannot be said to have contributed much further clarification regarding the analogous uses of "act" or "action", which could have helped to articulate the relation of creaturely free actions to that freedom proper to the creator. This mode of approach to the question, however, may have paved the way for Ghazālī's approach to these questions, and his cautious observations regarding two senses of "act" and "agent". Yet before considering Ghazālī and Razī, as later *kalām* figures, we should briefly review the "philosophers" with whom they expressly interacted.

THE *FALĀSIFA* ON ORIGINATION

The clearest picture here is given by Fārābī, whose adaptation of Plotinus' Neoplatonic scheme whereby all things emanate from the One offered an enticing model for articulating the qur'anic creator paradigm.[15] (It was also his commentary on Aristotle's *Metaphysics* which succeeded in unlocking its secrets for Avicenna.[16]) In the spirit of Plato's *Republic*, Fārābī's *Virtuous City* holds up the pattern of cosmic origination for the ideal leader of a human polity to emulate. The leader whom he has in mind, of course, is the Prophet, and the cosmic scheme displays the source of the Prophet's authority: an intellectual emanation from the unique source of being and of truth. Indeed, what distinguishes the Messenger of God from Plato's "philosopher king", now overtly recast in Neoplatonic terms, is that the divine emanation reaches well beyond his intellect into his imagination, so that the idiom of the Qur'an will not be limited to those who have undergone a rigorous intellectual training, but is eminently comprehensible to all who hear it. Yet by adopting the emanation scheme to model creation, these thinkers were carried into a set of presuppositions which proved to be at variance with the creator paradigm they sought to use the scheme to articulate. Indeed, the very logical elegance which attracted philosophical spirits to the emanation scheme would prove inimical to parsing the key phrase "God says 'Be!' and it is." For the controlling dictum "from one only one can come" clearly bespeaks the logical character of the model, so that the One from whom all things come will be assimilated to the unitary and immensely fruitful grounding axiom of a system from which the rest of the premises ineluctably follow. For all this, however, it remains a model, so we need not think of this One as an axiom, but could endow It with the rich intentionality of the very One who bestowed the Qur'an through Muḥammad. Yet models have an inner logic as well, so the intentionality of the source could not extend to freedom of action without contradicting the very logical elegance which had recommended it in the first place.

These tensions were soon to emerge with respect to specific questions, such as the relation of this timeless emanation to time: has the universe always been or is there an initial moment of time which marks its beginning? Must the dictum 'from one only one can come", which determined a step-wise emanation following the actual cosmological pattern of the nine planets, dictate a mediated origination of all things from the One? Can such a One ever be without the universe emanating from it? Merely posing questions like these allows any serious inquirer to query the effort of these thinkers to assimilate the qur'anic creator to this One. So it was only a matter of time before a Ghazālī arose to question the orthodoxy of the Avicenna who had elaborated Fārābī's scheme into a full-blown system for explaining the cosmos. Yet the infelicities of the scheme itself should not obscure its intent: to render an account of the origin of the very being of things. If *kalām* thinkers had been wary of presenting God's activity in creating as *causing* the universe to be, that was because they thought of causation as enmeshing the creator in a system of necessities. That would also be the result of the emanation scheme of the *falāsifa*, of course, yet the philosophers' intent had been to move our minds beyond one who makes individual things come to be, to the very "cause of being", even while the multiple names for a creator in the Qur'an include the Fashioner (*al-Muṣawwir*), which connotes God's shaping each thing as it comes to be. Indeed, an intentional creator who acts freely cannot but be pictured anthropomorphically, and so impedes the intellectual ascent to a "cause of being". So if the concerns surrounding God's freedom to create (with its corollary of utter transcendence), as well as the prophetic insistence on an initial moment of time, were to sideline this mode of thought for Islamic theology and return it to the *kalām* speculation we have seen, something invaluable would have been lost. Yet that is the picture we are often given: in the wake of Ghazālī's *Incoherence*, philosophical inquiry was rendered terminally suspect in Islam.[17] We shall see, however, that there are other Ghazālīs than the one intent on deconstructing the *falsafa* which he saw as threatening the qur'anic creator paradigm. In fact, the constructive Ghazālī felt free (or was intellectually constrained) to incorporate a great deal of Avicenna in his own attempt to articulate the relation of creator to creation, notably under the rubric of *tawḥīd*: faith in the divine unity from which all that is comes to exist. Yet the negative picture of *falsafa* which Ghazālī was supposed to have promulgated in his work of deconstruction could well have been facilitated by the fierce opposition of Averroes to that work, evidenced in his ensuing *The Incoherence of the Incoherence* (*Tahāfut al-Tahāfut*), which contains the entire text of Ghazālī's original work in order to excoriate what nefarious influence it might have. That Averroes' reaction may ironically have had the opposite effect of reinforcing Ghazālī's work of deconstructing *falsafa* for religious purposes can be suggested from the author's inattention to creation, in this or any other work. In fact, it requires a good deal of intellectual probing to determine what creation meant for Averroes, which is perhaps unsurprising given his utter devotion to Aristotle.[18] But how does Ghazālī manage to incorporate the very philosophy he criticised when he proceeds in a more constructive fashion?

LATER *KALĀM* THEOLOGIANS: GHAZĀLĪ AND RĀZĪ

Ghazālī's intellectual and spiritual odyssey, *The Deliverer from Error* (*al-Munqidh min al-ḍalāl*), details his quest for an understanding which will not turn out to have been in vain: either because one has been deluded into believing what is not the case, or by reason of the vanity inherent in learning itself.[19] The first fear is cast in sceptical terms, and permits us to draw parallels with Descartes's *Discourse on Method*; the second addresses a more spiritual issue: what is the point of it all? Reflecting in the wake of his intellectual and professional crisis on his early formation in *kalām*, he notes that those who have engaged in it

> did indeed perform the task assigned them by God: they ably protected orthodoxy and defended the creed which had been readily accepted from the prophetic teaching and boldly counteracted heretical innovation. But in doing so they relied on the premises which they took over from their adversaries, being compelled to admit them either by uncritical acceptance, or because of the Community's consensus, or by simple acceptance [*taqlīd*] deriving from the Qur'an and the Traditions ... This, however, is of little use in the case of one who admits nothing at all except the primary and self-evident truths. So *kalām* was not sufficient in my case, nor was it a remedy for the malady of which I was complaining.[20]

Here the malady can be voiced in sceptical terms, though "one who admits nothing at all except the primary and self-evident truths" could hardly expect a cure in terms so stringent. In fact, as he relates it, even

> accept[ing] the self-evident data of reason and rel[ying] on them with safety and certainty ... was not achieved by constructing a proof or putting together an argument. On the contrary, it was the effect of a

> light which God Most High cast into my breast. And that light is the key to most knowledge. Therefore, whoever thinks that the unveiling of truth depends on precisely formulated proofs has indeed straitened the broad mercy of God.[21]

So it was predictable that Ghazālī would not find what he was looking for in any of the six parts of philosophy either: "mathematical, logical, physical, metaphysical, political, and moral".[22] Nor could he see in the physical sciences the central point of the qur'anic creator paradigm:

> that nature is totally subject to God Most High: it does not act of itself but is used as an instrument by its Creator. The sun, moon, stars, and the elements are subject to God's command: none of them effects any act by and of itself ... [But] it is in the metaphysical sciences that most of the philosophers' errors are found. Owing to the fact that they could not carry out apodeictic demonstrations according to the conditions they had postulated in logic, they differed a great deal about metaphysical questions. Aristotle's doctrine on these matters, as transmitted by Fārābī and Ibn Sīnā, approximates the teachings of the Islamic philosophers. But the sum of their errors comes down to twenty heads, in three of which they must be taxed with unbelief, and in seventeen with innovation.[23]

To accuse someone of unbelief (*kufr*) in an Islamic society was a stark judgement, which could result in banishment or death for one found guilty; innovation (*bid'a*) was far less stringent a charge. The positions which Ghazālī deemed tantamount to unbelief were "[1] that men's bodies will not be assembled on the Last Day ... [2] their declaration: 'God Most High knows universals, but not particulars' ... when 'there does not escape from Him the weight of an atom in the heavens or in the earth' (Qur'an 34:3), [and 3] their maintaining the eternity of the world, past and future".[24]

Yet it will not suffice to be disillusioned with philosophers who had been brought to contradict divine revelation; one must go on to ascertain the truth of that revelation in ways which the philosophers have been unable to do. So the dimensions of his crisis moved well beyond that of scepticism, and demanded of him a pilgrimage whose "beginning ... was to sever my heart's attachments to the world by withdrawing from this abode of delusion and turning to the mansion of immortality and devoting myself with total ardour to God".[25] Now he would address the second and more telling fear: that life (and especially the life of inquiry) has no point at all. Realising that this would demand a total disengagement from his work and status, he vacillated for six months until "the matter passed from choice to compulsion", so that the renowned teacher found himself

> completely unable to say anything. As a result that impediment of speech caused a sadness in my heart accompanied by an inability to digest; food and drink became unpalatable to me ... Then, when I perceived my powerlessness, and when my capacity to make a choice had completely collapsed, I had recourse to God.[26]

Entering Damascus and residing there for nearly two years,

> my only occupation was seclusion and solitude and spiritual exercise ... with a view to devoting myself to the purification of my soul and the cultivation of virtues and cleansing my heart for the remembrance of God Most High, in the way I had learned from the writings of the Sufis.[27]

In consequence, "what became clear to me of necessity from practicing their Way was the true nature and special character of prophecy".[28] That is, faith in divine revelation is a form of knowing as well, though it is hardly self-evident but requires sustained efforts at purification. After engaging in these, he can insist: "I believe with a faith as certain as direct vision that there is no might for me and no power save in God, the Sublime, the Mighty; and that it was not I who moved, but He moved me; and that I did not act, but He acted through me."[29] It is this conviction, founded in his own pilgrimage, which he will extend to the cosmos as well: what faith in divine unity (*tawḥīd*) effectively means is that "there is no power or might but in God". Yet he did not turn to *kalām* occasionalism to make this point philosophically; he rather had recourse to a model close to that of Avicenna's, though grounded in the *sunnat Allāh*, the order bestowed on the universe by its free creator.[30] That ordering permits a fresh approach to causality, as evidenced in the following portion from his section on "Faith in Divine Unity and Trust in Divine Providence" in his *Revival*:[31]

> Now you may object: how can there be any common ground between faith in divine unity and the *sharī'a*? For the meaning of faith in divine unity is that there is no agent but God Most High, and the meaning of the law lies in establishing the actions proper to human beings [as servants of God]. And if human beings are agents, how is it that God Most High is an agent? Or if God Most High is an

agent, how is a human being an agent? There is no way of understanding "acting" as between these two agents. In response, I would say: indeed, there can be no understanding when there is but one meaning for "agent." But if it had two meanings, then the term comprehended could be attributed to each of them without contradiction, as when it is said that the emir killed someone, and also said that the executioner killed him; in one sense, the emir is the killer and in another sense, the executioner. Similarly, a human being is an agent in one sense, and God is an agent in another. The sense in which God Most High is agent is that He is the originator[32] of existing things [*mukhtari' al-mawjūd*], while the sense in which a human being is an agent is that he is the locus [*maḥall*] in which power is created after will has been created after knowledge has been created, so that power depends on will, and action is linked to power, as a conditioned to its condition. But depending on the power of God is like the dependence of effect on cause, and of the originated on the originator. So everything which depends on a power in such a way as it is the locus of the power is called "agent" in a manner which expresses that fact of its dependence, much as the executioner and the emir can each be called "killer," since the killing depends on the power of both of them, yet in different respects. In that way both of them are called "killer," and similarly, the things ordained [*maqrūrāt*] depend on two powers ... So the Most High clarifies it, saying: "You [Muslims] did not kill them, but God killed them," and further: "You [Muḥammad] did not throw when you threw, but God threw" (8:17). On the surface this amounts to a denial and an affirmation together, but its meaning is: you did not throw in the sense in which the Lord can be said to throw, since you threw in the sense in which it belongs to a human to throw – and the two senses are different.

So it is that "acting" is fraught with different senses, and these meanings are not contradictory once you understand [that fact] ... Anyone who relates all there is to God Most High is unquestionably one who knows the truth and the true reality, while whoever relates them to what is other than Him is one whose speech is laced with figurative expressions and metaphors. Figurative expression is on one side while true reality is on another, yet the author of language determined the term "agent" to mean the one who originates [*mukhtari'*], so those supposing human beings to be originators call them "agents" according to their power.[33] For they suppose that human beings actualize [*taḥqīq*], so they imagine [*tawahhum*] that "agent" is attributed to God Most High metaphorically, as the killing was attributed [in the example] to the emir, yet metaphorically so when contrasted with that attributed to the executioner. Yet in the measure that the truth is revealed to those inquiring, they will know that things are quite the opposite, and they will say: O linguist, you have posited the term "agent" to signify the one who originates, but [in that sense] there is no agent but God, so the term belongs properly to Him and metaphorically to whatever is other than Him. That is, you must bear with the way in which linguists have determined it …

You may still object: it is now clear that all is coerced [*jabr*]. But if so, what can these mean: reward or punishment, anger or complete approval [*riḍā*]?[34] How can He be angry at His own deed? You should know that we have already indicated the meaning of that in the Book of Thanksgiving [Book 32 of the *Revival*], so we will not proceed to a long repetition here. For this has to do with the divine decree [*qadar*], intimations of which we saw with respect to the faith in divine unity which brings about the state of trust in divine providence, and is only perfected by faith in the benevolence and wisdom [of God]. And if faith in divine unity brings about insight into the effects of causes, abundant faith in benevolence is what brings about confidence in the effects of the causes, and the state of trust in divine providence will only be perfected, as I shall relate, by confidence in the trustee [*wakīl*] and tranquillity of heart towards the benevolent oversight of the [divine] sponsor. For this faith is indeed an exalted chapter in the chapters of faith, and the stories about it from the path of those experiencing the unveiling go on at length. So let us simply mention it briefly: to wit, the conviction of the seeker in the station of faith in divine unity, a conviction held firmly and without any doubt: [that] all this happens according to a necessary and true order, according to what is appropriate as it is appropriate and in the measure that is proper to it; nor is anything more fitting, more perfect, and more attractive within the realm of possibility[35] … Now this is another sea immensely deep, with vast extremities and chaotic swells, nearly as extensive as the sea of faith in divine unity, and the boats of those whose capacity is limited flounder in it, for they do not know that this is something hidden, not to be grasped except by those who know. The lore regarding this sea is the secret of the divine decree which confuses the many, and those to whom it has been unveiled

> are forbidden to disclose its secret. The gist of it is that good and evil are determined by it, and if they were not, then what comes about would have to follow a prior volition in such a way as not to contradict His wisdom and yet not to follow upon His judgment and His command. But everything, small or large, is recorded and carried out by Him according to the divine decree as an object foreseen, and if you were not afflicted you would not make progress, and were you not making progress you would not be afflicted. But let us cut short these allusions to ways of knowing through unveiling which are themselves the basis of the station of trust in divine providence, and return to the knowledge of practices – God Most High willing – and let us praise God.[36]

Ghazālī holds on to what he deems to be the properly grammatical sense of "acting" as "originating" or "creating", yet once the term has been acknowledged to be analogous, then it becomes a matter of which analogate to privilege as primary. The burden of this treatment is to attempt to articulate a created universe in relation to its creator, in the clear recognition that one will be unable to do so properly. For what is paramount is the transcendence of the creator, so that the manner of "determining" by the "divine decree" (*qadar*) remains inexpressible, and hence cannot be read as "determining" in our sense of the term. To be consistent, he will not be able to espouse either the created determining "volition" of Ash'arī or the necessitating scheme of Avicenna, much as he may employ that scheme to illustrate his point of divine ordering. In this case, however, he will be employing it as a metaphor, understanding that divine ordering cannot be comprehended in any human scheme.[37] In the context of the book in question, which responds to Ghazālī's own development, what cannot be articulated conceptually can nonetheless be worked out in the way one lives, so the faith in divine unity (*tawḥīd*) which reminds us forcibly that the prime analogate for "agent" is the creator, can be lived out in a life of trust in divine providence (*tawakkul*).

Rāzī, a century later than Ghazālī, resisted even the use of the terms *kasb* and *iktisāb* to refer to the human contribution to human acts, doubtless on account of their ambiguity, while he also acknowledged that the Qur'an could be cited on all sides of the question, so that rational discourse must prevail.[38] In his case, that amounted to an analysis of human actions in terms of their prevailing causes, summarised in his commentary on Qur'an 6:102: "Creator of all things":

> In this way, conclusive rational proof supports the truth of the literal sense of this verse because action depends on motivation which is

> created by God. And when power and motivation are joined, the action necessarily occurs. Now this requires that God be the Creator of the creatures' acts. And if this conclusive rational proof supports the literal sense, then all problems and ambiguities cease.[39]

Or as Gimaret puts it boldly: "Rāzī does not hesitate to declare himself a Jabrite", given his insistence that "because these acts can be done only if God creates the power and the motivation to do them, the combination of the two necessarily brings about the emanation of the act from the creature".[40] As for the reward for good deeds, he is consistent in holding that God is in no way bound to supply this, thereby returning us to divine generosity and mercy. Evil actions, of course, make the question yet more acute, leading Rāzī to qualify his "Jabrite" position severely:

> It is as though this question is located in a field of contradiction, founded on contrary evidence as well as reasoning regarding the necessity of exalting God in His power as well as His wisdom, affirming His oneness and his exemption from evil; or one simply remains grounded on the proofs issuing from revelation. For these reasons it is a difficult question, at once obscure and deep. Let us ask God Most High to bring us to the truth of it.[41]

LATE MYSTICISM: SUHRAWARDĪ, IBN ʿARABĪ AND MULLĀ ṢADRĀ

If Islamic philosophers point us towards a "cause of being", while later *kalām* thinkers, notably Ghazālī, try to rescue that source-of-all from being enmeshed in causal necessities, what remains to be expressed is the utter uniqueness of the creator/creature relation. The Qur'an had insisted upon it; what idiom can help us to articulate its *sui generis* character? That will be the task of the thinkers who emerged, after the decisive accusations of Ghazālī, to restore Islamic philosophy in the original heartland, the "East", hence its title, *ishrāqī*, picking up the associations of sunrise with illumination. It fell to Shihāb al-Dīn al-Suhrawardī (d. 1191) to introduce a new paradigm for the doing of philosophy.[42] While it is accurate to call that paradigm Platonist rather than Aristotelian, one must also call attention to the way in which spiritual exercises came to be seen as integral to the philosophical inquiry, perhaps under the influence of Ghazālī's *Deliverer* yet also consonant with that dimension of ancient philosophy underscored by Pierre Hadot.[43] The metaphor of light allowed Suhrawardī to account for the emanation of all things from the One in such a way as to finesse the necessitarian implications of Avicenna's scheme while retaining his emphasis on essence. Mullā Ṣadrā reoriented Suhrawardī's legacy so as to give primacy to existence, in the light of the reflections of Ibn 'Arabī, so that creation came to be recognised properly as the bestowal of existing. He puts it succinctly:

> Now contingent beings, [that is, those not necessary in themselves], need something proper to them constituting what they are in themselves [*huwiyyāt*], for should one consider them apart from the One who originates them by that very fact they must be considered to be empty and impossible. [That factor proper to them, then, must be] the act constituted by the One who originates them, much as the quiddity of a composite species is constituted by its difference. For the *ratio* [*ma'nā*] of being an existence which is necessary is that it belongs to it properly to exist, without needing to be united with an originator nor have any receptacle to receive it; while the *ratio* of being an existence which exists [that is, contingent] is that it is something attained, either by itself or by an originator.[44]

It would be fair to say that *existence* (*wujūd*) plays the role which light had played for Suhrawardī, yet by exploiting Avicenna's celebrated distinction of *essence* from *existence* in this way, Mullā Ṣadrā moved the issue beyond the metaphorical, opening a way of seeing the relation of creator to creatures as the One who bestows existence to all-that-is, in such a way that God alone *exists* in Himself, while everything else which exists does so "from God". That emanation need not be "necessary", however, as it had to be for Avicenna, but can be thoroughly intentional; while the relation of everything-that-is to the originating One must be inherent to each thing, and so will be different from any relation within the created universe. The term of art, *non-duality*, seems best suited to express this unique "non-reciprocal relation of dependence", signalling Mullā Ṣadrā's debt to Ibn 'Arabī as well as offering some suggestive connections with Shankara's Hindu idiom as well as that of Thomas Aquinas.[45] Moreover, by moving us into the world of Shī'ite philosophical reflection, Mullā Ṣadrā's suggestive focus on existence helps to round out our survey of models for creation in Islamic theology. If the relation of creator to creatures turns out in the end to escape conceptual articulation, and to require a set of spiritual exercises to move both mind and heart to further enlightenment, that would seem to reflect the nature of this inquiry more accurately.

Further reading

Arnaldez, Roger, "Khalḳ", in *Encyclopedia of Islam*, 2nd edn, 12 vols. (Leiden, 1986–2004), IV, pp. 980–8.

al-Bayḍāwī, 'Abdallāh, *Ṭawāli' al-anwār min maṭāli' al-anẓār*, tr. Edwin E. Calverley and James W. Pollock, *Nature, Man and God in Medieval Islam* (Leiden, 2002), pp. 603–39.

Frank, Richard M., *Creation and the Cosmic System: Al-Ghazālī and Avicenna* (Heidelberg, 1992).

"Two Islamic views of human agency", in George Makdisi *et al.* (eds.), *La notion de liberté au moyen âge: Islam, Byzance, Occident* (Paris, 1985), pp. 37–49.

Al-Ghazālī: The Ninety-Nine Beautiful Names of God, tr. David Burrell and Nazih Daher (Cambridge, 1992).

Gimaret, Daniel, *La doctrine d'al-Ash'arī* (Paris, 1990).

Théories de l'acte humain en théologie musulmane (Paris, 1980).

Nispen tot Sevenaer, Christian van, *Activité humaine et agir de Dieu: le concept de "Sunan de Dieu" dans le commentaire coranique du Manār* (Beirut, 1996).

Notes

1. Parallel texts in the Qur'an: 3:47, 59; 6:73; 16:40; 36:82; 40:68.
2. *Ghazālī: The Ninety-Nine Beautiful Names of God*, tr. David B. Burrell and Nazih Daher (Cambridge, 1992).
3. *Summa Theologiae* 1.1. Prol.
4. Robert Sokolowski, *God of Faith and Reason* (Notre Dame, IN, 1982; Washington, DC, 1990); see David Burrell, "The Christian distinction celebrated and expanded", in *The Truthful and the Good: Essays in Honor of Robert Sokolowski*, ed. John Drummond and James Hart (Dordrecht, 1996), pp. 191–206.
5. Ian Netton, *Allah Transcendent: Studies in the Structure and Semiotics of Islamic Philosophy, Theology and Cosmology* (London, 1989), p. 22. For a critical appreciation of this massively erudite treatise which also calls attention to its pointedness, see Richard Taylor's review in *Middle East Journal* 44 (1990), pp. 521–2.
6. My source here is Richard Frank's detailed account, "*Kalām* and philosophy: a perspective from one problem", in Parviz Morewedge (ed.), *Islamic Philosophical Theology* (Albany, 1979), pp. 71–95, with abundant references to primary sources.
7. Ibid., pp. 78–9.
8. Daniel Gimaret, *La doctrine d'al-Ash'arī* (Paris, 1990), p. 443. On this significant difference, see Richard M. Frank, "Two Islamic views of human agency", in George Makdisi *et al.* (eds.), *La notion de liberté au moyen âge: Islam, Byzance, Occident* (Paris, 1985), pp. 37–49.
9. Gimaret, *La doctrine*, pp. 443, 416.

10. Richard M. Frank, "Moral obligation in classical Islamic theology", *Journal of Religious Ethics* 11 (1983), pp. 204–23, esp. p. 218 n. 19, with Gimaret's rejoinder in *La doctrine*, p. 371, n. 1.
11. Richard M. Frank, "The structure of created causality according to al-Ash'arī", *Studia Islamica* 25 (1966), pp. 13–76; citations at pp. 44, 43.
12. Christian van Nispen tot Sevenaer, *Activité humaine et agir de Dieu: le concept de "Sunan de Dieu" dans le commentaire coranique du Manār* (Beirut, 1996), p. 367. The author signals a key article by Michael Schwarz, "Acquisition [*kasb*] in Early Kalām", in *Islamic Philosophy and the Classical Tradition: Essays presented to Richard Walzer* (Oxford, 1972), pp. 355–87; as well as Richard M. Frank's review of Gimaret's *Théories* (see next note) in *Biblioteca Orientalis* 39 (1982), cols. 705–15.
13. For references to this and other sources, see Daniel Gimaret, *Théories de l'acte humain en théologie musulmane* (Paris, 1980), pp. 175–231; as well as W. Madelung, "al-Māturīdī", in *Encyclopedia of Islam*, 2nd edn, VI, pp. 846–8.
14. Gimaret, *Théories*, p. 179.
15. *Fārābī on the Perfect State*, ed. and tr. Richard Walzer (Oxford, 1985).
16. See the translation by Thérèse-Anne Druart, "Le Traité de Fārābī sur les buts de la *Métaphysique* d'Aristote", *Bulletin de Philosophie Médiévale* 24 (1982), pp. 38–43.
17. al-Ghazālī, *The Incoherence of the Philosophers*, ed. and tr. Michael E. Marmura (Provo, UT, 1997).
18. See Barry Kogan, *Averroës and the Metaphysics of Causation* (Albany, 1985).
19. Richard McCarthy's translation and notes have been reissued as *Ghazālī's Path to Sufism* (Louisville, KY, 2000).
20. Ghazālī, *Deliverer*, in McCarthy, *Ghazālī's Path*, p. 26.
21. Ibid., p. 23.
22. Ibid., p. 31.
23. Ibid., p. 35.
24. Ibid., p. 36.
25. Ibid., p. 53.
26. Ibid., pp. 54–5.
27. Ibid., pp. 55–6.
28. Ibid., p. 59.
29. Ibid., p. 72.
30. For the model, see Richard M. Frank, *Creation and the Cosmic System: Al-Ghazālī and Avicenna* (Heidelberg, 1992); and for an elucidation of *sunnat Allāh*, see Christian van Nispen, *Activité humaine*, part 1, pp. 57–251.
31. *Ghazālī on Faith in Divine Unity and Trust in Divine Providence*, tr. David B. Burrell (Louisville, KY, 2001).
32. This term is not qur'anic, nor is it a name of God; cf. L. P. Fitzgerald, "Creation in *al-Tafsīr al-Kabīr* of Fakhr ad-Dīn al-Rāzī" (PhD dissertation, Australian National University, 1992), p. 34.

33. This assertion regarding the primary meaning of the term "agent" reflects the presumption in Ghazālī's Ash'arite milieu that identified *agency* with the activity of creating.
34. For the sense of *riḍā*, see Marie-Louise Siauve's translation of the *Revival*'s "Book of Love": *Le Livre de l'amour, du désir ardent, de l'intimité et du parfait contentement* (Paris, 1986), pp. 247–68.
35. This is Ghazālī's celebrated claim regarding the universe: that it is "the best possible", a claim whose reception has been examined in detail by Eric Ormsby, *Theodicy in Islamic Thought* (Princeton, NJ, 1984), with a clarifying réprise in "Creation in Time in Islamic Thought with Special Reference to Ghazālī", in David B. Burrell and Bernard McGinn, *God and Creation: An Ecumenical Symposium* (Notre Dame, IN, 1990), pp. 246–64. See also Frank, *Creation*, pp. 60–1.
36. Burrell (tr.), *Ghazālī on Faith in Divine Unity*, p. 276.
37. This is my way of acknowledging Richard Frank's delineation of Ghazālī's extensive use of Avicenna (in his *Creation and the Cosmic System*), while demurring from the necessitarian conclusions he draws in "Currents and countercurrents", in Peter Riddell and Tony Street (eds.), *Islam: Essays on Scripture, Thought and Society: A Festschrift in Honour of Anthony H. Johns* (Leiden, 1997), pp. 113–34.
38. For a detailed treatment of Rāzī, complete with sources, see Gimaret, *Théories*, pp. 134–53.
39. *al-Tafsīr al-Kabīr* to 13:122, tr. in Fitzgerald, "Creation in *al-Tafsīr al-Kabīr*", p. 99.
40. *al-Tafsīr al-Kabīr* to 9:159, tr. in ibid., p. 103; Gimaret, *Théories*, p. 142.
41. *al-Tafsīr al-Kabīr* to 2:52, tr. in Gimaret, *Théories*, p. 153.
42. For Suhrawardī, see John Walbridge and Hossein Ziai's translation and commentary, *The Philosophy of Illumination* (Provo, UT, 1999), as well as Ziai's study of this book, *Knowledge and Illumination* (Atlanta, 1990), and John Walbridge, *Leaven of the Ancients: Suhrawardī and the Heritage of the Greeks* (Albany, 2000).
43. Arnold Davidson has translated key essays of Pierre Hadot in *Philosophy as a Way of Life* (Oxford, 1995). John Walbridge suggests why Sufi practices tended to eclipse natural philosophy as a path for understanding, in his *Leaven of the Ancients*, pp. 215–20.
44. Henry Corbin, *Le livre des pénétrations métaphysiques* (Teheran, 1964), par. 42; see my comparative study, "Thomas Aquinas (1225–1274) and Mullā Ṣadrā Shīrāzī (1572–1640) and the primacy of *esse/wujūd* in philosophical theology", *Medieval Philosophy and Theology* 8 (1999), pp. 207–19.
45. For Ibn 'Arabī, see William C. Chittick, *The Self-Disclosure of God: Principles of Ibn al-'Arabī's Cosmology* (Albany, 1998); for Shankara, see Sara Grant, *Towards an Alternative Theology: Confessions of a Non-dualist Christian*, ed. Bradley Malkovsky (Notre Dame, IN, 2001).

8 Ethics

STEFFEN A. J. STELZER

The end of action is to serve God.

(Ibn Ḥanbal)

Following the Aristotelian example in the field of metaphysics, it is often preferable not to accept received wisdom as to what a discipline is, but, after inquiring into the possibility of its existence, to go instead in search of it. This is certainly advisable in a field like Islamic ethics, where the very concept of such a science has not originated in the place in which one looks for its manifestation. In this case, instead of insisting on an already established understanding of ethics gained from ancient Greek philosophy and from its interpretations in the course of Western philosophy and then transplanting these into Islamic theologies of ethics, one should rather go so far as to risk their failure. Such failure can, of course, attain the concept of the ethical itself. But the price paid can be a gain when it opens the ear to an unheard-of version of ethics. If one prefers, however, to begin from a common root, then there will be two minimal assumptions to be made: that ethics is a science, a knowledge, in the Greek sense of the word, and that the object of this science is human action.

That much said, when one starts to inquire into Islamic ethics, one will soon notice where ways begin to part. Any knowledge, any "science" in Islam, as well as the initiative and the ways to practise it, must be derived from the Holy Qur'an, the Word of God, and from hadith, the reports of the sayings of the Prophet of Islam. The body of rules formulated from both is called *Sharīʿa*, commonly translated as "Islamic law". *Fiqh* (Islamic jurisprudence) and *kalām* (theology) are, thus, not so much original sources of knowledge as ways (*madhāhib*) of taking from the original sources. Both are born of a precarious situation where authority passes from someone whose actions and words are believed to be unquestionably true because his knowledge is not derived from himself, but from the source of all knowledge, from God, to one whose qualification consists in two things: his following of the former authority to the highest degree of perfection possible for a human being and his best use of the instrument that God gave him for the purpose of "measuring for Him", that is, reason (*'aql*). But because there is always the possibility that reason may lose sight of the limits imposed on her as an instrument of knowledge and mistake herself for both the chief subject and object, not only the sources of knowledge but also the procedures of knowing must be formulated on the grounds of divine and prophetic authority. In other words, reason may not always be able to determine by herself whether she "follows reason".

The event that accounts for the necessity of *fiqh* and also, though to a lesser extent, *kalām*, is the "death of the Prophet". It should, however, be immediately added that this expression is not unproblematic, because "death" should be understood here from two angles: from the perspective of prophecy, and also from that of humanity, where each angle effects a change in meaning.

Islam as (a) "religion" (*dīn*) describes a situation where human beings cannot know themselves through themselves; where, thereby, the end of their actions is not in their reach; where, in addition, both the command to know their end and the means for such knowledge are not issuing from themselves; and where, lastly, they accept this situation as true and binding. As such the "death of the Prophet" refers first of all to the absence of a human being who, when alive, was accepted as absolutely trustworthy (*amīn*) in matters of knowledge about human existence in its relation to the divine. It means, in other words, the absence of an advisor in divine matters whose closeness to the source of divine knowledge was beyond compare.

To give advice (*naṣīḥa*) is, according to a prophetic saying, "religion" (*al-dīn naṣīḥa*).[1] To be an advisor is, however, difficult, because it requires a very high degree of sincerity (indicated in the use of *naṣaḥa* in Qur'an 9:91). The important characteristic of "advice" understood in this way is that it makes interpretation superfluous. When an advisor with such authority is thought no longer to be available, then not only other advisors but also other modes of advice must be sought. What offers itself readily as "another mode" is one's own reason. But there is more that changes with this change than just a mode. Islamic legists and theologians were quite aware of this.

The most striking differences between the various schools of jurisprudence as well as between the main schools of theology lie in their views about the sources of knowledge concerning human action. It has often been stressed that both *fiqh* and *kalām* are responses to attempts at breaking up the unity of the community of believers, the *umma*, which occurred quite early in the history of Islam. This is certainly correct. But it should not be forgotten that the political events were born of and took advantage of an element that lies dormant in the very formulation of religion as we find it in Islam. This is indicated by many prophetic sayings concerning authority, which warned of the events that were coming to pass.

In this sense, *fiqh* and *kalām* can be understood as attempts to answer two kinds of insecurities. In the case of *fiqh*, once the groundwork for the assessment of human actions has been laid (through the *Sharī'a* derived from the Qur'an and the *sunna*), there remains the task of applying these guidelines to particular actions and situations and, thereby, establishing the means available and acceptable for formulating particular rulings. *Kalām*, on the other hand, can be seen as an attempt to answer a basic insecurity regarding knowledge of the nature of acts themselves. This insecurity is born of a tension inherent in the ascription of acts. The Qur'an names as agents of acts both God and man and, furthermore, ascribes responsibility for acts to man. This situation of tension is quite testing for any believer. As long as he understands responsibility only in terms of ownership, that is, as long as he can conceive of being responsible only for that which is his, in this case, his own acts, he lives in this tension without being able to resolve it. Faith will not contribute to its solution, but it allows him to carry the weight.

It becomes, then, important to join to the question which Aristotle sees as central to ethics, that is, the question about the end of (human) action, another one, namely: who acts? In view of one's usual awareness of oneself, this question certainly sounds odd and, perhaps, it cannot ultimately be answered by a human being. It is, then, all the more puzzling that we are able to ask it.

According to the dominant view among Western specialists, Islamic ethics, where it went beyond the mere listing of virtues and vices, was first of all concerned with evaluation and assessment. The "values" for such an evaluation were given in the authoritative texts, the Qur'an and the collections of the prophetic sayings, and consequently, tools had to be devised and applied to particular acts in order to determine the category under which they should fall. Yet such a search could proceed only within given parameters, that is, within *ḥudūd Allāh*, the limits set by God. These can be in the most general way described as His commands. The divine commands, very much like the two types of qur'anic verses, namely, the "clear ones" (*muḥkamāt*) which should be taken as given, and the "ambiguous ones" (*mutashābihāt*) which invite interpretation, are of two kinds: those which, simply given, are to be followed as given and for the mere fact that they are given, and those which invite the use of reason and reflection (*'aql* and *fikr*) in order to arrive at an understanding which leads to their acceptance. The first kind of command refers, broadly speaking, to acts, which address that which is beyond human perception and conception. Such are all recognisable acts of worship. Prayer, pilgrimage and recitation of the Qur'an are examples. The second kind of command refers, again broadly speaking, to acts that address the apparent (*ẓāhir*). Here, man is invited to use his *'aql*, that is, the means he was given by God, and to do so for the purpose it was given, namely, mindfully to direct his actions in such a way that through them he realises or serves God.

Two things become clear. First, we are in the midst of a subtle play of rotation between "the apparent" (*ẓāhir*) and "the hidden" (*bāṭin*) around the axis of the Unseen. It is essential that this configuration be kept firmly in view in any serious reflection about religion, as it lies at the heart of faith itself. If one can say that ethics in a religious context is concerned with actions as acts of worship, then it must take account of both apparent acts of worship and hidden ones. Secondly, the use of what is often called "independent reason" is here not the result of a "free" decision. It follows the divine permission to do so and it is to be exercised "to measure for God and not to measure Him" (Ibn 'Arabī). Permissions are, however, double-edged swords and sometimes more of a trial than of a blessing. They let loose while holding back, a fact which in the original enthusiasm about being able to run on one's own feet is easily overlooked. Reason is no exception. Once it is allowed to indulge in the exercise of its capabilities and grows strong through it, it easily becomes its own object of enjoyment, its own pride and measure. In other words, it forgets, and this forgetting expresses itself as conflict.

Accordingly, the main positions in both *fiqh* and *kalām* as they had crystallised in the so-called "classical period" of Islamic civilisation are seen by many scholars as revolving around the two poles of "reason" and "revelation", or "reason" and "tradition". Although both formulations situate the two poles in different ways and places, they share the terms as marks around which the various theological and jurisprudential schools are grouped.

The main schools of Islamic theology which are of relevance for the discussion of classical Islamic ethics are the Mu'tazila, the Ash'arīs, and, to a certain extent, the Māturīdīs. However, these are not as clearly distinguishable from one another as the names suggest. There are representatives for each school who are known to have changed affiliations, and sometimes the outlines of a particular school have become apparent only through its critical description by another. Perhaps this could serve as an incentive to shift attention from the distinguishing of one group from another and the weighing of one against the other to more relevant considerations, such as: to what extent are all theological schools deposits of one faith? And what significance is there in the fact that, whatever the theological differences and alliances, each text on the matter of ethics begins with the glorification of God and the Holy Prophet?

The interpretations of Islamic moral thought which to this date have shaped the most prominent view of ethics in Islam begin from the assumption that ethics occurs in Islamic theology first and foremost as a matter of the assessment or the evaluation of acts; this differs from Western philosophical thought where the ethical occurs first of all in regard to the constitution of an act. Accordingly, in Islamic moral thought "ethical" refers to a knowledge which allows us to locate a particular act on a predefined scale of categories, while "ethics" denotes the science which defines the means for such a localisation. The scale is distilled from the Qur'an. Whatever the particular categories are, be they "*ḥasan*" and "*qabīḥ*" ("good, acceptable" and "detestable"), or "obligatory" (*wājib*), "recommended" (*mandūb, mustaḥabb*), "permissible" (*mubāḥ*), "offensive" (*makrūh*), and "unlawful" (*ḥarām*), they are always acceptable or non-acceptable to someone, and that someone is not myself, but God. The central question for this interpretation of Islamic ethics is, therefore, not only "What does God want me to do?", but also, and perhaps more importantly, "Which means do I have to find this out?"

Once the question about the means of evaluating action is asked in this systematic way, another one follows inevitably for the rationalist discourse: what mode of existence does the "value" of a particular action have, or, more precisely, where does it reside? If the value resides in the action itself, then reason is capable of knowing it. If it does not reside in the action, no amount of reasoning will be able to detect it. It has to be sought in its place of residence which, in the case of Islamic ethics, is the divine will, and by means conducive to hearing this will. G. F. Hourani calls the former position (where value resides in the action itself) "objectivism" and the latter (where it does not) "ethical voluntarism" or "theistic subjectivism", and identifies the former with Mu'tazilī theology and the latter with Ash'arism.[2]

It should be noted that the aforementioned classification is based on a certain concept of reason, one that sees reason as that which recognises what is present in its object and is, thus, capable of "evaluation". The name of this presentation, or rather, re-presentation, is "rationalism", and thus Mu'tazilī theology is seen as rationalist. Secondly, the concept of "evaluation" originates in nineteenth-century Western ontologies which interpret being as "value". This ontology implies an evaluator in front of or over against the thing to be evaluated. To be truly evaluating, or, precisely, to be "objective", this evaluator must be "in control", that is, must speak in such a way that in its evaluation the object of its "evaluation" speaks for itself. It is highly doubtful if such a situation can be unproblematically assumed for Islam and for Islamic theology because it implies a degree of sovereignty that is hardly possible for a "servant of God". It is thus only fair and necessary to ask which possibilities a religion offers to evaluate, be it one's own acts, be it those of others, or those of God. The question, if the predicament from which the theological debates between the two main theological schools of medieval Islam (the Mu'tazilites and Ash'arites) resulted was a matter of evaluation, is therefore not settled but open.

Ash'arite theology, on the other hand, while being recognised as the most widely accepted school of Sunnī theology, does not provide such a clear-cut picture. The reason for this does not lie in any obscurity of its theological tenets, but in the fact that it brings to the fore a concept central to Islamic ethics which is difficult to understand in a purely rationalistic way (the concept of "obligation"), which, furthermore, it presents in quite an uncomfortable way. Within the scheme of this classification, Ash'arite theology is registered under "theistic subjectivism". It holds, in other words, that values are not just "objectively" present in human actions and readily available to reason, but that they are the result of the divine will. Such a will cannot be known by reason, or not to an extent that would allow the formulation of judgements based on such knowledge, but must be taken from the sources through which this knowledge speaks: divine scripture, prophetic saying. The function of reason, in the Ash'arite approach, is to see that in referring to these sources their status is respected in the best way possible. The ideal will always be "to say what He says", "to command what He commands", because, in the end, the correct interpretation of a divine word is known only by the divine speaker Himself.

For the rationalist discourse on Islam the significance of Ash'arite theology can best be seen in the fact that, against Mu'tazilite "rationalism", it pointed to the relevance of "tradition" or "revelation". This view helps to sustain a certain idea of Islam, or, for that matter, religion in general, which allows the discrimination of "forward-looking" (rationalist) from "backward-looking" (traditionalist) theologies, the assignment of a "value" to each, and then offering a choice between the two. However, theology in general, and Ash'arite theology in particular, is more interesting than that. It is, for instance, conceivable that the Ash'arites stress "tradition" or "revelation" not only because they see that these are *per se* to be preferred over reason, but because reference to tradition and revelation is of theological relevance, that is, of relevance for faith and its unity, for the unity of the fellowship of believers, the *umma*. In this sense, Ash'arite theology has more to offer than just a "position", and the question of why this theology should have become the main representative of Sunnī Islam turns out to be less mystifying than it appears to its rationalist interpreters.

Ash'arite theology is of particular relevance for the discussion of Islamic ethics, not so much for its advocacy of tradition as because it contributes to this discussion in two ways which point to the heart of the matter: it directs attention to the nature of human action in a universe characterised by divinity, and it stresses obligation. These two points are, of course, connected. If the "value" of human action for the apparent agent (the human being) is decided by the evaluation of "another", if "permissible action" means "as found permissible by someone else", if "disliked" means "disliked by someone else", and so on, then anyone who considers himself as the owner and origin of his action may wonder what exactly his role in this action might be. Who is the agent of my action? In which sense can I take it to be "my" action? In which sense can I think that I "act" at all? If, furthermore, one is bound to such an "action" and held responsible for it, then what means does one have to understand such an obligation?

Comparing Aristotelian philosophical ethics and Islamic theological ethics, scholars of Islam have pointed out that the most noticeable difference between the two lies in the prominence that obligation as the main criterion for ethical action gains in the latter over "the end of man" in the former. This prominence is due to the fact that humans are seen in Islamic ethics, or in Islam generally, as standing before the law. Ancient Greek philosophy places humans before themselves and thus makes them concerned with their own end rather than with their obligation towards God.

This comparison implies that, for Islam, humans who want to know the "value" or the quality of their actions are placed in front of the divine law with two "gifts", one in each hand. They may either use the gift of reason to understand how the law defines their actions and, thus, how it wants them to act, or they may refer themselves to "the divine commands" as documented in the Qur'an and hadith. The Mu'tazilite position favours reliance on reason. It bases this on the view, justifiable through certain verses of the Qur'an and through our common perception of ourselves, that we are the agents of our actions. The ontological (though not theological) equivalent to this position assumes that the "value", that is to say, the "being", of an action lies in the action itself. The Ash'arite position, on the other hand, favours reliance on "the divine command", justifying its position through other verses of scripture and through a belief in a creator of whom one may have an intuition but no perception. To accommodate the perception of oneself as agent of one's actions to the view of God as the creator of one's actions, Ash'arite theology derives from qur'anic sources the concept of *kasb*, of "acquisition". In this view, humans "act", though not as agents or creators of their actions but as "receivers". Again, the ontological translation/interpretation of this theological position states that the "value" of an act lies not in itself but in the decree of a divine will ("ethical voluntarism").

There are, of course, various intermediate positions; as many, in fact, as the spectrum of reason allows. However, they all share a shortcoming inherent in their basic construction, namely, that attention is so strongly focused on humans that the divine law occurs only secondarily, only with respect to humans. The rationalist discourse on Islamic ethics implies correctly that, according to Islam, humans are "before the law" and, therefore, in relations of contract, punishment, reward and retribution, and that they are thereby distinguished from the "man" of Greek philosophy; but it does not really deal with the particularity of "the divine law". This has two consequences. First, such a view does not reach into the heart of Islamic ethics. Secondly, it places Islamic moral thought further away from Greek philosophical ethics than is needed or may be fruitful.

To gain a perspective on the matter of the divine Law and to derive from it a standpoint which may benefit an inquiry into Islamic ethics, it is useful to refer to the mystic Ibn 'Arabī's description of *tanzīl al-kitāb*, the "descent of the Book", or the "descent of the divine Word". This description is of particular relevance because it does not just repeat the principle that the Qur'an is the inspiration of all learning in Islam and that all Muslim sciences must take their knowledge from it and then leave these sciences to themselves. On the contrary, Ibn 'Arabī's description of the "descent of the Book" sees them as particular manifestations of the divine Word; it keeps them "in the company" of that Word. Furthermore, it stresses that the descent of the divine Word is not a historical process but an ever-recurrent epiphany. Finally, it roots the law, and thus ethics, firmly in the Word.

According to Ibn 'Arabī, the divine Word on its descent manifests first as "throne" (*'arsh*), then further on as "footstool" (*kursī*), and then splits into "ruling" (*ḥukm*) and "report" (*khabar*). Each "foot" of these pairs splits again into two: the "ruling" into "command" (*amr*) and "prohibition" (*nahy*). The various branches of the two categories of "ruling" finally form all the categories of "evaluation" of the *Sharī'a*.

What one should learn from this description is twofold. First, the divine law is a manifestation of the divine Word. The implication of this statement for ethics is that the human being as an ethical being is a being of the word. Secondly, because "ruling" and "report" form in this descent the first duality, the Law can be described as the (divine) Word of, or in, the world of opposition. Its characteristics as well as the sciences of the law themselves give ample proof of this. Humans can therefore not be adequately understood in their ethical dimension as already constituted beings "before the Law" who are then asked to find out by which means they will reply. Or rather, they can be understood in this way only because the law as a particular manifestation of the divine Word constitutes them *by way of word*. This dimension is altogether absent from the rationalist analyses of Islamic ethics, and it needs to be detailed here further.

In order to understand how humans are constituted "before the law", one must take into account that the law as a particular stage of descent of the divine Word marks one of three levels of the manifestation of divine "unity" (*tawḥīd*). In reverse order, the third level is the level of "the unity of acts" (*tawḥīd al-af'āl*), the second the level of "the unity of names" (*tawḥīd al-asmā'*), and the first the level of "the unity of essence" (*tawḥīd al-dhāt*). It appears from this description that "ethics", insofar as it is "a science of action", has its object in the third level. But ethics cannot be *understood*, if one remains on the level of actions. To become a science, a knowledge, one must move it to the next, higher level, that is to say, to the world of names. For the world of actions is, according to Islamic cosmogony, only a crystallisation of the world of divine names or attributes which, in the Qur'an's teaching, God taught humankind so that they could call upon Him. Ibn 'Arabī's description of the ethical situation of humans is based on this step. He says: "What in fact takes place is that one divine name prescribes the Law for another divine name, addressing it within the locus of an engendered servant. The servant is then called 'the one for whom the law is prescribed' (*mukallaf*) and the address is called 'prescribing the law'."[3]

The prescription of the law is first of all a linguistic event. It introduces "address". Without address there would be no one who could be held responsible for his actions or any possibility of knowledge regarding such actions: that is, there would be no ethics. Secondly, the addressee is not a particular human being or mankind in general, but a divine name. The law does not address "me". Or, to put it differently, I am addressed by the Law only because "I" is the place for this address from name to name. This is the meaning of *taklīf*, of ethical responsibility. Therefore, one's ethical responsibility does not lie in one's capacity to answer (the rulings of) the law through one's actions or in finding out which means are the most appropriate to that answer. Rather, any action or any responsibility on one's part lies in shouldering the address. It should be added that the role of reason is, thereby, not diminished; on the contrary, it is made clearer.

Accordingly, the schools of *kalām* should be seen as manifestations of concerns for the divine Word that appear once this Word reaches on its descent the stage of multiplicity, duality, opposition and thus what is called "the world of human actions". Insofar as the knowledge of these schools is situated on this stage, and to the extent that they are fixed in it, they must bear its marks. That is, they must be multiple and fixed in opposition to each other. When the Ash'arites regard another group of Muslims as "Mu'tazilites", meaning "seceders", when they argue back and forth against one another, each one claiming to know better regarding the matter of actions, then this is an expression of their station. As Ibn 'Arabī has remarked, each position on this level is both "right" and "wrong" (or "blind"). Furthermore, each school bases its own position on certain verses of the Qur'an which it accepts without interpretation and then proceeds to interpret the verses on which the opponent bases himself. When the Mu'tazilites say that man is the agent of his acts, this accords with one's perception of oneself and is to this extent correct. This perception is, however, "blind", not because it sees something that is not true, but because it does not see what it sees. It does not recognise that the reason for perceiving oneself as the agent of one's acts lies in the fact that one is created "in His image" (*'alā ṣūratih*). In a similar way, the Ash'arite theologians who hold that God is the creator of one's acts are also correct because such a view can be substantiated both by scripture and by one's thought. At the same time, the Ash'arites are "blind" because they do not witness this. They say something that reason "tells" them, namely, that there must be a creator, a "maker", behind all that is made. Yet they do not *see* this, because reason can show them only what is not the creator. In other words, both opponents are locked within their positions and within the level of the divine Word they share. Ibn ʿArabī's critique of the term *kasb* can be understood from this angle. Once the Ashʿarites had stated their position, that "one's acts are created by God", they still had to accommodate the perception one has of oneself as agent of one's actions. They did this by saying that humans "acquire" what God creates. Such a formulation may indeed satisfy the rational mind, but for Ibn ʿArabī it contains "a darkness towards knowledge which no one sees but the insightful: well, there is no relationship between what is built from that and what is realised of His essence – Majestic, High and Great!"[4]

The "darkness towards knowledge" lies here in two things. First, the concept of acquisition, while seeming to open to man in a world where actions are basically God's creation a way to contribute to these actions, in fact fixates the human element on itself through giving in to the human desire for priority, and thereby closes the possibility of humans' openness towards their creator. Secondly, the "human being" of *kasb* cannot recognise his shortcomings by himself. This can be best illustrated by the particular vicissitudes the main protagonist, reason, undergoes.

The human being who is accountable for his or her deeds is called in Islamic law *ʿāqil* (usually translated as "reasonable" or "endowed with reason"). The Arabic root *ʿQL* means "to bind", "to tie", "to tether". Reason is understood as that which allows a creature, here a human being, to bind himself, to hobble emotions which otherwise might sweep him away and thereby to become capable of "sane", "reasonable" judgement and action. This understanding is implied in the rationalist interpretations of Islamic ethics which see the main argument of the various theological schools as one of identifying the principle which should take the leading role in determining the validity of one's actions: reason or revelation, reason or scripture. But, as employed in rationalist discourse, "reason" and "revelation" cannot really fulfil the function of decisive players in this argument because they are *both* born of the same concept of reason. Furthermore, as long as the assumption of reason as "tie" does not lead to the next question, namely, What should this reason (*ʿaql*) which ties be tied to? or in other words, What is the reason of reason?, it is quasi-suspended, left to itself. One ends then with a false duality: one (1), as *ʿāqil*, as a morally responsible person, ties (via reason) (2′) oneself to reason (2″). It is obvious that this is not a true duality. It seems that the doubling of reason fulfils a requirement for triplicity which can be seen as the basis of "relation" in general and of ethical relation in particular ("one (1) binds oneself (2) to reason (3)"), but it is equally apparent that it allows it only falsely and as a false triplicity, that is, that it rejects it in reality. This falseness becomes clear when Ibn 'Arabī states that the *'āqil* is "the one who binds himself to Allah", thereby producing a true rational triplicity: one (1) binds oneself (through reason: 2) to Allah (3).

The correction of this false duality (inherent in all thought based on the classical subject–object dichotomy) is ethically important because, besides clarifying the ethical position of a human being "before God", it introduces a distinction between thoughts in view of their sources. Ibn 'Arabī says that the *'āqil*s, those who bind themselves to God, to "His command and His prohibition, and [to] what God has dictated in [their] innermost self ... distinguish among the incoming thoughts of their hearts, between the ones which are from Allah and those which proceed from their own selves, or the suggestions of angels, and the suggestions of Satan". And he adds that those are the "[real] human beings".[5]

Obviously, such a view does not criticise or minimise the validity of rational deliberation in ethics. No theological school in Islam has done this. It points, however, to the necessity of anchoring reason. For without such an anchor, reason is easily bandied about by the very thing from which she claims to be most distant, namely, emotion, while remaining fully convinced of her "reasonableness". And because this "reasonableness" is won from a doubling, from an insistence on itself, from a kind of stubbornness, the matter soon becomes insoluble. The danger outlined here is present both in Islamic moral thought and in the "rationalist" descriptions of this thought. In the former this is, however, recognised and mitigated by the fact that the founders of *kalām* were usually firmly rooted in one of the four traditional *madhhab*s (the four main schools of Sunnī jurisprudence); moreover, the founders of these *madhhab*s in turn consulted spiritual advisors. In a word, the proponents of the various schools of ethical thought in Islam knew very well that their "science" marked only a particular stage in the descent of the divine Word and that in order to be of any scientific relevance this science could not disrupt its connection with previous links in the chain of descent. Such disruption, or rather erosion of the previous stages, has occurred only in modern Islamic theologies.

The rationalist interpretations of Islamic ethics, on the other hand, are very ill prepared to counter this danger, and the more they find their value in themselves or in their own rationality, or the less they are aware of any other possible instance of knowledge, the more vulnerable to this danger they are. A good illustration for this is supplied by the term which stands in the very centre of Islamic ethics, namely "obligation".

Echoing from afar Kant's discussion of "duty" as the principle of ethics, obligation addresses the issue of "binding". In other words, recognition of the value of one's action, be it through reasoning or through revelation, is ethical only if it binds one to act in accordance with this recognition. Hence the challenge becomes the quest for a principle of self-binding. Kant's asking whether there is a reasonable principle in which and through which reason can oblige herself is echoed in the question about "whether one can ever have an obligation towards oneself".[6] It is significant that "obligation towards others" is perceived as much less problematical. This perception can be explained by the fact that reason's fascination is with herself, or put differently, by the fact that she is ever in search of a concept that can found her. For Western scholars, the benefit of positioning "obligation" in the centre of Islamic ethics lies in its assumed capacity to supply a pre-Islamic, "rational" basis for Islamic ethics in a historical perspective. Of course, if it founds Islamic ethics, it must then, in a certain way, be "before" Islam. If this can be shown, then the centre of gravity of Islamic ethics would lie both inside and outside of it.

The rationalist thesis is this: most humans may not be able to explain why, but they are very much aware that they feel "obliged" without anyone telling them so. They do not need sacred scripture to inform them about the existence of obligation. It is, therefore, remarkable that religion repeats in her own terms (revelation, Word of God, etc.) what one, as a human being, already knows. And it proves both religion, through the fact that she accords with our thinking, and us, through the fact that we always thought what she says. This gives the rationalist interpretation of Islamic ethics a much-needed historical perspective, because through it Islam can be believed to provide an illustration of the "anteriority" of reason to herself, that is, of an arch-reason located before its split into (religious) reason and revelation. There is one particular act which thus becomes the act of all acts, or *the* ethical act, namely "thanking the Benefactor" (*shukr al-mun'im*).[7]

Why, of all possible actions, this one? Why "thanking the Benefactor"? The main reason seems to lie in its capacity to lend itself to constructing a continuity between a pre-Islamic, pre-revelational mindset and Islam (or revelation) itself. If the terms of this act (*shukr al-mun'im*) could be found in pre-Islamic usage, then it would be sufficient simply to follow the changes in meaning they received in the various stages of Islam, and one would have thereby established a fair understanding of Islamic moral thought as a continuation of pre-Islamic *rationality*. Or, if it turns out that the terms involved in the act are terms central to Islam itself, one would have managed to "place" it, to confirm it as a religion.

Central to the act of "thanking the benefactor" is that it involves "obligation". The pre-Islamic usage, or, as it is called, the usage of "Arab humanism", is reconstructed in terms of *ni'ma* (benefaction, kindness; *al-mun'im*, the benefactor, is an active participle), as meaning "sparing a person's life". *Shukr*, thanking, is taken to mean "publicly to acknowledge the benefaction". The stress lies here on the "public" aspect of this acknowledgement. It implies that thanking is done not so much to the particular individual who spared my life without having to do so, as to or for "the public". The other, quite important, aspect of this matter is that "the refusal to recognise that obligation was, in pre-Islamic times, called *kufr*".[8] Now, *kufr* is commonly translated as "unbelief". The implications are not difficult to draw: *īmān*, faith itself, although not mentioned in this context, must then be found in the neighbourhood of this public acknowledgement of having been spared. In other words, religion, or more precisely Islam, translates the meanings these terms have "before revelation" into revelation: the Arab humanist, or human benefactor, certainly the one who gives life but, as we may assume, more relevantly the one who spares my life, is inflated until he becomes "The Benefactor", "God"; and "belief in God", or "religion" becomes the "public acknowledgement of having been spared" on a larger scale, that is, with God as the public.

The inerrant instinct with which rationalist-historicist discourse about Islamic ethics targets Ghazālī's view of "obligation" and "thanking the benefactor" permits us to recognise, however, that the historical construction of rationality, that is, here, of a logic of continuity from pre-Islamic rationality to Islamic rationality, is not unproblematic. The following quotation from Ghazālī is interesting here:

> Gratitude to a benefactor is not necessary by reason, contrary to the Mu'tazilite. The proof of this is that "necessary" [*wājib*] has no meaning but what God the Exalted has made necessary [*awjabahu*] and commanded with threat of punishment for omission; so if there is no revelation what is the meaning of "necessity"? This argument is confirmed as follows: Reason should make gratitude necessary either for some benefit or for none. It is impossible that reason necessitates it for no benefit, for that would be useless and foolish. If it is for a benefit, it must be either for the One served, but

> that is impossible, since He is too Exalted and Holy to have ends, or for the servant. The servant's benefit must either be in this world or in the next. But there is no benefit to him in this world, rather he is [only] wearied by study and thought, knowledge and gratitude, and deprived by them of desires and pleasures. And there is no benefit [known by reason] in the next world, for Reward is bestowed as a favour from God, and is known by His promise and His announcement; and if He did not announce it how would it be known that there is to be Reward?[9]

Hourani's reply to Ghazālī's critique of reason as a valid means for recognising "obligation", that is, as the source of ethics, is essentially that Ghazālī misses the point. Accordingly, the Mu'tazilite theologians would not have to prove that reason can see the *benefit* of acts for agents, but only their "obligatoriness". There seems to be a divergence, then, as to the function and status of reason. Whereas for Ghazālī the function of reason is precisely to measure benefits in this world ("obligation" lying beyond reason's scope because it is not a matter of benefit or not a matter of benefit as reason can conceive it), for Hourani reason is nobler than that: it can conceive "obligatoriness". What exactly is introduced with this divergence?

Alternatively, what precisely is the status of "thanking the Benefactor"? Is it such a central, self-contained element that one could build the whole edifice of Islamic moral thought upon it? The following lines from the Sufi writer Jalāl al-Dīn Rūmī (1207–1273) give a more intricate and exciting taste of Islamic ethics:

> If outwardly I neglect to thank you or express my gratitude for the kindnesses, favours, and support you give both directly and indirectly, it is not out of pride and arrogance, nor is it because I do not know how one ought to repay a benefactor in word or deed, but because I realise that you do these things out of pure belief, sincerely for God's sake. And so I leave it to God to express gratitude for what you have done for His sake. If I say that I am grateful, and acknowledge my admiration for you in praise, it would be as though you had already received some of the recompense that God will give you. Humbling oneself, expressing gratitude, and admiring another are worldly pleasures. Since you have taken pains in this world to bear the burden of monetary expense and social position, it would be better for the recompense to be wholly from God. For this reason I do not express my gratitude, as to do so would be this-worldly.[10]

Several things appear from these lines. First, the matter of "thanking the Benefactor" is certainly of relevance for Islamic *akhlāq* (manners) but it is *per se* not constitutional. Secondly, gratitude can be expressed "in word or deed". To express it in one way or in the other is of itself not decisive. More decisive than this word/deed distinction is the issue of *who* expresses gratitude and *to whom* such gratitude is expressed. As it is put here, actions done "out of pure belief" for the sake of God gratify God. It is not only humans who are "thanking", be it pre-Islamically as an announcement to the public, or Islamically, as belief in God. God Himself may "express gratitude" and does so, in fact, when the action is truly ethical, truly done for His sake.

It follows from these observations that "expressing gratitude" by itself does not constitute an action as "ethical" or "moral". If it is possible to express gratitude, be it to another human being or to God, as "a worldly pleasure", then the ethical dimension of this gesture is not constituted by the act itself but by its *address*. The fact that reason may itself have a concept of obligation, or "obligatoriness", does not constitute an ethical dimension for Islam, nor does it raise reason into the touchstone for recognising the ethical validity of actions. Rūmī even goes so far as to say that the best measure for assessing the ethical validity of actions could very well be "not to express my gratitude in word or deed". If, however, one should express gratitude and should thank the benefactor, or The Benefactor, *in this world*, then this is so not because reason informs us of the obligation but because God *commands* us to do so: "and as for thy Lord's blessing, declare it" (Qur'an 93:11). Thanking, declaring your Lord's blessings in this world, is described in Islam as a matter of "courtesy with God" (*adab ma'a'llāh*) and it constitutes a major ingredient in the knowledge of God. Herein, in *adab*, lies a truly significant and little-explained feature of Islamic ethics. It appears, for instance, in the command, difficult to understand on rational grounds, to ascribe "bad" (*sharr*) to oneself and "good" (*khayr*) to Allah, although one is told that everything occurs by divine leave.

Worth noting in terms of thanking the benefactor is that in Islamic teaching "the One who gives thanks" and "the Benefactor" are divine attributes. Accordingly, one would have in "thanking the benefactor" – as Ibn 'Arabī noted – the address of a name to another name in the locus of the engendered servant. The "engendered" or created servant is the place that allows the address of one name to another. The servant is neither the addresser, the one who thanks (*al-shakūr*), nor the one thanked (*al-mashkūr*). He/she serves the address, the names. And in order to do that, one must allow each name its full weight, which is to say that one must "abide by the Law".

It seems that the rationalist interpretation of Islamic ethics which takes "thanking the benefactor" to be its central principle is more interested in the one who thanks than in the benefactor. And the one who thanks is, in this interpretation, most likely not God. God is tied by this way of thinking, bound to the gratitude of the one who thanks. Or, so it appears, because this is, of course, not possible. And, thus, the same "false" duality seems to be at work again.

What if one were to ask: what is the character of the ground on which it is established that the ethos of a religion (here Islam) is rational? Is it itself rational? In other words, is what tells me that "I am obliged to the one who spares my life" really so rational, or might it not resound from different recesses? Further, is that which makes one *recognise* this voice as the voice of reason itself so rational? These are not very sound grounds on which to base ethical thought. Rūmī's description of "not thanking the benefactor" hints at this grey zone and displays a deeper wisdom in dealing with it. It hints, thereby, at an Islamic ethics that, discovering the treacherousness of the so-called rationalistic foundations, proposes not to leave the circle of reason but, on the contrary, to deepen it.

Immediate effects of such a deepening include what one might call the "freeing of realms to themselves", or, in Islamic terms, the "giving everything that has a right what is its right" (*ītā' kulli dhī ḥaqqin ḥaqqah*). Reason in this world is, thereby, freed from its admixture with metaphysical elements and becomes clearer and more astute. Traditional Islamic sciences like *fiqh* and *kalām* illustrate this. What belongs to heaven, on the other hand, is returned to heaven, and both are allowed "to be good neighbours", as the Taoist phrase goes.

All ethics is, in the end, moved by the question formulated by Plato and repeated by Aristotle: "Can virtue be learnt"? If the answer is that "unlike the *technai*, *aretē* [virtue] is not teachable" and that "traditional ethical and moral customs are based not so much on teaching and learning as on taking someone as an example and emulating that example",[11] then one would like to know what happens "after Socrates". How did Plato become virtuous? If being in the company of Socrates made him good (and, maybe, the Platonic dialogues are more than anything else a sign of this), then what happened "after Plato"? We might remember that the same issue, the "death of the Prophet", led to the formulation of Islamic jurisprudence and, eventually, theology. Should one not ask, then, what happened to the companionship of those who became virtuous through being in the company of the Prophet (*ṣaḥāba*)? It is strange that such a patent fact, the necessity of companionship for becoming an ethical, virtuous human being, escapes one although one knows it so well. Indeed, the more deeply entrenched one is in one's "rationalities", the less one is aware of the role of company (*ṣuḥba*) in ethics. The more sensitive interpretations of Islamic ethics or of the transmission of knowledge in a traditional Islamic context acknowledge at least the significance of the divine Word and, therewith, of all words. But although the Prophet of Islam is reported as saying that every prophet had a miracle, and his miracle was the Qur'an, it seems that even these interpreters cannot comprehend that words are not only something transmitted "from line to line, or mouth to mouth", but also, and most importantly, "from breast to breast".

Further reading

Abdullah, M. Amin, *Kant and Ghazālī: The Idea of the Universality of Ethical Norms* (Frankfurt, *c.* 2000).

Fakhry, Majid, *Ethical Theories in Islam* (Leiden, 1991).

Frank, Richard M., "Moral obligation in classical Islamic theology", *Journal of Religious Ethics* 11 (1983), pp. 204–23.

Gardet, Louis, and Anawati, George C. *Introduction a la théologie musulmane: essai de théologie comparée* (Paris, 1948).

Gimaret, Daniel, *Théories de l'acte humain en théologie musulmane* (Paris, 1980).

Hourani, George F., *Reason and Tradition in Islamic Ethics* (Cambridge, 1985).

Jackson, S. "The alchemy of domination? Some Ash'arite responses to Mu'tazilite ethics", *International Journal of Middle Eastern Studies* 31 (1999), pp. 185–201.

Reinhart, A. Kevin, *Before Revelation: The Boundaries of Muslim Moral Thought* (Albany, 1995).

Sajoo, Amyn B., *Muslim Ethics: Emerging Vistas* (London, 2004).

Winkel, Eric, *Islam and the Living Law: The Ibn 'Arabī Approach* (Karachi, 1997).

Notes

1. Bukhārī, Īmān, 42; Muslim, Īmān, 94.
2. George F. Hourani, *Reason and Tradition in Islamic Ethics* (Cambridge, 1985).
3. Muḥyī al-Dīn Ibn 'Arabī, cited in William C. Chittick, *The Sufi Path of Knowledge: Ibn al-'Arabī's Metaphysics of Imagination* (Albany, 1989), p. 208.
4. Eric Winkel (tr. and ed.), *Mysteries of Purity: Ibn al-'Arabī's Asrār al-ṭahārah*, (Notre Dame, 1995), p. 178.

5. Winkel, *Mysteries of Purity*, p. 511.
6. Hourani, *Reason and Tradition*, p. 14.
7. A. Kevin Reinhart, *Before Revelation: The Boundaries of Muslim Moral Thought* (Albany, 1995), p. 109.
8. Ibid.
9. Ghazālī, *Mustaṣfā*, quoted in Hourani, *Reason and Tradition*, p. 156.
10. Wheeler M. Thackston, Jr (introd. and transl.), *Signs of the Unseen: The Discourses of Jalaluddin Rumi* (Boston and London, 1999), p. 114.
11. Hans-Georg Gadamer, *The Idea of the Good in Platonic-Aristotelian Philosophy* (New Haven and London, 1986), p. 46.

9 Revelation

YAHYA MICHOT

The concept of "revelation" is usually considered to have for correspondents, in the Arabic language, words formed on the basis of two different roots: *WḤY* and *NZL*. In English translations of the Qur'an, *waḥy* is commonly understood as "revelation" and *awḥā* as "to reveal" or, sometimes, as "to inspire" or "to incite". In non-religious contexts, however, a fundamental meaning expressed by the root seems to be that of a sound or noise, rapid and blustering like thunder. Words derived from the second root, like *nazala, nuzūl, nazzala* and *anzala*, all relate to the ideas of "coming down", "descending", or "sending down", and have a strong place-related physical connotation. In the Qur'an, they are used much more often than the words derived from *WḤY*. Once examined together, the various qur'anic occurrences of these two groups of terms convey the clear image, not of the "unveiling" evoked by the word "revelation", but rather of a solemn or even awe-inspiring communication, literally originating "from on High": "If We had sent down this Qur'an upon a mountain, you would have seen it humble itself and split apart by the fear of God" (59:21).

The affirmation that such a transcendent communication takes place in the history of mankind is most often conceived in Islam through the dimensions of prophethood and messengership, from which it is therefore sometimes difficult to distinguish the thematic of revelation. The latter should, however, not be studied exclusively in relation to its recipient but also from the viewpoint of its divine origin and of the modalities of its transmission. This means, first and foremost, that a proper understanding of God as "revelator" must be developed.

God is of course the unique creator of the universes. All His creatures, good or bad, are submitted to His creative power and governed by Him. He is their sole Lord, their sole Master and their sole King, from whose decision and decree they cannot escape: what He wills is, even if they do not want it; and what they want, if He does not will it, is not. He makes humans live and die as He pleases, whereas they are essentially in need of Him, simply in order to be and to act. This ontological situation of total dependence on God's lordship is common to all – believers and unbelievers, libertines and good-doers. In the Qur'an, even the Devil says "O my Lord!" to the creator.

To proclaim the unique and exclusive lordship of God and to approach Him from the viewpoint of His rulership does not, however, introduce the real essence of God *qua* God. In order to do so, one must leave ontology in favour of ethics, and ascribe to God's moral will, which He expresses through revelation, at least as much importance as is to be ascribed to His creative lordly will. Manifestly, the world was not created in vain. Creation, as such, however, is not an end in itself, and there is no self-justification for it. Rather, it is as if creation were nothing but an occasion for revelation, which alone will lead to its completion. Just as the power to create belongs to none but God, He alone is entitled to be served, worshipped, adored, feared and trusted. In other words, it is relative to religion, not metaphysics, and thus beyond His seignioriality, that God's godhead can properly be investigated. Godhead (*ilāhiyya*), the Damascene theologian Ibn Taymiyya (d. 1328) explains, is not the power to create of a God (*al-ilāh*), understood in the sense of the active participle *ālih*, "creating". *Al-ilāh*, "the God", is to be understood in the sense of the passive participle *al-ma'lūh*, "the divinised one", or "the divinisable one", which is to say, He who has the exclusive right to be made divine (*uliha*) and is the only one entitled to be worshipped and loved.[1] It is revelation which, beyond creation, inaugurates such a relation and, by doing so, gives the first all its sense. Beyond the realm of what the Lord creates, the dimension of what God says should be given even more importance, as it is exclusively according to this other uncreated reality that the fullest kind of relation can be developed with the divine. It is revelation that brings some moral distinctions into the created reality, with its commands and its prohibitions, and thus initiates, through religion, the differentiation between good and evil, between virtue and sin, between God's friends and His foes.

However great His creative power would be, a God who would not do anything else and, specifically, would not communicate with humans, would be a remote abstract principle closer to the prime mover of Aristotle's metaphysics than to the God of the Qur'an. The latter has indeed frequently spoken and has been the source of innumerable revelations in different ages. The first man was also the first prophet to whom a revelation was given, as the creation of the world and, *a fortiori*, of mankind, would not have been accomplished without a further manifestation of God's will, this time the ethical and religious one, beyond his ontological *Fiat*. Inspired mainly by Plato's political philosophy, Fārābī, Avicenna and other classical Muslim philosophers and theologians considered prophethood necessary as a means to establish a just society. In contradistinction to this, the necessity of revelation, and of a divine accompaniment throughout the history of mankind by means of revealed scriptures, prior to sealing prophethood with Muḥammad, is in Islam a dogma directly related to a proper understanding of the nature of God Himself.

The Qur'an refers to different types of revelation or divine speech, not all of which can be linked to prophethood. "And your Lord revealed (*awḥā*) to the bee: 'Build your homes in the mountains'" (16:68); "And We revealed (*awḥaynā*) to the mother of Moses: 'Suckle him!'" (28:7); "And when I revealed (*awḥaytu*) to the Apostles: 'Believe in Me and in My messenger!'" (5:111); "On that Day, the Earth will tell her news: for that your Lord will give her a revelation (*awḥā*)" (99:5). Concerning such processes in which God addresses the earth, animals or some humans who are not prophets in order to give them instructions, Ibn Taymiyya speaks of an "equivocal" (*mushtarak*) form of revelation which is its lowest form.[2] This nevertheless demonstrates that God continues to intervene in the world after its creation not just ontologically but with His words, which are evidently not exclusively reserved for prophets.

This being so, it would be a mistake to expect the divine revelation typically to be communicated directly to every human being, through his or her reason, for example. Such a possibility was envisaged by the famous philosopher and physician Abū Bakr al-Rāzī (d. 925 or 935). As a theist denouncing all historical prophets as impostors, he trusted human reason to be the most appropriate vehicle for God's ethical will. This rationalisation and universal dilution of revelation was, however, deemed as extreme as the simple negation of the phenomenon would also have been, and Rāzī's views were unanimously condemned. Preferring once again to follow a *via media*, the orthodox doctrine thus remained one of a revelation essentially passing through a finite number of prophets or lawgiving messengers, elected by God so as to act as intermediaries between Him and His servants. The modalities of this process of prophetic revelation are alluded to in Qur'an 42:51: "It is not granted to any human that God should speak to him except through revelation or from behind a veil, or by sending a messenger to reveal, with His permission, whatever He wills."

According to Ibn Taymiyya, the three ways God speaks to a man can be understood in the following manner. First, inspiration (*ilhām*) in the awakened state or during sleep: the true vision of a prophet is indeed a kind of revelation. Secondly, words addressed from behind a veil, as was the case with Moses, when God called him at Sinai, made him draw near to Him and spoke to him but did not let him see Him (Qur'an 19:52; 7:143). Finally, words that God communicates by sending an angelic messenger who reveals, with His permission, whatever He wills. Concerning this last mode of revelation, the Qur'an says: "It rests upon Us to assemble it and to produce it; and when We produce it, follow its production" (75:17–18). Exegetes sometimes diverged in their interpretation of the various elements of this verse. Nevertheless they all agreed on God's authorship of the message and on Gabriel's involvement in its communication. According to a famous Companion, Ibn 'Abbās, "and when We produce it" referred to the archangel's reading of the revelation to the Prophet. As for "follow its production", Ibn Taymiyya understands it to mean, "Listen to it until Gabriel finishes reading it!"[3]

The revelation of the Qur'an itself spread over some twenty-three years (609–32 CE). It all started during a month of Ramaḍān, during a spiritual retreat of Muḥammad on Mount Ḥirā', outside Mecca. Gabriel appeared to Muḥammad and then taught him the first verses of *sūra* 96. According to 'Ā'isha, reporting directly from the Prophet whom she would later marry, it happened in the following way:

> The angel came to the Prophet and asked him to read. The Prophet replied, "I do not know how to read." The Prophet added, "The angel then caught me and pressed me so hard that I could not bear it any more. He then released me and again asked me to read, and I replied, 'I do not know how to read.' Thereupon he caught me again and pressed me a second time till I could not bear it any more. He then released me and again asked me to read but again I replied, 'I do not know how to read (or what shall I read?).' Thereupon he caught me for the third time and pressed me, and then released me and said, 'Read in the name of your Lord, who has created [all that exists], has created man from a clot. Read!, and your Lord is the Most Generous.'"[4]

Following a pause, during which the Prophet became depressed to the point of considering suicide, revelation resumed with the sending down of *sūra* 74, or 93. It then came upon the Prophet frequently and regularly until the end of his life, and under the most diverse circumstances, sometimes when he was asked for an opinion or a decision, or while he was riding, or was eating or preaching. According to his own reports, revelation sometimes came to him as a sound, of metal being beaten, of bees humming near his face, or the ringing of a bell. "This kind is the most painful," he recalled. "When it ceases, I retain what was said."[5] It could also be an angel speaking to him as a man whose words he would retain. Or revelation would approach him in the form of a young man handing it down to him. For people around the Prophet, it was easy to become aware that something extraordinary was going on. He could start shaking his head as if he tried to understand what was said to him, or (until he was told not to do so by 75:16) he moved his lips as soon as the revelation began. Even on very cold days, sweat dripped from his forehead. Sometimes his colour grew livid or he fell into a lethargy, swoon or trance. It was obvious that receiving revelation could cause him great pain and suffering. When he received 4:97, his thigh pressed so heavily upon that of the companion sitting next to him that the latter feared it would break. On one occasion when the Qur'an came down upon him while he was riding, the beast became unable to bear the weight, so he had to descend from it.

The peculiarities of the qur'anic revelation process just depicted triggered important theological and social developments.

A first question could have been phrased, "Who is speaking?" As recorded by the Qur'an, the Prophet's fellow Meccans accused him of being *majnūn*, a madman possessed by a *jinn* (15:6; 26:2; 37:36, etc.). God Himself confirmed that this was not the case: "So, remind [people]: by the grace of your Lord, you are neither an oracle nor possessed by a jinn!" (52:29; also 68:2; 81:22). And for the few scholars accepting the historicity of the incident of the "satanic verses", as soon as the Devil started interfering with the transmission of the revelation, the Prophet was warned by God and thus protected (*ma'ṣūm*) from persistence in sinning.[6] For some theologians, al-Ḥallāj, the controversial mystic executed in Baghdad in 922 for saying, "I am God", had experienced satanic states and was indeed possessed by a *jinn*. To claim – as people favourable to him do – that it was God who was speaking for him when he uttered his famous saying would be pure unbelief: God does not speak for a man as *jinn*s speak by possessing epileptics and using their tongues. Similarly, when Pharaoh, as narrated in the Qur'an (79:24), said, "I am your highest lord!", God was not speaking through his mouth. This being so, could it ever be said that God is speaking through Muḥammad? If what is meant thereby is that God inhabits His Prophet, absolutely not! God does not dwell within humanity and does not speak for a man, through his tongue. If, on the other hand, what is meant is that God sends with His words messengers who say for Him what He orders them to communicate, then this is the proper understanding of revelation in Islam. God speaks through His messenger, through his mouth and tongue, in the specific sense that the prophet speaks on His behalf. Between the extremes of possession and incarnation, there is room for a truly prophetic understanding of revelation, without the person chosen to receive and transmit the message losing any dimension of his humanity or becoming any kind of supernatural being. Muḥammad is the perfect man, but even in the highest spiritual station into which he is introduced by his Lord in order to receive the revelation, he essentially remains His servant. "He revealed to His servant (*'abd*) that which He revealed" (53:10). In no way would receiving revelation ever provide a reason to be associated with God as a partner in His godhead.

The idea of the Prophet speaking in the name of God led early Muslim theologians into a second debate, this time concerning the human or divine nature of the revealed speech itself. What was the part effectively played by the Prophet in the phrasing and wording of the qur'anic revelation? For fifteen years (833–48) the Abbasid caliph al-Ma'mūn and his successors imposed the dogma of a created and non-eternal Qur'an promoted by Mu'tazilism. This *miḥna* (ordeal) imposed on the community failed and the vast majority of Muslims have since proclaimed the uncreated and eternal nature of the Qur'an. As this doctrine affirmed, the Messenger thus loses all authorship of the Qur'an. In Islam, the Book is indeed never named after him as, for example, the Gospels bear the names of the Evangelists. With time, the interpretation of the qualificative *ummī* given to the Prophet in the Qur'an (7:157–8) evolved from its probable original meaning of "Gentile" to "unlettered", as a further confirmation that he could not possibly have authored it. Moreover, on the thin scriptural basis of a non-unanimously accepted way of reading of the last syllable of *sūra* 85, greater importance came to be given to the idea of a "Well-Guarded Tablet", in which the Qur'an would have been eternally inscribed and preserved. Finally, from the ninth century onwards, insistence was laid on the linguistic and stylistic inimitability, or insuperability (*i'jāz*), of the Qur'an already affirmed in some of its verses (for example in 17:88) as a way to add strength to the dogma of its exclusively divine nature. For Muslims, the revelation received by the Prophet is really what it says it is and its written copies have to be respected as such: "This is indeed a noble Qur'an, in a book safeguarded, which none shall touch except the purified, something sent down from the Lord of the Worlds" (56:77–80).

If the Prophet is so important in the eyes of the Muslims, it is due to his divine election, to his total humility as conveyer of God's speech, and to his perfect, paradigmatic implementation of this message, not because he partakes in its production. In this respect, apart from some modernists, today's Sunnīs are still convinced that, in this extraordinary intervention of the transcendent in human history signified by sending down the Qur'an to Muḥammad, the part played by God is worthy of infinitely greater consideration than that played by His Prophet.

They notably have no difficulty with psychological analyses of the mental process of reception of a revelation. Long ago, classical Muslim thinkers like Fārābī and Avicenna or, in their wake, the theologians Ghazālī and Fakhr al-Dīn al-Rāzī, did not hesitate to explore scientifically the phenomenon of prophecy with the conceptual tools they had developed in studying Greek philosophy, in particular Aristotelian psychology. For Avicenna,[7] after a purely immaterial contact between, on the one hand, the soul of the Prophet and, on the other, the angelic intelligence or the heavenly soul in charge of our sublunar world, the mental faculties at work in shaping the revealed message into a human discourse as imaged and evocative as the Qur'an are exactly the same as those active in dreams and follow similar patterns. Only the nature of the original data and, *a fortiori*, of their ultimate source, is essentially different. Revelation proceeds from the transcendent God whereas, usually, oneiric or psychological realities are to be traced back to particular physiological conditions. As the Prophet was chosen by God Himself, these conditions are optimal in his case, and his psyche perfectly transposes the divine message into the speech most appropriate for his human audience, without any distortion resulting from his mediation. The Prophet's statements and the reports of people close to him on the changes occurring in him and in his physical appearance while he was receiving revelation confirm how his whole self was then mobilised for the operation. It is no wonder that the crescent became the symbol of Islam! Just as the moon illuminates the night by doing nothing but reflecting the light that it receives from the sun, the Prophet draws humans out of darkness by humbly conveying a revelation that, fundamentally, is not his.

Muslims are also not that interested, generally, in a historical criticism of the Qur'an of the type to which the Bible was submitted during recent centuries in the West. They do not ignore, however, the importance of the various circumstances and events in the context of which particular verses and *sūra*s were revealed to the Prophet for a proper understanding of his message. During the first centuries of Islam, a science devoted to the study of these occasions when the Qur'an was sent down came into being under the name "occasions of revelation" (*asbāb al-nuzūl*). Ultimately, in a prophetic religion, it is nevertheless God's involvement in the originating of the revealed Book that seems to deserve all the attention, rather than the extremely modest role man had in the process. By contrast, in an incarnationist religion based on the apotheosis of humans, it is quite logical to expect the interest to shift from the transcendent to humans. Seen from this theological viewpoint, historical criticism of holy scriptures could well follow from a typically Christian concern rather than be a demand for truth of universal value.

Someone believing in the power of ideas to mould the course of history should not underestimate the consequences that the traditional Sunnī view of the Qur'an as divine speech, and of the role of the Prophet in its conveying as that of a *causa serva* only, had on the shaping of Muslim societies. In a religious environment encouraging an unconditional acknowledgement of the sole reality of God and of His exclusive rights, this dispossession of the Messenger from his message, by divinisation of the latter, surely contributed to the emergence of a humanism that could be called, in contradistinction to Nietzsche's "death of God", a humanism of the "extinction of man". In Islamic history, there are indeed other central cases of such a paradoxical process of divinisation of a human achievement or reality to man's own detriment. One thinks, for example, of the famous answer of the great Sūfi master al-Basṭāmī (ninth century) to a person knocking on his door and asking, "Abū Yazīd, are you there?": "There is nobody here but God!" Al-Ash'arī, one of the most representative theologians of mainstream Sunnī orthodoxy, could also be referred to as he denies man's agency and calls his actions "creations of God". In both instances, humans in some way acquire a divine status but themselves become extinct and disappear.

A third important question resulting from the specificities of the sending down of the Qur'an has to do with the fact that it was done in Arabic. For the contemporary Arab poet Adonis,

> the Qur'an, as of its oral state, had been perceived by the Arabs as a linguistic shock. They were conquered by the beauty of its language and the innovativeness of its aesthetics. This language was the key opening the gates that were to bring adhesion to a new religion: that of Islam. This is why it is impossible to trace a line of demarcation between Islam and the Arabic language. One can say that the first Muslims, those who constituted the hard core of the new religion, adhered to the Qur'an not because they found in it the explanation of the mysteries of the universe or of the human being,

> or a new system of life, but because they saw in it a model of eloquence and a hitherto unknown and unanticipated form of writing. It is the language which transformed their interior being, and it is this which changed their lives.[8]

This judgement is of course excessive. The substantial, intrinsic bond that it points to between the revelation sent down upon Muḥammad and the Arabic language is nevertheless a fact underlined in the Qur'an itself. "We have sent it down as an Arabic Qur'an, in order that you may think" (12:2). "With it came down the Truthful Spirit, upon your heart, that you may be among the warners, in plain Arabic language" (26:193–5). "Thus We revealed to you an Arabic Qur'an" (42:7). For a theology dreading all anthropomorphist approaches to the divine essence, a God who speaks is already something of a conundrum; *a fortiori* when the divine speech is so indivisibly attached to a particular language. Rather than a chosen people, would God have a chosen language, in this case Arabic?

What is certain is that sciences of the Arabic language and its use in the Qur'an – grammar, lexicography, rhetoric, the science of the proper enunciation of Arabic letters and of the various readings traditionally accepted for some parts of the Book, the science of writing even – all became central sciences of the religion. As Ghazālī writes, "in themselves, linguistic science and syntax are not of the sacred sciences, but it has become necessary to engage in their study because of the law since this law has come in the language of the Arabs".[9] Apologetic justifications for God's choice of Arabic rather than any other idiom were also discovered through a comparative study of the qualities and merits of languages. For al-Shāfiʿī, "of all tongues, that of the Arabs is the richest and the most extensive in vocabulary". For Ibn Taymiyya, Arabic is far superior to the Greek language so praised by the philosophers whom he attacks, because of "its [ability] to express detailed meanings and to distinguish between the subtle ones and the main ones by special terms that enunciate the truth. In perfection, it is followed by the Hebrew language. So, where [can one find] this in the case of the language of your barbaric companions, who carry on using long terms while what is meant is light?"[10]

That its signifier is such an important part of its signified contributes in making the Qur'an a much richer reality than a mere book to be read and studied. Of course, even before being a scripture, the revelation sent down to Muḥammad is a speech. And as God Himself explains, the words of this speech operate in many ways. They are not supposed to affect minds only. "They only are the believers whose hearts tremble with fear when God is mentioned. When His verses are recited to them, they make their faith increase and they put their trust in their Lord" (8:2). "When the verses of the Compassionate are recited to them, they fall down in prostrate adoration, weeping" (19:58). "God has sent down the most beautiful speech as a Scripture ... whereat the skins of those in awe of their Lord shiver, and then their skins and their hearts soften to God's remembrance" (39:23). "We send down, as the Qur'an, something that is a healing and a mercy for the believers" (17:82). This healing power of the revelation is understood literally by many, not just spiritually. The qur'an was thus sometimes also used physically for curing ailments: a piece of paper with a qur'anic inscription was dipped into water; once the ink was diluted, the qur'anically enriched water was drunk. By means of amulets, talismanic shirts and other artefacts covered with qur'anic inscriptions, often in conjunction with astrological or magical devices or practices, the revelation came to be put to all kinds of uses, not always strictly orthodox. By procedures reminiscent of the Cabbala, the letters of the Arabic alphabet and their numerical values themselves played an important role in Muslim mysticism, esotericism and the divinatory arts. This is particularly true of the seventy-eight "mysterious" letters opening twenty-nine of the qur'anic *sūras* (2–3, 7, 10–15, 19–20, 26–32, 36, 38, 40–6, 50, 68) and which, once they are reduced to the fourteen of which they are combinations, represent the various basic consonantal forms of written Arabic, hence of the whole Arabic alphabet.[11]

The fact that through qur'anic psalmody and calligraphy the most manifest ways of celebrating God's revelation have given rise to arts that are among the most representative of Islam, if not the two major Islamic arts, is also to be explained as an aspect of what the Algerian Malek Bennabi rightly called "the Qur'anic phenomenon". Be it through architecture, decorative arts, the media or other aspects of everyday life, the divine revelation conveyed in Arabic by the Prophet continues to be as present in the public sphere as it is in the hearts of the millions of those who, in their childhood, learn it by heart, often entirely. And just as Arabic is *per se* part of the Qur'an, the latter impregnates it to the point of making it impossible for non-Muslim Arabic-speakers not to be, in some way, linguistically Islamised.

There are some differences of opinion between Muslim scholarship and serious Orientalists on the way the revelations received by Muḥammad over twenty-three years were collected during his lifetime and soon afterwards recorded in a written form. All, however, agree in acknowledging two amazing facts: the rapidity of the process which led to the production of the so-called vulgate of 'Uthmān, the third caliph (d. 656), and the total invariability of this vulgate over the centuries. This second fact deserves more attention here, as it had directly theological connotations, with important societal implications.

The Arabic script, in manuscripts of the Qur'an, evolved greatly towards a more precise and detailed notation of several consonants with dots, vowels and peculiarities in the pronunciation of some letters. As a uniform way of reciting various passages of the text never achieved unanimity, a certain number of readings received a canonical status. However, this evolution and this multiplicity never jeopardised the permanence of the vulgate's organisation and content as they had been defined during the time of the Prophet and of his Companions, without a single word of the Qur'an being deleted, added or changed in fourteen centuries. As God had stated: "It was We who sent down the Reminder, and We will be preserving it" (15:9). In fact, just as the creation and the religion in general belong to God, so does His speech. And just as the Prophet conveyed the message without interfering with it, no man after him had any right to change it in any way. For some theologians, this notably meant that, apart from what the Prophet himself said, there was no better way of speaking about God – and therefore no better theology – than quoting what God Himself says about Himself in the Qur'an. Even for less exclusively scripturalist scholars, it also meant that nothing valid could be said concerning the creed and practice of Islam in any idiom other than Arabic, with the obvious consequence that a translation of the Qur'an is not *the* Qur'an. At best, a translation may be considered an essay to render its meanings, with all the other essential aspects of the qur'anic reality already alluded to being lost in the process. Once more, the situation is reminiscent of the Jewish Bible rather than of the Bible known to Christians.

The sacral nature and irreplaceability of the language of the revelation in Islam undoubtedly helped in the shaping of Muslim societies, especially Arabic-speaking ones. With the Qur'an, it was also, indeed, a linguistic norm that Muslims started integrating into their lives and communities. They of course disobeyed it often, and Arabic dialects were – and are still – spoken here and there. As for replacing this norm by another, nothing less than the revelation itself made it impossible. Nowhere was any of these dialects ever accorded a status that would have enabled it to replace qur'anic Arabic, with the revelation being "translated" into it, thereby sacralising it, and thus paving the way for a nationalistic division of the *umma*. One would search in vain for an

Islamic equivalent either of Luther's German Bible or of King James's Authorised Version.

The presence of rhyme, assonanced prose, regularly repeated formulas, and even refrains characterises the style of the Qur'an. Sometimes the revelation takes the form of oaths, curses or threats, praise formulas, prayers, declarations or articles of faith, rhetorical questions, statements resolving disputed matters or interrogations, commands and prohibitions, regulations and prescriptions, narratives and parables. Among other things, various accounts are proposed of the history of past prophets – Biblical or not – messengers, cities and peoples. Attention is drawn towards the signs of God manifest in His creation – man as well as nature and the cosmos. Vivid or dramatic depictions are given of human origins, of death and of eschatological realities. The way is paved for the organisation of the individual and collective lives of the believers, as well as of their relations with other religious communities, in particular Judaism and Christianity. Various passages relate exclusively to Muḥammad or concern the revealed Book itself.

This multiplicity of styles, literary forms and content of the Qur'an made it an urgent requirement, among theologians, Sufis and even philosophers, to define a rule for its interpretation. How was it possible to make sense of such a diversity? What in fact were God's intentions in sending down such a revelation? How were the "reminding", the "warning", the invitation to "think and reflect", the "teaching" and the "guidance leading out from darkness towards the light" repeatedly evoked in the new scripture to be effectively understood? Was the revelation a call to some knowledge of an esoteric type, or mainly a pragmatic message aimed at establishing an ethical order within human societies? Could symbols opening to inner, esoteric truths be found in it? Alternatively, was it an exhaustive exposition of the religion to be followed literally, without going beyond its outer meaning? The way Islam would develop as a comprehensive system of life depended on the kinds of answer given to these hermeneutical questions.

One of the most interesting and radical positions was adopted by Avicenna in a short but seminal work, the influence of which can be felt in later debates on the subject. "Concerning the law", the Iranian philosopher wrote, "one ought to know one single rule [*qānūn*], that is, that what is wanted by the law and religion that have come to us through the tongue of any of the prophets is to address all the crowd." It is "to address the crowd about things that they understand, bringing things that they do not understand closer to their imaginations by striking likenesses and similitudes. If matters were otherwise, the laws would be of no use at all." Asking the *vulgum pecus* to believe in truths that it would not be able to grasp would lead it into doctrinal discussions dangerous to the public order and the stability of human societies. With its apparent anthropomorphisms about God and its physical descriptions of the hereafter, the Qur'an has fortunately "come up with the most eminent and the most perfect things that laws could possibly come up with. It was therefore right for it to be the Seal of the laws and the last of the religions." Given its primary audience, "somebody wanting to be a member of the elite of humans, not of the commonalty", should realise that "the outer meaning of the laws cannot be used as an argument" in matters like eschatology and theology.[12]

In Avicenna's opinion, God's purpose in sending messengers is thus mainly practical, having to do with collective action and justice rather than with knowledge of the Truth in itself. All forms of scripturally based theology or eschatology consequently become illegitimate and can be dispensed with. Very useful for policymakers, the revelation is of no immediate interest to philosophers able to discover the truth by their own rational means. And it is the philosophers themselves who recognise images of this truth in the letter of the revelation. To claim that the purpose of the outer meaning of the Qur'an is to introduce the commonalty to some esoteric meaning is wrong. Likewise is the idea that it would do so *per se*.

Esotericism in interpreting the Qur'an nevertheless appealed to many, and still does today. For some, it is not only in doctrinal matters but also in ritual and legal ones that Muslims should deactivate the literality of the revelation in favour of their own interpretations of its real intentions, either for elitist reasons reminiscent of those of Avicenna or, more recently, as esotericism is now giving way to historical relativism, under the influence of modern humanities and ideologies. Yet, the great majority of traditional scholars and ordinary believers reject all essentially utilitarian understandings of the revelation as guidance conceived for mobilising imaginations and to be followed by the populace in its literality but which would be unacceptable as a source of knowledge for defining any kind of creed. First, without denying the infinite semantic depth of the revealed message, they indeed have no epistemological problem in reading it literally and founding their beliefs and practices upon it. According to them, there is, for example, room for a *via media* between the excesses of the apophatic, negationist, theologies of Mu'tazilism or *falsafa* and, at the other end of the doctrinal spectrum, the anthropomorphist assimilation of the creator to His creatures. This is the path of mainstream Sunnism which, faithful to clear scriptural and prophetic statements, asserts the reality of the divine names and attributes as well as God's absolute transcendence, acknowledges man's incapacity to grasp the modalities of these aspects of the divine nature and sees no advantage in entering into excessive scholastic discussions about them. Secondly, it is precisely because the manifest meaning of the qur'anic revelation, in its outward appearance accessible to anybody, corresponds so well to the truth knowable to humans that Islam, as Avicenna rightly indicates, is such a successful religion and contributes to the implementation of so much justice and order in human societies. Truth and ethics are not incompatible. On the contrary, they support each other, and the message "sent down" upon the Prophet came with both in the most ideal and complete form, reconciling the outer and inner dimensions of reality.

"Muḥammad is not the father of any man among you, but the Messenger of God and the Seal of the prophets" (33:40). With the Prophet's death in 632, the sending down of the Qur'an was completed and prophethood was "sealed" for ever. Is it nevertheless true that the phenomenon of revelation *per se* has thereby also come to an end? In fact, an extra-qur'anic form of divine speech can be found in the particular genre of the Prophet's authentic sayings traditionally called "holy traditions" (*ḥadīth qudsī*). These are some ninety sayings, sometimes transmitted in different versions, preserving first-person statements attributed to God by the Prophet, yet not included in the Qur'an. The beginning of a famous example runs: "O My servants, I have forbidden injustice to Myself and made it forbidden among you."[13] Muḥammad's holy hadith confirm that God's revelatory activity is, in his case, not limited to the sending down of the Qur'an. Does, however, such a process of non-scriptural revelation continue after 632?

In cases of indecision over difficult choices, Muslims were advised by the Prophet to let God inspire them during their sleep after a prayer called *istikhāra*, "search, or request, for what is better". The Qur'an (2:186) states: "When My servants question you about Me, I am surely close. I answer the call of the caller when he calls Me." The Prophet also affirmed: "The veridical dream-vision of the believer is one forty-sixth part of prophecy."[14] The Companion 'Ubāda ibn al-Ṣāmit is credited with the words: "The dream-vision of the believer is a speech by which the Lord speaks to His servant in his sleep."[15] Important forms of communication in which God speaks to humans do thus still exist after the "sealing" of prophethood. Although scholars prefer to analyse them in terms of inspiration (*ilhām*) rather than of revelation (*waḥy*), they can sometimes even be of a relatively prophetic nature. Classical Muslim thinkers developing a philosophical model for the reception of revelation could be expected to show a great interest in such potentialities. They saw in them a confirmation of their theory that the Prophet was in fact extraordinary in that he alone actualised perfectly psychological powers belonging *per se* to the essence of man, with the consequence that, although Providence did not lead most human beings to live their essence fully, prophethood was seen as consisting, in theory, of powers accessible to everybody.

For people preoccupied by qur'anic hermeneutics, the idea that God can in a way continue to speak to some beyond His last Messenger provided the most welcome solution to their problem. It could indeed mean that, after the historical completion of the sending-down of the Qur'an, it was God Himself who, through individuals whom He chose to inspire, was in charge of guaranteeing the adequate interpretation of the Scripture, the permanence of its performance among His servants, and the Muslim community's final salvation. For Shī'ites, these divinely guided mediators had to belong to the family of the Prophet. Muḥammad, God's Messenger, was the city of knowledge, but his cousin and son-in-law, 'Alī, the Friend (*walī*), or Saint, of God, was the gate to this city. He knew the true inner meaning of the revelation and, after him, his charisma was transmitted to eleven other Imams among his offspring (the Ismā'īlīs recognised only seven Imams). A somewhat similar approach to post-Muḥammadan divine inspiration also appeared among some later Sufis, with the consequence that they were sometimes accused of promoting a Shī'ism without Imams. Often influenced by Avicennan prophetology, some spiritual masters indeed claimed to be divinely spoken to during their ecstasies and given special sciences or prodigious powers. Also considered Friends (*walī*) or Saints of God by their followers, they became in their eyes the true heirs to Muḥammad, the best interpreters of the qur'anic revelation and the most enlightening guides to follow on the Prophet's path.

Obviously, the further away the true meaning of the Scripture is said to be from its literality, the more indispensable and useful post-Muḥammadan mediators can claim to be. From this point of view, the growth of gnosticism and esotericism, either in Shī'ism or in some types of Sufism, did not come as a surprise. However, in none of these particular Islamic ways of thought did the gulf between the Qur'an and its supposedly true meaning – inner or other – widen to the point where the revelation sent down to Muḥammad was effectively deposed and replaced by its so-called exegesis, whose author would then become a new prophet or messenger. As soon as such a development took place, as was effectively the case with Bahā'ism and Qādiyānism at the end of the classical period, it would inevitably have already excluded itself from Islam.

Mainstream Sunnīs have a special respect not only for the Companions of the Prophet but also for his family and all the true Friends of God, the righteous believers who fear Him. This being said, it is mainly through the community itself that they believe that God acts since the completion of the sending-down of the Qur'an and the sealing of prophethood in 632. Dream-visions, divine inspirations, answers to prayers, and, to say it simply, God's "being with" (*ma'iyya*) each of His servants are all true facts. Yet, a sound collective understanding of the revelation, and its continuing implementation in the world on the path traced by the Prophet, are not entrusted by God to any particular group or class of people (charismatic, ecstatic or political), but are the responsibility of the entire *umma*, animated and counselled by its scholars so as to reach the widest possible forms of consensus (*ijmā'*). "The consensus of the community", Ibn Taymiyya writes, "dispenses with the necessity of the infallibility of imams." Or, "what the Muslims agree on is a truth brought by the Prophet"[16] – that is to say, it has the same value as his divine message. Such devolution of responsibility to the believers themselves is all the more logical as Sunnīs generally consider the religious message revealed in the Qur'an to be essentially clear, self-explanatory and complete, in need of little elaboration beyond its literality. In a prophetic, non-incarnationistic religion like Islam, whose founder was told more than once by his Lord to say, "I am but a man like you, to whom it has been revealed that your God is only One God" (18:110; see also 21:108; 41:6), it would moreover have been rather contradictory to have anybody in particular legitimately claiming to have better knowledge and more authority. It is in fact revelation itself that makes Islam a religion of liberation for mankind, freeing God's servants from all forms of sacerdotalism, ecclesialism, caesaro-papism, Ma'mūnism, esotericism or neo-Mu'tazilism.

Further reading

Encyclopedia of Islam, 2nd edn, 12 vols. (Leiden, 1986–2004), articles "i'djāz", "al-Ḳur'ān", "lawḥ" "miḥna", "nubuwwa", "ummī ", "waḥy".

Caspar, Robert, *A Historical Introduction to Islamic Theology: Muḥammad and the Classical Period*, tr. P. Johnstone (Rome, 1998).

Cragg, Kenneth, *The Weight in the Word: Prophethood, Biblical and Qur'ānic* (Brighton and Portland, 1999).

Nadwi, Abul Hasan Ali, *Islamic Concept of Prophethood*, tr. M. Ahmad (Lucknow, 1979).

Notes

1. Yahya Michot, "Textes spirituels d'Ibn Taymiyya, XVI: La réalité de l'amour (*maḥabba*) de Dieu et de l'homme (suite)", *Le Musulman* 29 (1998), p. 25. See also Fritz Meier, "The cleanest about predestination: a bit of Ibn Taymiyya", *Essays on Islamic Piety and Mysticism*, tr. John O'Kane with the editorial assistance of Bernd Radtke (Leiden, 1999), pp. 309–34.
2. Yahya Michot (tr.), *Ibn Taymiyya: Lettre à Abū l-Fidā'* (Louvain-la-Neuve, 1994), p. 48.
3. See ibid., pp. 45–8.
4. Muhammad Muhsin Khan, *The Translation of the Meanings of Sahih Al-Bukhari*, 9 vols. (Beirut, 1405/1985), I, p. 3.
5. Ibid., I, p. 2.
6. See Shahab Ahmed, "Ibn Taymiyyah and the satanic verses", *Studia Islamica* 87 (1998), pp. 67–124.
7. See Yahya Michot, *La destinée de l'homme selon Avicenne: Le retour à Dieu (*ma'ād*) et l'imagination* (Louvain, 1986), pp. 133–58.
8. Adonis, *La prière et l'épée: Essais sur la culture arabe* (Paris, 1993), p. 111.
9. Al-Ghazālī, *The Book of Knowledge*, tr. N. A. Faris (Lahore, 1961), p. 39.
10. For both references, see Yahya Michot, "A Mamlūk theologian's commentary on Avicenna's *Risāla Aḍḥawiyya*: being a translation of a part of the *Dar'al-Ta'āruḍ* of Ibn Taymiyya, with introduction, annotation, and appendices", Part II, *Journal of Islamic Studies* 14/3 (2003), p. 344.
11. See Pierre Lory, *La science des lettres en Islam* (Paris, 2004).
12. Michot, "A Mamlūk theologian's commentary", pp. 173–7.
13. William A. Graham, *Divine Word and Prophetic Word in Early Islam: A Reconsideration of the Sources, with Special reference to the Divine Saying or Ḥadīth Qudsī* (The Hague and Paris, 1977), p. 205.
14. Bukhārī, Ta'bīr, 2.
15. See Michot, *Abū l-Fidā'*, p. 48.
16. See Yahya Michot, "Textes spirituels d'Ibn Taymiyya, XII: Mongols et Mamlūks: l'état du monde musulman vers 709/1310 (suite)", *Le Musulman* 25 (1995), p. 30.

10 The existence of God

AYMAN SHIHADEH

WHENCE THE NEED FOR PROOF?

The problem of whether or not belief in God should be founded in reason has a complex history in Islam. Both *kalām* exponents and philosophers showed a keen interest in advancing arguments for the existence of God, which was born of diverse motives, chiefly the need to establish this most crucial doctrine within their broader metaphysical systems, to respond to physicalist atheism, and to support and enrich the belief and piety of believers. Yet the epistemological view that rational proof is needed to recognise the existence of God was not held universally: while some propounded discursive reasoning, others advocated fundamentally non-rational "methods" (sing. *ṭarīqa*) to this end, such as spiritual discipline, said to provide direct, experiential knowledge of God. Some, moreover, maintained that only one correct method should be followed exclusively, whereas others allowed for a hierarchy of different methods. Related to this was the question of whether lay people must follow essentially the same route as theologians, or whether, if they are incapable of doing so, they may adhere to simple, uncritical belief instead. Let us first briefly consider some historical solutions to this complex of questions.

Most early *mutakallimūn* typically maintain that rational reflection (*naẓar*) is the only method that provides knowledge of God, to the exclusion of all other, fideist or fallacious, methods and stances. It follows that everyone, theologians and lay believers alike, ought to learn, not only the main creeds, but more primarily their key theological proofs.[1] Abū Hāshim al-Jubbā'ī (d. 933), a prominent early Mu'tazilite, went so far as to argue that the primary duty of each person is to rid oneself of traditional, uncritical belief by doubting God's existence, before attempting to prove it.

Most traditionalist theologians took the contrary view, holding that having a rationally unjustified belief in God, which accords with scriptural creeds, will suffice. For them, *kalām* proofs were at once reprehensible innovations and too obscure and precarious to serve as reliable bases for sound belief.

According to Ibn Taymiyya, man knows God immediately and intuitively by virtue of his innate, primordial nature (*fiṭra*), instilled in him by God. Those with a sound *fiṭra* are able to bear witness to God's existence without reflection. Yet he accepts that *fiṭra* is easily corruptible in unhealthy environments, especially when influenced by misguided or heretical doctrines and methods, such as those found in *kalām* and philosophy. For those with an unsound *fiṭra*, Ibn Taymiyya prescribes a different mode of theological knowledge, akin to an argument from design, namely the contemplation of God's "signs" in nature, through which one will be able to recognise God's existence immediately.[2]

Ghazālī, primarily a Sufi, secondarily a *mutakallim*, likewise maintains that man knows God through *fiṭra*, without discursive reasoning.[3] Resorting to proofs may become compulsory upon some, especially those plagued by doubts. Yet, for him, the most superior method of knowing God, which provides direct experience of "witnessing" Him and renders all other methods superfluous, is that of Sufi spiritual discipline. Thus, much more mildly than Ibn Taymiyya, Ghazālī too expresses some aversion to purely rational proofs for the existence of God, which he considers ultimately mediocre and primarily therapeutic.

Notwithstanding the great variety of stances, in the present chapter we are concerned only with some of the rational proofs expounded in the theological tradition, especially in *kalām*. Rather than attempting to account comprehensively for all proofs and their historical development, we shall consider some representative (but not always obvious) examples of the main proofs. A convenient starting-point will be a categorisation of proofs provided by Fakhr al-Dīn al-Rāzī (d. 1210), an outstanding philosopher and *mutakallim*, who surveyed and assessed the previous philosophical and theological dialectic more systematically and insightfully than did his predecessors. He distinguishes between four categories: (1) arguments from the creation of the attributes of things (a subspecies of the argument from design); (2) arguments from the creation of things; (3) arguments from the contingency of the attributes of things (a subspecies of the argument from particularisation); and (4) arguments from the contingency of things.[4] The first type will be discussed below under "Common teleological arguments"; the second and third under "*Kalām* cosmological arguments"; and the fourth under "Avicenna's argument from contingency".

First, however, a preliminary problem, already hinted at, merits consideration. How do the *mutakallimūn* justify their contention that theological reflection constitutes a duty (*wājib*)? The problem is fundamentally ethical, turning on the contentious question of the nature and grounds of ethical obligation. In the remainder of this section, we shall consider two contrasting solutions: one from Mu'tazilite ethical realism, the other from Ash'arite divine command ethics.

The Mu'tazilite position

How do the Mu'tazila justify their contention that undertaking reflection with a view to knowing God is obligatory? Al-Malāḥimī (d. 1141), a later Basran Mu'tazilite, puts forth two representative arguments in this regard.[5]

First, he argues that reflection offers the agent who is devoid of the foregoing knowledge the hope of allaying an inevitable *fear* resulting from a certain "motive" (*khāṭir*), which appears in his heart in one of several ways. If the sensible person hears or reads theological discussions and encounters warnings of afterlife punishment for unbelievers, he will experience fear as he realises that the world indeed betrays evidence of an intelligent Maker, confirming that His existence is a real possibility. If no such external factors effect this motive, God will, by necessity, produce it directly in the agent's heart.[6] Once the inevitability of this eschatological fear is established, the duty to reflect is affirmed through the Mu'tazilite ethical premise that it is obligatory on the agent to avoid any unjustified harm that he expects to befall him. Mu'tazilites consider this to be a duty in a realist sense: harming oneself is evil because it is a form of wrongdoing, and wrongdoing is intrinsically evil.[7]

The second argument runs as follows. Possessing knowledge of God's existence itself constitutes a duty for the agent; reflection is necessary for attaining this knowledge; an act that is necessary for fulfilling a duty itself becomes a duty; therefore, reflection is a duty. Malāḥimī justifies the premise that the agent is obligated to possess this knowledge on the ground that knowing that there exists a deity, who will punish evildoers and reward the doers of good, will motivate the agent to do good and avoid evil; all that serves this end will consequently be a duty.

Reflection, for Mu'tazilites, is thus neither intrinsically obligatory, nor an end in itself.[8] Rather, it is a duty on account of the foregoing ethical considerations, envisaged within the standard Mu'tazilite framework of ethical realism. By this, they attempt to demonstrate that theological reflection is a rational duty, without recourse to revelation, the acceptance of which presupposes belief in God.

Yet Mu'tazilites go on to maintain that reflection in order to know God is the most "primary" (*awwal*) duty of all. This contention seems to run into serious difficulties: evidently, the thrust of the above arguments is that this duty is neither absolute nor known immediately, but is conditional on the foregoing ethical duties, which indeed appear more primary.[9]

The Ash'arite position

Early Ash'arites, too, contend that reflection constitutes a duty. Yet, to them, it is a religious (*shar'ī*) duty, since they maintain that duties can be engendered only by revealed religion to the exclusion of unaided reason or any other sources.[10] One who lives on a remote island and has never heard of any revealed religions will not be under an absolute obligation to reflect in order to know God, or to do good and omit evil. Only when a religion is established through prophecy will knowing God and adhering to various forms of conduct become obligatory on those who receive it.[11]

The Mu'tazila object that this would allow the non-believer to argue that since he accepts neither God's existence nor the instructions of His purported prophet, he is in no way obligated to reflect in order to know Him. For Ash'arites, however, one need not accept a prophet's claims to fall under this obligation. Juwaynī (d. 1085) responds that a prophet's performance of miracles will habitually (*fī'l-'āda*) provide sufficient motivation for people to consider his claims seriously and to reflect upon the theological matters he refers to.[12] "The truthfulness of prophecy", therefore, "does not depend on reflection, but on miracles." The sensible person does not have to accept that God exists, that He could send prophets with His word, and that this particular man is a genuine prophet, to have sufficient reasons, and even to find it necessary, to investigate these matters.

Ash'arites also provide an argument *ad hominem* in reply to the foregoing Mu'tazilite objection, by highlighting a similar problem in their opponents' position. Since Mu'tazilites do not consider the duty to reflect to be known immediately, they argue that reflection is a duty because knowing God is a duty, and what is necessary for fulfilling a duty itself becomes a duty (Malāḥimī's second argument above). However, since this will be known through reflection, the non-believer will know that reflection is a duty only once he reflects; so he can simply refuse to reflect in the first place.[13] The Mu'tazilite contention – that if external circumstances do not motivate one to reflect, God will necessarily produce a motive in his heart – is dismissed as an utterly unsubstantiated claim.[14]

Although this Ash'arite argument *ad hominem* may seem merely topical, it underscores a more profound point: that no cognition or action possesses intrinsic qualities that make it obligatory on non-adherents. Religion, according to Ash'arites, addresses both believers and non-believers, obliging all to recognise the existence of God. Believers will readily accept this. Non-believers will, if presented with adequate evidence and inducements, perceive the gravity and persuasiveness of this obligation. The fact that they do not readily recognise it as an obligation makes it no less obligatory on them.

Later Ash'arism came hugely under the influence of Fakhr al-Dīn al-Rāzī, who departs from early Ash'arite divine command ethics in favour of a subjectivist, consequentialist ethics, whereby value is defined with reference to the consequences of acts for the agent. For Rāzī, a rational person who hears the doctrines of a revealed religion, especially the possibility of punishment in the afterlife, will find it prudentially necessary to check their veracity.[15] Reflection may thus be deemed "obligatory", not in any fundamentally religious sense, but in a subjective, prudential sense – the antithesis to the Mu'tazilite objectivist position.

COMMON TELEOLOGICAL ARGUMENTS

An argument from design, or a so-called teleological argument, is one which argues from manifestations of order or providence in the world to a God who produced them.[16] The Qur'an constantly invites to this type of reasoning; for instance 2:164:

> In the creation of the heavens and earth; in the alternation of night and day; in the ships that sail the seas with goods for people; in the water which God sends down from the sky to give life to the earth when it has been barren, scattering all kinds of creatures over it; in the changing of the winds and clouds that run their appointed courses between the sky and earth: there are signs in all these for those who use their minds.[17]

With a primarily qur'anic inspiration and endorsement, arguments from design have become extremely popular in general religious literature and among lay believers. They serve, not only as proofs for the existence of God as such, but often primarily as pointers to evidence for various attributes of the creator, to be contemplated pietistically by believers. The qur'an here merely provides the theologian with guidance on what kind of evidence and arguments to employ;

hence such qur'anically inspired arguments are not premised on the revealed nature of the text, which otherwise would entail circularity.[18]

Numerous works have been dedicated to the argument from design; yet we still have a very sketchy understanding of its history in Islam. One early book plausibly attributed to al-Jāḥiẓ (d. 869), the Mu'tazilite theologian and litterateur, draws on pre-Islamic Greek sources,[19] whereas another by his contemporary al-Qāsim ibn Ibrāhīm (d. 860) has a primarily qur'anic inspiration.[20] The list of exponents of the argument from design later comes to include some of the foremost philosophers and theologians in medieval Islam, including Abū Bakr al-Rāzī (d. 925), Ibn Ḥazm (d. 1064), al-Ghazālī, Averroes, and Fakhr al-Dīn al-Rāzī.

In what follows, we will focus on discussions of this argument by Fakhr al-Dīn al-Rāzī. On this he writes:

> Whoever contemplates the various parts of the higher and lower worlds will find that this world is constructed in the most advantageous and best manner, and the most superlative and perfect order (*tartīb*). The mind unambiguously testifies that this state of affairs cannot be except by the governance (*tadbīr*) of a wise and knowledgeable [being].[21]

Here and in other places, Rāzī distinguishes between two types of evidence of design. First, he refers to signs of providence, that is, advantages (*manāfi'*) provided to conscious beings, which indicate the existence of a God attributed with beneficence (*iḥsān*), who is responsible for them. Second, he refers to signs of order, or masterly production (*iḥkām, itqān*), in the world, which point to a God possessed of wisdom (*ḥikma*) and power. When explicated in detail, the latter signs of order or beauty observable to us in the created world are often referred to as "marvels" (*'ajā'ib*), or "wonders" (*badā'i'*).[22]

These signs may be gleaned, according to Rāzī, by directing attention to different "loci of discernment" (sing. *maḥall al-i'tibār*) in the cosmos. In the lower world, these are: (a) the human body, (b) the human psyche, (c) animals, (d) plants, (e) minerals, (f) meteorological phenomena, (g) the elements, and (h) "marvels that occur because of the discernable expediencies among these things, and the manner in which each assists in preserving the species of the other".[23] In the higher world, they are: (i) the natures of the celestial spheres and the planets, (j) the magnitudes of each, (k) their complex motions and the way in which these motions influence the lower world in a manner advantageous to creatures, (l) the way in which daily, monthly and annual cycles are dependent on the motions of celestial bodies, (m) the manner in which things in this world depend on the sun's motion, and (n) marvels that can be observed in both fixed and moving stars.

The marvels in each of these fields are explicated in their respective disciplines; for example, those of the human body in anatomy, and those of plants in botany. Rāzī's *Great Commentary* on the Qur'an also abounds with such discussions. He furthermore dedicates his little-known work *Secrets of Revelation* (*Asrār al-tanzīl*) to proofs for the existence of God from features in the observable world, including proofs from design and proofs from particularisation. Being qur'anically inspired, this book provides a different set of categories of loci for evidence: (a) the heavens, (b) the sun and the moon, (c) the stars, (d) man, (e) animals (the book is incomplete and ends here), (f) plants, (g) meteorological phenomena, (h) seas, and (i) mountains.[24]

Let us consider the following representative example.[25] Although the human body is tremendously complex, Rāzī reasons, it is generated from simple sperm. Let us first assume that the body emerges from sperm purely by virtue of its natural properties, as naturalists (*ṭabīʿiyyūn*) claim. Now either sperm is homogeneous (according to Aristotelian biology), or it consists of components drawn from, and corresponding in their natures to, the various different organs of the human body (the so-called "pansomatic" view dominant among earlier physicians). However, if sperm is homogeneous, it should produce an equally simple effect, namely a homogenous spherical object. Naturalists, however, maintain that sperm is inhomogeneous and that each of its components, purely by virtue of its latent natural disposition, produces a specific organ in the human body. Rāzī replies that, by the same foregoing analysis, each component would produce a simple effect – in which case a conglomerate of homogenous spherical objects would result – and that nothing among these components would determine the correct relative position of each organ in the body, guaranteeing, for instance, that the heart does not appear in the brain's position and vice versa. Therefore, sperm cannot develop into a fully fledged human body simply by the impulse of its natural properties. This development will require the agency of a wise (*ḥakīm*) creator who is able to produce objects with such complex and perfect features. As nature, Rāzī contends, lacks the wisdom to produce such sophisticated effects, the physicalist atheism of the naturalists will appear irrational.

He then quotes the philosopher-physician Abū Bakr al-Rāzī on the reasoning that underlies arguments from design. If one considers the design of a jug, he opines, which serves the function of containing water and pouring it controllably, one will have certainty that "it did not acquire its composition by virtue of a nature that lacks consciousness and perception"; rather, one will ascribe this jug to a knowledgeable and powerful agent who knew that benefit is achievable only when the jug has this particular composition. Abū Bakr al-Rāzī then explicates the signs of divine power and wisdom discernible in the human body, before concluding: "These marvels and wonders in this body's composition cannot be produced except by a powerful and wise [God], who created this composition with His power and fashioned it in a masterly manner with His wisdom."[26]

In many arguments from design, it is difficult to separate evidence of providence from evidence of order. Since some theologians conceived man as the centre and *telos* of the universe, they tended to interpret the cosmic order in terms of provisions to man. Yet Fakhr al-Dīn al-Rāzī provides a different rationale behind the combination of these two trends in qur'anic arguments from design: he has the reader in mind. Most evidences (*dalā'il*) provided in the Qur'an, he writes,

> are in one respect evidences, and in another respect blessings [*ni'am*]. Such subtle evidences are more efficacious in the heart, and more effective in the soul; for *qua* evidences they provide knowledge, whereas *qua* blessings they lead to surrender to the Benefactor, thankfulness to Him and submission to His majesty's might.[27]

The combination of these two respects provides a cognitive recognition of God's existence and attributes, especially knowledge, power and unity, as well as soteriological advantages to man – an analysis that accords perfectly with Rāzī's notion that the "method [*ṭarīqa*] of the Qur'an" is to combine demonstrative and rhetorical modes of discourse for maximal efficacy in humans.[28] Arguments from design, moreover, draw much strength from being cumulative (*muta'āḍida*) and from involving faculties of sense and imagination alongside reason.[29] For these reasons, Rāzī contends in his later works that arguments from design are superior to all other arguments for the existence of God, namely the classical arguments of *kalām* and philosophy (below), which are subtle and address reason alone.[30] By this, he explains the fact that although arguments from design are easy to devise and often lack formal rigour, they are normally the most powerful and widespread.

KALĀM COSMOLOGICAL ARGUMENTS

The early *mutakallimūn* developed characteristic doctrines and methods of argument (some of which we will encounter below), which formed the speculative frameworks in which they expounded their proofs for the existence of God. Generally, arguments from design were either omitted or accorded secondary importance in *kalām* works, since they proved only the existence of a "designer", but not the generation of matter and hence creation *ex nihilo*, and because they were often seen to lack methodological rigour. Instead, the *kalām* argument *par excellence* became the argument from creation *ex nihilo*, or temporal generation (*ḥudūth*),[31] and the closely related argument from particularisation – both cosmological arguments, since they prove the existence of God starting from the existence of other beings.

Arguments from creation *ex nihilo*

The basic argument from creation goes as follows. The world is temporally originated (*ḥādith*). All that is temporally originated requires a separate originator. Therefore, the world requires a separate originator.

This originator must be pre-eternal. Otherwise, if it too is generated, then, by the same reasoning, it will require another originator; and ultimately the existence of a pre-eternal originator has to be admitted.

Both premises in the argument were surrounded by complex discussions, both among theologians, and between them and the philosophers. In what follows, some of the discussions that appeared among the *mutakallimūn* surrounding the two premises in this proof are examined.

That the world is temporally originated

Several arguments were advanced in support of this doctrine (the minor premise in the above proof) mostly on the basis of the early *kalām* physical theory that, apart from God, all beings are bodies consisting of both atoms and accidents present in them.[32] The most commonly used is the so-called argument from accidents (*a'rāḍ*), apparently developed by the Mu'tazilite Abū Hāshim al-Jubbā'ī, which establishes the generation of atoms on the basis of four principles, as follows:

(a) Accidents exist in bodies.
(b) Accidents are generated.
(c) Bodies cannot be devoid of, or precede, accidents.
(d) What cannot be devoid of, or precede, what is generated is likewise generated.[33]

Earlier *mutakallimūn* seem to hold that the generation of the world follows from these contentions directly. Yet, as Averroes points out, this line of reasoning involves an equivocation: what is found to be generated in the fourth principle is the single body that necessarily has a particular accident known to be generated, rather than bodies as such, and consequently the world as a whole, as in the conclusion.[34] Indeed, he points out, it will still be conceivable for the world to be pre-eternal, involving infinitely regressing series of temporally originated things (*ḥawādith lā awwala lahā*).

Later *mutakallimūn*, as Averroes notes, became more aware of this gap in the proof, and attempted, apparently starting from Juwaynī, to address it by arguing that a pre-eternal series of accidents is inconceivable.[35] Several arguments are found in later works of *kalām* that support this contention; the following two are recorded in a later Mu'tazilite source.

For instance, it is argued, rather opaquely, that the whole must be characterised by the same attributes that necessarily characterise each of its individual parts; for instance, if something consists entirely of black parts, it too must be black. Therefore, since each part of the world is generated and has a beginning, the whole world too must be generated and have a beginning.

The infinite regress of accidents is also refuted using proofs from the impossibility of an infinite number, some of which were apparently adopted from John Philoponus (d. *c.* 570).[36] For instance, it is argued:

> When today's events are combined with past events, these will increase; without today's events, they will diminish. Increase and diminution in what is infinite are inconceivable. This indicates that [the series of past events] is finite with respect to its beginning. This is the proof also for the finiteness of the magnitude of the earth and other bodies; for it is possible to conceive of increase and diminution in them.[37]

Many later Ash'arites adopted Juwaynī's modified version of the argument for creation *ex nihilo*, which most theologians treated as an article of faith. Yet this doctrine soon became the centre of conflict between the theologians and most philosophers, who defended the pre-eternity of the world, as the interaction between the two traditions increased. Doubts were raised around the arguments for creation, to the extent that in one of his latest works Rāzī examines all the relevant arguments and counterarguments and admits that no rational or revealed evidence proves either the creation or pre-eternity of the world.[38] Under his influence, it seems, Ibn Taymiyya asserts that no rational or revealed evidence proves the inconceivability of the infinite regress of accidents, apparently suspending judgement on the subject.

That what is temporally originated requires an originator

Concerning the nature of the major, causal premise in the argument from creation, Rāzī distinguishes between two contrasting views, both made chiefly by Mu'tazilites. Some consider the premise self-evident, others consider it discursive.

The former position, writes Rāzī, finds support among many Muslims, and is defended notably by the early Baghdad Mu'tazilite al-Ka'bī (d. 931), who points out that "when rational people sense the occurrence of a thing, they will look for its cause without hesitation or reflection".[39] When we see a building, we will know immediately that it had a builder. Rāzī, however, rejects establishing this premise on such observable phenomena, which are too simplistic. He objects that if this premise is known to us immediately in this manner, we will also have immediate knowledge of two other concomitant facts that make it inapplicable to proving the existence of God: (a) that every temporal event has a temporal cause (whoever hears a sound will look for its temporal cause, rather than assume that it was due to the sky being above us and the earth beneath us!); and (b) that it is preceded by time and matter. Therefore, the claim that this premise constitutes immediate knowledge will only imply the infinite regress of temporal causes and the pre-eternity of time and matter, and cannot be used in proving that the world had a pre-eternal creator who is completely other than it.

By contrast, most Mu'tazilites, including 'Abd al-Jabbār (d. 1025), consider this premise to be discursive, and argue for it by a complex analogy (*qiyās*) with human action, as follows.[40] Human action requires an originator because it is temporally originated; the world too is temporally originated; therefore, it requires an originator. In this archetypical *kalām* analogy (an instance of inferring the "unobservable" from the "observable", *istidlāl bi'l-shāhid 'alā'l-ghā'ib*), the "original case" (*aṣl*) is "human action"; the "secondary case" (*far'*) is "the world"; the "judgement" (*ḥukm*) is "requiring an originator"; and the "ground" (*'illa*) is "being temporally originated". The analogy will be complete once it has been shown, first, that the judgement applies to the original case because of this ground, and second, that this same ground can be found in the secondary case; consequently the same judgement will equally apply to the latter case.[41] But how can both judgement and ground be affirmed in the original case here?

My act requires me (its originator), we are told, because it occurs according to my motives; this connection affirms the judgement in the original case. But in what respect exactly does my act depend on me? Does it depend on me *because* it is temporally originated, or for some other ground? This question is answered in several ways, most notably using two other standard *kalām* forms of argument.[42] (a) "Investigation and disjunction" (*al-sabr wa'l-taqsīm*): we first list all conceivable grounds for my act's dependence on me (the effect's continual existence, its ethical value, temporal origination, etc.), then disprove as many as we can; if one remains (in this case, temporal origination), it will be the true ground. (b) The "coextensiveness and coexclusiveness" (*al-ṭard wa'l-'aks*) of the event's dependence on me and its coming into being, which implies that the latter is the ground for the former: for the event depends on me only at the point of its coming into being, but ceases to depend on me when it continues to exist and "no longer comes into being". Therefore, my act depends on me in this respect only, and the ground will thus be affirmed in the original case.

It may seem strange to argue for the existence of God from human acts, rather than from the need of natural events generally for causes. Yet this oblique way is forced on those Mu'tazilites who employ this argument by their physics: many of them reject natural causality, and affirm that God creates all generated things, except accidents produced by the power of living creatures. Hence, when I move my pen, my power will generate the accident of motion in it; however, when running water moves a pebble, the accident of motion in the pebble will be generated by God's power, not by the water. Our acts, therefore, provide the only case where we can observe both the originated thing and its originator and conclude that the former is generated by the latter. The existence of the creator will then be the only explanation for the generation of the existence of other accidents and all atoms, as 'Abd al-Jabbār writes: "Everything that is [beyond the capacity of created beings] is evidence for Him."[43]

Mu'tazilites criticised Ash'arites on account of their contention that human acts are generated by divine, rather than human, power: since they cannot affirm that power generates things in the "observable" realm, they cannot affirm the same in the "unobservable" realm. They will be unable to accept the causal premise in the argument, and will thus fail both to explain the world as a divine act and to prove the existence of God. Juwaynī retorts that Ash'arites use the closely related particularisation argument, which does not resort to the above analogy.[44] Ash'arites indeed rarely use this basic argument from creation, involving the major premise, "What is originated requires an originator", except in an informal and non-technical manner. Rāzī attacks each step in the above analogical argument, arguing at length that "coming into being" cannot be the ground for a thing's requiring a cause.[45]

Arguments from particularisation

This is the main form of argument used by early Ash'arites, and is often used by Mu'tazilites and later Ash'arites. It turns on the notion of particularisation (*takhṣīṣ*), which has its background in a trend distinctly characteristic of classical *kalām*, stemming from the sense that randomness of any kind, in either quantity or quality, is inconceivable. Every seemingly random fact about the world or things therein thus calls for explanation. Different instances of this type of proof cite different facts. The earliest arguments were relatively simple and departed from the atomist framework of classical *kalām*, as in the following two arguments advanced by the Ash'arite theologian al-Bāqillānī (d. 1013).

He argues that we observe identical things coming into being at different times. If the occurrence of one thing at a particular moment is due to an intrinsic quality thereof, all similar things should occur at the same time. It thus appears that nothing intrinsic to the thing itself could make it more likely to occur at a particular moment rather than at another moment, or more likely to occur at a given moment than another, similar thing. Therefore, there must be an external voluntary effecter, who causes particular things to occur at particular moments.

Bāqillānī further argues that objects in this world have different shapes, since they consist of different arrangements of atoms. Yet it is conceivable for each object to have an arrangement different from the one it actually has:

> What is square can be round, and what is round square. What has the shape of one particular animal can have that of another. Each object may lose its shape to take on a different shape. It is inconceivable that what has a certain particular shape will have it by virtue of itself, or because it is possible for it to have it. Otherwise, if [the latter] were the case, [the object] would have to take on every shape that it may possibly take, all at the same time, so that it would acquire all dissimilar shapes simultaneously.[46]

The absurdity of this, Bāqillānī continues, proves that the shapes of objects must have been determined by a "shaper", possessed of will.

Both arguments are occasionalistic and presuppose classical Ash'arite atomism and a rejection of natural causality. Things, we are told, do not come into being at particular moments with particular characteristics because of any natural factors, such as intrinsic properties therein or a causal nexus between one moment and another. There is no natural necessity determining the way things actually are. All things, rather, consist of identical atoms and of different accidents present in them, which come in and out of existence at every moment. At each moment, therefore, every atom will have endless possibilities and will hence require an external factor to determine its properties and the accidents to be generated in it. This, it is argued, must be God.

As mentioned, the general particularisation argument can take different types of facts as its point of departure. The foregoing examples focus on the *when* and *how* with respect to the generation of things. In later, more sophisticated, arguments advanced by Juwaynī, the same lines of reasoning are applied to the world as a whole, which allows him to transcend the occasionalistic bias of earlier particularisation arguments.

He argues, first, that since the world is generated, it must have come into being at a particular point in time. This implies that a separate particularisation agent must exist to select this particular moment for creating the world out of other possible moments. Such selection can only be made by a voluntary agent. An unchanging, non-voluntary pre-eternal cause will necessitate its effect and will thus produce a pre-eternal world; yet the world, Juwaynī argues, has been shown to be temporally originated.[47] This argument faces the problem that it implies that time existed before creation, a doctrine that was subject to much debate.[48]

Elsewhere, Juwaynī also argues that if we observe the world, we find that it consists of things that have great variety in their attributes, composition and circumstances. None of these, however, is necessary, as the mind can imagine all things being otherwise. It becomes evident, he continues, that since the world is possible, "it will require a determinant [*muqtaḍī*], which determines it in the way it actually is". What could exist in different possible ways cannot exist randomly (*ittifāqan*), without a determinant, in one particular way.[49] Again, the determinant has to be a voluntary agent; for a non-voluntary factor will necessitate a uniform, undifferentiated effect, whereas this world consists of highly complex parts, which do not behave in simple, uniform ways.[50] Ghazālī writes with reference to the notion of particularisation: "The world came into existence whence it did, having the description with which it came to exist, and in the place in which it came to exist, through will, will being an attribute whose function is to differentiate a thing from its similar."[51]

Such particularisation arguments, which refer to characteristics of the world or things therein differ crucially from arguments from design. The latter focus on aspects of perfection, masterly production, or providence in the world. Particularisation arguments, by contrast, depart from the mere fact that existents in this world, regardless of their perfection, imperfection, goodness or badness, are possible, since they exist in one particular way rather than another, and thus require an external factor to select this possibility over all other possibilities. Such arguments aim only at proving that the world has a voluntary producer, whereas arguments from design seek to prove that the world must have a wise, powerful and good producer.

Finally, Juwaynī goes further to develop a third argument by applying the particularisation principle to the fact that the world exists. In this crucial modification to the particularisation argument, he frees it completely from the constraints of atomist physics. He first demonstrates that the world is temporally originated, then writes:

> What is temporally originated is a possible existent (*jā'iz al-wujūd*); for it is possible to conceive its existence rather than its non-existence, and it is possible to conceive its non-existence rather than its existence. Thus, since it is characterised by possible existence rather than possible non-existence, it will require a particularising factor (*mukhaṣṣiṣ*), viz. the Creator, be He exalted.[52]

The argument departs from the fact that the world exists, regardless of what it consists of and the way in which it exists. Since it is equally possible that the world did not exist, the fact that it does exist points to an external factor which effected one of the two possibilities.

In this argument, Juwaynī marries the argument from creation *ex nihilo* to the particularisation argument, which allows him, as an Ash'arite, to argue that the world requires an originator because it is temporally originated, without resorting to the Mu'tazilite analogy from human action. More crucially, Juwaynī's modified argument brings the particularisation argument close to Avicenna's argument from contingency, paving the way for a synthesis of the two arguments in later *kalām*.

AVICENNA'S ARGUMENT FROM CONTINGENCY

The central proof for the existence of God that Avicenna puts forth is the proof from contingency (*imkān*). In line with the Neoplatonic tradition, he attempts to prove an ultimate efficient cause for bringing the world into being, rather than a cause for motion in the world, as Aristotle does. Unlike most other proofs, this proof depicts God as a non-voluntary First Cause, which produces the world from pre-eternity by Its essence. Thus, despite its great influence on later Muslim thought, the proof had to be adjusted to conform to more orthodox conceptions of God.

Avicenna claims to advance a purely metaphysical proof (as opposed to a physical proof), one that rests purely on an analysis of the notion of existence *qua* existence, without consideration of any attributes of the physical world.[53] He writes:

> Reflect on how our proof for the existence and oneness of the First and His being free from attributes did not require reflection on anything except existence itself and how it did not require any consideration of His creation and acting even though the latter [provide] evidential proof for Him.
>
> This mode, however, is more reliable and noble, that is, where when we consider the state of existence, we find that existence inasmuch as it is existence bears witness to Him, while He thereafter bears witness to all that comes after Him in existence.[54]

If true, this characterisation would set the proof apart from all contemporaneous, cosmological and teleological proofs. In contemporary terminology, it would qualify it to be an ontological proof, that is to say, a proof which argues for the existence of God entirely from *a priori* premises and makes no use of any premises that derive from our observation of the world. Recent studies of Avicenna's proof, however, differ on whether the argument is cosmological or indeed ontological.[55] As we will see, doubt with regard to the purported fundamental novelty of Avicenna's proof was expressed centuries ago.

The proof rests on conceptions that, Avicenna contends, are primary in the mind, intuited without need of sensory perception and mental cogitation, namely "the existent" and "the necessary". The conception "the possible", being what is neither necessary nor impossible, is either equally primary, or derived directly from the conception "the necessary".

An existent, by virtue of itself, is either possibly existent, or necessarily existent. If we posit an existent that is necessary in itself, then, Avicenna argues, it will have to be uncaused, absolutely simple, one and unique. If we posit an existent that is possible in itself, it will have to depend for its existence on another existent. The latter will be its cause, not in the sense of being an antecedent accidental cause for its temporal generation, but as a coexistent essential cause for its continuous existence. If this cause is itself a possible existent, it will have to exist by virtue of another. The series of actual existents, Avicenna argues, cannot continue *ad infinitum*, but must terminate in an uncaused existent that is necessary in itself.

But why does a possible existent require a cause to exist? Avicenna proves this using the argument from particularisation, apparently borrowed from *kalām*. A possible existent can exist or not exist. It will exist only once "the scale is tipped" by an external cause such that its existence becomes preponderant over its non-existence. When this occurs, its existence will be "necessitated" by its cause.

Now, the proof for the existence of God runs as follows. There is no doubt that there is existence. Every existent, by virtue of itself, is either possible or necessary. If necessary, then this is the existent being sought, namely God. If possible, then it will ultimately require the necessary existent in order to exist. In either case, God must exist.[56]

Apparently based entirely on an analysis of *a priori* conceptions and premises, the proof will appear ontological. However, other considerations suggest that the proof is fundamentally cosmological. For instance, the deliberately abstract and unexplained premise, "There is no doubt that there is existence", appears to derive from our knowledge that "there is no doubt that something exists", or it may even mean the same as the latter statement.[57] When the proof then goes on to appeal to the dichotomy of possible existence and necessary existence, it branches into two hypothetical directions: that this indubitable existence is either possible or necessary. But this then begs the following question: if our indubitable knowledge that there actually is existence is examined, will this existence turn out to be possible or necessary? In other words, will this knowledge derive from our awareness (no matter how primitive and abstract) of possible existents or necessary ones? Of course, we cannot be aware of necessary existents; therefore, our indubitable knowledge of existence must relate to our awareness of possible existence. Inevitably, it seems, the proof reasons on the basis of possible existence using the causal premise, which explains the existence of possible existents by reference to a necessary existent. It hence appears to hinge on the existence of things other than God to prove His existence.

Indeed, eight centuries ago, Rāzī wrote that all proofs for the existence of God depart from facts about the world, except that Avicenna had claimed to have advanced a fundamentally new proof purportedly based on a consideration of existence *qua* existence, without consideration of things other than God. He quotes Avicenna's above statement to this effect. This claim, however, invites two objections from Rāzī. First, this proof depends on a causal premise: the proof in fact "infers the existence of the necessary [existent] from the [actual] existence of the contingent". Second, even if it proves a necessary existent, one will still need to demonstrate that it is other than the physical things perceptible in this world (this recalls the series of proofs, already referred to, which Avicenna advances for the simplicity, oneness and uniqueness of the necessary existent).[58] In other words, the argument presupposes these different considerations about the world: one should prove that the world is not necessarily existent, but contingent, and that a contingent requires a necessary existent to exist, before concluding that God, therefore, exists. A good proof indeed, Rāzī would add, but not an ontological one. Nevertheless, even if such criticisms are accepted, Avicenna should nonetheless be credited with the first attempt ever to advance such a proof.[59]

Further reading

Primary texts in translation

al-Bayḍāwī, 'Abdullāh ibn 'Umar, *Ṭawāli' al-Anwār*, tr. Edwin E. Calverley and James W. Pollock, in *Nature, Man and God in Medieval Islam*, 2 vols. (Leiden, 2002), esp. vol. II, pp. 727–48.

al-Ghazālī, Abū Ḥāmid, *The Jerusalem Epistle* [*Al-Qudsiyya*], tr. A. Tibawi, in *Islamic Quarterly* 9 (1965), pp. 62–122, esp. pp. 96–9.

Ibn Rushd, Abū l-Walīd, *Faith and Reason: Averroes' Exposition of Religious Arguments* [*Al-Kashf 'an manāhij al-adilla fī 'aqā'id al-milla*], tr. I. Najjar (Oxford, 2001), esp. pp. 16–38.

al-Jāḥiẓ, 'Amr ibn Baḥr, *Chance or Creation* [*al-Dalā'il wa-l-i'tibār*], tr. M. A. S. Abdel Haleem (Reading, 1995).

al-Juwaynī, 'Abd al-Malik, *A Guide to Conclusive Proofs for the Principles of Belief* [*Al-Irshād*], tr. Paul E. Walker (Reading, 2000), esp. pp. 11–18.

al-Qāsim ibn Ibrāhīm, *Kitāb al-dalīl al-kabīr*, tr. Binyamin Abrahamov, in *Al-Ḳāsim b. Ibrāhīm on the Proof of God's Existence* (Leiden, 1990).

Secondary texts

Craig, William, *The Kalam Cosmological Argument* (New York, 1979).

Davidson, Herbert, *Proofs for Eternity, Creation and the Existence of God in Medieval Islamic and Jewish Philosophy* (New York and Oxford, 1987).

Goodman, Lenn, "Ghazâlî's argument from creation", *International Journal of Middle East Studies* 2 (1971), pp. 67–85, 168–88.

Hallaq, Wael B., "Ibn Taymiyya on the existence of God", *Acta Orientalia* 52 (1991), pp. 49–69.

Marmura, Michael E., "Avicenna's proof from contingency for God's existence in the *Metaphysics* of the *Shifā'*", *Mediaeval Studies* 42 (1980), pp. 337–52.

Mayer, Toby, "Ibn Sīnā's 'Burhān al-Ṣiddīqīn'," *Journal of Islamic Studies* 12 (2001), pp. 18–39.

Morewedge, Parviz, "A third version of the ontological argument in the Ibn Sīnian metaphysics", in Parviz Morewedge (ed.), *Islamic Philosophical Theology* (New York, 1979), pp. 188–222.

Yaran, Cafer S., *Islamic Thought on the Existence of God* (Washington, 2003).

Notes

1. This view found expression in a dedicated genre on what every Muslim ought to believe in, represented by Muḥammad ibn al-Ṭayyib al-Bāqillānī, *al-Inṣāf fī mā yajibu iʿtiqāduhu wa-lā yajūzu al-jahl bih*, ed. Muḥammad al-Kawtharī (Cairo, 1963).
2. See Wael B. Hallaq, "Ibn Taymiyya on the existence of God", *Acta Orientalia* 52 (1991), pp. 49–69.
3. Al-Ghazālī, *The Jerusalem Epistle* [*Al-Qudsiyya*], tr. A. L. Tibawi, in *Islamic Quarterly* 9 (1965), p. 98.
4. Fakhr al-Dīn al-Rāzī, *al-Maṭālib al-ʿāliya mina'l-ʿilm al-ilāhī*, ed. Aḥmad al-Saqqā, 8 vols. (Beirut, 1987), I, p. 71. He gives two other types, which he then includes under these four. For greater chronological accuracy, the arguments are presented here in reverse order.
5. Maḥmūd ibn Muḥammad al-Malāḥimī, *al-Muʿtamad fī uṣūl al-dīn*, ed. Martin McDermott and Wilferd Madelung (London, 1991), pp. 79–81.
6. On the background to this Muʿtazilite view, see Harry Wolfson, *The Philosophy of the Kalām* (Cambridge, MA, 1976), pp. 624ff.; Josef van Ess, "Early Islamic theologians on the existence of God", in Khalil I. Semaan (ed.), *Islam and the Medieval West* (Albany, 1980), pp. 64–81, at pp. 75–7.
7. Cf. Mankdīm Shashdīw ['Abd al-Jabbār], *Sharḥ al-uṣūl al-khamsa*, ed. 'Abd al-Karīm 'Uthmān (Cairo, 1965), p. 67.
8. Cf. ibid.
9. Cf. Malāḥimī, *Muʿtamad*, pp. 81–2; Mankdīm, *Sharḥ*, p. 69.
10. See Ayman Shihadeh, *The Teleological Ethics of Fakhr al-Dīn al-Rāzī* (Leiden, 2006), pp. 49ff.
11. 'Abd al-Malik al-Juwaynī, *al-Shāmil fī uṣūl al-dīn*, ed. 'A. al-Nashshār *et al.* (Alexandria, 1969), p. 115. Cf. Juwaynī, *A Guide to Conclusive Proofs for the Principles of Belief* [*Al-Irshād*], tr. Paul E. Walker (Reading, 2000), pp. 5–7.
12. Al-Juwaynī, *Shāmil*, pp. 118–19, reading *jarat* for *kharq*, and *ḥālih* for *ḥāla*.
13. Al-Rāzī, *Muḥaṣṣal afkār al-mutaqaddimīn wa'l-muta'akhkhirīn min al-ʿulamā' wa-l-ḥukamā' wa'l-mutakallimīn*, ed. H. Atay (Cairo, 1991), pp. 134–5.
14. Al-Juwaynī, *Shāmil*, p. 117.
15. Rāzī, *Muḥaṣṣal*, p. 134; cf. Shihadeh, *Teleological Ethics*, pp. 56ff.
16. I here apply the conventional Kantian classification of arguments for the existence of God into teleological arguments, cosmological arguments and ontological arguments (cf. Immanuel Kant, *Critique of Pure Reason*, B 618–19). The last two types are defined below.
17. *The Qur'an*, tr. Muhammad Abdel Haleem (Oxford, 2004).
18. Cf. Juwaynī, *Shāmil*, pp. 277, 287.
19. Cf. Herbert Davidson, *Proofs for Eternity: Creation and the Existence of God in Medieval Islamic and Jewish Philosophy* (New York and Oxford, 1987), pp. 219ff.
20. English translations of both texts are available (see "Further reading").

21. Rāzī, *Maṭālib*, 1, p. 233.
22. See also Averroes, *Faith and Reason: Averroes' Exposition of Religious Arguments* [*Al-Kashf 'an manāhij al-adilla fī 'aqā'id al-milla*], tr. I. Najjar (Oxford, 2001), p. 33, who distinguishes between the argument from design (*ikhtirā'*) and the argument from providence (*'ināya*).
23. Rāzī, *Maṭālib*, 1, p. 234.
24. Rāzī, *Asrār al-tanzīl wa-anwār al-ta'wīl*, ed. M. Muḥammad *et al.* (Baghdad, 1985), p. 151.
25. Rāzī, *Maṭālib*, 1, pp. 218–24.
26. Ibid., 1, pp. 224–5. On Abū Bakr al-Rāzī's notion of God, see Michael E. Marmura, "The Islamic philosophers' conception of Islam", in R. Hovannisian (ed.), *Islam's Understanding of Itself* (Malibu, 1981), pp. 87–102.
27. Rāzī, *Asrār*, p. 151; cf. *Maṭālib*, 1, p. 216.
28. On this notion, see Shihadeh, *Teleological Ethics*, pp. 142ff.
29. Rāzī (*Maṭālib*, 1, p. 239) also recognises the importance of cumulating arguments more generally for the existence of God. Even if each separately does not provide certainty, their cumulative force may achieve this. For a recent defence of such a strategy, see Richard Swinburne, *The Existence of God* (Oxford, 1991), pp. 13–15.
30. Rāzī, *Maṭālib*, 1, pp. 216, 236.
31. "*Ḥudūth*" is rendered as either "generation" or "temporal origination", depending on context.
32. On proofs for the existence of accidents, see Davidson, *Proofs*, pp. 180ff.
33. 'Abd al-Jabbār, *al-Majmū' fi'l-muḥīṭ bi'l-taklīf*, ed. J. Houben, 2 vols. (Beirut, 1965), 1, pp. 28–67; Malāḥimī, *Mu'tamad*, pp. 84–154; Davidson, *Proofs*, p. 140.
34. Averroes, *Faith and Reason*, pp. 25–6; cf. Davidson, *Proofs*, pp. 143–4.
35. Juwaynī, *Shāmil*, pp. 215ff., and *Guide*, p. 15; Davidson, *Proofs*, pp. 143–6.
36. See Davidson, *Proofs*, pp. 87ff., 117ff.
37. Malāḥimī, *Mu'tamad*, pp. 151–2.
38. Rāzī, *Maṭālib*, Book 4; Muammer Iskenderoğlu, *Fakhr al-Dīn al-Rāzī and Thomas Aquinas on the Question of the Eternity of the World* (Brill, 2002), pp. 69ff. In his earlier works, Rāzī defends the doctrine of creation *ex nihilo*.
39. Rāzī, *Maṭālib*, 1, p. 207. This view was also taken by Ghazālī, *al-Iqtiṣād fi'l-i'tiqād*, ed. Ibrahim Agah Çubukçu and Huseyin Atay (Ankara, 1962), pp. 25–6.
40. Cf. 'Abd al-Jabbār, *Majmū'*, 1, pp. 68–93. The analogy is summarised by Malāḥimī (*Mu'tamad*, pp. 172–4) and Rāzī (*Maṭālib*, 1, pp. 210–12), both of whom reject it.
41. On analogy in *kalām* cf. Ayman Shihadeh, "From al-Ghazālī to al-Rāzī: 6th/12th century developments in Muslim philosophical theology", *Arabic Sciences and Philosophy* 15 (2005), pp. 141–79, pp. 165ff.
42. On these forms of argument, see Shihadeh, "From al-Ghazālī to al-Rāzī", pp. 165–7; Josef van Ess, "The logical structure of Islamic

theology", in G. von Grunebaum (ed.), *Logic in Classical Islamic Culture* (Los Angeles, 1967), pp. 21–50, *passim*.
43. 'Abd al-Jabbār, *Majmū'*, p. 28.
44. Juwaynī, *Shāmil*, pp. 276–7, 285–6.
45. Rāzī, *Maṭālib*, I, p. 214; IV, pp. 231–9.
46. Muḥammad al-Bāqillānī, *Tamhīd al-awā'il wa-talkhīṣ al-dalā'il*, ed. 'I. Ḥaydar (Beirut, 1987), pp. 43–4.
47. Juwaynī, *Shāmil*, pp. 263ff., and *Guide*, p. 17; Juwaynī *al-'Aqīda al-Niẓāmiyya*, ed. M. al-Kawtharī (Cairo, 1948), p. 20.
48. Cf. al-Ghazālī, *The Incoherence of the Philosophers*, tr. Michael E. Marmura (Provo, UT, 1997), p. 31.
49. Juwaynī, *Niẓāmiyya*, p. 16.
50. Ibid., p. 17.
51. Ghazālī, *Incoherence*, p. 22.
52. Juwaynī, *Luma' al-adilla*, ed. Fawqīya Ḥusayn, Maḥmūd (Cairo, 1965), pp. 80–1.
53. Abū 'Alī ibn Sīnā, *The Metaphysics of The Healing*, tr. Michael E. Marmura (Provo, UT, 2005), p. 4; cf. Davidson, *Proofs*, pp. 284ff.
54. Ibn Sīnā, *al-Ishārāt wa'l-tanbīhāt*, ed. Sulaymān Dunyā (Cairo, 1938), p. 482; tr. Michael E. Marmura, "Avicenna's proof from contingency for God's existence in the *Metaphysics* of the *Shifā'*", *Mediaeval Studies* 42 (1980), pp. 337–52, at p. 340.
55. Ontological, *a priori* proof: Marmura, "Avicenna's proof"; Parviz Morewedge, "A third version of the ontological argument in the Ibn Sīnian metaphysics", in Parviz Morewedge (ed.), *Islamic Philosophical Theology* (New York, 1979), pp. 188–222. Cosmological proof: Herbert Davidson, "Avicenna's proof of the existence of God as a necessarily existent being", in ibid., pp. 165–87. See also Toby Mayer, "Ibn Sīnā's 'Burhān al-ṣiddīqīn'", *Journal of Islamic Studies* 12 (2001), pp. 18–39, which engages in this debate.
56. The above summary of Avicenna's arguments is based on his *Ishārāt*, *Najāt* and *Shifā'*; Marmura, *Avicenna's Proof*; Davidson, *Proofs*, pp. 281–310.
57. The latter statement, for Avicenna, would still constitute *a priori* knowledge, since he maintains, first, that "existence" is a primary concept, and second, that one has *a priori* knowledge of the existence of one's own self, which is clearly less primitive than knowledge that something exists.
58. Rāzī, *Maṭālib*, I, pp. 53–4.
59. This debate continues after Rāzī. For instance, Jalāl al-Dīn al-Dawwānī (d. 1502) advances a slightly modified version of Avicenna's argument, and attempts to answer the objection that it indeed starts from the existence of possible existents: *Risālat Ithbāt al-wājib al-jadīda*, in *Sab' rasā'il*, ed. Aḥmad Tūysirkānī (Tehran, 2001), pp. 115–70, at pp. 118–19.

11 Worship

WILLIAM C. CHITTICK

Worship can be defined as the appropriate human response to the divine. Having said this, we might jump to an analysis of the rites, rituals and other activities classified as "worship" in the Islamic tradition. But that approach would ignore the basic theological questions: what exactly is "God" that he deserves to be worshipped? What exactly are "human beings" that worship should be demanded of them? What exactly makes the human response "appropriate"? It is to these questions that I turn my attention here. To keep the discussion within bounds, however, I limit myself to notions connected with the Arabic word *'ibāda*, which is normally translated as "worship" or "service".

'Ibāda is a gerund from the verb *'abada*. In his *Arabic–English Lexicon*, E. W. Lane offers a range of English equivalents for the religious meaning of this verb, such as rendering God service, worship, or adoration, and obeying God with humility or submissiveness. The verb also means to be or become an *'abd*: a slave, servant, or bondsman.[1] This word is familiar to those who do not know Arabic because of its common usage in the names of Muslim men (*'abd* + divine name; e.g. 'Abd Allāh, "the servant/slave of God"). Generally, *'abd* designates the proper situation of a human being before God. It is often discussed as the complement of the divine name Lord (*rabb*), though it is also paired with Master (*sayyid*) and Patron (*mawlā*). The word is a near synonym of the active participle *'ābid*, but the latter can better be translated as "worshipper". The texts sometimes highlight the complementarity of Lord and servant by using the past participles, *ma'būd* or "object of worship", as an equivalent for Lord and *marbūb*, "vassal" (literally, "the one who is lorded over") as an equivalent for servant.

Whether *'abd* should be translated as "slave" or "servant" has often been debated. The different meanings of the two English words reflect a constant tension in Islamic theology between divine omnipotence and human freedom. Those who would like to stress the absolute power and authority of God seem to prefer "slave". Those who would like to stress human responsibility opt for "servant". Others have used "bondsman", perhaps attempting to suggest a subtler relationship.

In discussing worship (*'ibāda*), the texts often use a second gerund from the same verb, *'ubūdiyya*, which I translate here as "servanthood".[2] Both *'ibāda* and *'ubūdiyya* designate the activity denoted by the verb *'abada*, but *'ubūdiyya* is more associated with the activity of an *'abd* or servant, and *'ibāda* with the activity of an *'ābid* or worshipper. When discussion focuses on ritual activities, *'ibāda* is typically used, and then the plural, *'ibādāt*, designates acts of worship, such as prayer and fasting. In jurisprudence, the plural is typically contrasted with *mu'āmalāt*, "transactions" or "interactions". Thus *'ibādāt* are required or recommended acts done solely for God, and *mu'āmalāt* are interpersonal and social acts done with God's guidance.

Although *'ibāda* and *'ubūdiyya* (worship and servanthood) tend to have different usages, the line between the two is not clearly drawn, so any discussion of one demands a discussion of the other as well. Thus, when the Qur'an commands *u'budū'llāh*, this does not mean simply "Worship God", but also "Serve God" and "Be God's servants/slaves."

Generally speaking, worship and servanthood are discussed in two branches of Islamic learning: jurisprudence and "Sufism". As I use the latter term, it can perhaps better be called Islamic "spirituality", that is, a concern with the inner life of the soul. As such, "Sufism" is likely to be found in any Muslim, whether or not he or she has links with any institutional form associated with the name. Generally, authors with a Sufi orientation attempt to bring out the moral, ethical, psychological and spiritual implications of worship. In contrast, jurists delineate, describe and codify acts of worship and the prescribed duties or recommended behaviour of the servants.

The earlier texts discuss worship and servanthood largely in terms of a moral imperative. Many later texts, especially from Ibn 'Arabī onwards, ground the moral imperative in what can be called an "ontological imperative". This perspective includes discussion of the Divine Being, the structure of the cosmos, and the reality of the human soul. In modern times, most well-known Muslim authors have continued to cling to the moral imperative, but they have lost touch with the ontological imperative. Indignantly denying "the death of God", they nonetheless go along with its implications by embracing the demise of metaphysics. Instead of standing on the solid ground of Being, they attempt to root the moral imperative in the shifting sands of empirical science, political ideology and critical theory.

THE MORAL IMPERATIVE

The centrality of worship in Islam is demonstrated already by the very structure of *sūra* 1, known as the "Opener" (*al-Fātiḥa*), which is traditionally understood as the epitome of the Qur'an. After beginning in God's name, the Fātiḥa praises God in three verses. The final two verses offer the request of the servant. Verse 5, which is structurally the middle, provides the best-known and most often recited reference to worship in Islam: "Thee alone we worship/serve, and from Thee alone we seek help." Many commentators refer to the manner in which this specific verse situates human beings between God and the world. Worship, they tell us, is the nexus, the point of contact, between God and man, and it is the heart of the Qur'an.

Many explicit qur'anic commandments tell people to worship God. Both the imperative and its rationale are summed up in the sound hadith, "God's right (*ḥaqq*) over His servants is that they worship God and associate nothing with Him. The servant's right over God is that He not chastise anyone who associates nothing with Him."[3] This hadith puts the prophetic message in a nutshell: the One God holds human beings accountable. The criterion for judging whether or not the servants have lived up to their accountability revolves around the word *ḥaqq*, one of the most important terms in the Islamic sciences.

The Qur'an employs the word *ḥaqq* along with various derivatives about 300 times. In half a dozen cases, the word explicitly designates God, so it is included in the lists of divine names (in the Islamic languages, it is a virtual synonym for *Allāh*). As a noun, the word means truth, reality, rightness, appropriateness, worthiness, right, responsibility; the choice of an equivalent has more to do with English usage than the Arabic meaning. It is difficult to say in any given case that the word does not have all of these senses, especially when the Qur'an applies it to God, or to itself, or to the message of a prophet. The word *ḥaqīqa*, from the same root, is used in the Islamic sciences in a similar range of meanings. The goal of a science is to find *ḥaqīqa* – truth, reality, rightness, correctness – within the limits imposed by its tools and methodologies.

To talk of "worship", then, is to talk about the central issue of Islamic learning, which is *ḥaqq* in the absolute and relative senses of the word. In the absolute sense, the word designates God as reality, rightness, truth, and appropriateness; in the relative sense, it designates the created repercussions of the Divine *Ḥaqq*. One can also say that the central issue in Islamic learning is *ḥuqūq* – the plural of *ḥaqq*. Thus we have *ḥuqūq Allāh* and *ḥuqūq al-insān*, often translated (especially in modern political discourse) as "divine rights" and "human rights".

God has many "rights" over human beings, not simply one; but God's unity compresses all these rights into one right, and that right has no more appropriate name than "worship" or "servanthood". God's *ḥaqq*, His rightness, reality, truth, and worthiness, demands human "worship". God's "right" (*ḥaqq*) is man's "responsibility" (*ḥaqq*). Fulfilling that responsibility is to achieve the truth, reality and worthiness of human nature. It is to reach completion and fulfilment, the posthumous repercussion of which is called "Paradise".

If God's right over mankind is that "they worship God and associate nothing with Him", and if worship is to abase and humble oneself before God and to submit oneself to Him, then the first issue that needs to be clarified is the object of worship (*maʿbūd*), and the second the proper method of serving that object. Knowledge of the object of worship is provided most succinctly by the first Testimony of Faith (*Shahāda*), "No god but God", known as *kalimat al-tawḥīd*, "the word that expresses divine unity". The right manner of worshipping follows upon the second *Shahāda*, "Muḥammad is God's Messenger." The first *Shahāda* states the *ḥaqq* of God, the second reformulates this *ḥaqq* as it impinges upon human responsibility. In other words, the second *Shahāda* announces the correct and appropriate response, which is worship and servanthood. The Qur'an universalises these two dimensions of religion (*tawḥīd* and worship) by making them pertain to all the prophets: "We never sent a messenger before thee except that We revealed to him, 'There is no god but I, so worship/serve Me'" (21:25).

Islamic theology – God-talk in all its forms – is concerned with clarifying the reality of the Object of Worship, the Absolute *Ḥaqq*, so that people can relate to it in the right and appropriate manner. The importance of knowledge cannot be overstressed. The Qur'an and the tradition established on its basis represent, in Franz Rosenthal's memorable phrase, "knowledge triumphant".[4] A worshipper without knowledge of the object of his worship and the right and proper ways of acting toward the object is, as the Prophet is reported to have said, "like a donkey in a mill".[5] ʿAlī put it this way: "There is no good in a worship in which there is no knowledge, and there is no good in a knowledge in which there is no understanding."[6] Jaʿfar al-Ṣādiq, the sixth Imam of the Shīʿites and an authority for Sunnī scholars as well, defines intellect (*ʿaql*) – the faculty of knowing specific to human beings – as "that by which the All-Merciful is worshipped and the Gardens attained".[7] Ghazālī represents mainstream thinking when he explains the meaning of the verse, "I created jinn and mankind only to worship Me" (51:56), as follows: "That is, to be My servants. No servant will be a servant until he knows his Lord in His Lordship and himself in his servanthood. He must come to know himself and his Lord, and this is the final goal of God's sending the prophets."[8]

More than a statement about God, the first *Shahāda* is a methodology for coming to know God. The Qur'an, God's Speech, is His self-revelation. It is summed up in the epithets that God gives to Himself (the "ninety-nine most beautiful names"). Explaining the meanings of these names was one of the most important genres of theology from early times. The point of the exercise was first to understand exactly what the names designated and second to open up the way to an appropriate human assimilation of the qualities and characteristics designated by the names. Thus Ghazālī, in his commentary on the divine names, provides a long discussion of *al-takhalluq bi-akhlāq Allāh*, "assuming the character traits of God as one's own character traits",[9] an expression that was already well known in the literature and was sometimes attributed to the Prophet.

The formula of *tawḥīd* is divided into two parts: the negation ("no god") and the affirmation ("but God"). The general methodology was to negate divine qualities from all that cannot rightly (*bi'l-ḥaqq*) lay claim to them, and to affirm that these qualities belong rightly to God. God calls Himself "the Just, the Merciful, the Knowing". In what sense does our understanding of justice, mercy and knowledge apply? What needs to be negated from the imperfect applications of justice, mercy and knowledge that we find in the world and in ourselves, and what needs to be affirmed for God so that we can say, with correct and proper understanding, "There is none just but God, there is none merciful but God, there is none truly knowing but God"?

The process of assimilating *tawḥīd* into the human soul is called *ikhlāṣ*, which means to make pure or to be sincere (notice that *sūra* 112 is called both *al-Tawḥīd* and *al-Ikhlāṣ*). The Qur'an repeatedly uses derivatives of this word to describe true believers and worthy worshippers. "We have sent down upon you the Book with *al-ḥaqq*, so worship God, making the religion pure for Him [or "being sincere to Him in the religion"]. Does not pure/sincere religion belong to God?" (39:2–3). The process of achieving purity of worship demands that servants rid themselves of impure worship, which is wrongly directed worship; hence the imperative of knowledge.

When impure worship is contrasted with sincerity, it is typically called "hypocrisy" (*nifāq*). The basic sense of the Arabic word is to sell oneself, that is, to act for people's sake rather than for God's sake. A second qur'anic expression that is commonly used in the same meaning is *riyā'*, "eye-service", acting with the intention of being seen by others. In contrast, "sincerity" is to worship and serve God alone. It is to negate from Him everything inappropriate and to affirm for Him everything appropriate. The inappropriate – the not *ḥaqq*, the *bāṭil* (false, vain, wrong) – is summed up in one word: *sharīk*, partner or associate. According to one early commentator, the command "O people, worship/serve your Lord" (2:21) means "Declare His unity" (*waḥḥidūhu*, that is, acknowledge *tawḥīd*). Another says that it means, "Purify/make sincere the worship of your Lord by not taking any partner with Him."[10]

The word *shirk*, which designates the act of ascribing a partner to God or associating something with him, is taken as the opposite of *tawḥīd*. Just as "sincerity" is *tawḥīd* put into practice, so "hypocrisy" is *shirk* put into practice. And just as *tawḥīd* is the salvific content of the religious message, so *shirk* is a sure road to hell. According to Qur'an 4:48 and 4:116, *shirk* is the one sin that cannot be forgiven if taken into the grave. Qur'an 4:145 tells us that the hypocrites will be placed in the deepest pit of hell.

The texts are not much interested in "polytheism" in the literal sense of the English word, that is, the worship of several gods at once, because the unity of God was far too self-evident to need a great deal of defence. Polytheistic beliefs were ascribed to other religious communities and to unbelievers. Such beliefs were labelled *shirk jalī*, manifest or obvious association. Much more insidious and dangerous for Muslims was *shirk khafī*, "hidden association". When the Prophet heard some Companions discussing the Antichrist, he told them that there was something he feared much more than that: "Hidden *shirk*: in other words, that a man should perform the *ṣalāt* and do it beautifully for the sake of someone who is watching".[11] This is precisely "hypocrisy" and "eye-service". Most of the literature focuses on this sort of *shirk*. Ibn 'Aṭā's remark is typical: "*Shirk* is that you behold other than Him or that you see loss or gain from other than Him."[12]

The question of *shirk* brings us back to the issue of the object of worship. Whom in fact are we serving? The Qur'an stigmatises the false gods that people worship, but it comes down especially hard on *hawā*, caprice or whim. As Ghazālī puts it, "Whoever follows caprice is the servant of caprice, not the servant of God."[13] Junayd tells us that when something unexpected happens, "the first thought from which you seek help is your object of worship".[14] Abū 'Alī al-Daqqāq provides the key to discernment here: "You are the servant of him in whose bondage and prison you are. If you are in prison to yourself, then you are the servant of yourself, and if you are in prison to this world of yours, then you are a servant of this world of yours."[15]

In short, "to worship none but God" (Qur'an 3:64) is what Ibn 'Aṭā' calls "the realisation of *tawḥīd*".[16] "Realisation" translates *taḥqīq*, the second form gerund from *ḥaqq*. It means to put *ḥaqq* into practice, to establish the truth, right, reality and appropriateness of something, to actualise the *ḥaqq* of things in oneself. Its sense in the early texts can perhaps best be understood in terms of the well-authenticated hadith, "Your soul has a *ḥaqq* against you, your Lord has a *ḥaqq* against you, your guest has a *ḥaqq* against you, and your spouse has a *ḥaqq* against you; so give to each that has a *ḥaqq* its *ḥaqq*."[17] "Realisation" is to give oneself, one's Lord and all things their *ḥaqq*. So, if worship is "the realisation of *tawḥīd*", this means that it is to give God his due and to give his creatures their due in accord with the divine *Ḥaqq*. It is to be at once a sincere worshipper and a perfect servant.

To realise *tawḥīd* is to practise *ikhlāṣ*: to purify the mind, heart and intention from everything but the divine *Ḥaqq* and, on that basis, to attend to the rights of the creatures. The most important obstacle to giving God and things their *ḥaqq* is a false sense of reality and self-sufficiency. The general stand is that hypocrisy is caused by failing to recognise the absolute reality of God and ignoring the evanescence, instability and unreliability of the human situation. Creation is nothing in face of God; God alone is truth, reality, rightness and appropriateness in the real senses of these words. Seeing oneself as possessing reality and rights is *shirk*, associating a *ḥaqq* with *al-Ḥaqq*. As Junayd would have it, the *ṭāghūt* (idol) mentioned frequently in the Qur'an is one's own self; or, it is everything other than God.[18] As long as one keeps both God and self in view and worships God on that basis, one is associating one's own supposed *ḥaqq* with the absolute *Ḥaqq*. As Naṣrābādhī tells us, "Servanthood is to overthrow the seeing of one's own worship by contemplating the Object of Worship."[19]

That human beings are called upon to worship God implies an affirmation of human strength and a power to carry out the worship. No one denies that individual choice and initiative play an important role, but the texts are extremely concerned that the individual self be given only its *ḥaqq*, nothing more. There is a constant tension between God's absolute reality and human insignificance. It often comes up in commentaries on the fifth verse of the Fātiḥa: "Thee alone we worship, and from Thee alone we seek help." Ja'far al-Ṣādiq explains that the second half of the verse means that we ask help from God's strength and sufficiency to worship Him properly.[20] It is impossible for us to fulfil God's *ḥaqq* without His guidance and grace.

In a similar way, Junayd says, "Servanthood is to abandon two things: leaning on other than God and reliance on [one's own power of] movement. When you have thrown these two things from yourself, you have fulfilled the *ḥaqq* of servanthood."[21] Reliance on oneself and one's own strength leads to the idea that one can earn one's way into Paradise. But this cannot stand up to analysis. *Tawḥīd* tells us that guidance to right activity, the power to act and the actual activity are all given by God. In other words, no servant can fulfil God's right except by relying totally upon Him, by "purifying his religion" of everything but attention to Him alone. As al-Ḥasan al-Baṣrī put it, "No one worships Him with the *ḥaqq* of servanthood at the beginning or the end such that one must receive a reward."[22] Why then worship? al-Sulamī explains: "By Your command we worship You. Otherwise, what use would worship be to realise Your *ḥaqq*?"[23] The true servant is he who sees his own situation clearly: "He owns nothing and claims nothing for himself" (Abū 'Uthmān al-Maghribī).[24]

One of the constant themes running through discussion of worship is that the goal is to transform the soul and bring oneself into harmony with God. In other words, worship cannot be divorced from *akhlāq*, a word that is often translated as "ethics" but which means more literally "character traits". Moral transformation demands ridding oneself of vices and acquiring virtues. Thus al-Wāsiṭī tells us that worship is rooted in six moral attitudes: reverence, which leads to sincerity; shame, which helps servants guard over their thoughts; fear, which holds them back from sin; hope, which encourages them in acts of worship; love, which allows them to devote their acts fully to God; and awe, which helps them put aside the sense of self-sufficiency.[25]

The virtues were often seen as part of the help that God gives to His servants so that they can worship Him. We have already noted that acquiring virtue was often called "assuming as one's own character the character traits of God". Sulamī waxes especially eloquent in describing the virtues assumed by the true servant in his commentary on Qur'an 25:64, "The servants of the Merciful are those who walk in the earth modestly."

In the relevant chapter of his famous *Treatise* (*Risāla*), Qushayrī offers a succinct definition of the early notion of worship and servanthood: "Servanthood is to undertake the *ḥaqq* of the acts of obedience, on condition of full exertion; to gaze upon what comes from yourself with the eye that sees shortcomings; and to witness your good traits as coming from the divine determination."[26]

One of the earliest books to offer a systematic analysis of the moral imperative was *Observing the Rights of God* (*al-Ri'āya li-ḥuqūq Allāh*) by al-Ḥārith al-Muḥāsibī (d. 857). The basic question he addressed was how people can live up to their human responsibility "to worship God and associate nothing with Him". Although the book says relatively little about "worship" and "servanthood" *per se*, it provides a thorough analysis of the worshipping soul.

Observing the Rights of God is divided into nine parts. The first describes the key moral and spiritual dimensions of worship, and the somewhat longer second part explains the nature of hypocrisy and the ways to overcome it. The next two parts deal with the importance of proper companions and knowing one's own defects. The next four chapters provide long analyses of the major obstacles to proper worship: self-satisfaction (*'ujb*), pride (*kibr*), delusion (*ghurūr*), and envy (*ḥasad*). In a short final section, the author describes how the aspirant should keep his mind vigilantly upon God.

Muḥāsibī's text begins not with a discussion of worship itself, but with an analysis of *taqwā*, a qur'anic term that translators have rendered into English with words such as piety, dutifulness, godfearing, and righteousness. Its fundamental importance is made clear in verses like 49:13: "Surely the noblest of you in God's sight is the one with the most *taqwā*." The word combines the senses of fear, caution and self-protection, and it comes up constantly in discussions of worship. In his commentary on 2:21, "O people, worship your Lord", Sulamī can say, "Make the worship of your Lord sincere by not taking any partner with Him. Then unity and sincerity will take you to *taqwā*."[27]

Muḥāsibī defines *taqwā* as "being wary of *shirk*, of every lesser sin prohibited by God, and of neglecting anything necessary made incumbent by God".[28] Having reminded his readers of the many qur'anic verses that command believers to have *taqwā*, he tells them, "*Taqwā* is the first waystation of the worshippers, and through it they will reach the highest waystation."[29] He then turns to a question posed by the person for whom he wrote the book: "What is it that you command me to begin with?" He answers:

> That you know that you are a servant and a vassal and that you have no deliverance except through *taqwā* before your Master and Patron. Only then will you not perish.

> So remember and reflect: For what were you created? Why were you put into this fleeting abode? You will come to know that you were not created uselessly, nor were you left aimless. You were created and put within this abode for testing and trial, so that you may obey God or disobey Him, and then you will move on from this abode to endless chastisement or endless bliss ... The first thing necessary for the well-being [*ṣalāḥ*] of your soul and without which it has no well-being – and this is the first observance [*ri'āya*] – is that you know that your soul is a vassal [*marbūb*] and a worshipper [*muta'abbid*]. When you know that, then you will know that a vassal and worshipper has no salvation save in obeying his Lord and Patron. He has no guide to obeying his Lord and Master other than knowledge, and then putting His commands and prohibitions into practice according to their situations, causes and occasions. The worshipper will not find that save in the Book of his Lord and the *sunna* of His Prophet, for obedience is the path of salvation, and knowledge is the guide on the path.[30]

The great *summa* of the moral imperative is Ghazālī's *Revival of the Religious Sciences* (*Iḥyā' 'ulūm al-dīn*). The first of its four parts is dedicated to *'ibādāt*, "acts of worship"; but this should not lead us to conclude that the rest does not concern our topic. In fact, all four parts (a total of forty books) explain what it means to be a servant of God. Ghazālī is simply setting down explicitly the moral and spiritual implications of the qur'anic command to worship. The book is nothing if not a statement of God's right over human beings. His explanations, however, remain largely in the moral, ethical and psycho-spiritual spheres. He avoids both juridical discussions, which were amply dealt with by other authors (and by himself in some of his other works), and the ontological issues that were soon to become commonplace (and to which he paid some attention in other writings).

In explaining why he wrote the *Revival*, Ghazālī first condemns the scholars of his time for busying themselves with worldly affairs and using religion for their own ends. In other words, he begins by criticising hypocrisy. Then he explains that true and useful knowledge is knowledge that impinges on ultimate human destiny. It is "afterworldly" knowledge, which is to say that it paves the way for people to fulfil the rights of God and the rights of man and to achieve their goal in life, which is for God to deliver them from hell.

The book is divided into four parts because afterworldly knowledge has two basic sorts: that which concerns outward things, such as the body and the limbs, and that which concerns inner things, such as character traits and "the states of the heart". Acts pertaining to outward things can then be divided into acts of worship (*'ibādāt*) and customary practices (*'ādāt*). Acts pertaining to inner things can be divided into blameworthy and praiseworthy traits.

The headings of Ghazālī's chapters provide a rough survey of what is entailed by any thorough discussion of "worship". Notice that Part 1, on "acts of worship", begins with the book of knowledge, which analyses the creed. In other words, the first chapter unpacks the implications of the two halves of the *Shahāda*, the recitation of which is the first of the five pillars of Islamic practice. The remaining nine books deal with ritual purity, *ṣalāt* (second pillar), *zakāt* (third pillar), fasting (fourth pillar), Ḥajj (fifth pillar), recitation of the Qur'an, remembrance (*dhikr*) and supplication (*du'ā'*), and the recitation of litanies (*awrād*).

Part 2 of the *Revival* outlines the proper attitudes and comportment of true servants in daily activities. If these are not labelled "acts of worship", it is because that word is reserved for rites and rituals. But the broad path of guidance set down by the Qur'an and the *sunna* is by no means limited to ritual and cultic activities, and everything that Ghazālī discusses in this section is rooted in the guidance of these two sources and of the pious forebears. The topics of the books are eating, marriage, earning a living, the forbidden and the permitted, companionship and social relationships, seclusion (*'uzla*), travel, listening to music, commanding the good and forbidding the evil, and right conduct of living along with the character traits of prophecy.

Part 3 of the *Revival* is reminiscent of Muḥāsibī's *Observing the Rights of God* in that it focuses on blameworthy character traits. It begins with an especially important chapter called "Explaining the wonders of the heart", which is an analysis of the human soul and an explanation of the necessity of self-knowledge. In his *Alchemy of Happiness* (*Kīmiyā-yi sa'ādat*), which is a popularising Persian summary of the *Revival*, Ghazālī puts this section at the very beginning of the book. In the next nine chapters of Part 3, Ghazālī addresses the training of the soul; the regulation of the two appetites (the stomach and the pudendum); the blights of the tongue; the dangers of anger, rancour and envy; the attractions of this world; possessions and stinginess; social rank and hypocrisy; pride and self-satisfaction; and delusion.

The last part of the *Revival* delineates the character traits that need to be acquired to establish *taqwā* and sincerity. This part is reminiscent of many books written by the Sufis on the "stations" (*maqāmāt*) of the path to God. The ten chapters cover repentance; patience and gratitude;

fear and hope; poverty and renunciation; *tawḥīd* and trust in God; love, yearning, intimacy and contentment; intention, truthfulness and sincerity; introspection and self-accounting; meditation; and the remembrance of death.

THE ONTOLOGICAL IMPERATIVE

The Qur'an is by no means simply a set of moral injunctions and practical guidelines. It goes to great lengths to encourage people to meditate on the signs (*āyāt*) of God in both the natural world and the soul so as to gain insight into God's reality and rights. The Qur'an pays special attention to the divine names and attributes that become manifest in creation – life, power, consciousness, speech, wrath, justice – and the fact that these provide general categories of understanding and the means to communicate with God.

For centuries the major schools of thought (*kalām*, *falsafa*, jurisprudence and Sufism) had remained relatively distinct disciplines, though any given scholar, like Ghazālī, might be expert in two or more fields. Gradually, cross-fertilisation among the disciplines increased, and Ibn 'Arabī (d. 1240) brought them all together in one grand synthesis. His voluminous writings cannot be classified according to the old categories, but his enormous *Meccan Openings* (*al-Futūḥāt al-Makkiyya*) can be considered the great *summa* of the ontological imperative.

Near the centre of Ibn 'Arabī's approach lies the discussion of *wujūd*: existence or being. Before him, the word had been employed primarily in philosophy and *kalām*. Ibn 'Arabī confirmed that *wujūd* was another name for *al-Ḥaqq* in itself: God as Reality, Truth, Rightness and Appropriateness. Investigation of the implications of *al-wujūd al-ḥaqq* – the Real Being – meant paying a great deal of attention to ontology, metaphysics, epistemology, cosmology and spiritual psychology. To be sure, philosophers and *kalām* experts before him had investigated these fields, but none of them had put anywhere near the same amount of effort into integrating these topics into the moral and spiritual imperatives of the Qur'an.

Nothing is closer to the heart of Ibn 'Arabī's project than clarifying the path of servanthood. His basic question is, "What does it mean to be human?" And his basic answer is, "To be God's servant." The goal of human existence is to achieve what is right, proper and true, and this can be done only by fulfilling the rights of God. The person who achieves such a state, such as Muḥammad specifically and the other prophets generally, is called *al-insān al-kāmil*, "the perfect human being".

But equally and more basically, such a person is called *al-'abd al-kāmil*, the "perfect servant", or *al-'abd al-maḥḍ*, "the sheer servant", or *al-'abd al-muṭlaq*, "the unqualified servant". It had never been lost on those who explained the nature of servanthood, least of all Ibn 'Arabī, that Muḥammad's chief epithets are *'abduhu wa-rasūluhu*, "His servant and His Messenger", in that order. Only by achieving servanthood is it possible for human beings to live in harmony with God and to act on his behalf. This activity on his behalf is precisely the purpose of human existence, announced already in God's words concerning the creation of Adam: "I am setting in the earth a vicegerent (*khalīfa*)" (Qur'an 2:30).

Worship, it was said, is the appropriate human response to God. It is for man to acquiesce, yield and humble himself before the Real, the Right, the True and the Worthy. On one level, this is a moral injunction. On a deeper level, it is a statement of fact: by nature human beings and all creatures acquiesce in the Real and the Appropriate, and they can do nothing else. Ibn 'Arabī points out that if we look at all of reality, we see that it can be divided into two basic categories: worshipper and Object of worship.[31] He bolsters this sort of statement with philological evidence, philosophical and theological arguments, and reference to many qur'anic verses and hadiths. Thus, for example, the Qur'an tells us repeatedly that all things in heaven and earth glorify God, which is to say that they announce his greatness and their own insignificance. All things are "Muslim": "To Him is submitted (*aslama*) everything in the heavens and the earth" (3:83). All things are servants: "None is there in the heavens and the earth that does not comes to the All-Merciful as a servant" (19:93).

In other words, "worship" and "servanthood" designate the actual situation of every created thing. Things serve and worship their Creator simply by being what they are. All things are, quite literally, slaves of God. God is the Real, and the Real is designated by all positive qualities that become manifest in existence: life, power, knowledge, mercy, love. These are precisely God's names and attributes. They designate the nature of reality itself, *al-ḥaqq*, which gives rise to the universe and all existence. Everything is a sign of God, because all things announce, by being what they are, qualities of *al-ḥaqq*. Thus, says Ibn 'Arabī, all things walk on "a straight path" (*ṣirāṭ mustaqīm*), and that path leads them back to God, their creator (though whether to the Merciful or to the Wrathful remains to be seen). "The straightness demanded by God's wisdom permeates every engendered thing. God said, in confirmation of Moses, 'He gave each thing its creation' [20:50]. Hence each thing has an actual straightness."[32]

Does this mean that human beings are forced to worship God? Yes and no. As creatures, they are slaves and can do nothing but live out their created nature. They can only obey their Lord's "engendering command" (*al-amr al-takwīnī*), which is the divine imperative "Be!" (*kun*). "His only command, when He desires a thing, is to say to it 'Be!,' and it comes to be" (36:82). This sort of worship Ibn 'Arabī calls "essential" or "primary" worship, because it pertains to the very essence of what it means to be a creature. It is nonetheless true that human beings were made in the image of God, taught all the names (2:31), and given the power to choose between right and wrong. They freely accepted responsibility to carry the Trust (33:72). The worship that results from these considerations Ibn 'Arabī calls "accidental" or "secondary". It is addressed by the "prescriptive command" (*al-amr al-taklīfī*), which imposes the burden of worship on God's servants: "He has commanded that you worship none but Him" (12:40). Such worship is "accidental" because it does not pertain to the very definition of what it means to be human; it becomes obligatory at a certain point in human development (e.g. at puberty) under certain circumstances (e.g. rationality, or knowledge of prophecy); it can be accepted or rejected; and it comes to an end at death.

Those who discuss the ontological imperative begin by acknowledging the way things are: human beings are always and forever servants of their Lord, creatures of their creator. In this respect they are always and essentially servants. As an early Sufi put it, "Just as lordship is a description of the Real that never leaves Him, so servanthood is an attribute of the servant that will not depart from him so long as he remains."[33]

Death is waking up to the nature of things. It is to become aware (if one was not already aware) that worship and servanthood of God are woven into the stuff of reality. After death, people no longer have the choice not to worship, whether they end up in Paradise or in hell. Like the angels, they will not be able to disobey their Lord and they will be fully aware that everything they do is done in His service, and His service alone.

If, as Ja'far al-Ṣādiq said, intellect is "that by which the All-Merciful is worshipped", this is because true and right knowledge situates things in their proper places. Through it man comes to know who is Lord and who is servant, and what exactly lordship and servanthood entail. The first truth of lordship is that it rules over all reality, all existence, and all attributes and qualities that define the servant. And the first truth of servanthood is that the creature has no right to its own created nature, no claim upon the Real. The servant is essentially nonexistent and accidentally existent through the Real. In philosophical language, this situation was often expressed by speaking of the "Necessary Being" (that which is and cannot not be) and the "possible thing" (that which has no inherent claim on existence). For Ibn 'Arabī, to say that God is Necessary and humans possible is to say, "O people, you are the poor toward God, and God – He is the Rich, the Praiseworthy" (Qur'an 35:15).

Knowledge lies at the root of human responsibility. Islam begins with the two *Shahāda*s, which give witness to the truth the believer knows in his heart. But truly to know God is a never-ending task, because his infinite reality cannot be exhausted. By knowing the signs and marks, one can come to know God's names and attributes. This knowledge cannot be disengaged from practice. Knowing the Lord is not separate from knowing and actualising servanthood. This is the weight of *ḥaqq*: the word does not simply mean "truth" and "reality", it also means right, appropriate, worthy and due. Knowledge of Reality makes practical demands on the knowing soul: when servants know their actual, ontological status *vis-à-vis* their Lord, they find themselves called upon to put themselves right, to "worship God sincerely", to strip themselves of any claim to the rights of lordship. The goal of worship and servanthood is to give everything that has a *ḥaqq* its *ḥaqq*; this is precisely "the realisation of *tawḥīd*".

In order to recognise the *ḥaqq*s of things, all of which are servants, one must recognise the *ḥaqq* of the "Lord" of things. This divine name designates God inasmuch as He has "vassals" (sing. *marbūb*) or servants. As Ibn 'Arabī points out, the Qur'an mentions the name *rabb* about 900 times, but never without ascription to a servant or servants (e.g. "your Lord", "Lord of Moses", "Lord of the Worlds"). If we pay attention to the meaning of the word in Arabic, we see that to say that God is Lord is to say that He brings about the well-being (*muṣliḥ*) of His servants; he is their nourisher (*mughadhdhī*), nurturer (*murabbī*), master (*sayyid*) and owner (*mālik*).[34]

God is in fact "Lord" in respect of each of His names, which is to say that the divine names designate the various respects and modalities in which the creator deals with creation, in which Real Being gives rise to cosmic existence. Whatever name we have in view, Merciful, Pardoner, or Severe in Punishment, God is Lord of His servants in respect of that name and he exercises the various functions of lordship in its terms.

The question of human nature is central to the ontological imperative. It is no accident that the purported hadith, "He who knows himself knows his Lord", is increasingly cited from Ibn 'Arabī onward.

In order to know ourselves, we must know how we differ from other created things. This basic answer is that "God created Adam in His image". Ibn 'Arabī points out that it is the name *Allāh* that is employed in this hadith, not any of the other divine names. This name designates God inasmuch as He is named by all the names and synthesises their diverse meanings in His One Reality. It designates God as "Lord of the lords", the lords being the divine names designating the qualities and attributes of Real Being. All creatures other than human beings display only some of God's signs and manifest only a few of His names and attributes. Man alone was "taught all the names" (2:31).

The "knowledge" that God imparted to Adam is not information. Rather, it is the ability to recognise the *ḥaqq* of things, to see things rightly (i.e., in terms of the Real) and to act appropriately. By their very nature human beings have the capacity to recognise the designations of all of reality and to acknowledge the *ḥaqq* of everything that exists. They can actualise this, however, only by living up to their nature, and to do so they need God's help.

Human beings, then, are *essentially* servants of God. *Accidentally*, however, they may be the servants of any of the individual divine names, or of any cosmic or human reality that can be an "object of worship" (*ma'būd*), including the ideas and notions that establish goals and aspirations. This unlimited human capacity to serve anything at all helps explain the tremendous emphasis that the texts place upon "sincerity": purifying one's worship of everything but God. The magnitude of the task does not become obvious until one grasps the transcendence of God, the omnipresence of His signs and marks, the diversity and even contradictory nature of His names and attributes (the Exalter and the Abaser, the Forgiver and the Avenger), and the ease of falling into the worship and service of what is less than God.

From the Qur'an onwards, the exalted situation of those who achieve proper servanthood is emphasised. Muḥammad, the supreme human model, was not only "His servant", but also "His Messenger". Human beings were created not only to worship God, but also to achieve God's vicegerency through worthy service. Here the texts remind us that, although servanthood demands an utter and absolute differentiation between servant and Lord, it also attracts God's love. "Say [O Muḥammad!]: 'If you love God, follow me, and God will love you'" (3:31). The goal of worship is not to remain distant from the Lord, but to be brought into His proximity. It is characteristic of love to bridge the gap between lover and beloved and to bring about nearness, especially when God is the lover. Those who fail the test of living up to servanthood remain distant (hell), but those who pass the test are given nearness (Paradise).

If worship and servanthood represent sincere engagement with observing the rights of God and the rights of man, then "vicegerency" represents being brought into God's proximity by living up to servanthood. No one represents God who has not completely submitted himself to His authority. God's "authority" is not merely moral and legal; it is above all ontological and cosmic. It is the fact that He is the Real and the Right, and the fact that servants are submitted to the Lord by virtue of their essential lack of *ḥaqq*. It is the fact that God is the Necessary Being, and they are merely possible things, with no claim on existence.

Worship, then, does not mean simply abasing oneself before the Lord by observing His commands and prohibitions. It also means recognising one's own non-lordship. It means knowing that one is not one's own owner, sustainer, nourisher, nurturer and source of well-being. It means following in the footsteps of those who know how to observe the rights of the Lord. Only after having negated any claim to lordship and having fully embraced servanthood can one be brought into God's nearness. This is not a movement from place to place, but from a weak mode of being to a strong mode of being. It is the realisation of the divine form upon which human beings were created. It is the gradual actualisation of praiseworthy character traits, which are modalities of being and light harmonious with the Real. It is these traits that denote the servant who has been given "well-being" by his Lord.

Here some of the practical implications of knowing one's Lord become more evident. The theological dedication to enumerating and explaining the names of God was not simply theoretical. Conscious and aware servants know that they were given intelligence and awareness to worship the All-Merciful. Knowledge is the door to actualisation and realisation. True vicegerents have eminent and exalted characters, because they have assimilated the character traits of their Lord. When the Qur'an says to the Prophet, "Surely thou art upon a magnificent character (*khuluq 'aẓīm*)" (68:4), no one needs to be told that this character was a divine gift. The Qur'an itself is, according to 'Ā'isha, the "character of Muḥammad". If this is so, one sees a deeper meaning to the verse, "I am a mortal like you; to me it is revealed that your God is one God" (18:110). The telling difference between this mortal and that mortal is the divine grace, the bestowal of the eternal Word, the gift of knowledge and character that comes about when servants live up to their part of the covenant – to worship God alone, making their religion sincerely His. Only God's character is essentially and irrevocably "magnificent". If Muḥammad has a magnificent character, if he is "a light-giving lamp" (33:46), it is because he is a servant who asked help from no one but God, and realised *tawḥīd*.

Further reading

Cragg, Kenneth, "Worship and cultic life: Muslim worship", in *The Encyclopedia of Religion* (New York, 1987), xv, pp. 454–63.

al-Ghazālī, Abū Ḥāmid, *Worship in Islam: Being a Translation, with Commentary and Introduction, of al-Ghazzālī's* Book of the Iḥyā' *on the Worship* tr. Edwin Elliott Calverley, (Hartford, CT, 1923).

Murata, Sachiko, and Chittick, William C., *The Vision of Islam* (St Paul, 1994).

Nakamura, Kojiro (tr.), *Al-Ghazālī on Invocations and Supplications: Book IX of the Revival of the Religious Sciences* (Cambridge, 1990).

Padwick, Constance E., *Muslim Devotions: A Study of Prayer-Manuals in Common Use* (Oxford, 1996).

Renard, John, *Seven Doors to Islam: Spirituality and the Religious Life of Muslims* (Berkeley, 1997).

Rosenthal, Franz, *Knowledge Triumphant: The Concept of Knowledge in Medieval Islam* (Leiden, 1971).

Notes

1. The Qur'an employs four words from this root, in a total of 277 instances. It uses the verb *'abada* 124 times and the gerund form *'ibāda* 9 times; the word *'abd* in the singular and plural 130 times; and the active participle *'ābid* 12 times.
2. There is also the far less commonly used *'ubūda*, "servitude", which is discussed by Qushayrī and Ibn 'Arabī among others.
3. Bukhārī, Tawḥīd, 1; Muslim, Īmān, 49, etc.
4. Franz Rosenthal, *Knowledge Triumphant: The Concept of Knowledge in Medieval Islam* (Leiden, 1970).
5. Hujwīrī, *Kashf al-maḥjūb*, ed. V. Zhukovsky (Tehran, 1336/1957), p. 11.
6. Dārimī, 'Ilm, 29.
7. Muḥammad Bāqir Majlisī, *Biḥār al-anwār*, 110 vols. (Beirut, 1983), I, p. 116.
8. Ghazālī, *Iḥyā' 'ulūm al-dīn*, 6 vols. (Cairo, 1992), IV, p. 31.
9. Ghazālī, *al-Maqṣad al-asnā fī sharḥ ma'ānī asmā' Allāh al-ḥusnā*, ed. Fadlou A. Shehadi (Beirut, 1971), pp. 42ff. See also *Ghazālī: The Ninety-Nine Beautiful Names of God*, tr. by David B. Burrell and Nazih Daher (Cambridge, 1992), pp. 30ff. The translators render *al-takhalluq bi-akhlāq Allāh* as "conforming to the perfections of God". The word *akhlāq* means character traits, both virtues and vices. If one wants to translate it as "perfections", one might better translate the whole expression as "becoming perfect through God's perfections".
10. Abū 'Abd al-Raḥmān al-Sulamī, *Ḥaqā'iq al-tafsīr*, MS, commentary on Qur'an 2:21.

11. Ibn Māja, Zuhd, 21.
12. Sulamī, on 4:36; also in Paul Nwyia, *Trois oeuvres inédites de mystiques musulmanes* (Beirut, 1973), p. 45.
13. Ghazālī, *Iḥyā'*, III, p. 45.
14. Sulamī, *Ḥaqā'iq al-tafsīr*, on 4:36.
15. al-Qushayrī, *al-Risāla*, ed. 'Abd al-Ḥalīm Maḥmūd and Maḥmūd ibn al-Sharīf (Cairo, 1972), p. 430.
16. Sulamī, *Ḥaqā'iq al-tafsīr*; Nwyia, *Trois oeuvres*, p. 41.
17. Versions of this hadith are found in most collections; Arent Jan Wensinck *et al.*, *Concordance et indices de la tradition musulmane* (Leiden, 1936–88), I, p. 486.
18. Sulamī, *Ḥaqā'iq al-tafsīr*, on 2:256.
19. Ibid., on 17:23.
20. Gerhard Böwering (ed.), *The Minor Qur'ān Commentary of Abū 'Abd ar-Raḥmān as-Sulamī* (Beirut: 1997), p. 5.
21. Sulamī, *Ḥaqā'iq al-tafsīr*, on 17:3.
22. Ibid., on 15:99.
23. Ibid., on 15:99.
24. Ibid., on 18:1.
25. Ibid., on 4:36.
26. Qushayrī, *Risāla*, 429.
27. Sulamī, *Ḥaqā'iq al-tafsīr*, on 2:21.
28. al-Muḥāsibī, *al-Ri'āya li ḥuqūq Allāh*, ed. 'A. Maḥmūd and 'A. Aḥmad 'Aṭā (Cairo, 1970), p. 40.
29. Ibid., p. 49.
30. Ibid., p. 52.
31. Ibn 'Arabī, *al-Futūḥāt al-Makkiyya* (Cairo, 1911, repr. Beirut, n.d.), III, p. 78, tr. in William C. Chittick, *The Sufi Path of Knowledge* (Albany, 1989), p. 311.
32. *Futūḥāt*, II, p. 217; Chittick, *Sufi Path*, p. 301.
33. Abū 'Alī al-Daqqāq, cited by Qushayrī, *Risāla*, p. 432.
34. Ibn 'Arabī often talks about these five meanings of the name *rabb*: e.g. *Futūḥāt*, II, p. 251; III, pp. 383, 537; IV, p. 198.

12 Theological dimensions of Islamic law

UMAR F. ABD-ALLAH

INTRODUCTION

Law represented one of the earliest models of intellectual activity in Muslim culture, and traditionally lay at the core of Islamic learning. To be a "scholar" (*'ālim*), whatever else it meant, was invariably to be a scholar trained in God's sacred law. Although the legal scholar did not possess the gift of prophecy, he was deemed a "successor of the Prophet". By virtue of issuing independent legal opinions, the jurisconsult[1] (*muftī*) in particular occupied a social position which in some ways was reminiscent of that of the prophetic lawgiver himself.

Because of the centrality of law in the Islamic tradition, Muslim society and culture are best accessed through it. For more than a millennium, the religious law constituted the Muslim world's most constant, characteristic and unifying feature. Mainstream Sufism was the only other dimension of Islam that enjoyed a comparable influence, but (contrary to the misperceptions of an older generation of historians) it, too, was erected on the law's foundations. Today, when many aspects of traditional Islamic society are disappearing, the religious law remains central to the Islamic consciousness, even in Muslim nations that have adopted secular legal systems.

THEOLOGY AND THE RELIGIOUS CONTENT OF ISLAMIC LAW

Islam is "ruled by law". It is not theocratic but nomocratic in nature, and the religious law which underpins this is all-embracing. *Kalām* theology and law were independent disciplines, and many questions – today including issues such as abortion, environmental protection and interfaith relations – which Christians regard as theological, are, for Muslims, not matters of theology but fundamental questions of religious law.

The historical relationship between the sacred law and classical theology (*kalām*) must be distinguished from the law's inherently religious nature, its immense body of positive law, and the various Sufi paths of spiritual illumination. Islamic theological speculation exercised only a limited impact on positive law, but its influence on Islamic legal theory (*uṣūl al-fiqh*) was profound. The emergence of *kalām* and that of *uṣūl al-fiqh* were roughly coeval. Both disciplines matured centuries after the schools of Islamic law had formulated their distinctive corpuses of positive law. None of the schools of law systematically reformulated its established body of substantive law on the basis of the dialectics of later legal theorists, despite the centrality of legal theory in their legal curricula. Few failed to note the symbiosis which existed between *kalām* and legal theory, but, from the beginning, many jurists questioned the validity of linking the two disciplines. Most of them ultimately welcomed legal theory and revered it for the monumental scholastic achievement that it was, but despite legal theory's indebtedness to *kalām*, a significant number of other jurists regarded *kalām* as irrelevant to the art of positive law. Still others regarded its influence as harmful.

THE NATURE OF ISLAMIC LAW

The Muslim lives in a theocentric universe, "in surrender" (*muslim*) to God, seeking through the prophetic Law to discover and implement God's will. The law's primary sources, the qur'anic revelation and the prophetic model (*sunna*), are the material referents of God's will. From a modern perspective Islamic law is at once legal and meta-legal: a set of legislative rules within a moral system of "oughts" and "ought nots", defining outward standards, while addressing the inward state of the agent's heart.

David Santillana observes that "law and religion, law and morality are the two aspects of this same [divine] will by which it is constituted and by which the Muslim community governs itself; every question of law is also a matter of conscience, and jurisprudence is based on theology in the final analysis".[2] Henri de Wael remarks that to be a good Muslim is, first of all, to keep the rules of Islamic law faithfully. Consequently, the law does not allow itself to be reduced to a simple methodology for governing social relations but regards itself as expressing morality at the highest plane, for the law's fundamental purpose is to "enjoin the right and forbid the wrong".[3] Many acts are not subject to secular sanctions but await their rewards and punishments in the next world. This otherworldly emphasis of the law imbues it with a predominantly ethical tone. Law and morality merge into a general philosophy of life. Every social institution and human activity is imbued with religious significance.[4]

RELIGIOUS AND SECULAR LAW IN PERSPECTIVE

Throughout the course of pre-modern history, religion tended to involve all aspects of life. The relegation of religion to the private sphere is a decidedly modern phenomenon. In the West, secularism is often taken for granted as if it were a distinctive legacy, but the division between church and state is relatively recent. It did not emerge in an unbroken continuum from ancient Greece and Rome but was the product of revolutionary politics, beginning with the Glorious Revolution of the seventeenth century and reaching its apotheosis with the Russian Revolution over 200 years later.[5] Although Islamic law falls within the traditional pattern of embracing the private and public spheres, surprisingly, the separation between religious authority and the state – contrary both to common opinion and to contemporary Islamist ideology – was the norm in the Islamic world for more than a millennium.[6]

In its comprehensiveness, Islamic law is akin to the legal outlook of the Hebrew prophets, Rabbinic Jews and the Persian Mazdeans. In early Indic religion, the governing concept of *dharma* stood for the totality of religion, legality and morality. *Dharma* mirrored the natural order of the universe and permeated all human relationships, so that "the distinction between religion and law can be justified only from the European point of view; the two notions are one in the Indian *dharma*".[7] The origins of Greek and Roman law were religious; it was only later that they became secular. The priest of ancient Rome has been compared to the Muslim *muftī*, and Roman law did not remove itself from the precincts of the priestly collegiums until the latter part of the fourth century BCE.[8]

Like Islam, Rabbinic Judaism is distinctly nomocratic. Rabbinic Jews, like Muslims, govern their communities through a system of revealed law, and not through theocratic priesthoods as in the Biblical (pre-Rabbinic) or Mazdean traditions. Orthodox rabbis summon Jews to take on the "yoke of the Kingdom" in faith and moral conduct, meaning total submission to God's law at the individual and social levels.[9] Nevertheless, the legal implications of both the Islamic and Rabbinic systems, apart from what is unequivocally understood from revelation, are matters of extension by exegesis and cognate principles. Both religions combine revelation with reason as the path to legal knowledge, while rejecting exclusively human legislation.

The earliest Christian attitudes towards the law did not depart radically from the Old Testament worldview. It has been argued that "nothing which Jesus said or did which bore on the law led his disciples after his death to disregard it".[10] Jewish Christianity in particular was noted for its fidelity to Mosaic law: "Till heaven and earth pass away, not an iota will pass from the law until all is accomplished" (Matt. 5:18).[11] Pauline Christianity opposed this conviction. Yet Paul himself understood Christ in terms of the law, ascribing to him qualities which in Rabbinic Judaism were attributes of the law alone. Even for Paul, there was a distinction between God's law *per se*, which was good, and Pharisaic "legalism", which was not.[12]

In the mainstream Christian theology which developed after Paul, adherence to the Mosaic law came to be seen as theologically pointless, given Christ's vicarious sacrifice: the law had been an inferior dispensation, which the grace and liberty of the Gospel transcended.[13] Nevertheless, the churches developed vast bodies of canon law. The chief difference between these systems and the laws of Muslims and Jews was that canon law was theocratic and not nomocratic. Its ultimate legislative authority rested in priestly prerogative. During the Middle Ages, the canon lawyer enjoyed a pre-eminence not unlike that of Muslim and Jewish jurists in their own communities. Both Christianity and Judaism entered Europe with organised legal structures of positive religious law, and the survival of the Western church in the midst of Europe's barbaric kingdoms was in large measure due to its independent system of canon law.[14]

Canon law was no less prominent in Eastern Christianity, especially in lands where the church came under Muslim rule. Islamic law required each denomination to administer its community autonomously as a "protected religious community". The policy of *dhimma* (state protection of religious minorities) required the Eastern churches to provide comprehensive codes for their respective Christian judges, who presided over all spiritual and worldly affairs that did not fall under the jurisdiction of Muslim courts (such as legal disputes arising between Muslims and Christians). Canonical writing became a preoccupation of the Eastern churches; in the case of the Nestorians, it took precedence over all other types of literature.[15]

THE COMPREHENSIVENESS OF RELIGIOUS CONTENT IN ISLAMIC LAW

Ritual and secular concerns coexist in Islamic law. De Wael illustrates this fact by noting that the law may deem a prayer invalid or a sale reprehensible.[16] Coulson cites the law's prohibition of pork, intoxicants and usury. He observes further that Islamic law invalidates sales contracted at the time of Friday congregational prayers, threatens hellfire for one who misappropriates an orphan's wealth, and portrays a wife's conjugal obedience as virtuous.[17]

The law's fundamental concern with ritual is evident from the "five pillars" (declaration of faith, prayer, alms-tax, fasting, and pilgrimage). It extends to the definition of the clean and unclean, the unlawfulness of certain foods and drinks, and criteria for the slaughter of lawful meats.

The religious content of the law bears on other matters of secular consequence. Oaths and vows are technically matters of private conscience but often create the legal obligation of full implementation. The law sets guidelines for the dress of men and women. It declares the institution of marriage to be "half the religion" and intervenes in numerous issues of family law. The alms-tax requires set weights and measures as well as definitions of monetary units; it also calls for adequate accounting practices. The law's ethical concerns extend into the marketplace and even the world of banking and commerce.

Despite Islamic law's comprehensiveness, it distinguishes carefully between the ritual (non-secular) and the non-ritual (secular). Ritual acts require a good intention, while non-ritual acts require no conscious intention at all. Non-ritual acts need only conform to the formal provisions of the law, although any valid non-ritual act can be transformed into an act of worship in the sight of God if it is performed with a religious intention. Thus, a commercial enterprise undertaken with the aim of alleviating poverty for God's sake would be elevated to an act of immense religious merit.

As a rule, Muslim jurists considered strictly ritual matters to be beyond the purview of reason. Non-ritualistic matters, on the other hand, were accessible to reason, and such matters constitute the greater part of the law. Thus, "rationalism" is in a sense one of the law's basic characteristics. An important maxim states that "the foundational principle [of the law] is to have rationales (*al-aṣl al-taʿlīl*)". Ritual matters are an exception to this rule because of their intrinsic connection to the spiritual realm. They relate to the purification of the soul and winning God's pleasure. Fundamentals of ritual like the formalities of prayer or the rites of pilgrimage stand as they are and are not open to significant modification. Secular matters, on the other hand, fall clearly within the domain of *ijtihād* (legal interpretation) and legal review because they have rationales.

Naturally, the distinction between the ritual and the non-ritual is not always clear-cut. For example, the schools of law differ regarding religious ablutions. Most jurists hold them to be strictly matters of ritual, while others regard them as essentially a means to promote bodily cleanliness. On the first view, the act of ablution requires a conscious intention; on the second, it does not. The alms-tax displays the same ambiguity, since it serves the very tangible purpose of assisting the poor, debtors and the needy. Jurists who regard the alms-tax as strictly an act of ritual hold that attainment of legal majority is a prerequisite, since obligatory ritual acts generally require legal majority. For those who regard the alms-tax as falling somewhere between the ritual and non-ritual, it is defined as essentially a right of the poor binding upon the wealth of the rich. For them, legal majority is not relevant.

Whether acts are ritual or non-ritual in nature, Islamic law assesses all acts according to five classifications: obligatory, recommended, neutral, disliked and forbidden. Western writers often cite this ethical taxonomy as indicative of Islamic law's essentially religious nature. Because the five categories embrace everything human, Gibb regards them as moral rather than juridical categories.[18] According to Schacht, they transform "law proper" into a system of religious duties, although he observes that they also guarantee "unity in diversity".[19]

Islamic law designates certain rulings as divine "limits" (*ḥudūd*), which include rituals but extend beyond them to punishments and other matters. The *ḥudūd* denote all matters fixed by revelation. Generally speaking, they are formally applied as they were revealed. Those *ḥudūd* that overlap with non-ritual categories may, however, be open to judicial review and modification in some cases. Inheritance lots are among the *ḥudūd*, because they are specified in the Qur'an. The restriction of polygamous unions to four women falls within the same category. All punishments set by revelation (for adultery, slander, theft and brigandry) are *ḥudūd*. Most criminal law, however, lies outside the *ḥudūd* and belongs to the category of "disciplinary acts" (*ta'zīr*), which are determined in accordance with public interest, and are open to adjustment and judicial review. The enforcement of all punishments, whether *ḥudūd* or *ta'zīr*, is permissible only within an Islamic jurisdiction, and there is consensus among jurists that it is impermissible for Muslims to exact Islamic punishments in a non-Muslim state.

Islamic law divides legal obligations into two categories: the "rights of God" (*ḥuqūq Allāh*) and the "rights of humanity" (*ḥuqūq al-'ibād*). Rights of God entail all non-negotiable obligations, whether of a ritual or a non-ritual nature. The "rights of humanity", on the other hand, allow for options and modifications at the behest of rightful parties. In Islamic jurisprudence, the purpose of the rights of God is to uphold the ultimate objectives of the law: the preservation of religion, life, intellect, children and property.

All *ḥudūd* are rights of God, as are most other obligations established by revelation. It is a right of God that binding contracts be written in unambiguous language. The claim of the poor to adequate sustenance and the obligation to give homeless children adequate care are rights of God. Forbidden acts may also fall under this rubric, including the prohibition of bribes or of legacies that jeopardise the interests of lawful heirs.

Debts and warranties, on the other hand, belong to the rights of humanity, because they may be pardoned or written off. Punishments for slander and murder fall into this grouping. The slandered party may pardon the abuse and not seek legal action. Exacting punishment for murder also falls into this category, since the right to execute the guilty party rests not with the judge but with the victim's next of kin or guardians, who are given the option of granting full absolution or a partial pardon with financial compensation. Imprisonment and other forms of punishment short of execution, however, fall within the jurisdiction of the court. In the case of murder, the rights of God and humanity are said to overlap, since some degree of judiciary punishment is regarded as God's right.

Given the religious nature of Islamic law, the issue of innovation (*bid'a*) is critical. *Bid'a* carries negative, neutral and positive meanings. Its fundamental purpose is to serve as a regulatory mechanism to keep legal developments in conformity with Islamic principles; but this is counterbalanced by the creative imperative of *ijtihād* to enact new rulings and review older ones. For the majority of classical jurists, any core revision of credal axioms and ritual acts constituted *bid'a* in the negative sense. For many jurists, the domain of *bid'a* was restricted to matters of belief and ritual and did not include worldly affairs. The notion that *bid'a* stood for the categorical prohibition of change in ritual and non-ritual matters alike was regarded as absurd in traditional Islamic law. On the contrary, innovation in the practical disciplines of the world, like crafts and urban development, was required, and here *bid'a* took on a positive sense.[20]

Bid'a covered a range of different meanings in classical Islamic jurisprudence, since the varieties of *bid'a* fell within the five ethical categories of the law. Certain types of *bid'a* were prohibited or disliked, but others were obligatory, recommended or simply considered to be neutral. When tobacco-smoking first appeared in the Muslim world, some jurists classified it as a forbidden *bid'a*, while others held it to be reprehensible, depending on their estimation of its effect on health and other considerations. The establishment of educational institutions was assessed as an "obligatory" innovation (there had been no such institutions during the prophetic period). Shading marketplaces from the heat of the summer sun was a "recommended" *bid'a*, while novel refinements in food and drink were "neutral" as long as they were not excessive.

Ijtihād, on the other hand, was a dynamic, forward-looking component of the law. As Weiss observes, it demonstrated that God's law was not meant to be passively received and applied.[21] Santillana notes in his analysis of the ancillary instruments of *ijtihād* that the point of departure of the entire system was that God had instituted laws for the well-being of society and the individual. Human beings were not made for the law; the law was made for human beings.[22]

The domain of *ijtihād* encompassed non-ritual matters, since they had legal rationales and were open to review and modification according to circumstance. One maxim (*qā'ida*) of Islamic law stated: "Modifications of legal judgements will not be denounced when they reflect changing times, places, and circumstances."[23] A famous statement of the Prophet declared: "If a judge performs *ijtihād* and gets the right answer, he receives two rewards. If he is [honestly] mistaken, he gets one."[24]

Ijtihād was seen as a standing obligation in Islamic law; to neglect it was not merely a cause for censure but also an act of disobedience to God.[25] The widespread notion that the "door of *ijtihād* was closed" in later centuries as a matter of theological principle has been shown in recent scholarship to be without historical foundation.[26]

ISLAMIC LAW AND CLASSICAL THEOLOGY

Opinions differ regarding the influence of theology on Islamic law. Fazlur Rahman stresses that the origins of theology and of law were distinct, and that even in the case of the Mu'tazila there is no evidence that their theology affected their positions in positive law.[27] The profound influence of *kalām* was in classical legal theory; by contrast, in all legal schools, the content of positive law remained essentially untouched, regardless of the influence *kalām* was wielding upon legal theory.

Schacht notes, however, that since the earliest times a close conjunction existed between the pursuit of theology and the eponyms of major schools of law: Abū Ḥanīfa, Mālik, Shāfiʿī and Aḥmad ibn Ḥanbal, all of whom were attentive to the theological issues of their times.[28] Of these principal Imams, Abū Ḥanīfa and Ibn Ḥanbal were the most conspicuously engaged in theology. Abū Ḥanīfa's theological writings exercised a lasting influence and culminated in the Māturīdite school of Samarkand. The Ḥanafī scholars of Samarkand (Māturīdī himself being only one of the most prominent among them) saw themselves as the adepts of Abū Ḥanīfa, busy in the elucidation and elaboration of his teachings. Māturīdī's synthetic theology rightly assigned him a distinctive position in the history of Muslim theology, but the Ḥanafī theological legacy of Samarkand only came to be designated "Māturīdite" after a complex process that came to its conclusion centuries after Māturīdī's death.[29] It is worthy of note that Māturīdī, like his mentor Abū Ḥanīfa, was a master jurist, and wrote one of the earliest and most influential works on Ḥanafī legal theory, *Indicants of the Revelatory Laws* (*Ma'ākhidh al-Sharā'i'*).

Kevin Reinhart argues that Islamic intellectual history must be seen as a holistic development. Law did not develop in isolation but was tightly integrated from the beginning with the emergence of *kalām*, grammar, and qur'anic commentary, and he insists that it is "impossible to grasp the origins, significance, and implications" of the act classifications of Ḥanafī positive law outside the context of Islam's earliest theological debates.[30] Similarly, Fazlur Rahman contends that Shāfiʿī's dialectic regarding hadith was oriented, not at legal scholars *per se*, but at early Muʿtazilites.[31]

Discussions of the role of reason in Islamic law often confuse the theological rationalism of *kalām*, especially in its Muʿtazilite form, with *ra'y* (independent reasoning) in Islamic law. They mistakenly presume that Islamic rationalism in law was eclipsed by the ascendence of the "grand synthesis" of Shāfiʿī's legal philosophy. However, as Binyamin Abrahamov observes, all of the speculative theologians of classical Islam, whether they were Muʿtazilites, Ashʿarites or Māturīdites, were equally rationalist. Each group considered "reason the principal device or one of the principal devices to reach the truth in religion". The differences between the three schools are not easy to discern, yet the disparity between them and their traditionalist[32] rivals is clear.[33] The systematic theology of the Māturīdites in particular excelled in its rationalist methodology and richness of thought; their purpose was non-apologetic and sought to demarcate Islamic theology as a distinct form of rationalism predicated upon unassailable proofs in reason, revelation and empirically verifiable truth.[34]

During the formative period of Islamic law, *ra'y* was a broad, speculative manner of reasoning associated with *ijtihād*. A number of pragmatic instruments of jurisprudence developed from it, such as analogy (*qiyās*), equitable discretion (*istiḥsān*), preclusion (*sadd al-dharā'i'*), and general necessity (*al–maṣāliḥ al-mursala*).[35]

Shāfi'ī's well-known rejection of legal sources such as *istiḥsān*, *sadd-al-dharā'i'* and *al-maṣāliḥ al-mursala*, and his emphasis on explicit texts, including the controversial "solitary hadith" (*aḥādīth al-āḥād*), offer, indeed, an interesting parallel to the voluntarism underlying the Ash'arite doctrines of free will and the nature of good and evil.[36] But none of his positions was taken up by the other Sunnī schools: even Ḥanbalism, for all its emphasis on textual deduction, continued to subscribe in limited fashion to Mālikī and Ḥanafī instruments of *ra'y*. Although arguably the most formalistic of the four Sunnī schools, the Shāfi'īs espoused a textually based doctrine of specific public interest (*istiṣlāḥ*) (as opposed to the non-textual *maṣāliḥ mursala* of the Mālikīs).[37] Like other Sunnīs, the Shāfi'īs elaborated much of their positive law in a pragmatic spirit. In the course of Islamic intellectual history, Shāfi'ī jurists proved themselves to be pioneers in the genre of legal maxims, arguably the epitome of Islamic legal realism.[38]

The rationalism implicit in *ra'y* and its later derivatives must not be confused with the metaphysical rationalism of classical Islamic theology. As Abrahamov observes, "rationality turns to rationalism when reason is prior to revelation".[39] This was not the case with the rationality of early *ra'y* or its ancillaries in the Mālikī and Ḥanafī schools. Their adamant adherence to pragmatic realism was, to take an expression from Abrahamov, a type of "informal dynamism".[40] It derived its strength from a non-formalistic legal induction and pragmatic intuition based on a general understanding of the law and its well-established precepts and legal rationales.[41]

The historical relationship between Islamic legal theory and positive law has yet to be carefully studied. Sherman Jackson asserts that classical legal theory had little to do with positive law: "In the end, however, legal theory remains standing as a monumental but fairly empty ruin whose authority can only be sustained through a reliance upon a never-ending series of 'ad-hoc adjustments' and 'makeshift apologies'."[42] The theologically informed speculations of Islamic legal theory had little effect on the positive law of the schools, even among jurists who readily subscribed to rationalistic theology and its application to legal theory. Indeed, the influence of legal theory on positive law was so limited that some insist that it is irrelevant to the study of the law's substantive content.[43]

The Mu'tazilites set the framework of Islam's classical theological debates. They seem also to have been the first to introduce speculative theology into Islamic legal theory. It is noteworthy, however, that most Mu'tazilites adhered to Ḥanafī positive law, even after many of their non-Mu'tazilite legal colleagues took theological positions antithetical to their own.

In response to the Mu'tazilite challenge, towards the beginning of the eleventh century Bāqillānī introduced extensive material from Ash'arite dialectical theology into legal theory. As a theologian, Bāqillānī was central to the development of the Ash'arite tradition, but his insistence upon the relevance of theology to law stood in sharp contrast to the approach of Ash'arī himself.[44] Instead of envisioning an organic relationship between the two disciplines, Ash'arī had conceived of them as discrete fields of knowledge that should not trespass on each other.[45]

Not all legal theorists followed Bāqillānī's lead. For Ḥanafī legal theorists, his theoretical positions often contrasted sharply with their own, although, like Bāqillānī, they were not Mu'tazilites. Non-Ḥanafīs also took issue with Bāqillānī. An Andalusian contemporary, Abu'l-Walīd al-Bājī (d. 1081), preferred to exclude *kalām* from his writings on legal theory as much as possible. Another contemporary, the Shāfi'ī chief jurisconsult Abū Isḥāq al-Shīrāzī (d. 1083), scrupulously avoided formal theological topics in his legal theory, making an exception only of those ideas which he found it necessary to refute. Another Shāfi'ī jurisprudent of the same period, Ibn al-Sam'ānī, composed a work on legal theory with the explicit intention of avoiding the methods and terminologies of *kalām*.[46]

Nonetheless, the approach of Bāqillānī ultimately won wide acceptance, and most non-Ḥanafī works on Sunnī legal theory that have come down to us are based on his work and refer to him as "*the* Shaykh". Ghazālī accounted for the wide acceptance of Bāqillānī's type of theological speculation among later jurists and jurisprudents, via the curricula and pedagogical techniques of classical Islamic education. By Ghazālī's time, most jurists were receiving a rigorous training in *kalām* during their formative period, and this inclined them to adopt the methodology of *kalām* and acknowledge the importance of its principal metaphysical concerns.[47] Consequently, many later jurists and jurisprudents came to regard *kalām* as the principal underpinning of legal speculation, even to the extent that they regarded jurisprudence as a branch of theology.[48]

Ghazālī argued that only a few theological doctrines were relevant to positive law, and he held that these did not go beyond the most rudimentary postulates of theological speculation.[49] Among those questions that legal theory shared with *kalām* which were actually relevant to the law were preliminaries such as the standards for accepting or rejecting hadith, the utility of "solitary hadith", the definition and implications of the abrogation of one scriptural text by another, the semantics of commands and prohibitions, the question of whether or not commands imply their opposites, and issues pertaining to consensus (*ijmā'*), analogy (*qiyās*), and general assessments of legal reasoning.[50]

Accountability before God (*taklīf*) was among the shared issues, but its relevance to law was different from its implications in *kalām*. From the standpoint of positive law, the definition of *taklīf* had a bearing on the question of when Muslims were required to follow Islamic injunctions and when they were not. The juristic criteria for *taklīf* were straightforward: Islam, reason and legal majority, the latter being determined by puberty or a minimum age. Thus, a non-Muslim, a person lacking the power of reason, and a child, were not required to adhere to the injunctions of the law.

The dispute over the relationship of *taklīf* to revelation was one of the classical debates of Islamic theology. Like theologians, jurists also debated whether *taklīf* was contingent upon the reception of revelation, although many legal texts made no mention of the issue.[51] For jurists, the issue of *taklīf* had a practical bearing upon the status of Muslims whose ignorance of Islam resulted from the absence of means for adequate instruction. For theologians, it raised other concerns, which, however consequential they appeared to theologians, were largely irrelevant to the practical concerns of the law. The theologians speculated on what existential questions (the existence of God, for example) a person just attaining *taklīf* was morally required to reflect upon. It brought up the question of free will and the implications of the human capacity or incapacity to act freely for *taklīf*. The theologians wondered whether pure reason and the natural human disposition (*fiṭra*) were sufficient to make human beings morally responsible before God in the absence of revelation. They questioned whether non-Muslims who had no access to revelation would be punished in the next world and if God would hold them responsible for disbelief or deviation from the dictates of monotheism.[52]

The question of good and evil was a central concern of *kalām*. Was revelation required for their knowledge, or could they be apprehended in the absence of revelation by unaided reason? This issue found its way into legal theory. It was not, however, a significant problem for positive law, which generally continued, as before, to take rational considerations like general necessity as its basic premise.

One of the truisms of Islamic studies in the West until recently was the notion that the voluntaristic ethics of Ash'arite theology ultimately destroyed the rationalism of Islamic law as reflected in Mu'tazilite theology and the *ra'y* of early jurists. This misconception was rooted primarily in a confusion of legal rationality with the rationalism of speculative theology. It fails to take account of the history of positive law in Islam, and also neglects the ethical perspective of Māturīdite theology, the dominant theology of the Ḥanafī school.

The theological problem of good and evil in Islam was hardly a new dilemma. Plato had asked whether God commands because He knows a thing to be good, or whether a thing is good because He commands it. Mu'tazilite theology supported the first proposition; the Ash'arites held to the second; the Māturīdites took a nuanced position between the two. Even the Ash'arite view, at least among significant representatives of the school, was not categorical. Shihāb al-Dīn al-Qārāfī (d. 1285) contended that there were broad areas of agreement between all theological schools. The actual point of disagreement, in his assessment, concerned the merits and demerits of good and evil and the nature of reward and punishment in the hereafter.[53]

Although an Ash'arite, Juwaynī held that the good and evil of human acts could be assessed on rational grounds, even though the acts of God Himself lay beyond the purview of human reason. Ghazālī preferred this position, and Rāzī is reported to have adopted it towards the end of his life.[54] The Māturīdite position was similar to that of the Mu'tazilites but did not accept the same primary corollaries which the Ash'arites rejected. Māturīdite theology held that all analogies between God and the created world were false because of the utter discontinuity between the physical and the metaphysical planes. Yet such analogies were necessary for human thought; the Mu'tazilites, in their view, had placed exaggerated confidence in speculative reason at the expense of spiritual intuition (*ma'rifa*) and had drawn analogies between God and creation, especially regarding the issue of good and evil, where no such analogical correspondence was possible.[55]

THE NEED FOR REVEALED LAW

Muslim jurists were more concerned with practice than with theory. The primary purpose of Islamic law in their view was the well-being and salvation of the entire community, which required clear tenets of faith and practice, not abstruse matters that only theologians and the scholarly minded could understand. Sound adherence to the law was something that all Muslims could learn and potentially put into practice. From a legal perspective, conformity to God's commandments did not require an abstract intelligence or an elaborate education. The pathways of faith and practice lay within the grasp of the many and the few, the untutored and the elite.

For Mu'tazilite and Ash'arite theologians, however, God's purpose in revealing the law revolved around the abstract questions, such as the nature of *taklīf*. For the former, human reason knew good and evil. God could not create evil but was bound of necessity to do what was best for human well-being. The chief purpose of the revelatory law was to inform humanity of the compensation or retribution their acts would meet with in the next world. Those who did good would of necessity be rewarded; those who did evil would inescapably be punished; those who fell between the two categories would occupy an intermediate state (*manzila bayn al-manzilatayn*).

For the Ash'arites the law's purpose also rested on the issue of *taklīf* and the knowledge of good and evil. Humans know good and evil and their otherworldly consequences only through revelation. Since the will of God is utterly free, God will mete out judgement in the next world as He sees fit. He is not bound by necessity to reward or punish anyone. By virtue of His revealed promise, He will, in fact, reward good and punish or forgive evil, but this is not a cosmic imperative; it is utterly the workings of His will.[56]

For the Māturīdites, revelation, reason and empirical knowledge comprise complementary sources of truth regarding the Seen and the Unseen. The revelatory law is humanity's aid in this life and the next, but knowledge of good and evil is accessible to them through each of the three sources. Unlike the Mu'tazilites, however, the Māturīdites argue that it is fundamentally mistaken to make the principle of divine justice the cornerstone of theology. Sound theological speculation must begin and end with reflection on divine wisdom. God's wisdom permeates creation, explains the existence of good and evil and provides the prism through which the intricacies of God's justice become intelligible to human beings.

The Muslim scriptures sometimes seem to exist in tension with the grand speculations of medieval *kalām*. The Qur'an and hadith clearly teach the innate goodness of human nature (*fiṭra*), and its inherent aptitude to know God. It was widely held that natural faith was sufficient for the salvation of all children who died before majority, and for adults who died before receiving the prophetic teaching, if they lived in a way faithful to their natures. The Islamic declaration of faith ("legal faith") based on true knowledge of God and acceptance of his prophets complemented and perfected human nature. An account attributed to Ibn ʻAbbās, a Companion of the Prophet, held that God's primordial covenant with humanity (Qur'an 7:172–3) accounts for the essentially moral and spiritual proclivities of human nature:

> God took from [human beings] as a covenant the pledge to worship Him and to associate no partners with Him. The Hour [of the day of judgement] will not come until all humans are born who were given the covenant on that [first primal] day. Whoever encounters the second covenant [i.e. the Prophetic message] and fulfils it will profit from the first covenant. Whoever encounters the second covenant but does not fulfil it will not be benefited by the first. Whoever dies as a child before encountering the second covenant dies in the state of the first covenant in accordance with the natural human condition [*fiṭra*].[57]

The soul knows God instinctively, is conscious of His perfection and glory, and desires nearness to Him. It possesses basic knowledge of good and evil, a love of truth and a hatred of falsehood, a consciousness of justice and injustice, and even, according to some, an intuitive knowledge that good and evil will receive full recompense. ʻAlī al-Qārī (d. 1607) affirmed that human natures are intrinsically equipped for the knowledge of God and the distinction between right and wrong. If left in their original state without negative influences, they would continue for ever to live according to their upright primordial natures.[58]

Some understood humanity's inborn knowledge of moral and spiritual realities to be "subconscious". Consequently, it could be confounded, forgotten and lost. The self's capricious nature and its inclination towards passions and selfish interests are among the *fiṭra*'s greatest adversaries. Humans often turn away from their better natures, and require inducements to turn back to their natures and stimulate the goodness intrinsic to them. Ghazālī exemplified the *fiṭra*'s need of positive motivations by using the metaphor of digging a well. The water lies hidden within the earth, but only shovels (positive outside stimuli) make it accessible. He also invoked the images of extracting oil from almonds and water from roses; neither feat can be accomplished without an oil press.[59]

THE LAW AND SUFISM

The law is essential to the perfection of divine servitude. As such, it is also fundamental to Sufism and the spiritual disciplines of Islam. Santillana notes the marked mystical tendency of Islamic law, which he attributes to its concern for the life of body and soul as two complementary aspects of a single phenomenon:

> [Islamic] religion and law belong to two distinct orders, yet they integrate themselves into each other in turn because they are intimately united by the common goal they share, which is the well-being of man. The principles of the faith regulate the internal form and determine what man ought to believe in pursuing eternal life. The positive law imposes discipline upon human activity and, in this, directs it toward those precise mundane foundations and becomes the necessary complement – the body – of that organism which is made up of the faith and the soul.[60]

The masters of mainstream Islamic Sufism insisted upon the law.[61] A Moroccan Sufi master, Muḥammad al-'Arabī al-Darqāwī (d. 1845), wrote:

> Whoever desires that Freedom show him her face, let him show her the face of servitude [to God]. This means having upright intentions, truthful love, a good opinion of others, noble character, and careful adherence to what the law commands and prohibits without any alteration or change. [Freedom] will then show him her face, and veil it from him no more.[62]

Traditional Western scholarship sometimes supposed that rigorous adherence to Islam's outward (legal) tenets was antithetical to the spiritual pursuits of Muslim mystics. There were, without question, strong antinomian Sufi strains on the periphery of Islamic spiritual history, but the mainstream tradition associated with Junayd, one of the earliest mentors of Sufism, insisted upon adherence to the law. In the eyes of the Junaydī Sufis, their spiritual discipline corresponded to Islam's third and highest dimension, that of *iḥsān* (human perfection), and, therefore, was "the life-blood of Islam". Junayd said: "This knowledge of ours [Sufism] is built upon the foundations of the Qur'an and the Sunna."[63]

Historical evidence shows that early Sufi notables took both law and spiritual teaching seriously, and the endorsement of the law remained central to mainstream Sufi tradition. The characteristic genius of Islamic mysticism was its ability to strike a balance between the law and spirituality, and to insist upon the complementary nature of the "exoteric" and "esoteric" dimensions of Islam.[64] Shāṭibī, one of the most illustrious of medieval Islamic jurisprudents, censured his juristic colleagues for their laxity in the law, while charging that the Sufis of his day were excessively rigorous in its application.[65]

Sha'rānī (d. 1565), a renowned jurist and prominent Sufi, held that it was a matter of consensus among the mystics that none of them was qualified to preside over their path who lacked profound mastery of the religious law. Every mystic, he argued, must be a jurist, but not every jurist can be a mystic. In his eyes, the Sufis were beyond reproach regarding the religious law. It was, indeed, their adherence to the law that, in each case of individual enlightenment, had brought them into the presence of God.[66]

As a rule, the jurists of Islam were more comfortable with Sufism than with rationalistic theology. Mainstream Sufis of the Junaydī tradition insisted upon the inseparable bond between the law and the spiritual path; many of them were prominent jurists. In proverbial Sufi wisdom the world of spiritual enlightenment is compared to the oceanic flood of Noah. The esoteric knowledge of God and the realm of ultimate realities lies at the threshold of a boundless inward sea without a floor and without shores. The believer's spiritual quest may open upon that sea but none can survive it without an ark like Noah's. For the Sufis, that ark is the prophetic law.

Further reading

Abd-Allah, Umar F., "Innovation and creativity in Islamic law", <www.nawawi.org/downloads/article4.pdf>, accessed October 2006.

Abrahamov, Binyamin, *Islamic Theology: Traditionalism and Rationalism* (Edinburgh, 1998).

Anawati, Georges C., "Philosophy, theology and mysticism", in Joseph Schacht and C. E. Bosworth (eds.), *The Legacy of Islam* (Oxford, 1974), pp. 350–91.

al-Azmeh, Aziz, "Islamic legal theory and the appropriation of reality", in Aziz al-Azmeh (ed.), *Islamic Law: Social and Historical Contexts* (London and New York, 1988), pp. 250–65.

Black, Antony, *The History of Islamic Political Thought: From the Prophet to the Present* (New York, 2001).

Cerić, Mustafa, *Roots of Synthetic Theology in Islam: A Study of the Theology of Abū Manṣūr al-Māturīdī (d. 333/944)* (Kuala Lumpur, 1995).

Hallaq, Wael B., *A History of Islamic Legal Theories: An Introduction to Sunnī Uṣūl al-Fiqh* (Cambridge, 1999).

Heinrichs, Wolfhart P., "*Qawāʿid* as a genre of legal literature", in Bernard G. Weiss (ed.), *Studies in Islamic Legal Theory* (Leiden, 2002), pp. 365–84.

Makdisi, George, *The Rise of Colleges: Institutions of Learning in Islam and the West* (Edinburgh, 1981).

Melchert, Christopher, *The Formation of the Sunnī Schools of Law, 9th–10th Centuries* CE (Leiden, 1997).

Rahman, Fazlur, "Functional interdependence of law and theology", in G. E. von Grunebaum (ed.), *Theology and Law in Islam* (Wiesbaden, 1971), pp. 89–97.

Islam (Chicago and London, 1979); 2nd edn, (Chicago, 2002).

Reinhart, Kevin A., "Like the difference between heaven and earth: Ḥanafī and Shāfi'ī discussions of *farḍ* and *wājib* in theology and *uṣūl*", in Bernard G. Weiss (ed.), *Studies in Islamic Legal Theory* (Leiden, 2002), pp. 205–34.

Rudolph, Ulrich, *Al-Māturīdī und die Sunnitische Theologie in Samarkand* (Leiden, 1997).

Santillana, David, *Istituzioni di diritto musulmano Malichita con riguardo anche al sistema Sciafiita*, 2 vols. (Rome, 1926).

Schacht, Joseph, "Islamic religious law", in Joseph Schacht and C. E. Bosworth (eds.), *The Legacy of Islam* (Oxford, 1974), pp. 392–403.

The Origins of Muḥammadan Jurisprudence (Oxford, 1953).

"Theology and law in Islam", in G. E. von Grunebaum (ed.), *Theology and Law in Islam* (Wiesbaden, 1971), pp. 3–23.

Stewart, Devin J., *Islamic Legal Orthodoxy: Twelver Shiite Responses to the Sunni Legal System* (Salt Lake City, 1998).

Weiss, Bernard, *The Search for God's Law: Islamic Jurisprudence in the Writings of Sayf al-Dīn al-Āmidī* (Salt Lake City, 1992).

Notes

1. In this chapter, "jurist" stands for a scholar of Islamic positive law (*faqīh*); "jurisconsult" stands for a jurist trained to issue special legal opinions for individual cases (*muftī*); and "jurisprudent" is used for a scholar of Islamic legal theory (*uṣūlī*).
2. David Santillana, *Istituzioni di diritto musulmano Malichita con riguardo anche al sistema Sciafiita* (Rome, 1926), I, p. 5.
3. Henri de Wael, *Le droit Musulman: nature et évolution* (Paris, 1989), p. 52.
4. Noel J. Coulson, *Conflicts and Tensions in Islamic Jurisprudence* (Chicago, 1969), pp. 80–5.
5. John Henry Merryman, *The Civil Law Tradition: An Introduction to the Legal Systems of Western Europe and Latin America* (Stanford, 1969), pp. 15–17.
6. In the wake of the Mu'tazilite-inspired Inquisition under Ma'mūn, and the subsequent institutional consolidation of the schools of law, Muslim jurists assumed authority over Islamic religious discourse and legal institutions. Through subsequent centuries, this disparate and non-centralised body of men continued to exercise virtually exclusive religious authority at the expense of the state (see Devin J. Stewart, *Islamic Legal Orthodoxy: Twelver Shiite Responses to the Sunni Legal System* (Salt Lake City, 1998), p. 1). The rift between the political and religious establishments in Islam left a legacy of crisis over political legitimacy. There were notable exceptions, such as the Ottoman Empire, but most Muslim polities were plagued by their endemic need for

political legitimacy in the absence of religious endorsement. See Antony Black, *The History of Islamic Political Thought: From the Prophet to the Present* (New York, 2001), pp. 23–4, 30, 33, 38.

7. Austin B. Creel, *Dharma in Hindu Ethics* (Calcutta, 1977), pp. 1–3; and Ariel Glucklich, *The Sense of Adharma* (New York and Oxford, 1994), pp. 3, 7–9.
8. See Mario Bretone, *Geschichte des römischen Rechts: Von den Anfängen bis zu Justinian* (Munich, 1987), pp. 81–4; Michael Gagarin, *Early Greek Law* (Berkeley, 1986), pp. 1, 15–16.
9. Ze'ev W. Falk, "Jewish law and medieval canon law", in Bernard S. Jackson (ed.), *Jewish Law in Legal History and the Modern World* (Leiden, 1980), p. 78.
10. Philip S. Alexander, "Jewish law in the time of Jesus: towards a clarification of the problem", in Barnabas Lindars (ed.), *Law and Religion: Essays on the Place of the Law in Israel and Early Christianity by Members of the Ehrhardt Seminar of Manchester University* (Cambridge, 1988), p. 44.
11. Roger Tomes, "A perpetual statute throughout your generations", in ibid., p. 20.
12. F. F. Bruce, "Paul and the law in recent research", in ibid., pp. 115–18.
13. Timo Veijola, "Der Dekalog bei Luther und in der heutigen Wissenschaft", in ibid., pp. 66–7.
14. Falk, "Jewish law", pp. 78–80.
15. Hubert Kaufhold, *Die Rechtssammlung des Gabriel von Baṣra unter ihr Verhältnis zu den anderen juristischen Sammelwerken der Nestorianer* (Berlin, 1976), pp. 5–8, 13–4.
16. De Wael, *Le droit musulman*, p. 52.
17. Coulson, *Conflicts and Tensions*, p. 80–5.
18. H. A. R. Gibb and Harold Bowen, *Islamic Society and the West* (Toronto, 1957), pp. 9–10.
19. Joseph Schacht, *An Introduction to Islamic Law* (Oxford, 1964), p. 200.
20. Umar F. Abd-Allah, "Innovation and creativity in Islamic law", <www.nawawi.org/downloads/article4.pdf>, accessed October 2006, pp. 6–7.
21. Bernard Weiss, *The Spirit of Islamic Law* (Athens, GA, 1998), p. 89.
22. Santillana, *Istituzioni*, I, p. 55.
23. Ibn Qayyim al-Jawziyya, *I'lām al-muwaqqi'in in* (Beirut, 1998), III, p. 5. In Arabic, the maxim reads: "*la yunkaru taghayyur al-ahkam ma'a taghayyur al-azmān*". Ibn Qayyim parses it by adding: "in accordance with changing times, places, circumstances, intentions, and customary practices".
24. 'Alī ibn al-Qaṣṣār, *al-Muqaddima fi'l-Uṣūl* (Beirut, 1996), pp. 114–15; Abu'l-Walīd al-Bājī, *Iḥkām al-Fuṣūl* (Beirut, 1995), II, pp. 714–16.
25. Abd-Allah, "Innovation and creativity in Islamic law", pp. 8–9.
26. See George Makdisi, *The Rise of Colleges: Institutions of Learning in Islam and the West* (Edinburgh, 1981), pp. 4, 290; Wael B. Hallaq, *A History of Islamic Legal Theories: An Introduction to Sunnī Uṣūl al-Fiqh* (Cambridge, 1999), pp. 201–2 and n. 59; Christopher Melchert,

The Formation of the Sunnī Schools of Law, 9th–10th Centuries CE (Leiden, 1997), pp. 16–17.

27. Fazlur Rahman, "Functional interdependence of law and theology", in G. E. von Grunebaum (ed.), *Theology and Law in Islam* (Wiesbaden, 1971), pp. 89–97, at pp. 89–90.
28. Joseph Schacht, "Theology and law in Islam", in ibid., pp. 3–24, at p. 4.
29. Ulrich Rudolph, *Al-Māturīdī und die Sunnitische Theologie in Samarkand* (Leiden, 1997), pp. 25–6, 29–30, 84–5, 354, 357; Mustafa Cerić, *Roots of Synthetic Theology in Islam: A Study of the Theology of Abū Manṣūr al-Māturīdī (d. 333/944)* (Kuala Lumpur, 1995), p. 11.
30. Kevin A. Reinhart, "Like the difference between heaven and earth: Ḥanafī and Shāfi'ī discussions of *farḍ* and *wājib* in theology and *uṣūl*", in Bernard G. Weiss, ed., *Studies in Islamic Legal Theory* (Leiden, 2002), pp. 205–34, at pp. 205, 225, 230.
31. Fazlur Rahman, *Islam*, 2nd edn (Chicago, 2002), p. 51.
32. Abrahamov defines "traditionist" as a scholar of hadith, and a "traditionalist" as one who regards religious and theological truth as strictly revelatory and directly derivative, often in a literalistic fashion, from the Qur'an, Sunna and Consensus: Binyamin Abrahamov, *Islamic Theology: Traditionalism and Rationalism* (Edinburgh: 1998), p. ix.
33. Ibid., pp. viii, ix.
34. Rudolph, *Al-Māturīdī*, pp. 221–2.
35. For definitions and illustrations of these instruments of law and the divergent attitudes of the principal Sunnī schools toward them, see Umar F. Abd-Allah, "Mālik's concept of *'amal* in the light of Mālikī legal theory", 2 vols. (PhD thesis, University of Chicago, 1978), I, pp. 209–85.
36. Muḥammad Ma'rūf al-Dawālibī, *al-Madkhal ilā 'ilm uṣūl al-fiqh* (Beirut, 1965), p. 174.
37. Santillana, *Istituzioni*, I, pp. 55–7.
38. See Wolfhart P. Heinrichs, "*Qawā'id* as a genre of legal literature", in Weiss, *Studies*, pp. 365–84, at pp. 367–8, 371.
39. Abrahamov, *Islamic Theology*, p. x.
40. Ibid., p. 7.
41. See Abd-Allah, "Mālik's concept of *'amal*", I, pp. 209–85.
42. Sherman A. Jackson, "Fiction and formalism: towards a functional analysis of *uṣūl al-fiqh*", in Weiss, *Studies*, p. 184.
43. See Yvon Linant de Bellefonds, *Traité de droit musulman comparé* (Paris, 1965), I, pp. 7–9.
44. Muḥammad al-'Arūsī 'Abd al-Qādir, *al-Masā'il al-mushtaraka bayna uṣūl al-fiqh wa-uṣūl al-dīn* (Jeddah, 1410/1990), p. 12.
45. Rahman, "Functional interdependence", p. 90.
46. 'Abd al-Qādir, *Masā'il*, pp. 12, 15.
47. Ibid., pp. 15–16.
48. Hallaq, *History*, pp. 37–8.
49. Rahman, "Functional interdependence", p. 91.
50. 'Abd al-Qādir, *Masā'il*, pp. 12–13.

51. See Kevin Reinhart, *Before Revelation: The Boundaries of Muslim Moral Thought* (Albany, 1995).
52. 'Abd al-Qādir, *Masā'il*, pp. 12–13, 70–1, 94–5, 132–48.
53. Aḥmad ibn Idrīs al-Qārāfī, *Sharḥ tanqīḥ al-fuṣūl fi'l-uṣūl* (Cairo, 1306 AH), pp. 41–2.
54. 'Abd al-Qādir, *Masā'il*, pp. 78–9.
55. Rudolph, *Al-Māturīdī*, pp. 296, 298; cf. Cerić, *Roots*, p. 127.
56. 'Abd al-Qādir, *Masā'il* pp. 74–7.
57. Muḥammad ibn Jarīr al-Ṭabarī, *Jāmi' al-bayān 'an ta'wīl āī al-Qur'ān* (Beirut, 1995), VI, pp. 150–1.
58. 'Alī al-Qārī, *Mirqāt al-mafātīḥ* (Mecca, n.d.), I, p. 283.
59. Muḥammad al-Ghazālī, *Iḥyā' 'ulūm al-dīn* (Damascus, n.d.), I, p. 77.
60. Santillana, *Istituzioni*, I, pp. 6–7.
61. Melchert, *Formation*, p. xiii.
62. Muḥammad al-'Arabī al-Darqāwī, *Majmū'at rasā'il Abī 'Abd Allāh Muḥammad al-'Arabī al-Darqāwī* (Casablanca, n.d.), p. 47.
63. In 'Abd al-Wahhāb al-Sha'rānī, *al-Ṭabaqāt al-kubrā al-musammā bi-lawāqiḥ al-anwār fī ṭabaqāt al-akhyār* (Beirut, 1408/1988), I, p. 4.
64. William C. Chittick, *Faith and Practice of Islam: Three Thirteenth-Century Sufi Texts* (Albany, 1992), pp. xii–xiii, 168–70.
65. Hallaq, *History*, p. 163.
66. Sha'rānī, 'Abd al-Wahhāb, *al-Ṭabaqāt al-kubrā* (Cairo, 1965), I, p. 6.

13 Theology and Sufism

TOBY MAYER

INTRODUCTION

Concepts of God are mere simulacra. Such, in brief, was the teaching of the great Hispano-Arab mystical theologian Muḥyi'l-Dīn ibn 'Arabī (d. 1240). In his typically outspoken formulation, the conceptual God is just a "created God". He is, according to Ibn 'Arabī's expression "the God created in dogmas" (*al-Ḥaqq al-makhlūq fi'l-i'tiqādāt*).[1] In the Islamic ethos, such a deity is ultimately a deception. "All that you worship instead of God is nothing but names which you have invented, you and your forefathers, for which God has bestowed no warrant from on high!" (Qur'an 12:40). In a "civilisational event" charged with numinosity, at the conquest of Mecca on Thursday 20 Ramadan 8 (11 January 630), the Prophet enters the Great Sanctuary on his camel Qaṣwā, fully armed. He first touches his staff to the Black Stone in the north-east corner of the Ka'ba, magnifying God. In a deafening crescendo, the cry *Allāhu akbar* (God is most great) is taken up by the thousands of onlookers before the Prophet hushes them with a gesture. After making his *ṭawāf*, the seven ritual circuits of the Ka'ba, the Prophet next turns to face the surrounding idols of the pagan Arabs. There are 360 in all, standing for each degree in a vast circle of universal illusion. The Prophet rides slowly round, pointing his staff at each totem, and intones the verse of the Qur'an: "The Real has now come and the false has vanished: for behold, the false is bound to vanish!" (17:81). As he points, one idol after another lurches forward on its face.

Sufism drew its own radical consequences from this archetypal act of iconoclasm. It viewed not just stone but mental constructs with suspicion. It set aside man-made gods in favour of the living God, the palpable mystery encountered in the disciplines of the Sufi path through contemplation (*mushāhada* = *mystika theamata*). To be sure, Sufism has a theology, but one unlike the science of the speculative theologians (*mutakallimūn*). It is a "mystical theology" which flows from the transcendent experience of God in the lives of the saints. While Sufism strove, especially from the thirteenth century, to express its theology positively and systematically, it had earlier favoured quite different media: hagiography, spiritual ethics, the theopathic locution (*shaṭḥ*),[2] allusion (*ishāra*), paradox and poetry. Moreover, in common with other mystical theologies, it strongly inclined to an apophatic rather than a kataphatic approach to the divine mystery, expressing God through denial, not affirmation, through "unsaying" rather than saying. Thus Niffarī (d. after 977) reported that God said to him: "Do not speak, for he that reaches unto Me does not speak!" and "Name is a veil over essence."[3] For Ḥallāj (d. 922), even the attribution of unity to God (*tawḥīd*) by man in the end fell short of God's absolutely transcendent reality: "Unity is an attribute of the created subject who bears witness to it. It is not an attribute of the Object witnessed as one."[4] Apophasis had venerable roots in the Islamic tradition. The first caliph, Abū Bakr (d. 634), reputedly said: "The incapacity to attain comprehension [of God] is comprehending [God] (*al-ʿajz ʿan dark al-idrāk idrāk*)".[5]

But Sufism did not isolate itself from wider Muslim society and discourse. On the contrary, it underwent an extremely productive tension which was arguably the central dynamic of Islamic intellectual history: though Sufism constituted an esoterism of the highest order, with all the exclusiveness which that implies, it also had to reckon with the Islamic genius. The salient quality of that genius is *integrality*. In this there is a subtle but definite link between the unity of God and that of man, theological *tawḥīd* ("making one" – monotheism) implying societal *tawḥīd*. If Sufis found striking proof-texts for a distinction of esoterism from exoterism in the Qur'an and hadith,[6] they also had to contend with clear texts which muted the free social expression of such a distinction.[7] Moreover, Sufism claimed to lie at the core of Islam, and to have the vivifying role in the civilisation of the heart within a body. On these grounds, it could not divorce itself from Islamic society, despite constituting at times a radically esoteric movement.

A treatment of the relationship between Islamic mysticism and theology must note this tension. It is at work throughout the history of Sufism, but is more apparent in certain phases, and in particular from the ninth to the tenth century. This was the time in which the Islamic tradition was emerging from a brilliant process of formalisation through the development of a series of sciences (hadith, jurisprudence, theology, exegesis), each with its principles (*uṣūl*), authorities and schools (*madhāhib*). But this "fixation" unavoidably threatened to restrict and even alienate the role of spirituality, which had been central to the ferment of early Islamic religious culture. Parallel with this, certain representatives of spirituality in this period tended for the first time to suggest a radical incommensurability of the *via mystica* with exoteric norms: key figures such as the already mentioned Ḥallāj, and later Niffarī, Abū Yazīd al-Bisṭāmī (d. *c.* 875), Ḥamdūn al-Qaṣṣār (d. 884) and Abū Ḥafṣ ʿAmr al-Ḥaddādī (d. *c.* 874).

MUʿTAZILITE SUFISM

Let us explore the development of this situation. Mysticism, theology, jurisprudence and exegesis clearly formed a seamless unity in the apostolic period of Islam. Notwithstanding vexing questions of historicity, all the disparate sciences and groups of the classical Islamic universe trace their origins back to the "naked singularity" of this time. In the post-apostolic era, the era of the Successors (*tābiʿūn*), there is still a striking unity of impulse. A clear case in point is mysticism and theology – the subject of this chapter. It is well known that both trace their origins as distinct fields to the figure of al-Ḥasan al-Baṣrī (d. 728). A phalanx of "proto-Sufis" like Ibn Wāsiʿ, Farqad, Abān, Yazīd al-Raqqāshī, Ibn Dīnār, Bunānī and Ḥabīb al-ʿAjamī emerged from Baṣrī's circle.[8] As central a Sufi concept as *ḥāl* (pl. *aḥwāl*, a rapture or transitional spiritual state, as opposed to *maqām*, a stable station), may have started with Baṣrī. In addition, the key Sufi practice of systematic self-examination (*muḥāsaba*) appears to have been recommended first by him.[9] On the other hand, the first stirrings of speculative theology in its earliest Muʿtazilite form were also felt in his group. The two men held up as the founder figures of Muʿtazilite theology, Wāṣil ibn ʿAṭāʾ (d. 748) and Abū ʿUthmān ʿAmr ibn ʿUbayd ibn Bāb (d. 769), were both associated with his circle. It is noteworthy that both men were also well known for *askēsis*.[10] True, Wāṣil removed himself (or was banished by Baṣrī) from the circle. But for Massignon it was Baṣrī's own rationalist exegesis of scripture in particular which marks him down as the prototypical Muʿtazilite. For instance, he viewed the qurʾanic figures of Hārūt and Mārūt (2:102) as non-Arab princes (*ʿiljān*), not as fallen angels; and "with his critical mind" he held the salutations to right and left ending the formal prayer to be an islamisation of an earlier custom.[11]

In due course, this early link between Muʿtazilism and Sufism was so completely eclipsed as to seem improbable. For example (to jump ahead in time), Ibn Munawwar, the hagiographer of the great Central Asian Sufi saint Abū Saʿīd ibn Abiʾl-Khayr (d. 1049), typified his period in implying that Ḥanafite-Muʿtazilite rationalism was quite unsuited for

Sufism.[12] Nevertheless, in the meantime there had indeed been figures categorised as "Sufi Mu'tazilites" (*ṣūfiyyat al-mu'tazila*). The founder of the Baghdad school of Mu'tazilite theology, Abū Sahl Bishr ibn al-Mu'tamir (d. 825), numbered Sufis among his followers, such as Abu'l-Qāsim al-Balkhī; one of the most famous of all Mu'tazilite thinkers, al-Naẓẓām (d. 845), had students who were Sufis, such as Faḍl al-Ḥadathī and Ibn Khābiṭ; and the already mentioned major figures Bisṭāmī and Ḥaddādī were members of the Mu'tazila.[13]

The foreclosure of a Mu'tazilite Sufism was accelerated by the famous caliphal Inquisition (*miḥna*) between 833 and 851, in which the confession of the created status of the Qur'an was enforced by the Abbasid state in line with Mu'tazilite doctrine. Prominent contemporary Sufis resisted the policy in varying degrees. A major Baghdādī leader of the Sufi movement, Bishr al-Ḥāfī (d. 841 or 842) typically adopted a stance of "passive resistance", lauding Ibn Ḥanbal for not yielding to the pressure of the authorities, yet avoiding putting himself in direct jeopardy. But despite his high standing, Bishr was strongly criticised for his quietistic attitude, even by disciples.[14] Other mystics, such as the mysterious Dhu'l-Nūn al-Miṣrī (d. 860), resisted as actively as Ibn Ḥanbal himself, and underwent imprisonment for their intransigence.[15] At any rate, the period of the *miḥna* appears to have confirmed Sufism's already strong links with the "orthodox" Sunnī party (*ahl al-ḥadīth*). The latter triumphed under al-Mutawakkil's caliphate, and with the discrediting of Mu'tazilism the Sufi Mu'tazilite became an anomalous figure.

THE BAKRIYYA, SĀLIMIYYA AND KARRĀMIYYA

Baṣrī's main legacy to Sufism must be sought in a different quarter from the Sufi Mu'tazila. The important eighth-century proto-Sufi order known as the Bakriyya derived directly from his influence. This group, who were strongly aligned with the *ahl al-ḥadīth*, had their origins in a figure who was reputedly a student of Baṣrī, 'Abd al-Wāḥid ibn Zayd (d. 793), although the name *Bakriyya* derives from the latter's nephew and disciple Bakr ibn Ukht 'Abd al-Wāḥid ibn Zayd. The sect was strongly focused on the inner life of its adherents. An ascetic community of Ibn Zayd's followers established themselves at 'Abbādān, at that time an island between the estuaries of the Qārūn and Tigris rivers, where they used distinctive conical cells[16] for contemplative exercises. One of Ibn Zayd's main disciples was Abū Sulaymān al-Dārānī (d. 830), who is a significant link in the development of Islamic mystical thought insofar as he first tried to systematise the key Sufi concept of the state (*ḥāl*) and station (*maqām*) on the path to God.[17] Some of the great early Sufis were to be found at the 'Abbādān complex, such as the aforementioned Bishr al-Ḥāfī, Sarī al-Saqaṭī (d. 865) and Sahl al-Tustarī (d. 896).

Tustarī, a thinker of great importance in the history of Sufi thought, had been attracted to the community by its then head, a little-known figure by the name of Abū Ḥabīb Ḥamza ibn 'Abd Allāh al-'Abbādānī. He alone, Tustarī found, could answer the spiritual problem which had convulsed his life from his early teens. This, if Ibn 'Arabī is to be believed,[18] was the problem of the "prostration of the heart". Tustarī had become aware that his heart, his inner consciousness, was also in prostration to God, like his physical body in the formal prayer (*ṣalāt*). Unlike his body in the *ṣalāt*, however, Tustarī's heart refused to return to the stipulated standing position (*qiyām*). Only 'Abbādānī could confirm for him that it was perfectly correct for the heart of the mystic to be rendered prostrate, and never to recover. It was also in seclusion at 'Abbādān that Tustarī had the mysterious formative experience of his spiritual novitiate – his visions of God's "Supreme Name" (*ism Allāh al-a'ẓam*) filling the nocturnal sky.[19]

The noteworthy point about the Bakriyya is that it was as much a theological school as a spiritual movement. Moreover, the group's theology was moulded in opposition to the rationalist Mu'tazila and their influence in Basra. In other words, it was a self-consciously Sunnī theology which in certain respects foreshadowed Ash'arism.[20] The movement called the Sālimiyya, presently engendered by Tustarī through his disciple Muḥammad ibn Sālim and the latter's son Abu'l-Ḥasan Aḥmad ibn Sālim, was very similar. The Sālimiyya was one of the major Sufi movements of the late ninth century, but it is sometimes referred to in Muslim doxographical works as a theological (*kalām*) school. For instance, Baghdādī's *Distinction between the Sects* (*al-Farq bayn al-firaq*) refers to the Sālimiyya as a band of *kalām* scholars in Basra.[21] Theologically, the Sālimiyya's doctrines, like those of the Bakriyya, were opposed to Mu'tazilism. The movement was indeed broadly linked with the radical anti-Mu'tazilite perspective known to its enemies as the *ḥashwiyya* (approximately: the "stuffing-ists", i.e. the outspoken literalists). The *ḥashwī* perspective was formalised, above all, within Ḥanbalism and it is significant that the Sālimiyya sought refuge in the metropolis of Baghdad inside the Ḥanbalite quarter. The major contemporary Ḥanbalite scholar Abū Muḥammad al-Barbahārī (d. 941) had in fact been a disciple of Tustarī.[22] An important proposition of the Sālimiyya suggestive of an ethos analogous to that of Ḥanbalism is that when one recites the Qur'an, God Himself recites it by one's tongue, and when one listens to another reciting the Qur'an, one actually hears it from God.[23] Again, Tustarī vehemently upholds the reality of the attributes of God, or rather, in his curiously nuanced way of putting it, he upholds the reality of the attributes *of* the attributes. These "attributes of the attributes" are strongly affirmed by Tustarī and yet are declared by him to transcend human comprehension: "behind the names and attributes [are] attributes which the minds [*afhām*] do not pierce because God is a fire ablaze. There is no way to Him and no escape from plunging into Him."[24] The amodal affirmation of the divine names/attributes is a basic Ḥanbalī and Ash'arī response to Mu'tazilism. The latter sought to preserve divine transcendence by the negation (and metaphorical interpretation) of the attributes of God cited in the Qur'an. On the other hand, the "orthodox" correctives to Mu'tazilism (be they Ḥanbalī or Ash'arite) attempted to preserve both divine transcendence and the letter of scripture, by affirming the panoply of scriptural attributes in all their richness while simultaneously approaching them strictly amodally, or apophatically, thus raising them far beyond the reach of human understanding. The difference, such as it is, between the response to the issue of God's attributes in these orthodox Sunnī theologies and in Tustarī's mystical theology, is the palpably "experiential" element in the latter: "God is a fire ablaze" and "there is no escape from plunging into Him". This movement from the two-dimensionality of conception to the three-dimensionality of empirical experience marks a typical difference of emphasis between *kalām* and Sufism.

The "orthodox" party in theology did not refrain from criticism of the Sālimiyya for the school's less conformable teachings. This is evident in the (unextant) work condemning Aḥmad ibn Sālim by Ibn Khafīf al-Shīrāzī (d. 981). Ibn Khafīf was the direct disciple of the founder and eponym of the school of Sunnī "orthodox" theology *par excellence*, Abu'l-Ḥasan al-Ash'arī. Nevertheless, his attack on the Sālimiyya cannot be used as evidence of a general hostility of Ash'arism towards Sufism. For Ibn Khafīf was in fact one of the best-known Sufis of his generation in Baghdad. He thus shows, at the very historical inception of Ash'arism, just how closely this major *kalām* school and Sufism could be intertwined.

What general conclusions, then, might be drawn from the cases of the Bakriyya and Sālimiyya? First, these are glaringly the ancestors of the post-thirteenth-century Sufi orders. Moreover, they bear out that, true to the precedent of the Prophet and primitive Islam, spirituality and theology coalesce in the mystical movements of this formative period, since in the Bakriyya and Sālimiyya theological dogmata and spiritual agenda wholly combine. Louis Massignon long ago vouched for the idea that the theologies of these groups were actually explored and vindicated *through* their spiritual "experimentation".[25] Lastly, the theologies in question, while *sui generis* and sometimes subject to criticism by partisans of the *ahl al-ḥadīth*, are more in keeping with the latter's point of view and stand against the Mu'tazilite tendency to rationalise and figurate.

There is one other major school which, from the later ninth century, like the earlier Bakriyya and contemporary Sālimiyya, in Massignon's words "made a defense of orthodoxy based upon the experimental method of the mystics" and even "revised contemporary scholastic vocabulary in the light of the constants observed through mystical introspection".[26] This school was the Karrāmiyya. Again, counter-Mu'tazilite doctrine combined in the Karrāmiyya with a semi-cenobitic lifestyle and spiritual programme. The sect's eponym, Muḥammad ibn Karrām (d. 870), spent time studying at Balkh and other places at the then eastern extremity of the Muslim world where the remnants of Manichean or Buddhist religious institutions may have contributed to his idea of the *khānqāh* or convent. While the term became the normal word in the Persianate world for a Sufi convent, in the ninth century the institution was still so closely identified with Ibn Karrām's followers that they were sometimes called "Khanqāhīs".[27] Within his movement, the *khānqāh* was a place for spiritual retreat (*i'tikāf*) and ascetic exercises but also a centre from which Ibn Karrām's distinctive theological teachings could be propagated. The theology in question was presently anathematised, largely because Ibn Karrām veered towards gross corporealism (*tajsīm*), in reaction to the rationalistic abstraction of God (*ta'ṭīl*) by the Mu'tazilites. Nevertheless, the Karrāmite movement was in its time widely influential in eastern Islam, and many contemporary authorities within the Ḥanafite rite who rejected Mu'tazilism in *kalām* had defined themselves in terms of membership of Ibn Karrām's school.[28]

THE CHALLENGE OF ESOTERISM

Aside from bequeathing to Sufism the distinctive institution of the *khānqāh*, the influence of Karrāmism on Islamic mysticism is indirect. It should be remembered that Ibn Karrām's movement was not mystical *sensu stricto*. However, the violent asceticism of its exponents, which cast such a spell over the working classes of Khurāsānian towns such as

Nīshāpūr, provoked an epochal reaction amongst mystics in the ninth century. With Ḥamdūn al-Qaṣṣār and Abū Ḥafṣ ʻAmr al-Ḥaddādī at their head, their distinctive teaching emphasised the rejection of all spiritual ostentation (*riyā'*), against the histrionic otherworldliness of the Karrāmite ascetics. Spiritual striving was for God alone, or it was worthless. In the case of Ḥamdūn, this radical "introversion" might even involve actively seeking social blame, in line with the verse in the Qur'an which praises those who "struggle in the path of God and do not fear the blame of a blamer" (5:54). The new tendency emanating in particular from the mystics of Nīshāpūr was thus known as the Malāmatiyya, the People of Blame.[29] The Malāmatī ethic was fraught with danger. It predictably led some would-be mystics to legitimise outright antinomianism, and so threatened to discredit Sufism within Islam. Interpreted sincerely and conscientiously, however, the Malāmatī ethic remains a constant and moving undercurrent of Sufi spirituality and hagiography. ʻAbd al-Raḥmān al-Sulamī (d. 1021), author of one of the earliest esoteric commentaries on the Qur'an, formalised and structured Malāmatī spirituality in his *Malāmatī Treatise* (*Risālat al-Malāmatiyya*), and in the school of Ibn ʻArabī, the highest of all saints are in the Malāmatī ranks.[30]

Exponents of the Malāmatiyya were thus urged, through the negative example of the Karrāmiyya, to objectify what marked out a truly "esoteric" *askēsis* from its exoteric analogue. Their *askēsis* was wholly introverted and had no one but God for witness. The Malāmatī mystics are part of a larger convulsion which characterises Sufism in that period. Sufism (as the mystical movement was presently generalised) could not disguise a certain asymmetry between its teachings and wider religious norms. This asymmetry was visible in many areas, from Sufism's involved paraliturgical practices and the audacity of its goals, to its characteristic media. The pursuit of the Prophet's "good example" (*uswa ḥasana*) by Sufis unsatisfied with simple conformity to his precedent (*sunna*) in the routines of daily life, seemed to trespass on the very uniqueness of the Last Prophet. From the ninth century, for example, there were Sufis who spoke frankly of emulating the Prophet's ascension.[31] Saintly thaumaturgy – denied by Mu'tazilites but accepted unhesitatingly by the masses[32] – seemed to rival prophetic thaumaturgy. Neither was the supreme goal of the Sufi gnostic simply the fulfilment of the religion's legal obligations with a view to posthumous salvation, but was additionally God-realisation (*ittiṣāf*), no less, while alive. And the gnostic's encounter with God was expressed in Sufism in a unique medium, the theopathic locution. In such utterances, it was claimed that God Himself spoke through the mystic in enigmas akin to the ambiguities (*mutashābihāt*) found in the Qur'an. Like the qur'anic ambiguities, these locutions were to be accepted by the mass of believers in good faith, leaving their interpretation to an elite. Thus, in Carl Ernst's words, they shockingly amounted to a virtual "supplementary canon, formed by the uninterrupted contact which God maintains with the elect".[33] The most famous ecstatic who brought such readings of Sufism into the open, forcing the issue of their asymmetry with exoterism, was undoubtedly Manṣūr al-Ḥallāj.

There had already been trials of Sufis under the Abbasids, notably that of Abu'l-Ḥusayn al-Nūrī and his companions *c.* 878. The mystical "lover" Sumnūn (d. 910) had fallen foul of certain authorities for his amorous way of talking about God. Aḥmad al-Kharrāz (d. 899) was exiled from Baghdad at this time on account of his work *The Secret* (*Kitāb al-Sirr*), and later, after an eleven-year residence in Mecca, he found himself expelled again. But it is clearly the furore centring on Ḥallāj and his two trials (913 and 922) under the Abbasid caliph al-Muqtadir, which marks the moment when the tension most momentously broke surface.

What doctrines were specifically at stake in these persecutions? It appears that the Nūrī trial was founded on a vague allegation of *zandaqa* (crypto-Manichean heresy). This was enough provocation for the Ḥanbalite jurist Ghulām al-Khalīl to persuade the authorities to have him arrested and tried. For a figure like Khalīl, Nūrī's doctrine of divine love suggested an outrageous intimacy between creature and God, and implied an intolerable anthropomorphism. It is important, however, that when questioned by the chief judge of Baghdad, Nūrī spoke in particular about the saints who "see by God and hear by God" (the idea of *ittiṣāf*), causing the judge to weep with emotion. The same principle was the recurrent issue in the Ḥallāj trials. In the first of these, the main charge was that Ḥallāj had claimed divine lordship for himself and taught incarnationism (*ḥulūl*), by which the authorities concluded that the wandering thaumaturge was posturing as a messianic figure (*mahdī*).[34] This was deeply threatening to the state at a time when the extremist Shī'ite movement known as Carmathianism was in the air. In the second trial, although Ḥallāj's alleged replacement of the Ḥajj was decisive in his condemnation from the point of view of orthopraxy, nevertheless the vital issue from the viewpoint of orthodoxy was probably again *ittiṣāf*. It was the seizure of a text on this subject among Ḥallāj's effects which initially provoked the caliph to hand him over for cross-examination, and Ḥallāj's "thesis of [God's] witness" (*qawl bi'l-shāhid*) was the subject of a special session during the proceedings. In this last doctrine, it was claimed that witnessings (*shawāhid*) of God are obtainable in the person of the saints (*ahl al-ikhlāṣ*), who thereby become persuasive evidence of God in the midst of creation, drawing mankind to Him.[35] Ḥallāj evidently claimed as much for himself: "If you do not know Him, then at least know His signs! I am that sign and I am the Truth [*ana'l-Ḥaqq*]!"[36]

It must be noted that Ḥallāj himself rejected the concept of *ḥulūl*. But a *unio mystica*, in some sense, clearly lies at the heart of his teachings. Ḥallāj thus describes the realised saint as a manifestation (*ẓuhūr*) of God, but "not an infusion [*ḥulūl*] in a material receptacle [*haykal juthmānī*]".[37] The distinction is important and clearly eluded Ḥallāj's persecutors. The point is surely that through the saint's self-annihilation there is a thinning of the existential veils which hide God from the world, so that God in His infinity and transcendence may be contemplated through the saint, as the sky may be glimpsed through a window. There is no suggestion here of God incarnating, through a kenotic "descent" into an earthbound individual. Indeed, a recurring note of Ḥallāj's *Ṭawāsīn* is that God and the creature *never combine*. Be that as it may, the very notion of God-realisation, whatever its interpretation, appalled the Ḥanbalites, and obliged Sufis who used such language to qualify and carefully explain what they meant. A more circumspect view was that the saint was "invested" with one or another divine name or attribute (*ṣifa*). This was the so-called *ṣifātī* mysticism, initially developed by Ḥallāj's disciple Abū Bakr al-Wāsiṭī (d. *c*. 932) and popular in later Sufism. Another way in which the unitive experience of the mystic was explained was through the Sufi concept of *baqā'* ("enduring"), whereby the earthly adjunct of the mystic was readmitted subsequent to his annihilation (*fanā'*) in God – readmitted, however, in the light of that experience. The great contemporary mystic Junayd (d. 910), whose epistles are marked by a preoccupation with this whole problem, explains *baqā'* as follows: "[The mystic] is present in himself and in God after having been present in God and absent in himself. This is because he has left intoxication with God's omnipotence [*ghalaba*] and comes to the clarity of sobriety."[38] Junayd goes so far as to emphasise that the famous ecstatics like Bisṭāmī had all passed away only "in their imagination" (*'alā al-tawahhum*).[39] His insistence on the subjectivity of the experience of annihilation and the imperative of passing beyond it to a reinstatement of the creature–creator distinction became a feature of so-called sober (*saḥwī*) Sufism, and was later enshrined in the doctrine of *waḥdat al-shuhūd* ("the unity of witnessing", subjective theomonism).

THE RESCUE OF INTEGRALITY

Junayd thus heralds a reaction. His earlier observation of the Nūrī affair probably made him wary of Ḥallāj's strident form of esoterism, and many accounts point to his censure of Ḥallāj's outspokenness. It is not a matter of Junayd being more scrupulous in upholding the *Sharī'a*, for Ḥallāj himself was allegedly extremely meticulous in his religious observance and renounced all legal mitigations and concessions (*rukhaṣ*). Nonetheless, Junayd makes a reassertion of what has been referred to earlier as the Islamic genius for integrality, and he marks the beginning of a concerted effort to express Muslim esoterism in a way which contributed to, rather than undermined, the wider religion. Junayd's mysticism of "sobriety" perhaps received its strongest expression in a tradition of Sufism affiliated to the Ḥanbalite legal rite, though he himself had in fact adhered to the (presently defunct) rite of Abū Thawr al-Kalbī. Ḥanbalism's strict rejection of any superimposition on the Qur'an and hadith yields a form of Sufism in impeccable conformity with the consensual foundations of the tradition. This kind of Sufism might explore the tradition's agreed norms with eminently abnormal intensity, but it may never violate them in the name of esoterism. In keeping with Junayd's emphasis, Sufism has always had a significant Ḥanbalite and Ẓāhirite manifestation in figures like Junayd's contemporaries Ruwaym and 'Amr al-Makkī, and later figures like Khwāja 'Abdallāh Anṣārī and the great 'Abd al-Qādir al-Jīlānī. Ibn Qayyim al-Jawziyya, disciple of Ibn Taymiyya, would in due course be responsible for documenting this Ḥanbalite tradition of Sufism.[40]

The period from the later tenth to the eleventh century saw the production of a series of compilatory works and manuals, ever since viewed as classics, aimed at organising and defending the mystical movement. Unity was imposed on the different regional traditions, technical terms were defined, standard hagiographies were put together, and above all Sufism was shown to conform to "orthodox" Sunnī creeds and to be rooted in the Qur'an and the precedent of the Prophet and the first Muslims. The five key works in question were the Arabic *Food of Hearts* (*Qūt al-qulūb*) by Abū Ṭālib al-Makkī (d. 966), the *Book of Gleams* (*Kitāb al-Luma'*) by Abū Naṣr al-Sarrāj (d. 988), the *Disclosure of the Way of the People of Sufism* (*al-Ta'arruf li-madhhab ahl al-taṣawwuf*) by Abū Bakr al-Kalābādhī (d. *c.* 990), the *Generations of Sufis* (*Ṭabaqāt al-Ṣūfiyya*) by Abū 'Abd al-Raḥmān al-Sulamī (d. 1021), and the Persian work *Unveiling the Veiled* (*Kashf al-maḥjūb*) by 'Alī al-Hujwīrī (d. 1071 or 1072).

These texts represent a watershed, and a distinction should be drawn between the pre- and post-compilatory periods. An important result of such texts was the imposition of homogeneity. The term "Sufi" appears to have applied originally only to the Baghdad school, while the eastern tradition used the term *Malāmatī*, or *ḥakīm* (sage), for its representatives.[41] Especially noteworthy is the inclusion in these texts of formal Sunnī creeds. For example, Kalābādhī's *Disclosure* contains a lengthy preliminary section (chapters 5–30) which amounts to a detailed statement of Sufism's orthodoxy and conforms to the conventional order of Islamic catechisms (*'aqā'id*): first, correct teaching on the divine attributes; secondly, correct teaching on the Beatific Vision; and thirdly, correct teaching on theodicy.

Arberry claimed that Kalābādhī's creed was modelled on *al-Fiqh al-Akbar II*,[42] so named by Wensinck and identified by him as a Ḥanbalite creed of the ninth or tenth century.[43] But Watt has dismissed Wensinck's thesis, identifying this creed as basically Ḥanafite in character.[44] The facts that Kalābādhī was later listed as a famous Ḥanafite jurist,[45] and that Ḥanafism was the prevalent rite in the Sāmānid realm where he lived, confirm that the real dogmatic background of the *Disclosure*'s creed is Ḥanafism. Whatever the case, it propounds many of the core teachings of Sunnī *kalām* as formalised in Ash'arism and to a lesser extent in Māturīdism. It affirms that God has eternal attributes which are "neither He nor other than He" (a typically Ash'arite formula), and that these attributes are akin to God's essence in their unknowability: "As His essence is not caused, so His attributes are not caused: to attempt to display the eternal is to despair of understanding anything of the realities of the attributes or the subtleties of the essence [of God]." This is the same "apophatic assertion" (*al-ithbāt bi-ghayri'l-tashbīh*) of the divine attributes (versus the "apophatic denial" of them typical of Mu'tazilism) that was seen earlier in Tustarī's formulation. It is typical of Ash'arism. Kalābādhī adopts the same attitude in regard to the critically important attribute of Speech. Sufis, he claims, hold that God's Speech is "an eternal attribute of God contained in His essence, *in no way resembling the speech of created beings*". The author discusses the status of the Qur'an at some length, and concludes that since God affirms for Himself the attribute of Speech (e.g. Qur'an 4:162) and God's attributes must be eternal because He is eternal, therefore, the divine Speech cannot consist of letters and sounds since this would make it contingent and temporal. Nevertheless, by a kind of *epochē*, the Qur'an is affirmed to be truly God's Word and uncreated. What is interesting about such passages[46] is that they read like pure *kalām*, and are not "mystical theology" in any obvious sense, though Kalābādhī may quote Sufis in support of his position.

In his discussion of the *visio beata*, Kalābādhī again uses a typical *kalām* combination of scriptural texts and rational arguments to make another, essentially Ash'arite, affirmation: believers will have a true vision of God in the hereafter, but without any modality (*kayfiyya*) or circumscription.[47] Finally, the treatment of theodicy is typically Ash'arite. Jabrism (the theory of absolute compulsion) is formally denied but there is an affirmation of God's creation of every act of the creature as well as of its capacity (*istiṭā'a*) in acting. Kalābādhī, moreover, disapproves of the typically Mu'tazilite doctrine that God is determined by questions of welfare (*maṣlaḥa*).[48]

Credal statements like Kalābādhī's became a stock feature of a certain kind of Sufi literature, from Makkī's *Food of Hearts* to Ghazālī's *Revival* (which contains the *Jerusalem Epistle*, an Ash'arite catechism). It is simplistic to maintain that such creeds are artifices to win acceptance from the *Sharī'a*-minded, planted within works aimed at smuggling Sufism into "mainstream" Islam. Rather, such creeds are in the end symptomatic of the Sufis' own conviction that Sufism lies at the very heart of the religion, and is *sine qua non* for its spiritual vitality. It is the figure of Abū Ḥāmid al-Ghazālī who had the decisive historical role in bearing out this claim. He stands, above all, for the full confirmation of mysticism's centrality to Islam as a living theocratic civilisation.

GHAZĀLĪ AND THE SELJUK SYNTHESIS

This is not the place to rehearse the details of Ghazālī's life. Elsewhere in this volume, David Burrell has described how he came to confirm the centrality of Sufism through terrible inner traumata.[49] The result was that Ghazālī made his famous flight from Baghdad, dedicating himself to the contemplative disciplines of Sufism.

Ghazālī hyperbolises when he expresses himself in terms of an actual *disavowal* of the exoteric sciences. For the fruit of his conversion was of course a bold attempt to revive these very sciences through Sufism, as expressed in the title of his major work, *The Revival of the Religious Sciences*. Ghazālī thus aimed to generalise Sufism, in keeping with the spirit of integrality. He wanted Sufism to pervade society, guaranteeing its spiritual vitality. He wished, in other words, for a restoration of the primitive *theocratic* ideal of Islam: a society grounded in the living presence of God, in place of the (at best) *nomocratic* aspirations of the society he saw around him. It is noteworthy that in one of his last works, the famous *O Youth*, Ghazālī proposed that Sufism, euphemised as the "science of the states of the heart", was an "individual duty" (*farḍ 'ayn*) on Muslims and not merely a "duty of sufficiency" (*farḍ kifāya*).[50] Muslim society should not, in other words, be content to leave the internalising of religion to select individuals. This is breathtakingly radical. Yet it is closely mirrored in the *de facto* pervasion of Muslim society by organised Sufism in the period from the twelfth century onwards. With the propagation of the great Sufi orders (*ṭuruq*), a huge proportion of Muslims were involved in the mystical movement, albeit many as affiliates (*mutashabbihūn*) or "partakers in the blessing" (*mutabarrikūn*) of one or another order.

Ghazālī's is of course the consummation of a much older relationship between Ash'arism and Sufism. It is a story whose origins even pre-date Ash'arī himself, and go back to the prefigurations of Ash'arism in earlier counter-Mu'tazilite theology. In the century before Ash'arī, al-Ḥārith al-Muḥāsibī (d. 857) had been a figure of central importance in the formation of the Baghdad school of Sufism, but was also a self-consciously orthodox exponent of *kalām*. Like Ash'arī later, Muḥāsibī proposed combating Mu'tazilism on behalf of the *ahl al-ḥadīth* by using the dialectical tools of *kalām* in works like his (lost) *Reflection and Induction* (*Kitāb al-Tafakkur wa'l-i'tibār*). He was severely criticised for his approach by his contemporary, Ibn Ḥanbal, for whom all *kalām* was innovatory and suspect. Later, when Ash'arī's school emerged as a major force, a central figure like the aforementioned Ibn Khafīf could be both a well-known Sufi and a committed Ash'arite. This combination of Sufism and Ash'arism triumphed ultimately under Ghazālī's patrons, the Seljuks, the major Sunnī Turkish power operating in Iran, Iraq and Anatolia from the mid-eleventh century to the end of the twelfth (and to the beginning of the fourteenth century in Anatolia). Within the Seljuk context, Ghazālī is generally seen as completing the project already under way in the previous generation with al-Qushayrī (d. 1072), whose widely influential *Treatise* (*Risāla*) and esoteric commentary on the Qur'an assume an Ash'arite dogmatic framework. Even under the Seljuks, however, Sufism and Ash'arism did not prevail without tribulation. Despite Seljuk patronage of Sufism through the construction and endowment of *khānqāh*s, the trial and execution of Sufis were still not unknown, as in the case of 'Ayn al-Quḍāt al-Hamadhānī (d. 1131). Again, while Ash'arism became the official theology of the Seljuk domains, promoted in the newly founded Niẓāmiyya colleges all over the eastern lands of Islam in centres like Baghdad, Nīshāpūr and Merv, the theological school had earlier been persecuted and banned by Ṭughril-Beg's Mu'tazilite vizier, Kundurī, up until the latter's death in 1063.

But Ash'arite Sufism was undoubtedly the main intellectual bequest of the Seljuks to Islam. Its influence was primarily felt through the spread of Ghazālī's own works. Ghazālī became a normative voice in large areas of the Sunnī Muslim world, and the *Revival*, his *magnum opus*, became a text on which many Sufis founded their entire spiritual programme. There are many examples of this. It is known, for instance, that the *Revival* was the basic textbook of Ibn Ḥirzihim (d. 1165), teacher of the great North African saint Abū Madyan. A major figure in Persianate Sufism like Hamadhānī was thoroughly devoted to the *Revival* (at least, earlier in his career, before he took up more Avicennan ideas). But Ash'arite Sufism also continued to have major representatives without any obvious dependence on Ghazālī. The great visionary and mystical exegete, Rūzbehān Baqlī (d. 1209), was strongly Ash'arite in his theology, as is clear from his credal work *Road of Monotheism* (*Maslak al-tawḥīd*). In other texts, it is fascinating to see Ash'arite terms and ideas transposed by Baqlī into a purely mystical context. For instance, the difficult *kalām* issue of the *visio beata* is explored anew, no longer as an episode of the eschaton, or of the Prophet's ascension, but insofar as Baqlī himself claims to have encountered God "in the most beautiful of forms" in the privacy of his own home. He explains: "In my ecstasy and spiritual state my heart did not remember the story of anthropomorphism and abstraction, for in seeing Him, the traces of intellects and sciences are raised."[51] Baqlī typically uses the Ḥanbalite and Ash'arite formula "without how" (*bi-lā kayf*) in such visionary contexts: "He transcends change in His singleness and cannot be encompassed by His creation. I was watching God, awaiting the unveiling of attributes and the lights of the Essence, and God manifested His eternal face "without how" to my heart; it was as though I was looking at Him with the external eye, and the hidden world shone from the appearance of His glory."[52] Yet another representative of the synthesis under discussion is Abū Ḥafṣ al-Suhrawardī (d. 1234), whose work became the basic textbook of institutional Sufism in the Persianate world, but who also systematically defended Ash'arism against Ḥanbalism. Finally, in the Arab world, there is an example in the third master of the influential Shādhilī order, Ibn 'Aṭā' Allāh al-Iskandarī (d. 1309), whose Ash'arism was largely drawn from the *Book of Guidance* (*Kitāb al-Irshād*) of Ghazālī's teacher al-Juwaynī. Iskandarī's manual on invocation (*dhikr*), and his mystical aphorisms bear the unmistakable imprint of Ash'arite doctrine and terminology.

Clearly the term "Ash'arism" needs to be modulated when used in regard to Sufi thinkers like these. Ghazālī, for instance, has standard Ash'arite works which fall outside of Sufism altogether, like his *Just Mean in Belief* (*al-Iqtiṣād fi'l-i'tiqād*). He presents an analogous level of Ash'arism even in certain Sufi contexts, notably in the creed contained in the *Jerusalem Epistle*. This level of Ash'arism is purely catechistic, and is not Sufi *sensu stricto*, though it may pave the way for Ghazālī's mystical discourse. It should by no means be confused with the transcendentalised Ash'arism proper to that discourse.[53] It is Ash'arism in the latter sense which is of real interest to us in the study of thinkers like Ghazālī.

This transcendentalised Ash'arism must be exemplified. It is well known that a cornerstone of Ash'arism is atomism, according to which the world is made up of indivisible substances (*jawāhir*), which have no innate power of duration (*thubūt/baqā'*), and instead must receive it as an external accident directly from God at each moment of their existence. The structure of time itself, according to Ash'arism, is atomistic (compare the "chronons" postulated by certain modern physicists). Time too consists in nothing but discrete unextended moments (*awqāt*, or *ānāt* = "nows"). This Ash'arite doctrine is clearly meant to articulate God's omnipotence. For it denies, at each point in the duration of anything non-divine, that it has any intrinsic power of existence. God alone has such a power. Put differently, Ash'arism protests that we are quite right to ask at each point in the endurance of something, *why* it is there at all. Since it was not there in the past, it is never itself sufficient grounds to explain its presence. It must in fact be made present, *ab extra*, at every point of its duration. This leads to a radical occasionalism: the denial of secondary causes. The predictability, through time, of the cause–effect chains from which the world appears to be woven, in fact depends on "God's custom" (*'ādat Allāh / sunnat Allāh* = *potentia ordinata* versus *potentia absoluta*) and is not part of the intrinsic nature of the so-called cause and effect. Indeed, the Greek concept of "nature" (*physis* = *ṭabī'a*) is condemned outright by Ash'arism. God thus becomes the sole and absolute cause (*mukhtari'*) of the universe in its totality throughout its history. Creation is not restricted to a first moment of time, but the universe is perpetually created for as long as it is present in existence.

This occasionalist doctrine was developed by Ash'arism to confirm God's absolute power, against Mu'tazilism, which insisted that God, through surrender or delegation (*tafwīḍ*), might invest created beings with a capacity of their own. Created beings in Mu'tazilism have a certain independence. If this dialectical context partly explains the emergence of the Ash'arite teaching in question, it took on a life of its own in Sufism. For instance, a figure like Ghazālī harnesses it to Sufi ethics, when he recommends in *O Youth* that the best cure for ostentation is to keep in mind that people are really just inanimate objects (*jamādāt*).[54] But this is as yet a relatively modest application of the Ash'arite teaching. Ghazālī has much bolder uses for it, completely shifting the emphasis from causality to ontology, from denying power to creatures to denying existence itself to them, from occasionalism to theomonism. Thus, in Ghazālī's exegesis of the verse of the Qur'an "Everything is perishing except His Face" (28:88), he explains that it is not a matter of things perishing at some particular moment or other, but that they are perishing unceasingly and at every moment. This is a mysterious way of saying that created data have no ontological status of their own at any time, and therefore, that insofar as we speak of existence at all, it is a theophany. Ghazālī is quite frank about his drift, for he now says, "the only existent is the Face of God" (*fa-yakūnu'l-mawjūdu wajha'llāhi ta'ālā faqaṭ*).[55] While the original Ash'arite context is perhaps implied by Ghazālī's reference to "moments", there has been a bewildering transition. The discontinuous, cipher-like atomic substance (*jawhar*), which Ash'arism stripped of all influence but still formally maintained as the ground of the cosmos, has wholly dissolved. Ibn 'Arabī makes the same transition in the chapter on the prophet Shu'ayb in his *Bezels of Wisdom* (*Fuṣūṣ al-ḥikam*). The Ash'arites, he says, are on the right lines in their doctrine. But they fall short in maintaining the theoretical distinction between accidents and substances *within* the cosmos. In fact, the whole cosmos is a "sum of accidents" (*majmū' al-a'rāḍ*), involving nothing substantial. Insofar as we can speak of substance, it is not part of the cosmos, but is God Himself. God, not "atoms", is then the real ground of the cosmos. In this way, as Ibn 'Arabī puts it, "from the sum of what is not self-subsistent has come about what is self-subsistent... and what does not endure for two moments has come to endure for two moments".[56]

SPECULATIVE SUFISM

In speaking of a synthesis of Ash'arism and Sufism, it is not implied that Ash'arism was uniform. The terminology and basic intuitions of Ash'arism are stable, to be sure. But Ash'arism was undergoing a deep change during the Seljuk period. Ever since the magisterial corpus of Avicenna had been disseminated among the learned class, Islamic thought had been registering its impact. The Seljuk period has even been called a period of "Avicennan pandemic".[57] The first symptoms of change in *kalām* were to be seen in Mu'tazilism. The founder of the last great school of Mu'tazilism, Abu'l-Ḥusayn al-Baṣrī (d. 1044), already showed Avicenna's influence. The same trend entered Ash'arism through Juwaynī, Ghazālī's teacher. Ghazālī himself stood at the head of a wave of refuters of Avicenna in his *Incoherence*. But in weeding out key aspects of Avicennism which Ghazālī held to be incompatible with revelatory authority, he ironically assured its domestication within dogmatic theology. The whole style of the later Ash'arism of the "moderns" (*muta'akhkhirūn*) who came in Ghazālī's wake is strongly Avicennan in comparison with that of the "ancients" (*mutaqaddimūn*). The same markedly Avicennan influence is clear in Islamic mysticism, as will emerge. The result is generally called "speculative Sufism", and is above all bound up with the dramatic success of Ibn 'Arabī's teachings.

Clear evidence of the great scope of Ibn 'Arabī's success is to be found, paradoxically, among his opponents. His doctrine of "the unity of existence" (*waḥdat al-wujūd*, i.e. objective theomonism) was not without vehement opposition within Sufism. In particular, major figures like the great theoretician of the Kubrawī order, 'Alā' al-Dawla Simnānī (d. 1336) and the eminent Indian Naqshbandī thinker Aḥmad al-Sirhindī (d. 1624), believed that the theory of *waḥdat al-wujūd* bore responsibility for the undermining of the religious law. They claimed that the theory promoted antinomian forms of spirituality by demolishing the creator–creature distinction on which worship and moral accountability were predicated. Their response, after Sirhindī, was to become famous as the theory of *waḥdat al-shuhūd*, subjective theomonism, which retrieved the crucial *distinguo* by relativising the unitive experiences of the ecstatics. But this actually underlines the triumph of Ibn 'Arabī's speculative Sufism. For reformers like these combated Ibn 'Arabī by developing intricate speculative responses of their own, not by reverting to the pre-speculative Sufism of the classical period, as represented, say, by Ghazālī's *Revival*.

Despite the distinctively philosophical flavour of Ibn 'Arabī's Sufism, its precise relation with formal philosophy is awkward. The "Greatest Shaykh" had no truck with systematically syllogistic approaches, and tended to elevate the revealed canon and immediate mystical perception over reason. He never quotes philosophers, and sometimes displays a contemptuous ignorance of them, as in the account he gives of his reaction to Fārābī's *Virtuous City*, which he angrily flung in the face of the volume's owner.[58] Be that as it may, many features in Ibn 'Arabī's thought demonstrably borrow, albeit perhaps unconsciously, from philosophical sources, expecially from Avicenna. On the most superficial level, he clearly makes full use of philosophical *termini technici*. It is significant that Ibn 'Arabī is sometimes nicknamed "Ibn Aflaṭūn" – the "Platonist". His Platonism appears to boil down to his concept of the "fixed archetypes" (*a'yān thābita*) which are central to his thought. On scrutiny, these are not really Plato's universal *eidē* at all. They are rather Avicenna's quiddities (*māhiyyāt*), that aspect of individuals which receives existence, and which in itself is isolable from external existence. Again, Ibn 'Arabī's cosmogony is related to Avicenna's in its basically emanationist thrust, though there are important differences. Ibn 'Arabī's broad focus on existence and its emanation can be argued to mirror the focus of Avicenna's metaphysics.

Ibn 'Arabī's speculative approach is of course prefigured in some earlier Sufis. 'Ayn al-Quḍāt al-Hamadhānī has already been mentioned. There is a clear difference between Hamadhānī's Ghazālian work, the *Essence of Realities* (*Zubdat al-ḥaqā'iq*), and his later *Prolegomena* (*Tamhīdāt*). The Avicennism of the latter work is pronounced. It has been pointed out that it even embraces ideas from Avicenna's thought which Ghazālī (Hamadhānī's earlier authority) rejected as strictly incompatible with religious orthodoxy. These are specifically those ideas presented in Avicenna's *Risāla Aḍḥawiyya* which stress the pure spirituality of the afterlife, and interpret the corporeal imagery of revelation metaphorically.[59] An older speculative tendency, obviously owing nothing to the influence of Avicenna, can be seen long before this in the history of Sufism, for instance in a figure like Muḥammad ibn 'Alī al-Ḥakīm (= "the philosopher") al-Tirmidhī (d. *c*. 910), who was the representative of a pre-Avicennan, pre-"Hellenistic" Islamic theosophy, as well as bearing responsibility for laying the foundations for the Sufi theory of the hierarchy of saints.

There had been an earlier tradition of speculative Sufism in Ibn 'Arabī's Spain, going back to Ibn Masarra (d. 931). In the absence of Ibn Masarra's works such as the *Book of Letters* (*Kitāb al-Ḥurūf*) and the *Book of Apperception* (*Kitāb al-Tabṣira*), his thought was reconstructed by Asín y Palacios from the references of later writers.[60] On this reconstruction, Ibn Masarra's philosophy was primarily characterised by Asín as pseudo-Empedoclean. But the rediscovery of Ibn Masarra's works by Kamāl Ibrāhīm Ja'far has allowed this thesis to be discredited.[61] Nevertheless, it is clear that a strong Neoplatonic thread runs through this mystic's thought, and via the so-called "School of Ibn Masarra" he gave an essentially speculative stamp to the Sufism of the Iberian peninsula. The atmosphere of Ibn Masarra's school is directly felt in the followers of Shūzī of Seville, who were to be found up to Ibn 'Arabī's own day. Another major speculative Sufi thinker, Ibn Sab'īn (d. 1270), emerged from Shūzī's order during Ibn 'Arabī's lifetime. Ibn Sab'īn's school was still operating in Egypt in the fourteenth century. The actual term "unity of existence" in fact appears to originate with Ibn Sab'īn, not with Ibn 'Arabī.[62]

In this we have clear elements in speculative Sufism which fall beyond Avicenna's influence. Moreover, as has been said, Avicenna's impact on Ibn 'Arabī himself is elusive. Nevertheless, the broadly Avicennan character of speculative Sufism was to be strongly confirmed after Ibn 'Arabī's death, due to the special strengths of his foremost disciple Ṣadr al-Dīn al-Qūnawī (d. 1274). In an important correspondence[63] with one of Avicenna's greatest spokesmen, Nāṣir al-Dīn al-Ṭūsī, Qūnawī reveals a detailed grasp of Avicenna's work the *Allusions and Remarks* (*al-Ishārāt wa'l-tanbīhāt*), as well as of Ṭūsī's commentary on it. In the light of his knowledge of these texts, Qūnawī puts a series of difficult questions to Ṭūsī, and argues for the weakness of the rational faculty. When Ṭūsī sends his replies, Qūnawī writes a new treatise in response. But it is a typical feature of dialogical engagement that the tools and theses of the opposite party are partly accepted, and this is the case with Qūnawī too. Indeed, synthesis is to an extent Qūnawī's explict aim, for in detailing his objective in the correspondence, he explains that he wants to unite the knowledge yielded by philosophical demonstration (*burhān*) with the fruit of mystical perception.

What begins with Qūnawī, then, is the systematic formulation of *waḥdat al-wujūd* as a virtually philosophical perspective. Qūnawī's approach is transmitted through a series of direct master–disciple relations, becoming the prevalent reading of Ibn 'Arabī. Thus Mu'ayyad al-Dīn al-Jandī and Sa'īd al-Din al-Farghānī were Qūnawī's direct disciples; 'Abd al-Razzāq al-Kāshānī was Jandī's disciple, and finally Daūd al-Qayṣarī was in turn Kāshānī's disciple. This list contains the names of some of Ibn 'Arabī's greatest commentators. The ultimate results of Qūnawī's philosophical transformation of the Unity of Existence are clear in the important fifteenth-century Sufi thinker and poet, 'Abd al-Raḥmān Jāmī (d. 1492). Jāmī's work *The Precious Pearl* (*al-Durra al-Fākhira*) is an attempt to present Sufism (for which read Ibn 'Arabī) as a superior perspective to *kalām* and Avicennism, and presents Sufism's distinctive answers to a whole series of difficult issues in the philosophy of religion: the proof of God, God's unity, God's knowledge (or ignorance) of particulars, the nature of God's will, power and speech, the capacity of contingent beings, and the relation of multiplicity to unity. Jāmī's work, which was commissioned by the Ottoman sultan Meḥmed II, is meticulously built up by its author from syllogisms, with separate arguments detailed for each premise. It is more obviously a work of *ḥikma* philosophy than a Sufi work, and virtually presents the Unity of Existence as a school of philosophy. The pedigree from Qūnawī is clear. Extensive passages from Qūnawī's works, including his correspondence with Ṭūsī, are quoted.

The deep impact of Avicenna on the speculative Sufism of Jāmī's day emerges from an early passage of the *Pearl* in which the author rehearses an argument for God's existence. It begins thus:

> Know that there is in existence a necessary existent, for otherwise that which exists would be restricted to contingent being, and consequently nothing would exist at all. This is because contingent being, even though multiple, is not self-sufficient with respect to its existence.[64]

This argument is clearly rooted in Avicenna's type of proof for God, generally called the *Burhān al-Ṣiddiqīn* (the "proof of the strictly truthful"). Avicenna's argument contains both ontological and cosmological aspects, and Jāmī's argument here is traceable to its cosmological aspect. Avicenna's argument may be briefly summarised as follows.[65] Existence can be hypothesised in the mind in two ways. The mind can entertain either the idea of necessary existence or the idea of contingent existence. Contingent existence, for its part, is incapable of explaining itself. By their very definition, contingents always somehow depend on something outside of themselves in existing. An individual contingent might have other contingents preceding it, and the chain of them might conceivably regress without beginning. But as a "set" (*jumla*) they will retain the same dependence on something external which characterises an individual contingent. Moreover, to say "external", when we have mentally gathered any contingent whatsoever into a set, is to say non-contingent or necessary. Thus, even though the world may be temporally infinite, it cannot be without dependence on something which transcends it and stands apart from the contingency which characterises it. Thus far, we have the cosmological aspect of Avicenna's argument, which is fairly obviously the ancestor of Jāmī's proof. Especially noteworthy is the audacious Avicennan claim that the world might be beginningless. This is hinted at by Jāmī's statement that the contingent might be multiple (*muta'addid*), from which understand *indefinitely* multiple. Later in the *Pearl*, Jāmī surprisingly confirms that in his view the Sufis uphold the world's beginninglessness in time.[66]

Avicenna's argument, however, also has an ontological aspect. This follows from the first modality in which existence may be entertained in the mind, as necessary rather than contingent. Avicenna's claim about this is that it is contradictory to set up "necessary existence" in the mind, but then to deny it outside the mind. For then it would not be *necessary* existence. To paraphrase Psalm 14, only a fool would say "God" in his heart, and go on to deny such a being in the real world. For God's existence *in re* follows from God's nature *in intellectu*. Avicenna was especially proud of this aspect of his reasoning, insofar as it avoided basing the conclusion (God's existence) on any lesser being. He cites the Qur'an in evidence of the superiority of this "ontological" method in proving God: "We shall show them Our signs on the horizons and in themselves until it becomes clear to them that He is the Truth."[67] This verse is taken to refer to the inferior cosmological method in which God's existence is brought out via God's traces in the cosmos. But Avicenna sees the words immediately after these in the Qur'an as referring to the ontological aspect of his reasoning: "Does it not suffice that your Lord bears witness to everything?" That is, for an elite, God Himself is in principle a sufficient basis to reach any conclusion – including that of God's own existence. This elite consists of the "strictly truthful ones" referred to in the title of Avicenna's proof.

While Jāmī's Sufi proof has an Avicennan pedigree, it is in turn quite demonstrable that Avicenna's earlier proof was partly inspired by contemporary Sufism. The distinction of a superior "ontological" approach to God from an inferior "cosmological" one is firmly rooted in Sufi theory pre-dating Avicenna. The *distinguo* is indeed implicit in the very title of Kalābādhī's aforementioned Sufi compendium, the *Disclosure* (*Ta'arruf*). In Kalābādhī, the term *ta'rīf* ("making known") refers to what the world does to God – pointing to His existence "from the outside". Contrariwise, the reflexive form *ta'arruf* is what God does to Himself, making Himself known through self-disclosure. Clearly this is precisely the distinction at work in Avicenna's classification of proofs of God.

It is noteworthy that Kalābādhī's and Avicenna's lives overlapped and that Avicenna was raised in Bukhārā, a city in which Kalābādhī must have been one of the major living representatives of Sufism. It has been suggested that Avicenna may even have heard the distinction in question from the great Sufi theorist, in person.[68] The provenance of Avicenna's *distinguo* from Kalābādhī is probably confirmed by the fact that the latter refers to the very same verse from the Qur'an as used by

Avicenna in explanation: "The meaning of *ta'rīf* is that [God] shows them the effects of His power in the heavens and in the souls."[69] Moreover, in the Sufism of Kalābādhī's day, the *distinguo* already had the authority of tradition behind it. For Kalābādhī himself attributes the *ta'rīf/ta'arruf* dichotomy further back to Junayd. Even Junayd may have been passing on an idea which was already abroad in Sufi circles. This is clear in a story detailed by Hujwīrī in the course of his Sufi lexicon in the *Unveiling*. In explaining the antonymous technical terms *muḥāḍara* and *mukāshafa* ("presenting" and "unveiling"), roughly corresponding with *ta'rīf* and *ta'arruf* respectively, he quotes a story from Junayd's friend and contemporary, Kharrāz. Kharrāz and his companion Ibrāhīm ibn Sa'd al-'Alawī are wandering, it is said, by the seashore, when they stumble on one of God's friends. They pose for him a question: "What is the way to God?", and he replies that there are in fact two ways to reach Him, one being for the vulgar and the other for the elite. When they press him to explain himself he reproves them as follows: "The way of the vulgar is that on which you are going: you accept for some cause and you decline for some cause; but the way of the elect is to see only the Causer [God, who makes all causes what they are], and not to see the cause [outside of God]."[70]

CONCLUSION

Philosophy and Sufism thus influenced each other theologically. Sufism's impact on philosophy is yet more obvious later in its history, in the Ṣafavid period. Its influence pervades the thought of the most eminent Ṣafavid Shī'ite philosopher, Mullā Ṣadrā (d. 1640), who arguably represents the final importation of Ibn 'Arabī's ideas into philosophy. Mullā Ṣadrā's thinking as a whole is framed within the idea of four philosophical journeys, as in the title of his magnum opus, *The Four Journeys* (*al-Asfār al-Arba'a*), namely: from creatures to the Truth, from the Truth to the Truth by the Truth, from the Truth to creatures by the Truth, and from creatures to creatures by the Truth. In this we see the direct appropriation of a topos of speculative Sufism into a philosophical context. 'Abd al-Razzāq al-Kāshānī, for instance, presents four similar journeys, with definitions overlapping with Mullā Ṣadrā's, in his *Technical Terms of the Sufis* (*Kitāb Iṣṭilāḥāt al-Ṣūfiyya*).[71]

To summarise. Throughout its history, Islamic mystical theology undergoes a powerful creative tension between esoterism and the civilisational genius of Islam for integrality. Emerging from the period of the Prophet and Companions, mysticism and theology coalesce in early spiritual movements like the Bakriyya, reflecting the unity of impulse found in al-Ḥasan al-Baṣrī's circle. Later, this integrality begins to break down. This is partly through the hardening of the religious sciences into formal disciplines and schools of thought, excluding the vital spiritual element enshrined in Sufism. It is also owed to developments within Sufism itself. For example, a radically esoteric ethic appears in the Malāmatiyya and doctrines not obviously symmetrical with exoterism make themselves felt, notably, *ittiṣāf*. A confrontation gathers force through a line of ecstatics: figures like Bisṭāmī, Nūrī and Ḥallāj. There result the major Sufi trials of the ninth to the tenth century.

Integrality, for which Junayd is the original figurehead in this period of crisis, reasserts itself in the course of the following century. This is the period of the Sufi compilations. Notwithstanding the mystical teachings recorded in the works in question, they establish the orthodox credentials of Sufism, *inter alia* through the inclusion of credal statements conforming to the theological teachings of Sunnī traditionalism, notably as fixed by Ash'arism. Decisive confirmation of Sufism's centrality comes in Ghazālī, and the triumph of the Sufi-Ash'arite synthesis for which he stands is ensured through the support of the Seljuks. It is important, however, when approaching Ash'arism in Ghazālī's mystical writings or in those of any other Sufi, to separate the catechistic from the transcendentalised mode of doctrine. Ash'arism in the transcendentalised register found in Sufi discourse may be dramatically distinct from its analogue in *kalām* discourse.

Finally, partly through the unofficial spread of Avicenna's teachings in the Seljuk period, the expression of Sufism is transformed by *falsafa*, resulting in what is generally known as speculative Sufism. Its triumph is closely linked to the success of Ibn 'Arabī's teachings. The essentially philosophical tenor of speculative Sufism is underlined by Qūnawī. In fact, there had always been a definite relationship between Islamic philosophy and Sufism, as is clear even in the case of one of the high points of Avicenna's metaphysics, the "Proof of the Strictly Truthful".

What about the fate of integrality in the victory of speculative Sufism? Clearly, the *shuhūdī* mysticism of the Naqshbandī order is part of a seventeenth-century attempt to re-establish integrality against Ibn 'Arabī. Yet *waḥdat al-shuhūd* itself remains part of speculative Sufism. So speculative Sufism *per se* is by no means opposed to integrality; in fact it is strictly false that Ibn 'Arabī's own esoterism violates integrality. Sirhindī and his reformist predecessors fought a degeneration of Ibn 'Arabī's teachings: a crude pantheism conducing to the relativisation of the *Sharī'a*. But Ibn 'Arabī's mystical theology, for all its radicalism, had been self-consciously in keeping with the law. It is crucial that Ibn 'Arabī was traditionally held to have adhered to the most fiercely literalistic and anti-rational of all the legal rites, Ẓāhirism,[72] which had been promoted in Spain by Ibn Ḥazm of Córdoba (d. 1064).

Ibn 'Arabī had engaged in depth with Ibn Ḥazm's works, and a full list of the jurist's writings he studied is contained in his *ijāza* (scholastic licence).[73] That he undertook the project of abridging the Ẓāhirite thinker's vast, thirty-volume *The Adorned* (*al-Muḥallā*) is surely sufficient evidence of dedication. In transmitting Ibn Ḥazm's *Refutation of Analogy* (*Ibṭāl al-Qiyās*), Ibn 'Arabī provided it with an introduction in which he even recounts a visionary dream of the author and the Prophet embracing in a village near Seville. Ibn 'Arabī says that the dream helped him understand the enormous value of hadith.[74] Elsewhere, he explicitly mentions that people in his day identified him as a partisan of Ibn Ḥazm, and although it has recently been pointed out by more than one author that he is categorical that he did not conform to Ibn Ḥazm's positions,[75] on scrutiny this seems only to have been a protest that he follows nothing but the Qur'an, Hadith and consensus. It can be argued that this is, paradoxically, impeccably Ẓāhirite, since Ẓāhirism expressly condemns the superimposition of a legal theory on the God-given sources of religious law. It is a fact that Ibn 'Arabī privately adopted one of the cornerstones of Ẓāhirite law, the rejection of analogical reasoning, and held that the Mahdī would presently do likewise. Doubtless the Shaykh exercised authoritative independence in jurisprudence, and trying to prove that he upheld Ẓāhirism in detail is probably futile. But it is easy to miss the wood for the trees. That he was close enough to Ẓāhirism to have been identified as its exponent in his lifetime is sensational. The links of the pre-eminent Muslim esoterist with Ibn Ḥazm's literalist lawschool are impressive, and offer cause for reflection. In reality, his mystical thought itself can be shown to contain Ẓāhirite elements. The conventional word for esoteric interpretation, *ta'wīl*, is not a positive term in Ibn 'Arabī's lexicon, for it suggested to him a hermeneutic dictated by mere reason.[76] For the Shaykh, the revealed scripture (to repeat Chodkiewicz) must be respected as a text, not used as a *pretext*. Correspondingly, Ibn 'Arabī's intensely esoteric hermeneutic of the Qur'an is often strictly in line with the *literal sense of the text*. His interpretation of the words "There is nothing like unto Him" (42:11) offers a good example. Although the verse is routinely taken to underscore God's transcendence of all comparison, Ibn 'Arabī points out that not one but two "likening" words occur in this Arabic sentence. It literally says: "There is nothing like (*ka*) His likeness (*mithlihi*)." The expression thus actually affirms God's likeness, but denies that that likeness is in any way commensurable with anything else.[77] "God's likeness", according to Ibn 'Arabī, is the Perfect Man, that linchpin of late Sufi cosmology.[78]

In this it can be argued that Ibn 'Arabī's teachings amount to a superlative manifestation of esoterism as specifically expressed within the Islamic ethos. For his teachings stress, with unique intensity, that the heights of mysticism are inseparable from the text of the revealed tradition. In Ibn 'Arabī, esoterism and the civilisational genius for integrality are wholly married. Chodkiewicz has put his finger on this central characteristic of the Shaykh's hermeneutic, its "esoteric literalism". In a striking analogy, he suggests that the Qur'an, in Ibn 'Arabī's understanding, is akin to a Möbius strip. This is a geometric figure which seems to have two sides, an outer and an inner. In reality, however, the two sides are one and the same.[79] The analogy equally holds of the Shaykh's theology. For at its heart, too, is a God who is simultaneously, as the Qur'an puts it, "the Outward and the Inward" (57:3). His thought thus contains an implicit critique of forms of mysticism divorced from the revelatory tradition, a critique which is all the more potent for not being based on the ethos of that tradition *per se*, but on the deepest insights of mysticism itself.

Further reading

Chittick, William C., *The Sufi Path of Knowledge: Ibn al-'Arabī's Metaphysics of Imagination* (Albany, 1989).

Corbin, Henry, *Creative Imagination in the Sufism of Ibn 'Arabī* (Princeton, 1969).

Cordt, Hartwig, *Die sitzungen des 'Alā'ad-dawla as-Simnānī* (Zurich, 1977).

Elias, Jamal, *The Throne-Carrier of God: The Life and Thought of 'Alā' ad-Dawla as-Simnānī* (Albany, 1995).

al-Iskandarī, Ibn 'Aṭā' Allāh, *The Key to Salvation: A Sufi Manual of Invocation*, tr. M. A. K. Danner (Cambridge, 1996).

Izutsu, Toshihiko, *Sufism and Taoism* (Berkeley, 1983).

Knysh, Alexander, *Islamic Mysticism: A Short History* (Leiden, 2000).

Lewisohn, Leonard (ed.), *The Heritage of Sufism*, I: *Classical Persian Sufism from Its Origins to Rumi (700–1300)*; II: *The Legacy of Persian Sufism (1150–1500)* (Oxford, 1999).

Lewisohn, Leonard, and Morgan, David (eds.), *The Heritage of Sufism*, III: *Late Classical Persianate Sufism (1501–1750)* (Oxford, 1999).

Lings, Martin, *A Sufi Saint of the Twentieth Century: Shaikh Ahmad al-'Alawī: His Spiritual Heritage and Legacy* (London, 1971).

Radtke, Bernd, *Al-Ḥakīm at-Tirmiḏī: ein islamischer Theosoph des 3./9. Jahrhunderts* (Freiburg, 1980).

Ritter, Helmut, *The Ocean of the Soul*, tr. J. O'Kane (London and Boston, 2003).
Schimmel, Annemarie. *Mystical Dimensions of Islam* (Chapel Hill, NC, 1975).
The Triumphal Sun: A Study of the Works of Jalaloddin Rumi (London and The Hague, 1980).
Sells, Michael A., *Early Islamic Mysticism: Sufi, Qur'an, Mi'raj, Poetic and Theological Writings* (Mahwah and New York, 1996).
"The infinity of desire: mystical union and ethics in Sufism", in Barnard and Kripal (eds.), *Crossing Boundaries: Essays on the Ethical Status of Mysticism* (New York, 2000), pp. 184–229.
Trimingham, J. Spencer, *The Sufi Orders in Islam* (Oxford, 1971).

Notes

1. E.g. Ibn 'Arabī, *Fuṣūṣ al-ḥikam*, ed. Abu'l-'Alā' 'Afīfī (Beirut, 1365/1946), pp. 122, 178. Ibn 'Arabī also on occasion speaks of "the deity conditioned by dogma" (*al-ilāh al-mu'taqad*); M. Chodkiewicz, *An Ocean Without Shore: Ibn 'Arabī, the Book and the Law* (Albany, 1993), p. 128.
2. "Locution théopathique" is the term of the French scholar Louis Massignon, though interestingly "theopathy"/"theopathetic" is attested in English as early as the eighteenth century. Louis Massignon, *Essay on the Origins of the Technical Language of Islamic Mysticism*, tr. Benjamin Clark (Notre Dame, 1997), pp. xxiii–xxiv. For an introduction to the idea of *shaṭḥ*, see Carl Ernst, *Words of Ecstasy in Sufism* (Albany, 1985), pp. 9ff.
3. Muḥammad al-Niffarī, *The Mawāqif and Mukhāṭabāt*, ed. and tr. Arthur J. Arberry (Cambridge, 1978), pp. 158, 183; 154, 176.
4. Louis Massignon, *The Passion of al-Ḥallāj: Mystic and Martyr of Islam*, tr. H. Mason (Princeton, 1982), p. 316. Apophasis is a major concern in the thought of Ḥallāj.
5. The saying is often quoted by Sufis; e.g. Abū Naṣr al-Sarrāj, *Kitāb al-Luma'*, tr. Reynold Alleyne Nicholson (London, 1914), p. 36; Ibn 'Arabī, *Fuṣūṣ*, p. 62. The idea is also found in a whispered prayer (*munāja*) attributed to 'Alī Zayn al-'Ābidīn (d. 713/4): "Thou hast assigned to Thy creatures no way to know Thee save incapacity to know Thee!" Zayn al-'Ābidīn 'Alī ibn al-Ḥusayn, tr. William C. Chittick, *The Psalms of Islam: al-Ṣaḥīfa al-Kāmila al-Sajjādiyya* (London, 1988), p. 253.
6. A favourite basis for the division in the Qur'an was the story of Moses' encounter with the servant of God "whom We had given knowledge from Ourselves", identified on Ubayy ibn Ka'b's authority with the immortal figure al-Khiḍr ("the Green One"). Moses' understanding is confounded by the strange actions of this wisdom figure, until he finally rejects Moses: "This is the parting of the ways between me and you" (18: 64–82). An example of the division in hadith is the saying of the Companion Abū Hurayra: "I guard two receptacles from God's Messenger; as for the first of them, I have distributed it. As for the other, were I to distribute it this throat of mine would be slit" (Bukhārī, 'Ilm, 61).

7. "Verily, as for those who have broken the unity of their religion ..." (6:159); and in the hadith: "No monasticism in Islam!" Muḥammad ibn Aḥmad al-Qurṭubī, *al-Jāmi' li-aḥkām al-Qur'ān* (Cairo, 1387/1967), XVIII, p. 87 (to Qur'an 61:10).
8. Massignon, *Essay*, p. 137.
9. Massignon, p. 132, citing a quotation from Baṣrī in al-Ghazālī, Abū Ḥāmid, *Iḥyā' 'ulūm al-dīn* (Cairo: 1312/1894), II, p. 21.
10. Ignaz Goldziher, *Introduction to Islamic Theology and Law*, tr. A. and R. Hamori (Princeton, 1981), p. 87.
11. Massignon, *Essay*, p. 127.
12. Wilferd Madelung, *Religious Trends in Early Islamic Iran* (Albany, 1988), p. 46.
13. Massignon, *Essay*, p. 185; Ali Hasan Abdel-Kader, *The Life, Personality and Writings of al-Junayd* (London, 1976), pp. 28–9.
14. Florian Sobieroj, 'The Mu'tazila and Sufism', in Frederick de Jong and Bernd Radtke (eds.), *Islamic Mysticism Contested* (Leiden, 1999), p. 72.
15. Ibid., pp. 75–6.
16. Ar. *ṣawma'a*, pl. *ṣawāmi'*. The term is qur'anic. Qur'an 22:40 refers to "monasteries (*ṣawāmi'*), churches, synagogues and mosques in which God's Name is abundantly extolled".
17. Massignon, *Essay*, pp. 152–3.
18. As reported by 'Abd al-Ra'ūf al-Munāwī, *al-Kawākib al-Durriyya fī tarājim al-Sāda al-Ṣūfiyya* (Cairo: 1357/1938), I, p. 238.
19. Gerhard Böwering, *The Mystical Vision of Existence in Classical Islam: The Qur'ānic Hermeneutics of the Sufi Sahl al-Tustarī (d. 283/896)* (Berlin, 1980), p. 49.
20. Massignon, *Essay*, p. 151.
21. 'Abd al-Qāhir al-Baghdādī, *al-Farq bayn al-firaq* (Beirut, 1393/1973), p. 247.
22. Note, however, that many of the followers of the Sālimiyya were Mālikī.
23. Böwering, *Mystical Vision*, p. 95. This seems to evoke the famous Ḥanbalite doctrine that the pronunciation of the Qur'an is uncreated.
24. Tustarī, in Böwering, *Mystical Vision*, p. 167.
25. In Massignon's usage, the term means something like "active experience". See Benjamin Clark's introduction to Massignon, *Essay*, p. xxv.
26. Massignon, *Essay*, pp. 151, 177.
27. So described, for instance, by Sam'ānī in his *Kitāb al-Ansāb*.
28. A list of pro-Karrāmī scholars from the third Islamic century to the sixth is given by Massignon, *Essay*, pp. 178–9.
29. See Sara Sviri, "Ḥakīm Tirmidhī and the Malāmatī movement in early Sufism", in Leonard Lewisohn (ed.), *Classical Persian Sufism: From Its Origins to Rūmī* (London, 1993), pp. 583–613.
30. Michel Chodkiewicz, *Seal of the Saints: Prophethood and Sainthood in the Sufism of Ibn 'Arabī* (Cambridge, 1993), p. 172.
31. E.g. Bisṭāmī, cited in Sarrāj, *Kitāb al-Luma'* pp. 382, 384, 387.
32. Eminent representatives of Mu'tazilism like Jubbā'ī, Zamakhsharī and the Qāḍī 'Abd al-Jabbār ibn Aḥmad (*al-Mughnī fī abwāb al-tawḥīd wa'l-'adl*, XV, ed. M. al-Khuḍayrī and M.M. Qāsim (Cairo, 1965), pp. 270ff.) attacked al-Ḥallāj's miracles as charlatanry.

33. Ernst, *Words of Ecstasy*, p. 20.
34. The normal Muslim term for the Christian doctrine of incarnation is *ḥulūl*, in line with the fact that in Christian Arabic the verb *ḥall* ("to be infused") is sometimes used for the descent of the Word into human form. However, the technical term "Incarnation" in Christian Arabic is *ta'annus* or *tajassud*.
35. Massignon, *Essay*, pp. 521ff.
36. Manṣūr al-Ḥallāj, *The Tawasin*, tr. Aisha al-Tarjumana (Berkeley and London, 1974), p. 46.
37. Massignon, *Passion*, III, p. 45. From a quotation in Baqlī's *Sharḥ al-shaṭḥiyyāt*.
38. Abdel Kader, p. 90. Amended translation.
39. Massignon, *Essay*, p. 189.
40. Ibn Qayyim al-Jawziyya, *Madārij al-sālikīn*, ed. Muḥammad Kamāl Ja'far (Beirut, 1980–2002).
41. Sviri, "Ḥakīm Timidhī", pp. 592–6 . A legacy of the pre-compilatory distinction is that some later authorities still differentiate, within Sufism, the *Ṣūfiyya* and the *Malāmatiyya*, and tend to assert the superiority of the latter; e.g. Abū Ḥafṣ al-Suhrawardī, *'Awārif al-ma'ārif*.
42. Arthur J. Arberry (tr.), *The Doctrine of the Sufis* (Cambridge, 1977), p. xiv.
43. Arent Jan Wensinck, *The Muslim Creed: Its Genesis and Historical Development* (Cambridge: 1932), p. 246.
44. W. Montgomery Watt, *Islamic Creeds: A Selection* (Edinburgh, 1994), p. 62.
45. Arberry, *Doctrine*, p. xi.
46. Ibid., pp. 21–2.
47. Ibid., pp. 24–7.
48. Ibid., pp. 28ff.
49. See above, chapter 7.
50. Abū Ḥāmid al-Ghazālī, *Lettre au disciple* (*Ayyuhā al-Walad*), ed. and tr. into French by Toufic Sabbagh (Beirut, 1969), p. 55.
51. Cited in C. Ernst, *Ruzbihan Baqli* (Richmond, 1996), pp. 40–1.
52. Ernst, *Kuzbihan Baqli*, p. 39.
53. Sufi texts are explicit on the difference between catechismic and transcendentalised doctrine. E.g. "You must rectify your religious creed (*'aqīda*) to bring it into line with the doctrine of the initiates" (Ibn 'Aṭā' Allāh al-Iskandarī, *The Key to Salvation: A Sufi Manual of Invocation*, tr. Mary Ann Koury-Danner (Cambridge, 1996), p. 104).
54. Ghazālī, *Lettre au disciple*, p. 37.
55. Abū Ḥāmid al-Ghazālī, *The Niche of Lights*, tr. David Buchman (Provo, UT, 1998), p. 16.
56. Ibn 'Arabī, *Fuṣūṣ*, p. 126.
57. Michot, J. "La pandémie avicennienne au VIe/XIIe siècle", *Arabica* 40 (1993), pp. 287–344.
58. Claude Addas, *Quest for the Red Sulphur: The Life of Ibn 'Arabī*, tr. Peter Kingsley (Cambridge, 1993), pp. 107–8.
59. 'Afīf 'Usayrān, introduction to 'Ayn al-Quḍāt Hamadhānī, *Tamhīdāt*, ed. 'A. 'Usayrān (Tehran, 1962), pp. 66–77.

60. Miguel Asín y Palacios, *The Mystical Philosophy of Ibn Masarra and His Followers*, tr. Elmer Douglas and Howard Yoder (Leiden, 1978).
61. Kamāl Ibrāhīm Ja'far, "Min mu'allafāt Ibn Masarra al-mafqūda", *Majallat Kulliyyat al-Tarbiyya*, III (1972), pp. 27–63.
62. William C. Chittick, "Rūmī and *waḥdat al-wujūd*", in Amin Banani, Richard Hovanissian and Georges Sabagh (eds.), *Poetry and Mysticism in Islam: the Heritage of Rūmī* (Cambridge, 1994), p. 82.
63. Ṣadr al-Dīn Qūnawī, *al-Murāsalāt bayna Ṣadr al-Dīn al-Qūnawī wa-Naṣīr al-Dīn al-Ṭūsī*, ed. G. Schubert (Beirut, 1995).
64. Nicholas Heer (tr.), *The Precious Pearl: al-Jāmī's* al-Durrah al-Fākhirah *with the Commentary of 'Abd al-Ghafūr al-Lārī* (Albany, 1979), p. 57.
65. See Abū 'Alī Ibn Sīnā, *al-Ishārāt wa'l-tanbīhāt* (Cairo, 1957–60), III, pp. 447ff.
66. Heer, *Precious Pearl*, p. 57.
67. Qur'an 41:53, quoted in Ibn Sīnā, III, pp. 482–3.
68. Hermann Landolt, "Ghazālī and 'Religionswissenschaft': some notes on the *Mishkāt al-Anwār* for Professor Charles J. Adams", *Asiatische Studien / Études Asiatiques* 45 (1991), p. 51, n. 125.
69. Arberry, *Doctrine*, p. 47.
70. 'Alī al-Hujwīrī, tr. Reynold Alleyne Nicholson, *Kashf al-mahjûb: The Oldest Persian Treatise on Sufiism* (Leiden and London, 1911), p. 374.
71. 'Abd al-Razzāq Qāshānī, tr. N. Safwat, rev. D. Pendlebury, *A Glossary of Sufi Technical Terms* (London, 1991), pp. 80–1 (Arabic); pp. 57–8 (English).
72. Aḥmad ibn 'Alī al-Maqqarī, ed. Reinhart Dozy *et al.*, *Analectes sur l'histoire et la litérature des arabes d'Espagne* (Leiden, 1855–61), I, p. 567.
73. Ibid.
74. Ignaz Goldziher, *The Ẓāhirīs: Their Doctrine and Their History*, tr. W. Behn (Leiden, 1971), p. 170.
75. Mahmoud al-Ghorab, "Muhyiddin Ibn al-'Arabi amidst religions (*adyān*) and schools of thought (*madhāhib*)", in Stephen Hirtenstein and Michael Tiernan (eds.), *Muhyiddin Ibn 'Arabi: A Commemorative Volume* (Shaftesbury, 1993), p. 200; Michel Chodkiewicz, *An Ocean Without Shore: Ibn 'Arabī, the Book and the Law* (Albany, 1993), pp. 55ff.
76. Chittick, "*Rūmī*", p. 199.
77. Ibn 'Arabī, *Fuṣūṣ*, p. 111.
78. Chodkiewicz, *Ocean*, p. 37.
79. Ibid., p. 25.

14 Epistemology and divine discourse

PAUL-A. HARDY

INTRODUCTION

From the time of Aristotle to the present, philosophers have assumed that there is an intimate connection between literal meaning and truth. Recent discussions in the West, however, have challenged this link and its corollary that non-literal meaning is a departure from truth. A similar challenge was offered in classical Islam. Its origin is traceable to the "consensus of Muslims that the Creator of the world is a speaker (*mutakallim*)"[1] whose discourse consists of statement (*khabar*), command (*amr*), prohibition (*nahy*), question (*istikhbār*) and other such elements. Divine utterances, in other words, come in a number of varieties, distinguishable by what contemporary linguists call their "illocutionary force".[2] But if divine discourse consists of specific speech-acts, one would expect it to portray the same features as spoken human language. Such force after all is a property all spoken utterances bear and a condition for understanding any one of them.[3] If this is true, how can one maintain the traditional link between literal meaning and truth? Certainly, it is difficult to imagine well-established conditions for the truth of a command (*amr*), for example. Indeed, there is an entire range of divine utterances that do not describe anything to which truth-conditions can be applied. Rather, they constitute actions in themselves or speech-acts. This includes utterances that fall under the rubric of figure (*majāz*), such as metaphor and metonymy.

In the face of such considerations is the distinction between *ḥaqīqa* (literal meaning) and *majāz* or figural meaning tenable? Classical Muslim theology evolved a spectrum of positions here. On one side of the question we find Ghazālī the Ash'arite, and on another, the late Ḥanbalī theologian Ibn Taymiyya. For Ghazālī language's role in thinking was fundamental. Like Aristotle, he held a generic concept of thinking that included knowledge as one of its species. But to know the meaning of our thoughts insofar as they relate to reality is to know what the world would have to be like for the sentences expressing them to be literally true. On this view, it follows that cognition of meaning in the Qur'an is first and foremost a matter of understanding the truth and the literal character of divine utterance. If meaning and thought are modelled in this fashion, epistemic access to figurative meaning is asymmetrically dependent on the cognition of literal meaning.

Ibn Taymiyya put Ghazālī's theory under critical stress by arguing that all that hearers of divine discourse need know is how the divine discourser intended His speech to be taken. That is, one only has to grasp its illocutionary force arising from contexts (*qarā'in*) of use (*isti'māl*), plus the intention revealed in God's habit of address (*'ādat al-mutakallim*). Hence, the apprehension of figure in the Qur'an resides in the apprehension of force. But if this is the case, Ghazālī's view that epistemic access to figurative meaning is asymmetrically dependent on cognition of literal meaning is seriously undermined and the distinction between *ḥaqīqa* and *majāz* is utterly erased. Thus, for Ibn Taymiyya the question of epistemic access to figural speech does not really arise. Hermeneutics is the only matter of concern, that is to say, the interpretation of the pragmatic force of the divine utterance.

This chapter will sketch some of the main features of this debate. The issues it raises lie at the heart of modern discussions between Muslim traditionalists, who often side with Ghazālī, and fundamentalists whose champion is Ibn Taymiyya. But the question of how Muslims are to understand verses in the Qur'an that refer to God "sitting" or "descending" or having a particular spatial locus are at base matters of linguistic epistemology. Or rather, they concern the relation of epistemology to divine discourse.

AL-GHAZĀLĪ'S VERBAL EPISTEMOLOGY

In a work written towards the end of his life, *The Essential in Legal Theory* (*al-Mustaṣfā min 'ilm al-uṣūl*), Ghazālī defines divine discourse (*kalām*) as "either something a prophet hears from an angel or an angel from God or a prophet from God or a saint [*walī*] from an angel or the Muslim community from the Prophet".[4] That is, only to an appropriately qualified audience does divine speech bear significance. Hence, knowing what God means and how He means it when He speaks depends on who hears His voice. There is a difference, in other words, between the way prophets and saints hear the divine voice and the way the Muslim community (*umma*) including its scholars (*'ulamā'*) hears it.

The *umma* hears letters and sounds reported by the Prophet that signify the meaning of God's eternal speech (*dāll 'alā ma'nā kalām Allāh*) insofar as it has entered time. That is, what they hear is the expression of God's thoughts, since for Ghazālī God "is called a speaker from two aspects, from the aspect of sounds and letters and from the aspect of inner speech [*ḥadīth al-nafs*] devoid of sound and letters".[5] The latter corresponds to what Ash'arī called "interior discourse" (*kalām nafsī*). It is regarded as eternal, but what it expresses (*'ibāra*) is not. Moreover, they grasp it "by prior cognition of its assigned" or agreed-upon meaning or *waḍ' al-lugha* (prior imposition of language).[6] For Ghazālī believed that in the final analysis it makes no difference whether language originates from divine inspiration (*tawqīf*) or from a convention (*iṣṭilāḥ*) agreed upon by a community of primordial Arabic speakers.[7] He nevertheless saw language as essentially transcending the fate of the mortals who speak it. Deviations in particular contexts therefore represent a departure from a common standard. That is, they are deviations from a language envisioned as an established social institution or set of conventions.

By contrast, when prophets and saints hear the divine voice, God makes what He intends (*al-murād*) "known by creating in the hearer a necessary knowledge (*'ilm ḍarūrī*)",[8] that is, a knowledge which the hearer has no choice but to accept when it is presented to his or her mind.[9] When the prophet Moses heard God speak, his hearing had "no letter nor sound nor language established in such a way that one knows its sense (*ma'nāhu*) through prior cognition of its assigned" or agreed-upon (*mūḍa'a*) meaning. Instead, God creates the object of cognition or "what is spoken", the act of hearing His speech as well as the meaning "intended by His speech". For "every speaker needs to posit a sign to inform [others] of the content of his mind except God [who] is able to create a necessary knowledge without positing a sign; for His speech is not of the same genus as human speech." So "the act of hearing [His speech] that He creates for His servant is not of the genus of hearing sounds".[10]

But for Ghazālī, prior cognition of what expressions signify according to the conventions laid down in *waḍ' al-lugha* was not enough. The original speakers of Arabic did not establish conventions without having some reason for doing so. The motivation behind linguistic conventions is the communication of truth. Language, in other words, is founded in order to convey truth, not falsity. Now, the aim of logic is to fix the use of expressions by analysis of their contribution to determining the truth-value of judgements in which those expressions figure. So, it became

Ghazālī's view that logical norms ought to govern the way qur'anic expressions are used.[11]

But adherence to a logical analysis of qur'anic signification brought with it certain presuppositions, epistemological as well as metaphysical. In the latter case, it presupposed adopting an Aristotelian framework where all objects are seen as possessing universal essences allowing them to be defined in terms of genera and species. Epistemologically, this meant that the first moment in cognition, forming concepts or *taṣawwur*, is based upon knowledge of definition. Still, concepts by themselves have no truth-value until combined as subjects and predicates of judgements expressed by propositions (*qaḍāyā*) and sentences. Knowledge manifests its second element as *taṣdīq* or *takdhīb* (the cognition of truth or falsehood).

But if essences stand behind the concepts expressed by words in the Qur'an there is no real need to appeal either to meaning by *waḍ' al-lugha* or to interpretation (*ḥaml*) arising from actual contexts of use (*isti'māl*). Logical definition outstrips both. Consider the sentence "A lion is in the house", for example. Its figural interpretation, "A brave man is in the house", or its literal one, "There is a carnivorous feline in the house", is determined to apply when its context or its speaker's intention is known. But in logic neither context of use nor intention needs to be known. When you apply the concept of lion to "Leo", you by definition signify that "Leo" is also an animal. At the same time, you include thereby the act of signifying that "Leo" is also a mammal.

Ghazālī, following the philosophers, called these modes of signification respectively "signification by correspondence" (*dalālat al-muṭābaqa*) and "signification by inclusion" (*dalālat al-taḍāmun*). For logical purposes, he deemed them preferable to signification by implication (*dalālat al-iltizām*). They operate simply on what it means to be a lion, the essence expressed by "lion". "Implications [*lawāzim*]", by contrast, "are indefinite and unrestricted so that it leads to an expression being a sign (*dalīl*) for an infinite [number of] meanings."[12] Such implicit meanings, Ghazālī observes, are known from either linguistic,[13] rational or "situational contexts such as allusions (*ishārāt*), or symbols (*rumūz*)" which "are unlimited and unpredictable".[14]

The ideas sketched so far, however, form only part of Ghazālī's programme to link literal meaning to truth. After all, to him religious "faith (*īmān*) is *taṣdīq*" or assent to truth.[15] Accordingly, he theorises that in whatever way the predicates of qur'anic sentences signify, that is, whether they signify in an essential (*al-wujūd al-dhātī*), sensible (*al-wujūd al-ḥissī*), intelligible (*al-wujūd al-'aqlī*) or analogical (*al-wujūd al-shibhī*) fashion, they still preserve a meaning focused on *taṣdīq* or assent to truth. Or rather they preserve an existential sense; for the "essential nature (*ḥaqīqa*) [of *taṣdīq*] is recognition (*al-iʿtirāf*) of the existence of what the Messenger has reported (*akhbara ʿan*) about its existence."[16]

However, since this variation of predicates reflects only mental operations that supervene upon what amounts to a literal content, the same structure can illustrate the comprehension of figurative expression. For "every *majāz* [figural sense] has a *ḥaqīqa* [i.e. a literal sense] but it is not necessary that every *ḥaqīqa* have a *majāz*".[17] That is, a literal, factual or existential sense can be grasped behind any figure such that the figure is a departure from a literal meaning, but not vice versa. Figure is always asymmetrically dependent on a literal sense where the latter is conceived in terms of the conditions under which certain sentences are true. Literalness is thus linked to truth.

The theological consequences of Ghazālī's views proved in time to be controversial. For there comes with his commitment to logic a God whose mind could seem dissimilar to that of the author of the Qur'an. No longer is God pictured as communicating with the ordinary words of a human language like Arabic, words backed by human-like intentions. Rather, His words have to be backed up by essences. The language He speaks is a mental language of logical genera and species or universal natures, so His utterances reach out and decide every case of their application well in advance. For divine mental content embraces the details of every possible world.

If God prohibits the drinking of wine (*khamr*), for example, there must be written into the prohibition a selecting out of substances that share the essence of *khamr* in every possible context. The predicate "... is *khamr*" then governs its pattern of use in inferences connecting it with judgements employing other predicates such as "... is prohibited." In this way, cases not covered in the Qur'an are ruled out not as a matter of linguistic convention or textual probability but as a matter of logical necessity.

The motivating idea, however, is that one can give an account of what it is to have a thought without appealing to a speaker's ability to use expressions in ways appropriate to conventional use. Thoughts do not need linguistic representation. The idea echoes Avicenna, for whom thought had only an accidental connection to language. And while recognising that "it is impossible for internal reflection to put meanings into any order without imagining expressions for them", those imagined expressions accompany thoughts they do not embody. Was the God of

Avicenna's Neoplatonised Aristotelianism surreptitiously replacing the God of the Qur'an in Ghazālī's analysis?

But he did not need philosophy to tell him that God has an "inner speech [*ḥadīth al-nafs*] devoid of sound and letters". He knew, for example, that "every speaker except God needs to posit a sign to inform [others] of the content of his mind" and that "His speech is not of the same genus as human speech". So much he had from Ash'arism. The difficulty was this. If God's intentions were linguistically formulated, the extensions of the qur'anic words expressing them would have to be indeterminate as well. As the historian of religious and philosophical doctrines al-Shahrastānī (d. 1153) observed, "We know for certain that no text mentioned ever touches on every event nor is it ever conceivable that this should be so." For "texts are limited [but] facts [of life] are infinite, so the finite cannot embrace what is infinite". For Shahrastānī the Qur'an was clearly a text with gaps that needed to be filled by *ijtihād* (legally warranted personal interpretation). To that extent, the meaning of its words did not embrace every conceivable occasion of their application.

So a dilemma arises: either the thoughts of Ghazālī's God are totally devoid of linguistic representation and stand complete in every detail, or they are linguistically formulated and incomplete. Instead of speculating over Ghazālī's options for escaping this dilemma, however, we should note that he had another story to tell in his esoteric work *Niche of Lights* (*Mishkāt al-anwār*), written after the *Revival*. We will come to the picture painted there in due course.

IBN TAYMIYYA'S CRITIQUE

Meanwhile, we turn to Ibn Taymiyya's critique of the theory so far presented.[18] In his view, it can only be a fiction that the signs expressing divine speech occur without norm or context. "Meaningful discourse (*al-kalām al-mufīd*)" he declares, "is only conveyed by a complete sentence (*jumla*)", that is, in the context of a sentence.[19] So the fundamental unit of semantic analysis can never be the bare conceptual sign. To have a specific force, words must already stand in a fundamental grammatical relation to each other. For faith (*īmān*) at the outset assumes that sentences of the Qur'an are true, and sentences, not individual words, can be either true or false.[20] Thus, whoever hears or reads divine discourse must perceive it as "*al-kalām al-musta'mal*" or "discourse in use", that is, as sets of sentences uttered with an intended meaning, an intended force.

For Ibn Taymiyya, Ghazālī's vision of a language of thought internal to the divine mind replaces "*al-kalām al-musta'mal*" with an artificial "*al-kalām al-muqaddar*" or "hypothetical discourse".[21] The attempt to account for meaning in terms of the latter is a dead end. Since "*al-kalām al-muqaddar*" was never spoken by anyone, its existence is a matter of pure metaphysical speculation. Ibn Taymiyya thus makes an appeal to language as performance and to what people do with words in specific contexts of communication.

"Discourse in use" bases itself on the divine speaker's habit of discourse (*'ādat al-mutakallim*). No hidden essences lurk behind it to serve as the meaning of words. The meanings of words are immanent to the structure of their use (*isti'māl*). We know in a certain and decisive (*qaṭ'ī*) fashion what a speaker wills and intends to say simply by virtue of his habit of address. "The mere hearing of the expression without knowledge of the speaker and his habit", he writes, "signifies nothing", unless one knows "what is necessary for the speaker to signify by them." This is because the "signification of expressions is an intentional, volitional act signalling what the speaker means (*arāda al-mutakallim an yadulla bihā*) by them, [given that] expressions by themselves fail to signify".[22] To his student Ibn al-Qayyim (d. 1350), "the signification of the expression is constructed upon the habit of the speaker which he intends by his verbal expressions". If this were not true, no child would ever be able to learn language.

Ibn al-Qayyim argues that there is simply no scope for interpretive norms agreed upon (*muwāḍa'a*) prior to the actual contexts in which children learn to speak.

> After the child begins to distinguish [among sounds], he hears his parents or whoever raises him articulate a language and point to its meaning. In this way he understands that when a certain expression is used a certain meaning is intended ... [All that happens] without reaching an agreement with the child on a prior assignment (*waḍ' mutaqaddim*) in order to inform him of names' meanings.[23]

Ibn al-Qayyim concludes, "We know that this expression is primordially imposed only by virtue of *using* it ... in the sense [already imposed]."[24]

Both Ibn Taymiyya and Ibn al-Qayyim then totally reject the idea that "a group of scholars met together and imposed all the words to be found in their language and from that point proceeded to use the words assigned", that is, the theory that language originates from convention.[25] "On the contrary," Ibn al-Qayyim asserts, "inspiration suffices for the articulation of language without a prior assignment of names to things", and he adds, "If one calls this divine inspiration (*tawqīf*), then let it be called divine inspiration."[26]

At the same time, on Ibn Taymiyya's theory, there are no essences hidden behind God's words to determine their use in any particular context. When I hear the sentence "I saw her duck", for example, there is no universal "duckness" in my mind that constrains me to think of the bird "duck" rather than the verb "duck". In other words, meaning does not come in the form of a universal that fixes the extension of a term in every future case of its expression's future application. Meaning is nothing deeper than the use of ordinary words in particular contexts.

This does not mean that the future use of words revealed in the Qur'an is wholly unshaped. It indicates only that God provides nothing better than the Qur'an itself and the hadith of the Prophet to explain it. "The soundest method of commentary on the Qur'an", Ibn Taymiyya writes, "is to comment on it with the [words of the] Qur'an [itself]; for what is unclear in one place is explained in another and what is abridged in one place is set forth plainly in another."[27] All items of divine discourse, in fact, can be understood by an appeal to divine words as these have been given. There is no essence behind the use of "*khamr*" (wine) in the Qur'an that underwrites the right way of applying it in any given context.

ERASING THE LINE BETWEEN LITERAL AND FIGURAL MEANING

But if "a word (*lafẓ*) is never used alone (*muṭlaqan*)", that is, without a context, one must reject a symmetric priority of literal over figural meaning. When, for example, we hear the metonymic statement "The fish and chips wants his bill" it is literal when used by waiters in the context of a restaurant. If this is so, why is the metonymic phrase "Ask the village where we were ..." (12:82) any less literal when encountered in the Qur'an? Readers and hearers of divine discourse determine the meaning of its expressions from information arising from its context of use (*isti'māl*).

Ibn Taymiyya claims to trace his stance back to Abū 'Ubayda Ma'mar ibn Muthannā (d. *c.* 824), who observed in his *Metaphor in the Qur'an* (*Majāz al-Qur'ān*) that since

> the Qur'an has been revealed in "clear Arabic speech" the forefathers and those to whom [God's] revelations from the Prophet

were revealed did not need to inquire about its shades of meaning; for they were speakers of Arabic, and so could dispense with inquiring about its shades of meaning and about whatever it contains due to their immediate understanding of it.[28]

For Ibn Taymiyya, this argues that Muslims originally had no recourse to anything other than the very words God Himself uses in interpreting the Qur'an. For with the utterance of words, in his view, goes also how they are to be taken. No qur'anic utterance occurs without a specific force. "There is no part of the Qur'an or the hadith," he says, "that God and His Messenger have not made clear to their hearers and readers in such a way that they would require some other source of information to clarify their meanings."[29]

Finally, "how can one know for certain that the words that the Arabs were using to communicate with each other before and at the time of the Qur'an's revelation had not been used previously to convey different meanings?" We cannot. Furthermore, if we are "not certain that such words were not used differently at a previous time, then neither is it possible to know whether they bear a literal meaning in conflict with that upon which [people] have agreed".[30] The literal then may be a metaphor whose original figural sense has simply been forgotten.

Certainly, many lexical items prove to be dead metaphors that were alive and kicking at some time in the past. For an example, he observes that "the word *ẓaʿīna* was originally used to refer to a ... camel for riding, after which people came to apply the same word to the woman who rides on the camel's back in a litter".[31] Someone could use "*ẓaʿīna*" in a true sentence while his contemporaries continued to speak falsehoods with the same words.[32] If this is so, then what we call figural speech merely reflects a usage that is so far unfamiliar. We call "literal" those words we are able to handle based on our present and past knowledge. What we call "figural" then simply reflects our perception of what is unsuitable for use in any context we have known *so far*.[33] Once this is granted, it seems difficult to maintain that there exists a specifically figural as opposed to a literal meaning in divine discourse. But for Ibn Taymiyya literal meaning is all the meaning there is.

THE END OF EPISTEMOLOGY

Still, Ibn Taymiyya is himself not the most helpful guide for unpacking how much can be fitted into his concept of *al-kalām al-mustaʿmal*, or "discourse in use", or for that matter into the notion of intention insofar as the latter applies to divine speech. In his view, linguistic use is a thoroughly empirical notion. For divine discourse is linked with human language by a world of shared human experience which underlies both. As he says, "the expression 'experience' (*tajriba*) is used for what a person surveys with thought as well as with sense",[34] inasmuch as "in human action every sensation is tied to intellectual thought (*kull al-ḥiss al-maqrūn bi'l-'aql min fi'l al-insān*)".[35]

From the standpoint of Ghazālī's thinking in the *Niche of Lights* this means that Ibn Taymiyya's "discourse in use" restricts itself to only one level of meaning, the meaning revealed in the material world. But the same is true for Ghazālī's "inner speech". Its domain of reference is the same world. But the possible range of meaning (*ma'ānī*) nevertheless extends beyond that domain. For this world (*al-mulk wa'l-shahāda*) "parallel[s] the world of *malakūt* [the immaterial world of divine royalty]"[36] and "there is nothing in the former that is not a representation [*mithāl*] for something in the latter".[37] But he adds that "one thing perhaps is a *mithāl* for several things in the world of *malakūt*; perhaps a single thing in *malakūt* has many representations in the visible world".[38] Hence, "to enumerate all these representations would call for an exhaustive account of all the entities in both worlds in their entirety".[39] And for this task "human capacity is inadequate; it does not extend to its comprehension".[40]

There are then other possibilities of meaning beyond empirical and rational meaning, since words and sentences can signify realities in the "world of power" (*jabarūt*) contiguous to *mulk* and situated between the latter and *malakūt*. Hence, linguistic signs used in the Qur'an signify not simply because they share with the signs of ordinary language the ability to reflect a common world of experience. They point beyond that world to the "Preserved Tablet" (*al-lawḥ al-maḥfūẓ*) situated in the realm of *malakūt*. In the final analysis, this suggests that the order of intentions that inform divine discourse cannot be assimilated to ones only expressible in terms of human experience.

In consequence, an epistemology of divine discourse worked out only in terms of logic or even in terms of Ibn Taymiyya's analysis ultimately fails. The picture of divine discourse presented in the *Niche* does not portray the Qur'an as a static container of meaning. Rather, it is an arena where hearers and readers encounter the divine discourser, a point of ascent (*maṭla'*) from which fresh meanings can arise. The Qur'an is not an inert and self-contained artefact from the past. Recall that in *al-Mustaṣfā* Ghazālī says divine discourse (*kalām*) is "something a prophet hears from an angel or an angel from God, or a prophet from

God, or a saint (*walī*) from an angel or the Muslim community from the Prophet". That is, God's speech has real significance only to an appropriately qualified audience.

The rational thinker is restricted to knowledge (*'ilm*); but *'ilm* is analogical (*qiyās*). That is, *'ilm* emerges from the inferences made between propositions that come in the form of declarative statements or reports (*akhbār*, sing. *khabar*). Recall, "*taṣdīq* only applies to the *khabar*". Its "essential nature (*ḥaqīqa*) is recognition (*i'tirāf*) of the existence of what the Messenger has reported (*akhbara 'an*) about its existence". In contrast, the attitude of the Muslims at large not qualified by *'ilm* is *taqlīd*, or the imitation of established precedents.

However, for those who have reached a full perfection of knowledge through divine bestowal, the "knowers" (*'ārifūn*)[41] or saints (*awliyā'*, plural of *walī*), the epistemological situation shifts. Their mode of hearing divine speech is like that of prophets. Recall that Ghazālī in the *Mustaṣfā* says that the divine speech heard by Moses had "no letter nor sound nor language established in such a way that one knows its sense (*ma'nāhu*) through prior cognition of its assigned" or agreed-upon (*mūḍa'*) meaning. In the *Niche,* he offers an interpretation of the qur'anic verse where the prophet Moses exclaims "Lo! I see in the distance a fire" and says to those around him, "Perchance I shall bring you a report (*khabar*) from there or a brand from the fire that you may warm yourselves" (28:29). Ghazālī says that those who "may warm themselves" are the "knowers". Those who only hear a report or *khabar* are those who merely follow what it says by rote (*taqlīd*). For "only a person who has a fire of the prophetic spirit can warm himself, not the one who hears a report (*khabar*) about fire".[42]

For the *'ārifūn* there is no mediation of linguistic sign or symbol. As a result, as Ghazālī explains again in the *Niche,*

> The knowers (*'ārifūn*) do not need the day of resurrection to hear the Creator's proclamation, "Whose is the kingdom today? It belongs to the One, the Overwhelming" [40:16]. On the contrary, this proclamation never leaves their hearing. They do not understand the saying, "God is greater" to mean that He is greater than other things ... For there is nothing in existence along with Him than which He could be greater. Or rather, nothing other than He possesses the degree of "withness" (*ma'īya*); everything possesses "following after". In contrast, everything other than God exists only under the description of that which lies next. The only existent thing is His face.[43]

In support of this last claim Ghazālī cites the qur'anic verse, "Everything is perishing save His face" (28:88). To him this verse means that "there is none in existence save God ... since the essence of anything other than He is considered with respect to its essence; it is totally non-existent". To those who see nothing in existence except the One, knowledge (*'ilm*) as *taṣdīq* comes to an end. Its "essential nature (*ḥaqīqa*) is recognition (*i'tirāf*) of the existence of what the Messenger has reported (*akhbara 'an*) about its existence". But if everything other than God is non-existent, there is nothing about which one can make such epistemic claims.

The "knowers" then "see nothing in existence except the One, the Real", that is, God.[44] As Ghazālī explains, "Everything has two faces: a face turned towards itself and a face towards God." Only "from the standpoint of its own face, it has no existence".[45] But "from the standpoint of its face which is towards God, it exists (*huwa ... bi' 'tibār wajh Allāh mawjūd*)", or "is found there". "From the standpoint of its own face" includes also the self. "For he [*sc.* the *'ārif*] is aware neither of himself ... nor of any absence of awareness of himself", inasmuch as "awareness of unawareness is yet an awareness of self". They have arrived at the level of total self-extinction (*fanā'*). So at the level of "withness", spatiotemporal proximity and distance have no meaning. Everything arising from God's existence is perceived as equidistant from its ontological source. That is why he says that God's proclamation to the *'ārifūn* "never leaves their hearing" and their position thus differs from the *'ulamā'* or rational thinkers and the rest of the Muslim community. The latter hear divine discourse mediated by a report like a man who says, "I heard the poet Mutanabbī", and means by his claim that he heard Mutanabbī's poetry being recited by someone.[46]

THE SUBTLETIES OF ALLUSION

Yet, as the *Niche* continues, if nothing exists other than God, the "Light of the heavens and Earth" (24:35), "then the name 'light' for things other than the First Light [i.e. God] is sheer *majāz*".[47] Thus, "the *'ārifūn* ascend from ... *majāz* to ... *ḥaqīqa*", from the figural to the literal.[48] For "nothing possesses *huwīya* ('he-ness') other than He [*huwa*] except in a figural sense (*bi'l-majāz*)". "*Huwīya*", the abstract form of the third-person pronoun *huwa*, is one of the terms used in *falsafa* to render "existence". In his work *The Highest Aim* (*al-Maqṣad al-Asnā*), Ghazālī isolates "*huwa huwa*" and "*huwa ghayruhu*" as the basic form when one wants to say of something "It is ... " or "It is not ... "

(lit. other than ...)."[49] But for the *'ārif* the third-person pronoun *huwa* no longer functions simply at the literal level. "'*Huwa*'", he explains in the *Niche*, "is an expression (*'ibāra*) for an allusion (*ishāra*) to whatever [a thing] is, but there is no allusion to anything other than He [i.e. God]", so that "whenever you refer (*asharta*) to a thing, you in reality allude to Him, although ... you are unaware of it because of your ignorance of ultimate reality". So much follows from the earlier statement that "nothing possesses existence [he-ness, "*huwīya*"] other than He (*huwa*) except in a figural sense (*bi'l-majāz*)".

One might paraphrase the latter statement to say that whenever one says "It is ...", one indirectly speaks of God, although the sentence one formulates speaks of something else. After all, speakers can mean what they say, but can mean something more as well. In other words, *khabarī*, declarative or reported meaning, is what is meant when one says "*huwa huwa*" to refer to a thing. *Ishārī* or allusive meaning is what signifies indirectly. For example, whenever the *'ārif* refers to a thing using "*huwa*" he refers indirectly to God.

Earlier, we noted that Ghazālī classified this type of indirect speech-act as a form of signification by implication (*dalālat al-iltizām*). Implications (*lawāzim*) are known from linguistic, rational or "situational contexts such as allusions (*ishārāt*) and symbols (*rumūz*)". Signification by correspondence (*dalālat al-muṭābaqa*) and inclusion (*dalālat al-taḍāmun*) is best suited for signifying individuals and their properties in the material world. But this latter world "parallel[s] the world of *malakūt*". Furthermore, "there is nothing in the former that is not a representation (*mithāl*) for something in the latter", and in fact one thing in the former is a *mithāl* for several things in the world of *malakūt*, so that "a single thing in *malakūt* has many representations in the material world". Yet the possible range of meaning (*ma'ānī*) revealed to the saint extends beyond this world. This is why express meaning (*'ibāra*) is also inadequate. Accordingly, Ghazālī in the *Niche* tends to broaden his analysis of verbal signification to include the phenomenon of *ishāra*. It forms in fact the basis of his theory of mystical meaning.

Ishāra literally means "pointing", since by pointing one can signify all at once things it would need many words to express (*'abara*) verbally (*bi'l-lafẓ*).[50] In *al-Mustaṣfā* Ghazālī describes *ishāra* as "what one grasps from an expression [that] comes not from the expression [itself]", but the meaning "to which the expression extends without expressly intending it, e.g., what one understands by the speaker's allusion and by a gesture he makes while he speaks to give some hint that the expression by itself does not signify". However, "something not intended and not built upon the expression from the standpoint of grammar may [nonetheless] coincide with it".[51] We see this when a person says, "This hike is longer than I remember", and means primarily but not exclusively, "I need a rest." He communicates something in addition to, although clearly related to, the meaning the sentence conveys.

Hence, an *ishāra* will maintain the *'ibāra* (express meaning) but extend beyond it. For this reason, Ghazālī can say, "*'Huwa'* ['He'] is an expression (*'ibāra*) for an allusion (*ishāra*)." And Abū Ḥayyān al-Tawḥīdī (d. 1023), in his Sufi work *The Divine Allusions* (*al-Ishārāt al-Ilāhīya*), can exhort his readers "to lay hold of the *ishāra* buried within the *'ibāra*". The *ishāra* does not contradict the grammatical function of *'ibāra* (express meaning) or differ from it morphologically or syntactically. Rather, its grammatical, morphological and syntactic function is used to perform the act of *ishāra*. For, as Tawḥīdī asserts, *ishārī* or allusive meaning "is a concomitant feature of the composition of letters" making up the sentences of the qur'anic text, except that "the *ishāra* is beyond the rules governing names, verbs and circumstances".[52]

SUMMARY AND CONCLUSION

In the *Niche*, Ghazālī writes that "nothing possesses existence (*huwīya*) other than He [i.e. God] except in a figural sense (*bi'l-majāz*)" and "the knowers of God [who] ascend from ... *majāz* to ... *ḥaqīqa*". But in the *Mustaṣfā* he claims: "Every *majāz* [figural sense] has a *ḥaqīqa* [i.e. a literal sense] but it is not necessary that every *ḥaqīqa* has a *majāz*." Should we conclude that Ghazālī has simply reversed himself, that non-literal and literal are symmetrically interdependent? And if for Ibn Taymiyya literal meaning is all the meaning there is, then Ghazālī's *Niche* seems to take the opposite position: there are simply no literal truths to be told, at least not from the perspective of the saints.

How then does the *Niche* square with the idea that cognition of meaning in divine discourse is first and foremost a matter of literally understanding *what* the discourser said in the form of an assertion (*khabar*), rather than *how* it is said or its force? For faith (*īmān*) is assent to the truth (*taṣdīq*) of what the Prophet has reported to be the case. Meaning thus comes down to what is said or rather what is said to exist. This, at least, is the view put forth in Ghazālī's *Decisive Criterion* (*Fayṣal al-tafriqa*), that the use of sentences expressing essential, sensible, imaginal, intelligible or analogical senses presupposes an existential or factual meaning. Thus, qur'anic utterances always presuppose a literal assertion of existence.[53] And their variations of meaning result from mental operations performed upon this shared ontological content. However, here is the key to our mystery.

The possibility of performing such mental operations is what allows Ghazālī to maintain the two apparently incompatible claims: that figural meaning is asymmetrically dependent on literal meaning and that ultimately there are no literal truths to be told. The mental operations are the contents of specific speech-acts. One may then sum up Ghazālī's epistemology of divine discourse in two moments. In the first, he gives a logical account of the possible meanings of the sentences of the Qur'an, explained as a function of the meanings of their verbal components conceived as essences behind its words and their mode of combination in inferential structures. Divine discourse will in this way be seen as possessing a literal content linked with truth.

In the second moment, that literal content is placed at the disposal of various non-direct speech-acts (*ishārāt*) to effect utterances of a non-literal significance and of a specific non-assertoric or rather illocutionary force. *Ishārāt* are speech-acts performed with qur'anic sentences that already have a literal meaning. Hence, the Sufi jihādist against French colonialism, 'Abd al-Qādir al-Jazā'irī (1808–83) confessed, "Whenever [God] wishes to communicate to me a command or give me good news, warn me, communicate a piece of knowledge, or give me advice I have sought touching on some matter, He informs me of what He wishes by means of an *ishāra* through a noble verse of the Qur'an."[54]

Using a qur'anic verse as an *ishāra* therefore does not cancel out its *ẓāhir* or surface meaning. From the perspective of the rational thinker, for instance, a verse may have only legal import. At the same time, to the saint, the significance of the same verse will be mystical and symbolic.[55] Here the figural meaning and indeed, scriptural meaning in general become a matter of perspective. And if we have not in the phenomenon of *ishāra* an exhaustive account of the tropes found in the Qur'an, Ghazālī has at least outlined their structure from the standpoint of theological understanding.

What was important for him to stress was that "cancelling out the *ẓāhir* meaning" was not something he advocated. That was "the view of the *Bāṭinīya* [i.e. the Ismā'īlī Shī'a]" who have, as he asserts, "one blind eye and look only at one of the two worlds and do not recognise the parallel between the two nor understand its significance". But Ghazālī equally condemned "a cancellation of the secrets (*asrār*) ... which strips the *ẓāhir* meaning of its content", this being the path of literalists.[56] Only "those who bring the two together achieve perfection". Therefore, he can still maintain that cognition of meaning in divine discourse is first and foremost a matter of literally understanding *what* the discourser says, rather than its specific force as manifested in acts of *ishāra*. For the literal significance is preserved in *ishāra*, to be sure. Indeed, that literal significance is what motivates illocutionary uptake.

With Ibn Taymiyya only the latter is important, insofar as it displays the intention of the divine discourser revealed in His habit of address (*ʿādat al-mutakallim*). For the "signification of expressions is an intentional, volitional act signalling what the speaker means by them, [given that] expressions by themselves fail to signify". In fact, "the mere hearing of the expression without knowledge of the speaker and his habit signifies nothing" unless one knows "what is necessary for the speaker to signify by them".[57] In actuality, Ibn Taymiyya's focus is on the imperatival force of divine speech over its truth-stating power. For "it may very easily turn out", he reasons, "that someone may say, 'I know very well that what you say is true; nevertheless, I will not follow you but fight against you.'"[58] *Taṣdīq* is not tantamount to faith, as Ghazālī believed. God speaks to Muslims in order for them to obey Him, not to know that what He said is true. Hermeneutics and not epistemology is the foundation of his approach.

Despite their differences, the picture of divine discourse in both Ghazālī and Ibn Taymiyya portrays the Qur'an as a static container of meaning. This is the case, at least, with respect to the first moment of Ghazālī's verbal epistemology. And it is true because at that moment both he and Ibn Taymiyya find in the Qur'an a repository of unambiguous knowledge in which each sentence has the possibility of clear and literal meaning. To Ghazālī this is possible because his logic leads him to posit essences behind qur'anic words. They are the same essences God presumably thought as He spoke, the content of "interior discourse". They reach out and fix the meaning of words in the Qur'an wherever they are enunciated in every possible world of God's creation.

Ibn Taymiyya rejects this picture, as we have seen. Divine discourse contains itself within a hermeneutic circle: the best way of interpreting the Qur'an is by the Qur'an itself. There is no need to appeal to anything more than the meaning of qur'anic sentences and they reflect nothing deeper than the everyday use of the Arabic words that make them up. But the meaning of a word is determined by what people say and in what circumstances they say it. Therefore meaning cannot deviate from the world. That claim is true both for Ghazālī and for Ibn Taymiyya as long as "world" means perceptible objects continuous in space and time.

But Ghazālī holds that there are worlds of meaning beyond matter, such that Ibn Taymiyya's world is like that of a ring cast into the Sahara.

Hence, in the final analysis, the image of a static container of meaning fails really to capture the reality of divine discourse. For our earthly Qur'ans are mere reflections of the deeper reality of the Preserved Tablet situated in a world beyond. So our earthly Qur'an represents at best an arena where hearers and readers actually encounter the divine discourser, a point of ascent from which fresh meanings can constantly arise. In that arena, as described by the Ḥanbalite Sufi commentator on the Qur'an, Abu'l-'Abbās ibn 'Aṭā' (d. 919 or 920), in reality "[God] makes an *ishāra* from Himself to Himself since no one has the right to make an *ishāra* to Him except He Himself [... Thus,] whoever makes an *ishāra* to Him, only makes an *ishāra* to [God's] *ishāra* to Himself." And "whose *ishāra* is genuine owes its genuineness to divine glorification and protection", and "that person's *ishāra* is sound" and "coincides with the limits of [his own] rectitude", but "whose *ishāra* is pure pretence (*da'wā*) is invalid and far removed from ... reality".[59]

Further reading

Abu-Deeb, Kamal, "Studies in the *Majāz* and metaphorical language of the Qur'an: Abū 'Ubayda and al-Sharīf al-Raḍī", in *Literary Structures of Religious Meaning in the Qur'an*, ed. Issa J. Boullata (London, 2000), pp. 310–53.

al-Ghazālī, Abū Ḥāmid, *The Niche of Lights*, tr. David Buchman (Provo, UT, 1998).

Griffel, Frank, "Al-Ghazālī's concept of prophecy: the introduction of Avicennan psychology into Ash'arite theology", *Arabic Sciences and Philosophy*, 14 (2004), pp. 101–44.

Hallaq, Wael B., *A History of Islamic Legal Theories: An Introduction to Sunnī uṣūl al-fiqh* (Cambridge, 1997).

Ibn Taymiyya Against the Logicians (Oxford, 1993).

Jackson, Sherman, *al-Ghazālī's Fayṣal al-tafriqa bayna al-Islām wa'l-zandaqa: On the Boundaries of Theological Tolerance in Islam* (Karachi, 2002).

Stetkevych, Jaroslav, *Muḥammad and the Golden Bough: Reconstructing Arabian Myth* (Bloomington, 1996).

Notes

1. Abū Ḥāmid al-Ghazālī, *al-Mustaṣfā min 'ilm al-uṣūl*, ed. Ibrāhīm Muḥammad Ramaḍān (Beirut, 1414/1994), I, p. 737; cf. al-Ghazālī, *al-Iqtiṣād fi'l-i'tiqād*, ed. Ibrahim Agah Çubukçu and Huseyin Atay (Ankara, 1962), p. 114.
2. "Il" is prefixed to negate "locution" to show that il-locutions are actions that speakers perform with locutions. In the area of linguistics known as pragmatics a distinction is thus drawn between the locutionary act (what is said or asserted) and the illocutionary force (how the speaker intended

what was said to be taken: as a statement, a command, a threat, a promise, etc.). Cf. J. L. Austin, *How to Do Things with Words* (Cambridge, MA, 1962).

3. John Lyons, *Semantics* (Cambridge, 1977), II, p. 731.
4. Ghazālī, *Mustaṣfā*, I, p. 674.
5. Ghazālī, *Iqtiṣād*, p. 116.
6. Ibid.
7. Ghazālī, *Mustaṣfā*, I, pp. 659–62.
8. Ibid., I, p. 674.
9. Cf. Abū Bakr al-Bāqillānī, *Kitāb al-Tamhīd*, ed. Richard J. McCarthy (Beirut, 1957), pp. 7–14.
10. Ghazālī, *Mustaṣfā*, I, p. 674.
11. Cf. Wael B. Hallaq, *A History of Islamic Legal Theories: An Introduction to Sunnī uṣūl al-fiqh* (Cambridge, 1997), pp. 39ff.
12. al-Ghazālī, *Mi'yār al-'ilm fī fann al-manṭiq* (Beirut, 1983), p. 43.
13. E.g. the qur'anic verse 6:141: "Pay the due thereof upon the harvest day", which is contextualised by specifying that what is due is a tenth thereof; Ghazālī, *Mustaṣfā*, I, pp. 675–6.
14. E.g. the verse "The heavens are rolled up in His right hand", which is put in context by the hadith, "The heart of the believer is between two fingers of the fingers of the All-Merciful God"; ibid., I, p. 676.
15. al-Ghazālī, *Iḥyā' 'ulūm al-dīn*, ed. Abū Ḥafṣ ibn 'Imrān (Cairo, 1419/1998), IV, p. 351.
16. al-Ghazālī, *Fayṣal al-tafriqa bayna al-Islām wa'l-zandaqa*, ed. Sulaymān Dunyā (Cairo, 1381/1961), p. 77. Cf. Sherman Jackson, *al-Ghazālī's Fayṣal al-tafriqa bayna al-Islām wa'l-zandaqa: On the Boundaries of Theological Tolerance in Islam* (Karachi, 2002), Introduction; and Frank Griffel, "Al-Ghazālī's concept of prophecy: the introduction of Avicennan psychology into Ash'arite theology", *Arabic Sciences and Philosophy* 14 (2004), p. 125.
17. Ghazālī, *Mustaṣfā*, I, p. 679.
18. See Wael B. Hallaq, *Ibn Taymiyya Against the Logicians* (Oxford, 1993); and more recently Oliver Leaman, "Islamic philosophy and the attack on logic", *Topoi* 19/1 (2000), pp. 17–24.
19. Ibn Taymiyya, *al-Radd 'alā al-manṭiqiyyīn*, ed. Muḥammad 'Abd al-Sattār Naṣṣār and 'Imād Khafājī (Cairo, 1976), I, p. 114.
20. For Ibn Taymiyya's views on faith see Toshihiko Izutsu, *The Concept of Belief in Islamic Theology* (Tokyo, 1965), pp. 166–79 and *passim*.
21. Muḥammad al-Mawṣilī, *Mukhtaṣar al-Ṣawā'iq al-Mursala 'ala'l-Jahmīya wa'l-Mu'aṭṭila li'bni'l-Qayyim al-Jawziyya* (Beirut, 1405/1985).
22. Taqī al-Dīn Aḥmad Ibn Taymiyya, *Majmū' Fatāwā*, ed. 'Abd al-Raḥmān ibn Qāsim and Muḥammad 'Abd al-Raḥmān ibn Qāsim (Rabat, n.d.), XX, p. 496.
23. In Mawṣilī, *Mukhtaṣar*, p. 272, lines 4–10. Cf. Ibn Taymiyya, *Kitāb al-Īmān*, ed. Sayyid Jumaylī (Cairo, 1412/1993), pp. 83–4.
24. Mawṣilī, *Mukhtaṣar*, p. 254.
25. Ibn Taymiyya, *Kitāb al-Īmān*, p. 87.

26. Ibid., pp. 83–4.
27. Ibn Taymiyya, *Muqaddima fī uṣūl al-tafsīr*, ed. 'Adnān Zarzūr (Beirut, 1399/1979), p. 93.
28. Quoted in Ella Almagor, "The early meaning of *Majāz* and the nature of Abū 'Ubayda's exegesis", in Andrew Rippin (ed.), *The Qur'ān and Its Interpretative Tradition* (Aldershot and Burlington, VT, 2001), pp. 309–10. Also see Kamal Abu-Deeb, "Studies in the *Majāz* and metaphorical language of the Qur'an: Abū 'Ubayda and al-Sharīf al-Raḍī", in *Literary Structures of Religious Meaning in the Qur'an*, ed. Issa J. Boullata (London, 2000), pp. 310–53.
29. Ibn Taymiyya, *Kitāb al-Īmān*, p. 94.
30. Ibid., p. 88.
31. Ibid., p. 87.
32. On the linguistic change from *Jāhiliyya* to Islam see Jaroslav Stetkevych, *Muḥammad and the Golden Bough: Reconstructing Arabian Myth* (Bloomington, 1996), pp. 4–7.
33. Ibn Taymiyya, *Kitāb al-Īmān*, pp. 83–4.
34. Ibn Taymiyya, *Radd*, I, p. 208, lines 6–7.
35. Ibid., I, p. 204, lines 9–10.
36. "*Malakūt*" is derived from *malik*, "king", not *malak*, "angel".
37. al-Ghazālī, *Mishkāt al-anwār*, ed. Abu'l-'Alā 'Afīfī (Cairo, 1382/1964), p. 67; English tr. from the same edn by David Buchman, *The Niche of Lights* (Provo, UT, 1998), p. 27.
38. Ibid.
39. Ibid.
40. Ibid.
41. I avoid the frequent translation of *'ārif* as "gnostic" because such a translation superficially implies an association with an ancient movement with which Ghazālī had no known association.
42. Ghazālī, *Mishkāt*, pp. 69–70; tr. Buchman, p. 28.
43. Ibid., p. 56; tr. Buchman, p. 16.
44. Ibid., p. 57; tr. Buchman, p. 17.
45. Ibid., p. 56; tr. Buchman, p. 17.
46. Ghazālī, *Mustaṣfā*, I, pp. 674–5.
47. Ghazālī, *Mishkāt*, p. 54; tr. Buchman, p. 15.
48. Ibid., p. 55; tr. Buchman, p. 17.
49. Abū Hāmid al-Ghazālī, *al-Maqṣad al-Asnā fī sharḥ ma'ānī asmā' Allāh al-ḥusnā*, ed. Fadlou Shehadi (Beirut, 1971), pp. 21–4.
50. Cf. Pierre Cachia, *The Arch-Rhetorician or the Schemer's Skimmer: A Handbook of Late Arabic* badī' (Wiesbaden, 1998), p. 89.
51. Ghazālī, *Mustaṣfā*, II, pp. 219–20.
52. Abū Ḥayyān al-Tawḥīdī, *al-Ishārāt al-Ilāhīya*, ed. Wadād al-Qāḍī (Beirut, 1402/1982), p. 61.
53. Ibid.
54. 'Abd al-Qādir al-Jazā'irī, *Kitāb al-Mawāqif* (Beirut, 1966), I, p. 26.

55. This is not to say that no *ishāra* ever has legal import. For examples see Ghazālī, *Mustaṣfā*, II, pp. 219–21.
56. Ghazālī, *Mishkāt*, pp. 73ff.
57. Ibn Taymiyya, *Majmū' Fatāwā*, XX, p. 496.
58. Ibn Taymiyya, *Kitāb al-Īmān*, p. 227; cf. also the argument on p. 223.
59. *Tafsīr Abi'l-'Abbās ibn 'Aṭā'*, in *Majmū'-e āthār-e Abū 'Abd al-Raḥmān al-Sulamī*, ed. Naṣr al-Dīn Pūrjavādī (Tehran, 1369/1990 or 1991), I, p. 223.

15 Eschatology

MARCIA HERMANSEN

Given the great interpretive diversity within Islam and the absence of a central institution that might limit and define authoritative doctrine, throughout Islamic intellectual history the tension between literal approaches to revelation and the interpretive limitations of human reason as respective sources of truth has been a recognised constant. Even today, disagreements on eschatological teachings often echo the early debates of ninth-century Baghdad between the Mu'tazila and the literalist Ḥanbalites, or reflect other tensions that emerged at various intermediate points of that spectrum. While the Qur'an and the prophetic legacy are the shared sources of all legitimate Islamic doctrine and symbolism, they have throughout history been read in disparate ways, reflecting sectarian and interpretive divergences. It would therefore be futile to present Muslim theological positions on eschatology as if there were a consensus regarding each detail of what is expected at the end of time. By their very nature, eschatological doctrines test the limits of our rational and customary experience, thereby reminding us of the fragility of our attachment to conditions that strike us now as unquestionably real.

Eschatology embraces not only teachings about death, resurrection, immortality and judgement, but also the tradition's understanding of beginnings, the meaning of history and the direction and purpose towards which everything in creation tends. Theologically it orients our ultimate purpose, and this should be central in its interpretation. The various symbols and elements found in revealed sources or woven into the tradition throughout history invite exegesis. In terms of determining the authenticity of any given interpretation one may consult the opinions of recognised classical scholars, not so much in terms of the specifics of their individual allegorical paradigms, but rather on the epistemological foundations of their constructions of truth. For example, the Sunnī (and particularly the Ash'arite) position is to accept revealed truth, especially in matters pertaining to the realm of the

Unseen, without needing to take a specific position on precisely how that truth will be actualised. This stands in contrast to alternative interpretive positions which allow human reason greater scope, and may therefore prefer allegorising interpretations when confronted with texts that confound rationality. In the medieval period, a large majority of Muslim theologians stood by the view that the core eschatological doctrines and symbols must be held literally as tenets of faith. A smaller number derived inspiration from an intellectual tradition that constructed a dual truth system whereby archetypal or symbolic truth and material truth were asserted to be simultaneously distinct and compatible.

ESCHATOLOGY IN THE REVEALED SOURCES

Eschatology is a large subject. It possesses both an individual and a cosmic element in which the fate of the individual is inextricably bound up with the purpose and destiny of the entire creation within a religious vision. Sacred time finds its culmination, fulfilment and, ironically, its negation or deconstruction in the drama of the Last Things. Theologians typically held that it is among the three most fundamental Islamic doctrines – the unity and uniqueness of God (*tawḥīd*), prophecy (*nubuwwa*) and the ultimate "return" (*ma'ād*). Typically in late *kalām* manuals eschatological teachings are subsumed under the category of *sam'iyyāt*, "matters heard", or "received in faith", since unlike the other two great categories of theological concern, metaphysics and prophecy, they are considered to lie outside the reach of rational proof. The theologian's task here is simply to defend scriptural predictions from denial or misinterpretation rooted either in false scriptural exegesis or in an inappropriate extension of ratiocination into this uniquely revelatory area.

Islam gives a particularly important place to eschatology, partly because of its own self-understanding as the final revelation, but also because of the qur'anic stress on the intelligibility of history as well as on individual human accountability. Contemporary scholars of apocalyptic note its connection to theodicy, the concept that the things of this world will be brought to completion in a just way in which the good and true will be vindicated. But in addition, the end of things may be considered the binary or corollary of the beginning of things. Our discussion will begin with four important dimensions of the fact of creation which set the context for the specifically eschatological motifs within Islamic theology.

The creation motif: the day of "Am I not your Lord?"

Qur'an 7:172 recounts the establishment of what is sometimes known as "the Primordial Covenant" at a "time before time" when all souls implicit in the loins of Adam were asked by God, "Am I not your Lord?", to which they replied, "Yes, we testify!" The qur'anic assumption is clearly that humans in this life need to recognise and remember the divine truth they have already acknowledged. In this there is a resonance with other doctrinal topics such as the living out by humans of a destiny measured out (*qadar*) by God, as well as, in some *falsafa* and Sufi systems, the reawakening and development of qualities already implicit in the soul, a process that can lead to a saintly life which, although still lived in this world, is a sign of the life which the blessed will enjoy in the world to come.

The Islamic concept of time is frequently less linear than that of the Christian and Jewish traditions. However, it is marked by a similar concept of an *ex nihilo* creation and the destruction of the present world, with the intervening time being the unfolding of history. In addition, Islamic concepts of temporality include the idea of a pre-time (*azal*) in which the events of the future are determined and anticipated, a beyond-time or timeless realm (*lā zamān*), and a post-eternity (*abad*), which entails the realm of the afterlife.

The concept of a return to God – both personal and collective – is qur'anic (7:29). In this understanding, return (*ma'ād*) is both the process of return and the destination itself: the life to come. These ideas were particularly elaborated within philosophical and mystical approaches to Islamic theology which stressed personal transformation as the key epistemological method. According to this spiritual model, all human life in this lower world (*dunyā*) is viewed as a path of return. One may either consciously and spiritually participate in this process (voluntary return), or face an unavoidable physical death and bodily resurrection at its end (compulsory return).[1] Such an approach to eschatological teachings accepts their literal truth while positing further levels of Being accessible to correspondingly profound verifications of ultimate reality. Works by Muslim theologians who explicated the inner dimensions of religious teachings envision life as a process through which a person continually shapes his or her own soul, so that after death in the intermediary state (*barzakh*) this soul continues to exist as an imaginal form. At the archetypal level of the intermediate state this form of the soul is existentially real, as are the represented forms of human actions and all of the other eschatological symbols. This intermediary stage is comparable to a sleep from which one will be awakened at the resurrection, just as the present life also resembles a dream in comparison to the subsequent stages.[2]

Eschatology, while specifically addressing the end of things, is implicit during our passage as individuals through the life of this world. In answering the "why" question of creation with varying emphases, it structures a range of responses to the human condition. For example, if asked about the purpose of life, a Muslim scholar might reply with the qur'anic verse, "Indeed I have only created jinn and human beings in order to worship Me" (51:56). This supplies a deontological ethic in which obedience to the revealed law results in reward in the afterlife and fulfils the purpose of life. This, however, has not been the only Muslim response to this question. In a well-known passage, Ibn 'Arabī responded to the same issue by citing a tradition that God had said, "I was a hidden treasure and I wanted to be known, and therefore I created the universes."[3] In this case the ultimate human purpose is gnosis (*'irfān*) or realisation (*taḥqīq*) of the divine element immanent in all creation. Both positions are rooted in alternate qur'anic principles, one stressing the divine transcendence (*tanzīh*), and the other emphasising immanence (*tashbīh*); both uphold the concept of a chosen return to God, but one is implicitly dualistic while the other suggests a more humanistic orientation and an active participation in the eschatological project. These varying perspectives also displayed themselves in broader ethical perspectives on issues such as the ultimate source of evil.

Cosmic creation and the end of convention

The Qur'an speaks of the creation of the universe as either a process or an instantaneous response to the divine command "Be!" so that "it becomes" (*kun fa-yakūn*) (2:117; 3:47; 6:73 and elsewhere). Within the qur'anic formulations there are various aspects of the creative process, including the dimensions of creation *ex nihilo* (*ibdā'*), creation (*khalq*) that occurs through combining and developing elements that already exist, and God's continuous divine management (*tadbīr*) (32:4–5) of creation.

The idea that the natural order and physical creation as we know it will be transformed or overturned at the eschaton is found repeatedly in the Qur'an. Despite the incredulity of his unbelieving audience, in the epoch of the Prophet the concept of judgement and "the Hour" seems to have had a radical urgency. "How shall you know? Perhaps the Hour is near" (42:17). The eighty-first *sūra* forcefully describes how the natural order as humans know it will be overturned:

THE OVERTHROWING
In the name of God, the Beneficent, the Merciful.
When the sun is overthrown,
And when the stars fall,
And when the hills are moved,
And when the camels big with young are abandoned,
And when the wild beasts are herded together,
And when the seas shall rise,
And when souls are reunited,
And when the girl-child that was buried alive is asked
For what sin she was slain,
And when the pages are laid open,
And when the sky is torn away,
And when hell is lighted,
And when the garden is brought nigh,
Then every soul will know what it has made ready.

Here nature, a celebrated constant in the world of the pre-Islamic Arabs, is completely subverted. Descriptions of the earth's final cataclysm are particularly salient in such Meccan chapters of the Qur'an. These take the form of short dramatic outbursts of rhyming prose, and stress the need to repent and recognise God before the final days. The general picture of events leading up to the day of judgement is that great earthquakes will rock the earth, setting the mountains in motion, the sky will split open and the heavens will be rolled up like scrolls of parchment. The sun will be darkened, and the oceans will boil.

The creation of Adam and the Garden

The eschatological counterpart to the creation of the human prototype, Adam, would be the idea of the new or second creation (*khalq jadīd*) (14:39) which takes place at the resurrection. "As He originated you, so you will return" (7:29), and "As We originated the first creation so We will bring it back again – a promise binding upon Us, so We shall do" (21:104).

The doctrine of the resurrection of the body seems to have been difficult for the pre-Islamic Arabs to accept, as the Qur'an repeatedly asserts its reality and presents belief in it as a test of faith. Such incredulity did not vanish following the scripture's triumph: Avicenna took a psychological view of the resurrection, explaining that the return is to the same place whence one came, on the basis of the qur'anic verses

89:27–8, "O contented soul, return to your Lord, pleased and pleasing."[4] The human soul (*nafs*) possesses many aspects. For some commentators the level of "the contented soul" (89:27) represents a reunion with the archetypal, pre-existing source of a person's essential reality. For other thinkers, resurrection is the physical reconstitution of the human body and identity. Many theologians understood human experience in this life as a contest between the higher elements of human nature and the lower desires, often figured as angelic and animalistic tendencies. This is based on qur'anic anthropology, where humans are described on the one hand as having been created from "lowly mud" or a "clot of coagulated blood", while at the same time they share in the divine spirit that God breathed into Adam (15:29; 38:72). The story of the creation of Adam implies this, since it incorporates his quick disobedience to God. Yet according to 2:37 a repentant Adam turned to God and received words of guidance. This not only initiates Adam as a prophet but is taken to indicate that there is no Fall into original sinfulness within qur'anic anthropology. There can be no original sin since "every child is born with the sound original disposition (*fiṭra*)".[5] In fact God has created the human composite according to an ideal stature (95:4), and the words of guidance and modes of remembrance and God-consciousness (*taqwā*) received by humanity in the form of revelations and their elaboration into codes for life (*sharī'a*) are means for restoring rather than inaugurating this felicity.

Every element of creation is measured out by God, and has a divinely "determined term" (*ajal musammā*, 6:2). Once death comes, the human soul will exist, according to traditions of the Prophet, in the *barzakh* until the time of collective resurrection (23:100). On the basis of these traditions theologians developed doctrines of how an individual in this intermediary state will initially be examined by the angels, who will ask about his or her religious affiliation, the consequence being an experience in the grave which anticipates one's eternal destiny. Medieval debates occurred as to whether the "punishments of the grave" to be experienced in this state were in fact, physical, or occurred in the imaginative faculty, through psychological forms such as dreams and images.[6] Ash'arism and Māturīdism insisted on belief in this intermediary state as an article of faith; while most Mu'tazilīs, and perhaps the Khārijites, rejected it, the dispute hinging on the interpretation of the relevant scriptural passages.[7]

The creation motif: humans accepting the Trust (*amāna*)

A verse of the Qur'an states: "Indeed We offered the Trust (*amāna*) to the heavens, thc earth, and the mountains, but they refused to bear it because they were afraid of it. Yet the human being took it up; indeed he is oppressive and ignorant" (33:72).

The eschatological principle to be paired with this aspect of creation is the concept of judgement, either of individuals or of nations in history. Both individual humans and nations have their determined terms (10:49; 15:4–5). At the end of time a trumpet will sound twice (39:68), calling for the resurrection. The first blast will be like a wind that ends all life as we know it. The second blast signals the resurrection of the dead (*qiyāma*), also known as the "rising up" (*ba'th*). Once resurrected, all men and women will be assembled (*ḥashr*) on an immense and featureless plain. Many elements of the Ḥajj pilgrimage are held to be reminiscent of this final assembly, for example the huge crowds and confusion, as well as the uniform white garments (*iḥrām*) worn by males that resemble burial shrouds.

Further prophetic traditions indicate that after judgement punishment may be embodied in forms commensurable with a person's sins, so that avarice, for instance, will be embodied by a snake coiled around the miser's neck. At the same time all human actions are said to have been recorded (36:12), so that the judgement day is also known as the day of reckoning (*yawm al-ḥisāb*). At this time actions will testify for or against their agents, who will receive books in the right or left hand, witness their scrolls being unrolled, or hear their various limbs testify to the deeds they had committed (41:19–24; 69:19–26). The final judgement is depicted by a range of images. Each person's deeds will be weighed in scales (*mīzān*), the judged must walk over a narrow bridge (*ṣirāṭ*) stretched over hellfire, into which the guilty will plunge, while a heavenly pool (*ḥawḍ*) of the Prophet awaits the believers, who will be purified and have their thirst quenched.[8]

After the judgement, souls will be divided and assigned either to heaven, symbolised by a verdant garden (*janna*) or to hell (*jahannam*), also known simply as "the Fire" (*al-nār*). Qur'anic symbolism suggests further gradations of recompense such as that of the "People of the Heights" who are in neither heaven nor hell (7:46), and other specific terms for Paradise and hell that are in some cases interpreted by commentators as indicating ranks and levels in the afterlife.[9]

A further aspect of judgement is that of nations. This occurs within the course of history in terms of divine blessing or punishment being meted out to human communities that either fulfil or reject the teachings of God's messengers.

MESSIANISM

Belief in a figure who will come to the world in the end-time to combat the forces of darkness or evil is a theme common to the Western religious traditions. Meaning in history is brought to vindication through this potent image of a cosmic conflagration, succeeded by a just resolution and the ultimate victory of the good. The Muslim messianic figure, known as the Mahdī, or "guided one", is generally presented in hadith chapters called the books of crises, calamities or civil wars (*fitan*). For most Sunnīs the Mahdī concept has not been particularised around strong millenarian expectations, although in times of crisis it may be invoked, for example in various historical Mahdist movements, and in some Sufi-influenced, or politically driven movements featuring millenarian overtones. The last significant Mahdist movement was that of the Sudanese, Muḥammad Aḥmad ibn 'Abd Allāh (d. 1885). Among earlier (and very diverse) examples of millenarianism were the Abbasid revolution of the eighth century, Ibn Tūmart (d. 1130) of the Berber Almohads, and a South Asian movement, the Mahdawiyya, that revered Syed Aḥmad Jaunpūrī, a seventeenth century charismatic figure, as a messianic leader.

In Twelver Shī'ism the Mahdī is experienced in a more concrete way.[10] Since the Shī'ī Muslims existed as a minority and in an oppositional role for much of their history, it is understandable that the idea of vindication and deliverance from a marginal situation would evolve into a resonant theological concept. Therefore the Messianic doctrine of the Mahdī receives greater elaboration and devotional longing in this branch of Islam.

The Mahdī is identified by Twelver Shī'a as the twelfth Imam or spiritual and political successor to the Prophet Muḥammad. This Imam disappeared as a child in the year 939 and went into "occultation" (*ghayba*). Twelvers believe that as a guiding and inspiring spiritual presence he remains accessible to scholars and to his loyal devotees. He is known by additional apocalyptic titles such as al-Qā'im (the one who will rise up) and Ṣāḥib al-Zamān (ruler of the times). Most Shī'ite political theory in the pre-modern period posited that no political order could be legitimate in the absence of this returned Imam. In general, therefore, one may say that the expectation of a specific deliverer has led to political quietism for the bulk of Shī'ī history.[11]

As a counterpoint to the negative or fearsome elements connected with the eschaton, there exist in both Sunnī and Shī'ī understandings derived from the hadith corpus descriptions of a period in which the world will return to an ideal state during the Mahdī's reign. According to such hadith the Mahdī will come to restore justice, harmony and truth to all humanity by defeating the forces of evil, which will be led by a figure known as the Dajjāl.[12] The implications of this word entail falsehood and deception, as in the term "the false Messiah" (*al-masīḥ al-dajjāl*). This figure is said to be a deceiver and "one-eyed". Specific speculations about this "Antichrist" figure feature in genres of Muslim devotional texts and more recent apocalyptic allegory, reflecting particular historical anxieties rather than authoritative doctrine expounded in texts of *kalām*. The Qur'an itself does not refer to such a person, or to a millennium of any description.

Nonetheless, in Islamic history millenarian movements have at times arisen that read into particular cruxes of history the culmination or fulfilment of cycles, on the basis of symbolic divinations of an astrological or numerological type. Contemporary sociologists of religion analyse such movements as instances of how religion can rapidly transform into charismatic and affective rather than traditional forms.

There is a further concept of "centennialism", based on a prophetic tradition that a Renewer (*mujaddid*) would appear in the Muslim community at the beginning of every century. *Mujaddid*s have all been scholarly figures recognised after the fact; the list is not firmly established, and in contrast to Mahdism, this concept has not usually been used as an element in political mobilisation.

APOCALYPTIC

As the end of the world nears, various "signs of the Hour" are anticipated. Specific sequences of these are elaborated in the hadith, for example:

> You will not see the Hour before you see ten preceding signs.
> The first will be the sun rising from the West, then the Smoke, then the Dajjal, then the Beast,[13] three lunar eclipses,[14] one in the East, one in the West, and one in the Arabian Peninsula, the appearance of Jesus, upon whom be peace, then Ya'jūj and Ma'jūj,[15] and the last will be a fire coming out of Yemen, from the lower part of Aden.[16]

In the context of the early political and social turbulence of Islamic history, eschatological expectations combined with religious symbolism in generating a range of apocalyptic narratives, some of which achieved the status of admission to the hadith anthologies. Some of these reports suggest the Prophet's prior knowledge of the fates of the Roman and Persian Empires and predict the civil wars (*fitan*) that would disturb the emerging Muslim polity. An entire genre of apocalyptic literature developed, in many cases derived from a shared corpus of ancient Near Eastern motifs. Some of the hadith compilations of the third Islamic century include chapters devoted entirely to the topic of crises and civil wars (*fitan*), grouping hadiths predicting political struggles in this world (*malāḥim*) with other reports describing the trials and rewards of the next life. Entire volumes of reports such as the *Book of Seditions* (*Kitāb al-Fitan*) of Nu'aym ibn Ḥammād (d. 844) indicate the scale and popularity of this literature.

A further apocalyptic element is the second coming of Jesus, who will reappear before the day of judgement and, in a way that was never precisely adumbrated, assist the Mahdī in defeating the forces of evil. This was inferred from a set of hadith, and also from Qur'an 43:61, "And he [Jesus] shall be a sign of the [last] Hour". The precise Islamic position on this aspect of Jesus' Messiahhood is open to argument. It is clearly eschatological in its association with the closing episodes of sacred history. Muslim rejections of the crucifixion arise both from the fact that since there is no original sin, redemption is neither necessary nor possible, and the fact that as the "Messiah" Jesus would not be killed by his opponents (Qur'an 4:157). As a culmination, Jesus's return must reflect the Islamic reading of history as a site of multiple, fully saving divine interventions and ubiquitous and omnipresent signs; his second coming has nothing to do with any vindication of superseded Jewish or Christian claims. For this reason the hadith reports identify the returned Jesus as a Muslim who follows the law of the Qur'an. Jesus's humanity as one among God's prophets is affirmed by reports that he will die of natural causes before the judgement day, for "every soul shall taste death".[17]

THEOLOGICAL ISSUES

Theological issues arising from eschatological teachings include, significantly, the doctrine of intercession (*shafā'a*), which is treated in detail in the *kalām* texts, partly in consequence of early challenges to its validity. While the Qur'an states that "no soul shall bear the burden of another" (6:164; 17:15, and elsewhere), and explicitly rejects a redemptionist theology (2:48), it leaves the door open for some form of intercession in verses such as "no one shall intercede with Him except by His permission" (2:255). It seems that intercession by angels (53:26), true witnesses (43:86), or those who have made a covenant with God (19:87) may avail. A set of hadith regarded as sound by the traditional canons presented the Prophet as interceding for sinners of his community, both at the judgement day, and following the condemnation of some sinners to hell.[18] As this tension was debated, one source of particular difficulty was whether the Prophet will play an intercessory role for his community and whether additional sources of mediating spiritual aid (*wasīla*) such as the "friends of God" (*awliyā'*), might be efficacious. Sunnī Islam gave an affirmative answer here, reacting against the Mu'tazilite insistence that any form of intercession must compromise God's unity and justice. Sufi circles with a particular devotion to the Prophet as "the perfect human being" (*al-insān al-kāmil*) were particularly likely to uphold the intercessory possibility. Certain more recent positions such as those espoused by Wahhabism that emerged in the eighteenth century building on Ibn Taymiyya's hostility to intermediaries, or certain strands in twentieth-century rationalising Islamic modernism, have sought to reduce or eliminate any connection between this world and that of the departed, leading to a denial of intercessory powers and an aversion to practices and symbols of any sort of veneration.[19]

Controversies over intercession were inevitable in the context of a religion which set such store by the sole omnipotence of God, and which had emerged in prophetic tension with a polytheistic system. Yet it was clear to almost every Muslim that unless prayer on behalf of others is to be abandoned, some kind of intercessory devotional life must be part of Islam; and the hadith which affirmed the Prophet's intercession for his community clearly confirmed this. The Mu'tazilite alternative here, as on some other issues, seemed to reduce God to a calculating, merciless automaton, unresponsive to human prayer.

PROMISE AND THREAT

Symptomatic of this Ash'arite-Mu'tazilite divide was the largely Mu'tazilite topic known as the promise and threat (*al-wa'd wa'l-wa'īd*), which asserted that an individual's eternal fate may be at least to some extent rationally ascertained on the basis of God's promise to reward the good person and punish the evildoer. Ash'arites and Ḥanbalites contested this, asserting that it privileged human judgement based on reason over God's sovereign will. Fearful of vainglorious overconfidence in God's favour, Islamic piety has in general eschewed any concept of "being saved" or a sense of security about one's posthumous destiny. Significant reports of the Prophet caution about the possibility that even the most pious person might commit a grave sin before the last moment of life. At the same time, in the case of the sinner, God's mercy is said to outweigh His wrath,[20] and a particular good deed may carry salvific weight beyond any human expectation. A balance of hope and fear is therefore the general Muslim attitude towards one's eternal state, serving as both a deterrent against wrongdoing and an assurance of divine mercy. For some, the very notion of reward and punishment as a sufficient motivation for human behaviour has been open to critique. For example, al-Ghazālī states, "It is not proper that the bondman's quest for Heaven should be for anything other than meeting with his Lord. As for the rest of Heaven's delights, man's participation in them is no more than a beast let loose in a pasture."[21]

RESURRECTION

On the question of the nature of resurrection, issues engaged are the nature of the spirit or soul, and what exactly is to be resurrected. On this Muslim opinions have varied, with the great majority stressing the physicality of resurrection, given that nothing is impossible for God (cf. Qur'an 36:81).

A complete denial of resurrection is heretical, since it runs counter to the Qur'an's clear pronouncement in 75:1–6 and elsewhere. However, a denial of physical resurrection was upheld by certain Mu'tazilites and by *falsafa* practitioners such as Fārābī and Avicenna.[22] One aspect of the insistence on bodily resurrection arose from the fact that Islam rejected the usual Western body–mind distinction.

PARADISE AND THE FIRE

More than any other key postulate, the nature of heaven and hell has been subjected to a range of interpretations stretching from the purely literal to the utterly allegorical. Hell is a place of just chastisement for sin, which forms a temporary purgatory for sinning believers; whether any punishment there would be truly eternal was a matter of considerable dispute.[23] Paradise is presented as a garden (*janna*) arranged in levels, a verdant place where all wishes are fulfilled, and where the believers will enjoy celestial food and drink and be accompanied by beautiful clear-eyed maidens (*ḥūr*) who remain perpetually virginal. Some have suggested that the presence of earthly pleasures in heaven is to indicate the transformation of human nature in the next life so that those things forbidden in this world will no longer be sources of corruption and conflict. In fact, the state of satisfaction (*riḍwān*) from God is greater than such delights of the Garden (9:72). In recent times, the well-known poet-philosopher, Muḥammad Iqbāl (d. 1938), explained that heaven and hell were representations of inner character and states of mind rather than localities.[24] On the other hand, some Sufis claimed that one purpose of maintaining *erōs* in Paradise is to valorise it on earth, disclosing it as a sign of something higher.[25] This stands in stark contrast to the medieval Christian view, which regarded virginity, not marital life, as an anticipation of the life to come in heaven.

At the summit of Paradise, for those men and women who lived the religion to the full, there is the vision of God (*ru'ya*), which is unambiguously conceived as a spiritual reward higher than the material fulfilment of personal desires and wishes. This beatific vision was the site of a characteristic argument between Ash'arism and the Mu'tazilites. For the former, the hadith literature had clearly stated that "a veil shall be lifted, and the believers shall gaze upon the face of God".[26] God was therefore to be seen, in an ocular way that was nonetheless amodal (*bi-lā kayf*). For the Mu'tazilites, sight (*baṣar*) can only be a corporeal sense; and since God is not an accident or a body, it is axiomatic that He cannot be seen. God Himself had told Moses that he would not see his Lord (7:143); moreover "vision (*abṣār*) cannot attain Him" (6:104). Ash'arīs, Ḥanbalīs and Māturīdīs replied with the view that this latter verse applies only to complete perception; and that Moses might see God in the next life, even though God had chosen to veil Himself during that prophet's lifetime. They also denied that there was a logical reason why *baṣar* could not apprehend an entity that was neither substance nor accident.[27]

THE SALVATION OF NON-MUSLIMS

Islam emerged in the context of a prophetic dispute with pagan unbelievers, who were warned that the consequence of their practices and beliefs would be hellfire. Later in the Prophet's ministry the qur'anic challenge was extended to Jews and Christians also. Jews were told that their past disobedience to their own prophets, and more recently their rejection of Jesus and Muḥammad, would entail God's wrath.[28] Even more seriously, Christians had developed concepts of divine sonship and a three-fold understanding of the divine nature that impugned the core principle of *tawḥīd*, the monotheism without which there could be no salvation.[29] While the qur'anic critique of the earlier traditions was subject to varying interpretations, it was clear that God was now not merely bringing a version of monotheism that would suit peoples previously impervious to it, but was correcting in a radical way errors that had distorted the primordial monotheism received by the first disciples of Moses and Jesus. Throughout, the Muslim scriptures assume the existence of an *ur-monotheismus*, an ancient shared *tawḥīd*, which must have been delivered to earlier peoples as a reflection of God's desire to save his creatures, but which had been progressively lost or distorted (*taḥrīf*), unwittingly or deliberately, as scriptures and primitive doctrines were imperfectly transmitted.

Salvation has hence been available at many points in time and space; and it is a necessary corollary of the givens of divine love and justice that wherever God delivers it, it is full salvation. The emergence of Islam, therefore, was not thought to signal the opening of a radically new chapter in the history of salvation, but rather the reiteration of an ancient truth. The practices of Islam were understood as reminiscences of this cyclical process; in particular, the five daily prayers and the Ḥajj pilgrimage contain strong references to Abraham, who is the example *par excellence* of the prophet who invites his people back to the worship of the monotheistic God.

This understanding of salvation history made Muslim discussions with Jews relatively straightforward: the issue would revolve not around *tawḥīd*, but around the possibility of a non-Jewish prophet, and the arrival of a new law which would ease the burden placed upon the people of Moses. Islamic considerations of Christianity, by contrast, needed to be more intricate. Both religions began with the understanding that the Mosaic law need not be eternal, and with the assumption that God's purposes in history were merciful and just. Christianity's conclusion that those purposes were most fully realised in a single atonement was not, however, accepted by Muslims, who assumed that the divine love and justice required not one but many equally saving divine acts in history,[30] and that "no soul shall bear the burden of another" (6:164). This underlying gulf was seldom addressed directly on either side; instead, the considerable polemical literature, generated most often by *kalām* specialists, but sometimes also by Sufis and jurists, focused on the stability of the Biblical text, and the coherence of the doctrines of Trinity and the Incarnation.[31] Given this reluctance to address the underlying difference of emphasis, and the embryonic state of Biblical scholarship, it was inevitable that the debate was generally sterile.

A troubling internal issue for Muslim thinkers, however, was the possibility that the postulate of God's mercy and justice might be endangered by a view of history that regarded followers of abrogated monotheisms as damned. This latter interpretation was derived from qur'anic verses such as "Indeed the religion of God is Islam" (3:19) and "Whosoever desires a religion other than Islam it will not be accepted of him" (3:35). Yet if God's compassion ensured that sinning Muslims could be saved – at least on non-Mu'tazilite views – through God's forgiveness and the intercession of the Prophet, then there seemed to be a need to extend this compassion to non-Muslim monotheists, particularly where these had never had the opportunity to accept Islam, but had still led lives of virtue. The Qur'an itself can praise the virtues of Christian clergy: "You will find the nearest of them [Muslims] in affection to be those who say: 'We are Christians.' That is because there are among them priests and monks, and because they are not proud" (5:82). As a result, Ghazālī, the theologian who was perhaps most preoccupied with issues of divine providence, was able to allow salvation to the non-Muslims of his day, provided always that Islam had not been accurately presented to them, and that they had not wilfully refused it.[32]

In conclusion, the tenor of Islamic eschatology stresses the inexorable triumph of good over evil. God has created the universe and human nature as signs of His goodness; and the final Hour will reflect both His wrath at their subversion, and His final vindication of beauty and mercy. Needless to remark, in any religious tradition teachings and symbols related to final things are particularly susceptible to the workings of the human imagination. This imagination may be developed toward the most sublime and positive spirituality or may be employed to project more mundane and limited fantasies and anxieties. The Islamic spectrum has manifested all these possibilities abundantly. Yet the topic of eschatology, lying within the field of *sam'iyyāt*, illustrated how areas of theology that were deemed inaccessible to reason were not readily productive of unity based on acquiescence in scriptural reading alone; on the contrary, these were among the most hotly contested doctrines of all. Ash'arism here showed itself characteristically concerned with maintaining the omnipotence of God, but also insisted on doctrines which emphasised his sovereign mercy and forgiveness, notably the doctrines of prophetic intercession, the vision of God, and the desire of God to forgive sins outright, *bi-ghayri ḥisāb*: without reckoning.

Further reading

Arjomand, Said, *The Shadow of God and the Hidden Imam: Religion, Political Order and Societal Change in Shi'ite Iran from the Beginning to 1890* (Chicago, 1984).

Avicenna, *Epistola sulla vita futura (al-Aḍḥawiyya)*, ed. and tr. Francesca Lucchetta (Padua, 1969).

Chittick, William C., "Death and the world of imagination: Ibn 'Arabī's eschatology", *Muslim World* 78 (1988), pp. 51–82.

Cook, David, *Studies in Muslim Apocalyptic* (Princeton, NJ, 2002).

Eklund, Ragnar, *Life between Death and Resurrection according to Islam* (Uppsala, 1941).

al-Ghazālī, Abū Ḥāmid, *The Remembrance of God and the Afterlife: Book XL of the Revival of the Religious Sciences*, tr. T. J. Winter (Cambridge, 1989).

Haddad, Yvonne Y., and Jane I. Smith, *The Islamic Understanding of Death and Resurrection* (Albany, 1981).

Rahman, Fazlur, *Major Themes of the Qur'an* (Minneapolis, 1980).

Sachedina, Abdulaziz, *Islamic Messianism: The Idea of the Mahdī in Twelver Shī'ism* (Albany, 1981).

Saritoprak, Zeki, "The Mahdī tradition in Islam: a social-cognitive approach", *Islamic Studies* 41 (2002), pp. 651–74.

Notes

1. William C. Chittick, "Death and the world of imagination: Ibn 'Arabī's eschatology", *Muslim World* 78 (1988), p. 51.
2. Ibid., *passim*; cf. Abū Ḥāmid al-Ghazali, *Deliverance from Error*, tr. W. Montgomery Watt as *The Faith and Practice of al-Ghazzali* (London, 1953), p. 24.
3. Cf. Annemarie Schimmel, *Mystical Dimensions of Islam* (Chapel Hill, NC, 1975), p. 189.
4. Ibn Sīnā, *al-Risāla al-Aḍḥawiyya*, tr. Francesca Lucchetta as *Epistola sulla vita futura* (Padua, 1969), p. 19.
5. Bukhārī, Janā'iz, 80.
6. Abū Ḥāmid al-Ghazālī, *The Remembrance of Death and the Afterlife: Book XL of the Revival of the Religious Sciences*, tr. T. J. Winter (Cambridge, 1989), pp. 135–47.
7. A. J. Wensinck, *The Muslim Creed: Its Genesis and Historical Development* (Cambridge, 1932), pp. 117–21; Ragnar Eklund, *Life between Death and Resurrection according to Islam* (Uppsala, 1941); 'Abd Allāh al-Bayḍāwī, *Ṭawāli' al-anwār min maṭāli' al-anẓār*, tr. by Edwin E. Calverley and James W. Pollock, as *Nature, Man and God in Medieval Islam* (Leiden, 2002), II, pp. 1078–81.
8. Qur'an 36:66; 37:23–4; 101:6–11; cf. Ghazālī, *Remembrance*, pp. 217–18.
9. Ibid., pp. 222, 237; cf. T. O'Shaughnessy, 'The seven names for hell in the Qur'ān", *Bulletin of the School of Oriental and African Studies* 24 (1961), pp. 444–69.
10. Sevener Fāṭimid and Ismā'īlī theology upholds the need for a living guide (*imām*) to be present in the community, although some indications of cyclic fulfilment or high points are present.

11. Said Amir Arjomand, *The Shadow of God and the Hidden Imam: Religion, Political Order and Societal Change in Shi'ite Iran from the Beginning to 1890* (Chicago, 1984).
12. Cf. Abdulaziz Sachedina, *Islamic Messianism: The Idea of the Mahdī in Twelver Shī'ism* (Albany, 1981).
13. Possibly referred to in Qur'an 27:82.
14. Or earthquakes, in some interpretations.
15. Mentioned in Qur'an 18:94; 21:96; apparently a reference to Gog and Magog.
16. Muslim, Fitan, 128. As recounted in Imam al-Haddad, *The Lives of Man* (London, 1991), p. 51.
17. Qur'an 3:185. For more on the second coming, see Yvonne Y. Haddad and Jane I. Smith, *The Islamic Understanding of Death and Resurrection* (Albany, 1981), pp. 69–70.
18. Ghazālī, *Remembrance of Death*, pp. 210–16.
19. Richard C. Martin, Mark R. Woodward and Dwi S. Atmaja, *Defenders of Reason in Islam: Mu'tazilism from Medieval School to Modern Symbol* (Oxford, 1997), pp. 103–4, 126–8.
20. Hadith in Bukhārī, Tawḥīd, 15.
21. Al-Ghazālī, *Remembrance of Death*, p. 251.
22. Georges Anawati, *Études de philosophie musulmane* (Paris, 1974), pp. 263–89.
23. Haddad and Smith, pp. 142–4.
24. Muḥammad Iqbal, *Reconstruction of Religious Thought in Islam*, (Lahore, 1960), p. 123.
25. Sachiko Murata, *The Tao of Islam: A Sourcebook on Gender Relationships in Islamic Thought* (Albany, 1992), pp. 195–6.
26. Muslim, Īmān, 297.
27. Ibrahim Lutpi, "The problem of the vision of God in the theology of az-Zamakhshari and al-Baidawi", *Die Welt des Orients* 13 (1982), pp. 107–113; A. K. Tuft, "The *ru'yā* controversy and the interpretation of Qur'an VII:143", *Hamdard Islamicus* 6 (1983), pp. 3–41.
28. For Muslim understandings of Judaism see Camilla Adang, *Muslim Writers on Judaism and the Hebrew Bible: From Ibn Rabbān to Ibn Ḥazm* (New York: 1996).
29. Qur'an 9:31; for many scholars Christians were therefore idol-worshippers (*aṣḥāb al-awthān*); see Ibn Ḥajar al-'Asqalānī, *Fatḥ al-Bārī Sharḥ Ṣaḥīḥ al-Bukhārī* (Cairo, 1959), XXIV, p. 269.
30. Cf. Qur'an 13:7; 35:24.
31. Wadi Z. Haddad, "A tenth-century speculative theologian's refutation of the basic doctrines of Christianity: al-Baqillani (d. AD 1013)", in Yvonne Yazbeck Haddad and Wadi Z. Haddad (eds.), *Christian–Muslim Encounters* (Gainesville, 1995), pp. 82–94.
32. Cited in Tim Winter, "The last trump card: Islam and the supersession of other faiths", *Studies in Interreligious Dialogue* 9 (1999), pp. 149–50.

Index

abad 310
'Abādānī, Muḥammad al- 99
Abān 260
'Abbādān 261, 262
'Abbādānī, Abū Ḥabīb al- 262
Abbasids 113, 115, 315
'Abd al-Jabbār (d. 1025) 92, 93, 207, 208, 285
'Abd al-Malik ibn Marwān (d. 705) 38
'Abd al-Qāhir al-Baghdādī (d. 1037) 60, 84, 262
'Abduh, Muḥammad (d. 1905) 147
Abharī, Athīr al-Dīn al- (d. 1264) 68
Abraham 5, 28, 33, 321
Abū Bakr (d. 634) 22, 35, 36, 259
Abū Ḥanīfa (d. 767) 44, 51, 81, 86, 147, 245
Abu'l-Hudhayl al-'Allāf (d. 841) 47, 48, 49, 123
Abū Hurayra (d. 678) 284
Abū Ja'far al-Sharīf 111
Abū Madyan (d. 1197) 272
Abū Muslim al-Khurāsānī (d. 754) 58
Abu'l-Shaykh al-Iṣfahānī (d. 979) 52
Abū Thawr (d. 854) 268
accidents 129, 205, 273, 274, 320
Acquisition (*kasb*) 9, 45, 146–7, 168, 171
Active Intellect 63, 64, 70
adab 176–7
Adam 181, 230, 233, 310, 312–13
'adam 130
'āda 228, 273, 289, 294
Aden 316
Adonis 187
afterlife 78, 87, 91, 130, 201, 227, 238, 249, 250, 276, 308–24
agriculture 107
Aḥsā'ī, Ibn Abī Jumhūr al- (d. 1501) 94
ahl al-kitāb 28, 33
aḥwāl 48
'Ā'isha (d. 678) 35, 36, 183, 234
ajal 313, 314
'Ajamī, Ḥabīb al- 260
Akhbāriyya 94, 107
akhlāq 176, 225, 235 *see also* ethics
Alexander of Aphrodisias 61
Alexandria school 60, 61
Algeria 38
'Alī ibn Abī Ṭālib (d. 661) 35, 36, 40, 194, 221
allegory 129, 136, 137, 276, 309, 319
Almohads 315
amāna 313
Āmidī, Sayf al-Dīn al- (d. 1233) 127, 135
amr 134, 169, 231, 288
amr i'tibārī 71
al-amr bi'l-ma'rūf wa'l-nahy 'an al-munkar 48
'Amr ibn 'Ubayd (d. 761) 47
Āmulī, Sayyid Ḥaydar (d. 1385) 94
analogy 56, 59, 128, 129, 130, 137, 155, 207, 246, 249, 282, 298
Anatolia 12, 271
anatomy 203
Andalusia 69
angels 19, 20, 21, 24, 27, 183, 231, 260, 289, 313, 317
animals 202, 203
Ankaravī, Ismā'īl (d. 1631) 72
Anṣārī, Khwāja 'Abd Allāh (d. 1089) 5, 268
anthropomorphism 9, 10, 41, 44, 48, 52, 89, 111, 121, 122, 128, 135, 137, 149
Antichrist 223, 316
antinomianism 252, 265, 275

anti-Semitism 4, 15
Anūshirvān 58
apophatic theology 259, 269, 284; *see also bi-lā kayf*
'āqil 171
'aql 9, 11, 56, 69, 72, 83, 84, 135, 162, 163–4, 171, 182, 221
Arabic language 33, 125, 187–8, 290
Arabs, Arabia 11, 22, 29, 33, 114, 115, 174, 187, 312
a'rāḍ 46, 51, 205
a'rāf 314
al-'arḍ wa'l-'aks 208
argument from design 26, 198, 201–4, 210–11
Aristotle 11, 58, 61, 68, 70, 144, 150, 151, 163, 167, 177–8, 181, 186, 288–307
aṣālat al-'aql 55, 182
aṣālat al-waḥy 62
asbāb al-nuzūl 186
Ascension (*mi'rāj*) 14, 265, 272
aseity 133
Ash'arī, Abu'l-Ḥasan al- (d. 935) 52, 62, 66–7, 125, 129–31, 133, 187, 247
Ash'arism 9, 25, 56, 84, 85, 86, 88, 110, 113, 122, 128, 145, 147, 155, 164, 165, 200–1, 206, 208, 246, 249, 313, 320
  and Sufism 263, 272
atbā' al-tābi'īn 23
atheism 197, 203
atomism 46, 47, 50, 83, 144–5, 205, 209, 211, 273, 274
atonement 321
attributes of God 46, 52, 53, 121, 123, 169, 204, 229, 263, 269
  action 128
  creation 136
  essential 128
  hearing 128, 136
  knowledge 48, 60, 123, 128, 133–4, 136, 204, 230
  life 48, 123, 128, 136, 229, 230
  power 47, 123, 127, 128, 136, 146, 204, 229, 230
  sight 128, 136
  speech 49, 124, 128, 229, 269, 288
  unity 204
  will 123, 128, 136
Averroes (d. 1198) 68, 74, 78, 80, 149–50, 202, 205
Avicenna (d. 1037) 57, 65–6, 70, 131–2, 148, 149, 151, 157, 182, 185, 186, 191–3, 276, 292, 312, 319
  and Sufism 12, 152, 160, 274, 279
  The Healing 65
  influence of 11, 152, 211–14, 274
  relationship to *kalām* 11, 12, 79, 134, 135, 149, 160, 213, 275
'Awdī, al- 94
a'yān thābita 276
azal 127, 134, 151, 205, 278, 310

badā' 91, 92
badan mithālī 69
Baghdad 60, 91, 102, 111, 134, 145, 261, 262, 269, 271
Bahā'ī, Shaykh (d. 1621) 73
Bahā'ism 194
Baḥrānī, Maytham al- (d. 1300) 93
Bahshamiyya 92
Bājī, Abu'l-Walīd al- (d. 1081) 247
Bakriyya 261–2, 263
Balkh 264
Balkhī, Abu'l-Jaysh al-Muẓaffar al- (d. 977) 92
Balkhī, Abu'l-Qāsim al- (d. 931) 261
banking 241
Banū Mūsā 60
baqā' 267, 273
Bāqillānī, Abū Bakr al- (d. 1013) 60, 84, 209, 247
Baqlī, Rūzbehān (d. 1209) 272
baraka 111
Barbahārī, Abū Muḥammad al- (d. 941) 262
Barmecide 59
barzakh 310, 313
baṣar 320
Baṣra 39, 45, 88, 144, 262
Baṣrī, Abu'l-Ḥusayn al- (d. 1044) 93, 147
Basṭāmī, Abū Yazīd al- (d. 874) 187, 260, 261, 267
ba'th 314
bāṭin 121, 129, 164, 283
Bāṭiniyya 121, 129, 302
Bayḍāwī, 'Abd Allāh al- (d. 1286) 85
Bayt al-Ḥikma 74
Beast of the Apocalypse 316
Bennabi, Malik (d. 1973) 189
Bible 52, 190, 239, 321

Bidpai 58
bi-lā kayf 53, 89, 126, 127, 263, 270, 272, 309, 320
biology 203
Bishr al-Marīsī (d. 833) 46
Bishr ibn al-Mu'tamir (d. 825) 50, 261
Black Stone 258
body, human 202, 203–4, 312, 319
Bokhtishū' 58
botany 203
Buddhism 264
Bukhārā 279
Bukhārī, Muḥammad ibn Ismā'īl al- (d. 870) 24, 32, 51
Bunānī, Thābit al- (d. 744/5) 260
burhān 61
Burhān al-Ṣiddīqīn 278
Byzantium 74

Cairo 103, 111, 112, 117
canon law 240
Carmathianism 266
cataphatic theology 259
causality 60, 61, 144, 152, 154, 209, 274
centennialism 316
Chodkiewicz, Michel 283
Christians, Christianity 8, 33, 60, 190, 191, 195, 237, 310, 317, 320, 321–2
chronons 273
churches 285
command ethics, *see* theistic subjectivism
commerce 241
Companions (*ṣaḥāba*) 23, 178, 194
consequentialism 201
Constantinople 74
contingency, 65, 131, 157, 198, 211, 278
contracts 243
Corbin, Henry 5
Cordoba 69
cosmological arguments 204–11, 278, 279
creation 29, 60, 61, 75, 134, 136, 141–60, 148–50, 181, 231, 273, 276, 310, 311
  versus emanation 78, 132, 139, 157, 276
creed, creeds 8, 25, 44, 85, 93, 105, 269
cumulating arguments 216

dahr 38
Dajjāl 316
dalālat al-iltizām 291, 300
dalālat al-muṭābaqa 291, 300
dalālat al-taḍāmun 291, 300
Damascus 152
Daqqāq, Abū 'Alī al- (d. 1015) 223
Dār al-Ḥikma 117
Dārānī, Abū Sulaymān al- (d. 830) 261
Darqāwī, Muḥammad al-'Arabī al- (d. 1845) 252
dator formarum 64
dator scientias 64
Dawwānī, Jalāl al-Dīn al- (d. 1502) 217
day of judgement, *see* Resurrection
death 27, 29, 231, 308
debts 243
dervishes 112
Descartes 150
determinism 13, 26, 38–40, 41, 42, 44, 50, 141–60
devil 181, 184
dharma 239
dhimma 240
ḍidd 132
differentia 131
Ḍirār ibn 'Amr (d. 815) 45–6, 47, 50
doubt 198
dreams 182, 186, 193, 195, 282, 311, 313
dualism 2
dunyā 310

Eden 312
Egypt 103, 112, 114, 277
eidē 276
emanation 13, 61, 68, 132, 139, 148–50, 157, 276
epistemology 62, 73, 83, 88, 288
equivocal revelation 182
erōs 320
eschatology 191, 192, 308–24
essence/existence distinction 65, 82, 157
essence of God 121, 128, 133, 169
eternity 151
ethics 90, 147, 161, 181, 225, 234, 238, 242
Eurocentrism 2
Europe 78
evil 145, 147, 156, 160, 248, 249, 250, 251, 269, 315, 322

existence of God 26, 106, 141, 197–217, 248, 277, 278

face of God 6, 9, 122, 129, 130, 272, 274, 298–9
Faḍl al-Nawbakhtī 58
faith (*īmān*) 25, 44, 45, 46, 47, 50, 53, 86–8, 89, 152, 174, 250, 291, 293, 301, 303, 309
Fall, the 313
falsafa 3–4, 55–76, 79–80, 81, 84, 90, 93, 94, 110, 131–6, 148–50, 275
  decline of 11–14, 77, 81
  origins 55–6
fanā' 267, 299
faqīh 254
Fārābī, al- (d. 950) 60, 62, 63–5, 69, 73, 148, 151, 182, 185, 319
  Book of Letters 63
  Virtuous City 63, 148, 275
farḍ 'ayn 271
farḍ kifāya 271
Farghānī, Sa'īd al-Dīn al- 277
Farqad 260
faṣl 131
Fāṭima (d. 632) 35
Fāṭimids 91, 323
fatwā 113
fiqh 7, 162–3, 164
al-Fiqh al-Akbar I 44
al-Fiqh al-Akbar II 269
fitan 315, 317
fiṭra 198, 248, 250, 251, 313
Flying Man argument 65
forgiveness 24, 27, 49, 124, 128, 232, 233, 243, 322
fundamentalism 143, 289

Gabriel 20, 183
genus 132, 133, 292
Georgius ibn Jibrā'īl 58
ghayb 127, 164
ghayba 41, 91, 107, 315
Ghaylān 39
ghayriyya 130
Ghazālī, Abū Ḥāmid al- (d. 1111) 2, 6, 9, 10, 12, 84, 107, 145, 146, 148, 150–5, 156, 175, 186, 202, 222, 223, 247–8, 249, 270–4, 288, 319, 322
  Alchemy of Happiness 228
  and reason 11, 67–9, 77, 78, 143, 150–5, 198, 249
  and Sufism 152, 160, 198, 270–4
  Decisive Criterion 106, 301, 322
  Deliverer from Error 150, 156
  Highest Aim 299
  Incoherence of the Philosophers 13, 67, 132–3, 149, 275
  Just Mean in Belief 9, 273
  Niche for Lights 297–303
  Revival of the Religious Sciences 3, 7, 67, 90, 152–5, 227–9, 270, 272, 293
ghulām 100
ghuluww 7, 9
ghurūr 226, 228
Gimaret, Daniel 146
Gog and Magog 316
Gospel 28, 240
grammar 98, 106, 136, 144, 188, 293
gratitude to God 146
grave, punishment of 46, 47, 313
  visitation of graves 111–12
Greek 188

Ḥadathī, Faḍl al- 261
ḥadd 82, 132
Ḥaddādī, Abū Ḥafṣ al- 260, 261, 265
Hādī Sabzavārī (d. 1878) 69
ḥādith 205
hadith 21, 22–4, 59, 81, 98, 102, 105, 316, 318
  ḥadīth qudsī 193
  solitary hadith 246, 248
ḥadīth al-nafs 290, 293
Hadot, Pierre 156
Ḥāfī, Bishr al- (d. 842) 261, 262
Ḥafṣa (d. 665) 22
Ḥajj 103, 266, 314, 321
ḥakīm 57, 269
ḥāl 260, 262
Ḥallāj, Manṣūr al- (d. 922) 109, 184, 259, 260, 266–7, 268, 284, 285
Hamadhānī, 'Ayn al-Quḍāt al- (d. 1131) 271, 272, 276
Ḥanafīs 53, 86, 88, 245, 246, 247, 260, 264, 269
Ḥanbalism 9, 10, 11, 44, 45, 51–2, 62, 69, 78, 81, 82–3, 84, 87, 102, 109, 122, 124–7, 135, 246, 262, 268
hand of God 129, 130, 305
ḥaqīqa 220, 288, 292, 299

ḥarām 165, 242
Harawī, 'Abd Allāh al- (d. 1089) 5, 268
ḥarf 126, 131, 134, 293
al-Ḥārith ibn Surayj (d. 746) 44
Hārūn al-Rashīd (d. 809) 58
Hārūt and Mārūt 260
ḥasad 226, 228
ḥasan 165
al-Ḥasan al-Baṣrī (d. 728) 39, 225, 260, 261
al-Ḥasan ibn Muḥammad ibn 'Alī (d. 705) 43
al-Ḥasan ibn Zayd (d. 884) 93
ḥāshiya 90
ḥashr 314
ḥashwiyya 262
ḥawḍ 314
heaven 30, 44, 47, 231, 312, 319–20
Hebrew 188
Hegel 143
hell 30, 44, 87, 223, 231, 234, 312, 314, 318, 319–20
  eternity of 46, 47, 319
heresiography 8
heresy 6, 8, 59, 78, 81, 97, 102, 106, 108, 113, 114, 128, 266
hermeneutics 93, 121, 122, 124, 129, 130, 136–7, 191–4, 282, 303
  see also tafsīr; *ta'wīl*
ḥikma, ḥikmat 12, 57, 278
al-Ḥilla 94
Ḥillī, Ibn al-Muṭahhar al- (d. 1325) 93
Hindu 157
Ḥirā' 183
Hishām (d. 743) 39
Hishām ibn al-Ḥakam (d. 796) 41, 46, 91
hospitals 103
Hourani, George 165, 175
ḥudūd Allāh 163, 242
ḥudūth 205
ḥudūth al-alfāẓ 130
ḥudūth dahrī 68
Hujwīrī, 'Alī al- (d. 1072) 268, 280
ḥukm 169
Ḥunayn ibn Isḥāq (d. 873) 59
ḥuqūq Allāh 242
ḥuqūq al-'ibād 242
ḥūr 319
Ḥusayn ibn 'Alī, al- (d. 680) 40
Ḥusayn al-Najjār, al- 47
huwiyya 157, 299, 300
Ibāḍiyya 38, 39
ibdā' 311
Ibn 'Abbās, 'Abd Allāh (d. 686) 183, 251
Ibn 'Abd al-Wahhāb (d. 1792) 114
Ibn Abi'l-Khayr, Abū Sa'īd (d. 1049) 260
Ibn 'Arabī, Muḥyi'l-Dīn (d. 1240) 3, 6, 7, 10, 11, 12, 94, 157, 164, 168–70, 177, 219, 229–33, 235, 258–87, 311
Ibn 'Asākir 109
Ibn 'Aṭā', Abu'l-'Abbās (d. 920) 223, 224, 304
Ibn Bāb, Abū 'Uthmān (d. 769) 260
Ibn Badrān 126
Ibn Bājja (d. 1138) 69–70
Ibn Baṭṭa (d. 997) 127
Ibn al-Biṭrīq, Yaḥyā 74
Ibn Dīnār (d. 748) 260
Ibn Ḥammād, Nu'aym (d. 844) 317
Ibn Ḥanbal (d. 855) 32, 49, 51, 81, 126, 127, 161, 245, 261
Ibn Ḥazm (d. 1064) 16, 84, 202, 282
Ibn Ḥirzihim (d. 1165) 272
Ibn al-Jawzī (d. 1200) 109–10
Ibn Ka'b, Ubayy 284
Ibn Khābiṭ 261
Ibn Khafīf (d. 981) 263, 271
Ibn Khaldūn (d. 1406) 12, 86
Ibn Kullāb (d. 855) 52
Ibn Masarra (d. 931) 276–7
Ibn Munawwar 260
Ibn al-Muqaffa' (d. 757) 58
Ibn al-Murtaḍā (d. 1437) 93
Ibn al-Mu'tamir (d. 825) 50, 261
Ibn Muthannā, Abū 'Ubayda Ma'mar 295
Ibn al-Nadīm (d. 995) 57
Ibn al-Qayyim (d. 1350) 255, 268, 294–5
Ibn Qiba 92
Ibn Qudāma (d. 1223) 5, 108, 138
Ibn Sab'īn (d. 1270) 277
Ibn Sa'd, Ibrāhīm 280
Ibn Sālim, Aḥmad 262, 263
Ibn Sālim, Muḥammad 262
Ibn al-Sam'ānī 247
Ibn Sa'ūd (d. 1953) 114
Ibn Sīnā, *see* Avicenna
Ibn Taymiyya (d. 1326) 10, 69, 76, 82–3, 88, 181, 182–3, 195, 198, 206, 268, 289, 293–6, 303, 318

Ibn Ṭufayl (d. 1185) 69, 70
Ibn Ṭūlūn (d. 884) 112
Ibn Tūmart (d. 1130) 315
Ibn Wāsi' 260
Ibn Zayd, 'Abd al-Wāḥid (d. 793) 261
Ibn al-Zubayr, 'Abd Allāh (d. 692) 42
iconoclasm 258
iḍāfa 135
idolatry 5, 258
iḥrām 314
iḥsān 252
i'jāz 31, 185
ijāza 99, 100
Ījī, 'Aḍud al-Dīn al- (d. 1355) 10, 84, 85, 127, 136
ijmā' 8, 24, 108, 130, 150, 195
ijtihād 81, 138, 241, 244, 293
ikhlāṣ 222, 224, 228, 229
ilāhiyya 181
ilāhiyyāt 10
al-ilāh al-mu'taqad 284
ilhām 182, 193
illocutionary force 288, 302, 304
Illuminationism (*ishrāq*) 66, 68, 70–2, 82, 156
'ilm al-anwār 70
'ilm ḍarūrī 290
imagination 148, 267, 313, 322
imago dei 170, 231, 233
imāmat al-mafḍūl 41
immanence (*tashbīh*) 6, 128, 130, 311
impossibility 131
incarnation 5, 185, 187, 266, 267, 286, 321
India 239, 275, 315
infallibility 91
infinite regress 131, 206, 212
inheritance 242
innovation (*bid'a*) 6, 126, 150, 151, 243–4
al-insān al-kāmil 229, 283, 318
inspiration (*ilhām*) 182, 193
intention 87, 241
intercession (*shafā'a*) 49, 92, 317–18, 322
Iqbal, Muhammad (d. 1938) 81, 320
Iran 15, 67, 72, 91, 93, 108, 114, 239, 271, 272
Iraq 36, 91, 108, 271
'irfān 311
irjā', *see* Murji'ites
'Īsā ibn Shahlatha 59
Iṣfahān 56
Iṣfahān school 72–3
ishāra 259, 291, 300–1, 302, 304
Iskandarī, Ibn 'Aṭā'illāh al- (d. 1309) 272
islām 6, 29
ism 122
Ismā'īl ibn Ja'far al-Ṣādiq 41
Ismā'īlism 41, 51, 55, 56, 91, 93, 117, 134, 135, 194, 302, 323
isnād 24, 99, 108
istidlāl 'ala'l-ghā'ib bi'l-shāhid 129, 207
istiḥsān 246
istikhāra 193
iṣṭilāḥ 290
istiṣlāḥ 246
istiṭā'a 91, 270
i'tikāf 264
ittiṣāf 265, 266

Jabal 'Āmil 108
jabarūt 297
jabr (divine compulsion) 154, 156, 270
jadal, jadalī 80, 126
Ja'far, Kamāl Ibrāhīm 276
Ja'far al-Ṣādiq (d. 765) 221, 224, 231
jahannam 314; *see also* hell
Jāḥiẓ, al- (d. 869) 101, 202
Jahm ibn Ṣafwān (d. 746) 9, 44
jamā'a 8
Jāmī, 'Abd al-Raḥmān (d. 1492) 277
Jandī, Mu'ayyad al-Dīn (d. *c.* 1300) 277
Jaunpūrī, Syed Aḥmad 315
jawāhir 273, 274
Jazā'irī, 'Abd al-Qādir al- (d. 1883) 302
Jesus 25, 28, 316, 317, 321
Jewish Christianity 240
Jews, 28, 60, 190, 239, 310, 317, 320, 321
Jīlānī, 'Abd al-Qādir al- (d. 1166) 268
jinn 184, 222
jins 132, 133
jismiyya 130
Jubbā'ī, Abū 'Alī al- (d. 915) 51, 53, 106, 124
Jubbā'ī, Abū Hāshim al- (d. 933) 48, 106, 124, 197, 205, 285
Judaism 9, 28, 33, 191; *see also* Jews
judges 109, 112–13, 114, 243, 244

jumhūr 8
Junayd, Abu'l-Qāsim al- (d. 910) 223, 225, 252, 267, 268, 280, 281
Jundī Shāpūr 58
Jurjānī, al-Sharīf al- (d. 1413) 10, 85, 127, 136
justice of God 47, 49, 92, 94, 229, 250, 251, 321
Juwaynī, Abu'l-Ma'ālī al- (d. 1085) 78, 84, 109, 200, 206, 208, 210–11, 249, 272, 275

Ka'ba 258
Ka'bī, Abu'l-Qāsim al- (d. 931) 92, 207
Kalābādhī, Abū Bakr al- (d. 990) 268, 269–70, 279–80
kalām
  defined 2, 12, 81, 161, 164, 170
  late *kalām* 81, 85–6, 146, 150, 309
  opponents of 5, 52, 79–80, 81, 82–3, 109, 110, 132–3
  origins 45, 81, 84, 162
al-kalām al-muqaddar 294
al-kalām al-musta'mal 293–4, 296, 297
kalām nafsī 290
Kalīla wa-Dimna 58
al-kalimāt al-fi'liyya 134
al-kalimāt al-qawliyya 134
Kant 173, 215
Karājakī, al- (d. 1057) 92
Karbalā' 40, 114
Karrāmiyya 44, 135, 264, 265
Kāshānī, 'Abd al-Razzāq al- (d. 1336) 94, 277, 280
kathra 130, 132, 134, 170, 278
Kātibī, Najm al-Dīn al- (d. 1276) 85
khabar 122, 169, 298, 301
Khālid ibn Yazīd (d. 704) 57
khalīfa 36, 37, 60, 109, 230, 234
khānqāh 103, 113, 264, 271
Khārijites, Khawārij 7, 11, 36, 37–8, 39, 87, 313
Kharrāz Amad al- (d. 899) 266, 280
khāṭir 199
Khiḍr, al- 284
Khudāy Nāmeh 58
khums 107
kibr 226
Kindī, Abū Yūsuf al- (d. 866) 51, 61–2
Kubrawiyya 275
Kūfa 40, 43, 44
kufr, kuffār 38, 67, 78, 87, 109, 126, 127, 151, 174
Kundurī, al- (d. 1063) 272
Küng, Hans 7
kursī 169

lā zamān 310
lafẓ 126, 135, 285
lafẓiyya 126, 127, 130, 136
language 48, 51, 63, 71, 122, 125, 129, 136, 153, 288
Laqānī, Ibrāhīm al- (d. 1641) 85
law, see *Sharī'a*
al-lawḥ al-maḥfūẓ 126, 185, 297, 304
Lebanon 108, 114
legalism 240
Leucippus 144
lexicography 188
Libya 38
limbo 87
liturgy 8, 21, 265
logic 14, 50, 61, 63, 73, 78–9, 85, 90, 125, 135, 151, 292
love 229, 230, 233–4, 321
luṭf 47, 50, 94

ma'ād 309, 310
Ma'bad al-Juhanī (d. 699) 40
madhhab 7
madrasa, 72, 103–5, 113, 244
  curriculum 5, 72, 85
Maghnisāwī, Abu'l-Muntahā al- (d. 1532) 127
Maghribī, Abū 'Uthmān al- (d. 983/4) 225
maḥall 153
maḥall al-i'tibār 202
Mahdawiyya 315
mahdī 25, 266, 282, 315, 317
māhiyya 71, 131, 134, 276
ma'iyya 195, 298
majāz 288, 292, 299
Makkī, Abū Ṭālib al- (d. 966) 268, 270
Makkī, 'Amr al- (d. 903/4) 268
makrūh 165, 242
malāḥim 317
Malāḥimī, al- (d. 1141) 199
malakūt 297, 300
Malāmatiyya 265–6, 269
Mālik ibn Anas (d. 795) 42, 245
Mālikīs 53, 114, 246, 285

Mamlūk period 99, 102
Ma'mūn, al- (d. 833) 46, 49, 58, 59, 112, 116
mandūb 165, 242
Manichean 264
Mankdīm (d. 1034) 93
Manṣūr, al- (d. 775) 58
manuscript 98
manzila bayn al-manzilatayn 46, 47, 50, 250
maqām, maqāmāt 228, 260, 262
Marāgha 56
marji' al-taqlīd 108
marriage 241, 320
Marwān (d. 685) 58
al-maṣāliḥ al-mursala 246
Māsawayh 74
Mashhad 103
maṣlaḥa 270
Massignon, Louis 264
maṭla' 297
matn 24, 100
matter 132
Māturīdī, Abū Manṣūr al- (d. 944) 53, 86, 88, 147, 245
Māturīdism 9, 53, 85, 86–9, 110, 127, 147, 164, 245, 249, 250, 313, 320
mawālī 44
maẓāhir 134
Mazdeans 239
Mecca 19, 22, 27, 42, 103, 114, 183, 258
medicine 58
Medina 22, 35, 42, 43
Meḥmed II (d. 1481) 104, 278
mercy 5, 124, 151, 230, 319, 322
Merv 271
messianism 40, 91, 92, 315–16
meteorology 202, 203
metonymy 288
miḥna 49, 112, 113–14, 254, 261
milla ibrāhīmiyya ḥanīfiyya 5
millenarianism 315
Mīr Dāmād (d. 1630) 68, 73
Mīr Fendereskī (d. 1640) 73
miracle 31, 178, 200, 265
Miṣrī, Dhu'l-Nūn al- (d. 860) 261
mithāl 297, 300
mīzān 314
Möbius strip 283
Mollā Kestelli (d. 1495) 12
Mollā Ṣadrā (d. 1640) 73, 157, 280
monasteries 285
Mongols 71, 114
Mosaic law 321
Moses 28, 53, 126, 182, 183, 230, 284, 290, 298, 320, 321
mosque 23, 101–2, 114, 285
mu'āmalāt 219
Mu'ammar 124
Mu'āwiya (d. 680) 36, 38
mubāḥ 165, 242
Mufīd, al-Shaykh al- (d. 1022) 92
muftī 113, 237, 239, 254
muḥāḍara 280
Muḥammad ibn Abī 'Umayr 91
Muḥammad ibn al-Ḥanafiyya (d. 703) 40
Muḥammad ibn Karrām (d. 869) 44, 264
Muḥammad the Prophet (d. 632) 7, 8, 20, 21, 22, 33–4, 148, 162, 229, 233, 234–5, 265, 282
  eschatological role 49, 92, 315, 317–18, 321
  succession to 35–7, 237
  vocation 5, 19, 162, 183, 230
muḥāsaba 260
Muḥāsibī, al-Ḥārith al- (d. 857) 52, 226–7, 228, 271
muḥkam, muḥkamāt 127, 163
mujaddid 316
mukallaf 169
mukāshafa 280
al-Mukhtār al-Thaqafī (d. 687) 40
mukhtari' 153, 273
mulk 297
Mu'min al-Ṭāq 91
mumkin bi-dhātihi 131
murder 243
Murji'ites 42–5, 86, 88
Murtaḍā, al-Sharīf al- (d. 1044) 92
mushāhada 258
music 228
muslim 230
Musnad 32
Mustaḍī', al- (d. 1180) 109
mustaḥabb 165
muta'akhkhirūn 12, 275
Mutanabbī, al- (d. 965) 299
mutaqaddimūn 12, 275
mutashābih, mutashābihāt 127, 137, 163
Mu'taṣim, al- (d. 842) 49

Mutawakkil, al- (d. 861) 261
Mu'tazilism 7, 8, 9, 55, 105, 127, 132, 134, 164, 165, 168, 175, 199–200, 208, 244, 247, 249, 262, 313, 318
and Shī'ism 51, 89, 92
and Sufism 260–1
creation of Qur'ān 49, 51, 53, 114, 122–3, 130–1, 135, 145, 261
doctrine of *luṭf* 47, 50
Five Principles 47
free will 50, 52, 156
on creation 144–7, 250, 273
origins 11, 15, 38, 40, 44, 47–51
Muzanī, al- (d. 878) 106

Nahḍa 77
Nahrawān 36
nahy 169
Najd 22, 114
names of God 122, 127, 132, 141, 169, 220, 222, 229, 231, 232, 233, 234, 262
naql 9, 56, 73, 84, 164
Naqshbandiyya 275, 281
Nasafī, Abu'l-Ḥasan al- (d. 943) 41
Nasafī, Najm al-Dīn al- (d. 1142) 84, 85, 136
Naṣrābādhī, Ibrāhīm al- (d. 977) 224
naṣṣ (designation of Imām) 41, 91
nature 151, 273, 311, 312
Nawbakhtī 58, 92
Nawbakhtī, Abū Sahl al- (d. 923) 92
Naẓẓām, Abū Isḥāq al- (d. 835) 51, 101, 123, 261
Necessary Being/Existent 65, 93, 133, 134, 212, 232, 234, 278
necessity 131, 149, 155, 157, 174
negative theology 128
Neoplatonism 13, 41, 61, 93, 139, 148, 211, 276
Nestorians 240
Netton, Ian 143
nidd 132
nifāq 222, 227
Niffarī, Muḥammad al- (d. 976) 259, 260
Nīshāpūr 111, 265, 271
Niẓām al-Mulk (d. 1092) 111, 113
Nizārīs 93
Noah 253
nominalism 82
non-Muslims, salvation of 106, 248, 320–2
North Africa 91
Nūrī, Abu'l-Ḥusayn al- (d. 907) 266

oaths 241
objective theomonism 275; *see also* *waḥdat al-wujūd*
objectivism 165
obligation 173–4
occasionalism 2, 84, 152, 209, 273
Oman 38
omniscience 128
ontological argument 212, 278, 279
ontology 63, 65, 73, 83, 124, 274
optics 130
Orientalism 1–2, 163, 189, 249, 252
Orthodox Christianity 240
orthodoxy 3, 7–9, 10, 12, 14, 97–117, 150, 266, 268
Ottomans 16, 68, 71, 87, 89, 104–5, 113, 114, 278

paganism 27, 33
pansomatic 203
particularisation argument 198, 208, 209–11, 212
particulars, 82
God's knowledge of 78, 133, 135, 151, 277
Paul, apostle 240
personhood of God 124, 132
Pharaoh 184
Philoponus, John 206
plants 202, 203
Plato 12, 61, 63, 68, 148, 177–9, 182, 249
Platonism 60
Plotinus 61, 148
plurality of eternals 123
poetry 259
political thought 60, 63, 73, 80, 87, 91, 109–10, 112–15, 148, 239, 254–5, 315
polytheism 26, 38, 142, 223
Porphyry, 58, 61
possibility 154, 211, 232; *see also* contingency
potentia absoluta 273
potentia ordinata 273
prayer 27, 108, 111–12, 124, 164, 193, 228, 240, 241, 262, 318, 321

predication 63
primacy of quiddity 71
primordial covenant 251, 310
Proclus 61
prophecy 20, 62, 64, 65, 80, 106, 135, 152, 180, 181, 200, 221, 228, 309, 313
prophets 28, 229, 289, 290
providence 154, 202, 204
psychē 202; *see also* soul
purgatory 319

qabīḥ 165
Qadarites 38–40, 81
Qadiyānism 194
qā'ida 244
al-Qā'im 315
Qalandar 112
Qarāfa, al- 111
Qarāfī, Shihāb al-Dīn al- (d. 1285) 249
qarā'in 289
Qārī, 'Alī al- (d. 1607) 251
Qārūn 261
al-Qāsim ibn Ibrāhīm (d. 860) 93, 202
Qaṣṣār, Ḥamdūn al- (d. 884) 260, 265
Qatāda ibn Di'āma (d. 735) 39
qaṭ'ī al-dalāla 25
Qayṣarī, Dāūd al- (d. *c.* 1347) 277
qidam al-ma'ānī 131
qirā'a 99, 100, 126
qiyāma 314
quiddity, *see māhiyya*
Qum 91
Qūnawī, Ṣadr al-Dīn (d. 1274) 277, 278, 281
Qur'ān 11, 19–22, 33, 83, 129, 178, 180, 183–5, 234
  arguments of 34, 148, 279
  creation of 38, 44, 46, 49, 122–3, 136, 269
  exegesis of 88, 98, 129, 170, 191–4; *see also tafsīr*
  inimitability of, *see 'i'jāz'*
  theology of 6, 9, 24–31, 156, 163, 279
Quraysh 35, 36, 37
Qushayrī, Abū Naṣr al- (d. 1120) 111
Qushayrī, Abu'l-Qāsim al- (d. 1072) 225, 235, 271

rabbis 28
Rabī', al- 101
raj'a 92
Ramaḍān 183
rationality 81, 83, 85, 88, 106, 125, 150, 161, 197, 241, 245, 246, 299, 309
ra'y 245, 246
Rayy 100
Rāzī, Abū Bakr Muḥammad al- (d. 935) 182, 202, 203–4
Rāzī, Abū Ḥātim al- (d. 890) 100
Rāzī, Fakhr al-Dīn al- (d. 1210) 2, 14, 25, 84, 109, 135, 143, 145, 146, 155–6, 186, 198, 201, 202–4, 213–14, 249
Rāzī, Ibn Qiba al- 92
Rāzī, Sadīd al-Dīn 93
reason, *see 'aql*; rationality
redemption 317
Renan, Ernest 11, 15
repentance 151, 152, 228, 313
resurrection 26, 29–30, 34, 62, 64, 69, 93, 151, 308, 311–12, 314, 319
revelation 19–22, 137, 142, 152, 166–7, 168, 173, 248, 250
revivalism 90, 316
rhetoric 188
ribāṭ 103
Riḍā, al- (d. 818) 103
Riḍā, Rashīd (d. 1935) 147
riḍwān 320
riḥla 100
ritual 241, 242
riyā' 223, 265
Roman law 239
Rome 239, 317
Rosenthal, Franz 221
rukhaṣ 268
Rūmī, Jalāl al-Dīn (d. 1273) 13, 175, 176
Ruwaym (d. 915) 268

al-sabr wa'l-taqsīm 208
Sabzavārī, Hādī (d. 1878) 69
sacraments 7
sadd al-dharā'i' 246
Ṣadūq, al-Shaykh al- (d. 991) 91, 92
Ṣafavids 7, 72, 114, 280
Ṣaḥāba 23
Ṣāḥib 100
Ṣāḥib al-Zamān 315
saints 194, 265, 267, 276, 280, 289, 290, 298, 301
salaf 84, 85

Salafism 69
Sālimiyya 262–3
salvation history 321
samā' 99, 100
Samanids 269
Samarkand 147, 245
sam'iyyāt 10, 12, 309, 322
Sanūsī, Abū 'Alī al- (d. 1490) 85
Saqaṭī, Sarī al- (d. 865) 262
Sarrāj, Abū Naṣr al- (d. 988) 268
Satanic verses 184
Saudi Arabia 115
ṣawt 126, 131, 293
scriptures 24, 27–8
  corruption of 33, 321
seal of prophecy 193
Second Coming 317
sectarianism 8, 35, 106, 308
secularism 239
Seljuks 270, 271, 272, 275, 281
sermon 101, 111
Seville 69, 277, 282
Şeyhülislām 113
Shabīb al-Najrānī (d. *c.* 718) 39
Shādhiliyya 272
Shāfi'ī, Muḥammad ibn Idrīs al- (d. 820) 99, 101, 103, 106, 109, 245
Shāfi'īs 53, 81, 103, 109, 111, 112, 114, 245
Shāh Ismā'īl (d. 1524) 114
Shahāda 221, 222, 228, 232
Shahrastānī, Muḥammad al- (d. 1153) 84, 134–5, 293
Shāhrokh (d. 1447) 72
Shankara 157
Sha'rānī, 'Abd al-Wahhāb al- (d. 1565) 253
Sharī'a 3, 7, 10, 14, 60, 106, 152, 163, 167, 168, 169–70, 191–2, 237–57, 313
shaṭḥ 259, 265–6, 284
Shāṭibī, Abū Isḥāq al- (d. 1388) 252–3
Shaykh al-Islām 113
Shī'ism 43, 65, 69, 73, 90, 102, 110, 114, 157, 315; *see also* Ismā'īlism; Twelvers; Zaydiyya
  and the Qur'ān 32
  imāms 40, 41, 91, 92, 93, 94, 107, 135, 194, 315
  origins 9, 12, 36, 37, 40–1
Shīrāz 56
Shīrāzī, Abū Isḥāq al- (d. 1083) 247
shirk 27, 224, 226
Shu'ayb 274
shukr al-Mun'im 173–7
Shūzī 277
ṣifa 122, 267; *see also* attributes
Ṣiffīn 36
Simnānī, 'Alā' al-Dawla (d. 1336) 275
sin 313, 314, 317, 318, 319
ṣirāṭ 314
ṣirāṭ mustaqīm 230
Sirhindī, Aḥmad (d. 1624) 275, 281
slander 243
Socrates 178
soul 62, 229, 313, 319
spheres 202
Stoic 61
Strauss, Leo 12
subjective theomonism 267, 275
Successors (*tābi'ūn*) 23, 260
Sudan 315
Sufism 77, 83, 94, 103–4, 112, 113, 114, 152, 156–7, 194, 219, 228, 237, 318, 320
  and law 251–3
  relationship to theology 2–3, 6, 10, 12, 160, 198, 258–87
Ṣufriyya 38
ṣuḥba 100, 178
Suhrawardī, Abū Ḥafṣ al- (d. 1234) 272
Suhrawardī, Shihāb al-Dīn al- (d. 1191) 12, 68, 70, 156–7
Sulamī, 'Abd al-Raḥmān al- (d. 1021) 225, 226, 265, 268
Sumnūn (d. 910) 266
Sunan 32
sunna 22, 163, 238, 265
sunnat Allāh 152, 273
Suyūrī, al-Miqdād al- (d. 1423) 93
syllogism 82, 275, 278
symbols 291, 300, 308
synagogues 285
Syriac 58, 59

ta'alluq 135
ta'annus 286
ta'arruf 279
tābi'ūn 23, 260
Tabrīz 56
tadbīr 311
ta'dīb al-'āmma 8
tafaḍḍul 51
tafsīr 88, 98, 126, 129, 147, 194, 265

Taftazānī, Sa'd al-Dīn al- (d. 1389/90) 10, 12, 85, 136
tafwīḍ 127, 273
ṭāghūt 224
taḥqīq 311
taḥrīf 33, 321
tajassud 286
tajsīm 130, 264; *see also* anthropomorphism
takdhīb 291
takfīr 7, 15, 32, 106
takhṣīṣ, *see* particularisation argument
taklīf 170, 248, 250, 275
takwīn 147
Ṭalha ibn 'Ubayd Allāh (d. 656) 36
tamthīl 126, 128
tanzīl al-kitāb 168
taqiyya 134
taqlīd 125, 128, 150, 298
taqwā 86, 226, 228, 313
ta'rīf 279, 280
tarkīb 130
taṣawwur 291
taṣdīq 291, 292, 298, 303
ta'ṭīl 48, 264
ṭawāf 258
tawḥīd 26, 47, 121, 141–2, 149, 152, 169, 221, 222, 223, 232, 259, 309, 320
  tawḥīd al-af'āl 169
  tawḥīd al-asmā' 169
Tawḥīdī, Abū Ḥayyān al- (d. 1023) 301
ta'wīl 129, 138, 192, 282
tawqīf 290, 295
ta'zīr 242
Tehran 100
tekke 103
teleological argument, *see* argument from design
theistic subjectivism 165, 166, 201
theodicy 145, 147, 156, 160, 248, 249, 250, 251, 269, 270, 309
theopathic locution 259, 265–6, 284
Thomas Aquinas 157
throne of God 27, 44, 127, 169
Tigris 261
time 46, 132, 160, 210, 273, 279, 310
Tirmidhī, Abū 'Īsā al- (d. 892) 32
Tirmidhī, al-Ḥakīm al- (d. 910) 276
tobacco smoking 244
Torah 28
traditionalism 79, 81, 85, 94, 167, 245, 256
transcendence (*tanzīh*) 6, 9, 48, 121, 123, 129, 134, 263, 311
Translation movement, 1, 11, 13, 57–60, 61, 74
Trinity 5, 320, 321
Tughril-Beg (d. 1063) 272
Turkey 89–94
ṭuruq 7, 271
Ṭūs 67
Ṭūsī, Naṣīr al-Dīn al- (d. 1274) 93, 277
Ṭūsī, al-Shaykh al- (d. 1067) 91, 92, 108
Tustarī, Sahl al- (d. 896) 262
Twelvers 41, 51, 72, 91, 107–8

'Ubāda ibn al-Ṣāmit (d. 654) 193
'ubūda 235
'ubūdiyya 219, 252
'ujb 226
'ulamā' 23, 56, 69, 90, 97, 107, 108, 111, 112, 114, 115, 227, 237, 289, 299
al-'ulūm al-ṭabī'iyya 135
'Umar II (d. 719) 23, 38, 39
'Umar ibn al-Khaṭṭāb (d. 644) 23, 36
Umayyads 36, 40, 43
Umm Hāni' (d. 1454) 102
umma 35, 90, 115, 167, 190, 195, 289
ummī 185
universals 82, 83, 135, 151
ur-monotheismus 321
uṣūl al-dīn 81
uṣūl al-fiqh 238, 254
uṣūlī 254
Uṣūliyya 108
usury 241
'Uthmān ibn 'Affān (d. 656) 22, 36, 189

virginity 320
vision of God 25, 46, 47, 53, 130, 269, 270, 272, 320
voluntarism 165, 168
vows 241

waḍ' al-lugha 290, 291
al-wa'd wa'l-wa'īd 47, 318–19
waḥdat al-shuhūd 267, 275
waḥdat al-wujūd 275, 277, 278
Wahhābism 69, 84, 115, 318
waḥy 180; *see also* revelation
wājib 165, 174, 242

wājib al-wujūd 134
wājib al-wujūd bi-dhātihi 131, 133
wājib al-wujūd bi-ghayrihi 131
walāya, walī 91, 194, 289, 298
Walīd II, al- 39
waqf 103, 107, 113
waqt 132
wasaṭ 8
waṣf 122
Wāṣil ibn 'Aṭā' (d. 748) 47, 50, 123, 260
wasīla 318
Wāsiṭī, Abū Bakr al- (d. 932) 225, 267
Whitehead, Alfred North 3
Wittgenstein, Ludwig 79
women 24, 26, 102–3, 104, 241, 242
worship 164, 218–36, 275, 311
wujūd 71, 157, 229
al-wujūd al-'aqlī 291
al-wujūd al-dhātī 291
al-wujūd al-ḥaqq 229
al-wujūd al-ḥissī 291
al-wujūd al-shibhī 292
Yaḥyā ibn al-Ḥusayn (d. 911) 93
Ya'jūj and Ma'jūj 316
Yamāma 22
Yazīd III 39
Yazīd al-Raqqāshī (d. 733) 260
Yemen 91, 93, 316
Yūḥannā ibn Māsawayh (d. 857/8) 59
Yūnus ibn 'Abd al-Raḥmān 91

ẓāhir 121, 126, 129, 164, 268, 283, 302–3
Ẓāhirism 16, 84, 282–3
ẓa'īna 296
zakāt 228, 241, 242
Zamakhsharī, Abu'l-Qāsim al- (d. 1144) 285
Zanjān 56
zāwiya 103–4, 113
Zayd ibn 'Alī (d. 740) 40
Zaydiyya 41, 51, 91, 93
Ziai, Hossein 5
Zoroastrianism 33
Zubayr, al- (d. 655) 36
Zubayrids 42, 43
ẓuhūr 267

THE CAMBRIDGE COMPANION TO HANS URS VON BALTHASAR
edited by Edward T. Oakes, SJ, and David Moss (2004)
ISBN 0 521 81467 7 hardback   ISBN 0 521 89147 7 paperback

THE CAMBRIDGE COMPANION TO REFORMATION THEOLOGY
edited by David Bagchi and David Steinmetz (2004)
ISBN 0 521 77224 9 hardback   ISBN 0 521 77662 7 paperback

THE CAMBRIDGE COMPANION TO AMERICAN JUDAISM
edited by Dana Evan Kaplan (2005)
ISBN 0 521 82204 1 hardback   ISBN 0 521 52951 4 paperback

THE CAMBRIDGE COMPANION TO KARL RAHNER
edited by Declan Marmion and Mary E. Hines (2005)
ISBN 0 521 83288 8 hardback   ISBN 0 521 54045 3 paperback

THE CAMBRIDGE COMPANION TO FRIEDRICH SCHLEIERMACHER
edited by Jacqueline Mariña (2005)
ISBN 0 521 81448 0 hardback   ISBN 0 521 89137 x paperback

THE CAMBRIDGE COMPANION TO THE GOSPELS
edited by Stephen C. Barton (2006)
ISBN 0 521 80766 2 hardback   ISBN 0 521 00261 3 paperback

THE CAMBRIDGE COMPANION TO THE QUR'AN
edited by Jane Dammen McAuliffe (2006)
ISBN 0 521 83160 1 hardback   ISBN 0 521 53934 x paperback

THE CAMBRIDGE COMPANION TO JONATHAN EDWARDS
edited by Stephen J. Stein (2007)
ISBN 0 521 85290 0 hardback   ISBN 0 521 61805 3 paperback

THE CAMBRIDGE COMPANION TO EVANGELICAL THEOLOGY
edited by Timothy Larsen and Daniel J. Trier (2007)
ISBN 0 521 84698 6 hardback   ISBN 0 521 60974 7 paperback

THE CAMBRIDGE COMPANION TO MODERN JEWISH PHILOSOPHY
edited by Michael L. Morgan and Peter Eli Gordon (2007)
ISBN 0 521 81312 3 hardback   ISBN 0 521 01255 4 paperback

THE CAMBRIDGE COMPANION TO THE TALMUD AND RABBINIC LITERATURE
edited by Charlotte E. Fonrobert and Martin S. Jaffee (2007)
ISBN 0 521 84390 1 hardback   ISBN 0 521 60508 3 paperback

THE CAMBRIDGE COMPANION TO LIBERATION THEOLOGY, SECOND EDITION
edited by Christopher Rowland (2007)
ISBN 9780521868839 hardback   ISBN 9780521688932 paperback

THE CAMBRIDGE COMPANION TO THE JESUITS
edited by Thomas Worcester (2008)
ISBN 9780521857314 hardback   ISBN 9780521673969 paperback

Forthcoming

THE CAMBRIDGE COMPANION TO THE VIRGIN MARY
edited by Sarah Boss

THE CAMBRIDGE COMPANION TO ANCIENT CHRISTIANITY
edited by Rebecca Lyman